AF342526

ADVANCES IN
FINANCIAL PLANNING
AND FORECASTING

Volume 5 • 1994

ADVANCES IN FINANCIAL PLANNING AND FORECASTING

Editor

CHENG-FEW LEE

Rutgers University at New Brunswick

Editorial Board

ADVANCES IN FINANCIAL PLANNING AND FORECASTING

Editor: **CHENG-FEW LEE**

Department of Finance

Rutgers University at New Brunswick

VOLUME 5 • 1994

JAI PRESS INC.

Greenwich, Connecticut   *London, England*

CONTENTS

AGENCY COSTS, ASYMMETRIC INFORMATION,
AND ALTERNATIVE CAPITAL STRUCTURE:
THEORY AND EVIDENCE

CAPITAL BUDGETING AND ASYMETRIC INFORMATION

VALIDATION AND UNIFICATION OF MERGER
THEORIES: A CANONICAL CORRELATION APPROACH

MERGERS CAN REDUCE SYSTEMATIC RISK

GOVERNMENT FINANCING POLICIES FOR SMALL
AND MEDIUM SIZED BUSINESS IN TAIWAN:
A FURTHER ANALYSIS

INTERNATIONALIZATION OF TAIWAN'S FINANCIAL
MARKETS IN 1980s

THE INFORMATION CONTENT OF PRICE-BASED
EARNINGS FORECASTS

LIST OF CONTRIBUTORS

Ravija Badarinathi

Cameron School of Business
University of North Carolina, Wilmington

Samir K. Barua

Indian Institute of Management

Chung Chen

Department of Quantitative Methods
School of Management
Syracuse University

Robert A. Connolly

Kenan-Flagler Business School
University of North Carolina

William P. Dukes

College of Business Administration
Texas Tech University

Said M. Elfakhani

School of Business
Indiana State University

Jack Clark Francis

Department of Economics
    and Finance
Baruch College

Cheryl J. Frohlich

Department of Accounting
    and Finance
College of Business Administration
University of North Florida

V. Gopalakrishnan

Department of Finance
    and Real Estate
George Mason University

Srinivasan Kannan

Colorado State University

Ladd Kochman

Kennesaw State University

Beni Lauterbach   Bar Ilan Univeristy

Cheng-few Lee   Department of Finance
School of Business,
New Brunswick

Kevin J. Leonard   School of Business
and Economics
Wilfred Laurier University

K. Thomas Liaw   Department of Economics
and Finance
St. John's University

Larry J. Lockwood   Finance and Decision
Science Department
M. J. Neeley School of Business
Texas Christian University

Michael S. Long   Faculty of Management
Rutgers University

Ileen B. Malitz   Faculty of Management
Rutgers University

A.G. Malliaris   Department of Economics
Loyola University, Chicago

Larry J. Merville   School of Management
The University of Texas, Dallas

Tom Miller   School of Business
Kennesaw State College

Michael H. Morris   College of Business Administration
University of Notre Dame

Jihad S. Nadir   Faculty of Commerce
and Administration
Concordia College

Paul Newbold

Department of Economics
University of Illinois,
Urbana-Champagn

Shafiqur Rahman

Portland State University

Kevin Scanlon

Division of Business
  and Economics
University of Notre Dame

Jai-Dong Shea

Institute of Economics
Acedemia Sinica

L. Soundarajan

Department of Economics
  and Finance
Georgia College

Silvana Stefani

Faculty of Economics
  and Business
University of Brescia

Bernell K. Stone

School of Management
Brigham Young University

Robert K. Su

Business School
Department of Accounting
National Cheng-Chi University

Timothy F. Sugrue

Department of Finance
School of Business Administration
George Mason University

William M. Taylor

Department of Finance
School of Business
Rutgers University

Jayanth R. Varma

Indian Institute of Management

P. V. Viswanath

Graduate School of Management
Rutgers University

James B. Wilcox   College of Business Administration
                                     Texas Tech University

Chunchi Wu   Finance Department
                                     School of Management
                                     Syracuse University

Chau-Chen Yang   National Taiwan University

Eva C. Yen   Research Division II
                                     Taiwan Institute of Economic Research

Gili Yen   Research Division II
                                     Taiwan Institute of Economic Research

J. Kenton Zumwalt   Department of Finance and Real Estate
                                     Colorado State University

PREFACE

This is the fifth volume of *Advances in Financial Planning and Forecasting*. The main purpose of this publication is to promote high-quality theoretical and empirical research in financial analysis, planning and forecasting.

The contents of this publication will include original articles which:

1. present and develop finance theories that are innovative to financial analysis, planning and forecasting
2. contribute substantially to the development of new financial planning and forecasting models
3. examine or illustrate, through empirical analysis, the applications of important and useful statistical, econometric, mathematical, and computer techniques in financial planning and forecasting
4. present and analyze new and useful accounting, financial, and economic data for financial planning and forecasting in business policy decisions

This volume will include 5 papers. Overall, these papers show how accounting information, finance, theory, and management tools such as statistics, econometrics, and programming techniques can be combined to perform financial planning and forecasting. Inclusive there are six papers in this volume studying mutual funds and their performance.

Cheng F. Lee
Series Editor

COMMON FACTORS AND THE INTERTEMPORAL VARIABILITY OF MUTUAL FUND BETAS

Larry J. Lockwood and L. Soundararajan

ABSTRACT

This study examines the intertemporal variation in the systematic risk of mutual funds for the existence of common factors. Empirical Bayes estimates for beta are derived using a random walk prior process. Results of a factor analysis indicate that three common factors underlie variation in fund betas. Significant relationships between the common factors and risk-free rate changes, default risk premia, and term structure are found.

INTRODUCTION

Empirical results indicate that systematic risk follows a stochastic process over time (see, among others, Fabozzi and Francis, 1978; Lee and Chen, 1980; Sunder, 1980; Lee and Chen, 1982; Ohlson and Rosenberg, 1982; Bos and Newbold, 1984).[1] Collins, LeDolter, and Rayburn (1987) find that beta variability persists at

Advances in Financial Planning and Forecasting,
Volume 5, pages 1-15.
Copyright © 1994 by JAI Press Inc.
All rights of reproduction in any form reserved.
ISBN:1-55938-421-2

the portfolio level, suggesting that marketwide factors may be a source of beta instability. Moreover, theories developed by Galai and Masulis (1976), Turnbull (1977), and Bildersee and Roberts (1981) indicate that beta changes in response to changes in macroeconomic variables, such as the risk-free rate, default risk premium, term structure, inflation, and industrial production.[2]

Direct tests of the relationship between beta and common factors are provided by Ferson (1989) and DeJong and Collins (1985). Ferson (1989) provides evidence suggesting that beta may be a linear function of risk-free rates. Further, DeJong and Collins (1985) find that beta variability depends on the volatility of risk-free rates. They also find that beta variability is higher for firms with high leverage than for firms with low leverage.

This paper examines mutual fund returns to test whether intertemporal changes in fund betas are caused by common factors. An empirical Bayes estimator for random-walk betas is developed. The existence of common factors of beta variation is then examined by factor-analyzing the stochastic betas.[3] In identifying the common factors, we do not claim to examine an exhaustive set of macroeconomic variables, but instead propose to test the theories of Galai and Masulis (1976), Turnbull (1977), and Bildersee and Roberts (1981). Findings indicate that there are three common factors underlying intertemporal changes for mutual fund betas and that these factors are related to risk-free rate changes, default risk premia and term structure.[4]

Section II examines the problem of the portfolio manager attempting to maximize the utilityof the fund's shareholders. A linear model relating systematic risk and a set of common factors is developed. The testable propositions of the model are also presented. The data and methodology are discussed in Section III. Section IV presents the empirical results. Section V summarizes the major findings of the paper.

MACROECONOMIC FACTORS AND SYSTEMATIC RISK: A LINEAR MODEL

The Model

Jensen (1972) shows that the excess market return expected by the manager for period t is $E(R_m) + \pi_{it}^*$. The expected excess return and variance of return for the portfolio can be expressed as

$$E(R_{it}) = \beta_{it}[E(R_m) + \pi_{it}^*],\tag{1}$$

$$\sigma^2(R_{it}) = \beta_{it}^2\sigma_i^2(\pi_{it}^*),\tag{2}$$

where $\sigma_i^2(\pi_{it}^*)$ is the variance of the market factor forecast by manager i. The objective function for the manager becomes

$$\max_{\beta_{it}} U[\beta_{it}(E(R_m)+\pi_{it}^*),\ \beta_{it}^2\sigma_i^2(\pi_t^*)], \tag{3}$$

so that

$$\frac{dU}{d\beta_{it}} = \left[\frac{\partial U}{\partial E(R_i)}\right]\left[\frac{\partial E(R_i)}{\partial \beta_{it}}\right] + \left[\frac{\partial U}{\partial \sigma^2(R_i)}\right]\left[\frac{\partial \sigma^2(R_i)}{\partial \beta_{it}}\right] = 0, \tag{4}$$

or

$$\left[\frac{\partial U}{\partial E(R_i)}\right][E(R_m) + \pi_{it}^*] + \left[\frac{\partial U}{\partial \sigma^2(R_i)}\right][2\beta_{it}\sigma_i^2(\pi^*_{it})] = 0, \tag{5}$$

from which

$$\beta_{it} = -\frac{\left[\dfrac{\partial U}{\partial E(R_i)}\right][ER_m + \pi_{it}]}{\left[\dfrac{\partial U}{\partial \sigma^2(R_i)}\right]2\sigma_i^2(\pi_{it}^*)} \tag{6}$$

$$= \left[\frac{d\sigma^2(R_i)}{dE(R_i)}\right]\frac{[E(R_m) + \pi_{it}^*]}{2\sigma^2(\pi^*_{it})}$$

$$= g_{it}[E(R_m) + \pi^*_{it}],$$

where $g_{it} = [d\sigma^2(R_i)/dE(R_i)][1/2\sigma_i^2(\pi_{it}^*)]$.

Assume that $\sigma_i^2(\pi^*_{it})$ and $d\sigma^2(R_i)/dE(R_i)$ are constant. The latter term will be constant if investors have constant absolute risk-aversion. As pointed out by Jensen (1972), this assumption amounts to ignoring the second-order effects of changes in $E(R_i)$ and $\sigma^2(R_i)$ on $d\sigma^2(R_i)/dE(R_i)$. Thus, for small changes in $E(R_i)$ and $\sigma^2(R_i)$, $d\sigma^2(R_i)/dE(R_i)$ will be fairly constant. Equation (6) can be rewritten as

$$\beta_{it} = g_i[E(R_m) + \pi^*_{it}], \tag{7}$$

where g_i is a constant, $E(R_m)$ is the expected excess market return and π^*_{it} is the forecast by manager i of the market return from its mean for period t.

Managers will be assumed to forecast changes in the market return via an evaluation of selective macroeconomic factors thought to affect the market as a whole. The vector of selective macrofactors will be denoted as G and its value at time t as G_t. If π_{it}^* and G_t follow a multivariate normal distribution, then

$$E(\pi^*_{it}|G_t) = d_{0i} + d_{1i}G_t, \tag{8}$$

or

$$\pi^*_{it} = d_{0i} + d_{1i}G_t + \phi_{it,} \tag{9}$$

where ϕ_{it} is a zero-mean error term with $E(\phi_t,\phi_s) = \sigma_\phi^2$ for $t=s$ and zero otherwise; d_0 is the intercept, and d_1 is a row vector of slope coefficients. Substituting (9) into (7) yields

$$\begin{aligned} \beta_{it} &= g_i E(R_m) + g_i\pi^*_{it} \\ &= g_i E(R_m) + g_i[d_{0i} + d_{1i}G_t + \phi_{it}] \\ &= g_i[E(R_m) + d_{0i}] + g_id_{1i}G_t + g_i\phi_{it}. \end{aligned} \tag{10}$$

By defining $\beta_{io} = g_i[E(R_m)+d_{0i}]$ as the target beta, $a_i = g_id_{1i}$, and $c_{it} = g_i\phi_{it}$,

$$\beta_{it} = \beta_{i0} + a_iG_t + c_{it}. \tag{11}$$

Therefore, a multifactor beta model emerges in which beta is a combination of the set of common factors G_t and a fund-unique factor c_{it}.[5]

This paper will test the proposition that common factors underlie beta variability (H_1). The proposition that the common factors are related to the macroeconomic variables suggested by Galai and Masulis (1976), Turnbull (1977), and Bildersee and Roberts (1981) also will be tested (H_2). The variables considered in tests of H_2 are risk-free rate change, default risk premium, term structure, industrial production growth, and inflation change.

THE DATA AND METHODOLOGY

The Data

Monthly returns for 374 mutual funds for the period January 1978-December 1986 are used. All funds existed throughout the 108-month period. The sample consists of a wide range of growth/income objectives. The value-weighted CRSP index is used to proxy the market portfolio.

Monthly changes in 90-day Treasury bill rates are used to measure the monthly change in the risk-free rate. The difference between the monthly yields on corporate Baa-rated bonds and 20-year Treasury bonds is used to measure the default risk premia in a particular month. The difference between the yield on 20-year Treasury bonds in a particular month and the monthly return on 90-day Treasury bills in the previous month is used to measure the effects of the shape of the term structure.

The growth (difference in logarithms in two adjacent months) in the industrial production index is used to reflect industrial production uncertainty in the economy. Changes in the monthly growth in the consumer price index (CPI) are used as the inflation variable (which affects nominal cash flows as well as the discount rate). See Chen, Roll, and Ross (1986) for a discussion relating these variables to cash flow changes.

The monthly change in T-bill returns (RF), default risk premium (DRP), term structure (TS), growth in industrial production (IP), and change in inflation (INF) are used in the canonical correlation analysis to identify the common factors for the beta fluctuations. These data are collected from the *Federal Reserve Bulletin*.

Methods for Testing H_1

The first proposition, H_1, is related to the presence of common factors in beta variability. A direct test of H_1 can be derived by factor-analyzing the betas defined from (11) as $ß_{it} = ß_{io} + w_{it}$, where $w_{it} = a_i G_t + c_{it}$.

Factor analysis can be used to segment the sample correlation matrix of the $ß_{it}$ (estimated for all i and t) into common and unique factors. This section develops an empirical Bayes estimator (an unbiased, consistent, and efficient estimator) for the $ß_{it}$ and discusses how the $ß_{it}$ will be factor analyzed. Mutual fund betas will be assumed to follow a random-walk process.[6]

The Bayes Estimator for a Random-Walk Beta

For any fund i (subscript i omitted), consider the model,

$$R_t = \alpha + ß_t R_{mt} + \varepsilon_t \tag{12}$$

$$ß_t = ß_{t-1} + u_t, \text{ or} \tag{13}$$

$$ß_t = ß_o + w_t \tag{14}$$

where R_t is the excess fund return (over risk-free rate) in period t and R_{mt} is the excess return on the market index for period t; β_o is the starting point for β_t; and

ε_t and u_t and $w_t = \sum_{s=1}^{t} u_s$ are normally distributed disturbances for which $E(\varepsilon_t) =$

$E(u_t) = 0$, $E(\varepsilon_t \varepsilon_t) = \delta_{ts}\sigma_\varepsilon^2$, $E(u_t u_s) = \delta_{ts}\sigma_u^2$, and $E(\varepsilon_t u_s) = 0$, $\delta_{ts} = 1$ for $t = s$, zero otherwise.

Substituting (14) into (12) yields a mixed heteroskedastic model,

$$R_t = \alpha + ß_o R_{mt} + v_t, \tag{15}$$

where $v_t = R_{mt}w_t + \varepsilon_t$. The model, in matrix form, becomes

$$R = 1\alpha + R_m ß_o + v, \tag{16}$$

where R is the T-vector of R_t values, 1 is a T-vector of ones, R_m is the T-vector of R_{mt} values, and $v = Zw + \varepsilon$ is the T-vector of normally distributed disturbances, where Z is the $(T \times T)$ diagonal matrix whose tth diagonal element equals R_{mt}. The assumptions for u and ε imply that $E(\varepsilon\varepsilon') = \sigma_\varepsilon^2 I$, $E(ww') = \theta$, and $E(vv') = Z\theta Z' + \sigma_\varepsilon^2 I = \Omega$, where θ is a $(T \times T)$ matrix $\sigma_u^2((\theta_{ts}))$ and $\theta_{ts} = \min(t,s)$, or the minimum of observations t and s.

If (14) is regarded as the prior distribution for ß, the joint density of ß and R is

$$p(\text{ß},R) = (1/2\pi)^{T/2} \mid \theta \mid^{-\frac{1}{2}} \exp\{-1/2\,(\text{ß} - \mu)'\theta^{-1}(\text{ß} - \mu)\}(1/2\pi)^{T/2}(1/\sigma_\varepsilon)^T$$
$$\exp\{-\tfrac{1}{2}(r - Z\text{ß})'(r - Z\text{ß})/\sigma_\varepsilon^2\}, \tag{17}$$

where $\mu = 1\text{ß}_o$ and $r = R - 1\alpha$. After completing the square in ß, the exponent in (17) becomes

$$\exp\{\text{ß}'A\text{ß} - 2\text{ß}'C + r'r/\sigma_\varepsilon^2 + \mu'\theta^{-1}\mu + C'AC - C'AC\}, \tag{18}$$

or

$$\exp\{(\text{ß} - A^{-1}C)'A(\text{ß} - A^{-1}C) + r'r/\sigma_\varepsilon^2 + \mu'\theta^{-1}\mu - C'AC\}, \tag{19}$$

where $A = Z'Z/\sigma_\varepsilon^2 + \theta^{-1}$ and $C = Z'r/\sigma_\varepsilon^2 + \theta^{-1}\mu$. The marginal density of R, determined by integrating $p(\text{ß},R)$ with respect to ß, is

$$p(R) = (1/2\pi)^{T/2} \mid\theta\mid^{-\frac{1}{2}} (1/\sigma_\varepsilon)^T \exp\{-1/2(r'r/\sigma_\varepsilon^2 + \mu'\theta^{-1}\mu - C'AC)\}$$
$$\times \mid A \mid^{-\frac{1}{2}} \int (1/2\pi)^{T/2} \mid A \mid^{\frac{1}{2}} \exp\{-\tfrac{1}{2}(\text{ß} - A^{-1}C)'A(\text{ß} - A^{-1}C)\}d\text{ß}. \tag{20}$$

The term in the integral is a normal density of ß with mean $A^{-1}C$ and covariance matrix A^{-1}. Hence, the posterior density of ß given R is

$$p(\text{ß} \mid R) = p(R,\text{ß})/p(R) = (1/2\pi)^{T/2} \mid A \mid^{\frac{1}{2}} \exp\{-1/2(\text{ß} - A^{-1}C)'A(\text{ß} - A^{-1}C)\}, \tag{21}$$

which is a normal density with mean $A^{-1}C$ and covariance matrix A^{-1}. If a quadratic loss function such as the mean squared error, $E(\text{ß} - \hat{\text{ß}})'\,(\text{ß} - \hat{\text{ß}})$, is used to estimate ß, then the best estimate of ß is the mean of the posterior distribution (see DeGroot, 1975, p. 169),

$$\hat{\text{ß}} = (\text{ß} \mid R) = A^{-1}C = (Z'Z/\sigma_\varepsilon^2 + \theta^{-1})^{-1}(\theta^{-1}\mu + Z'r/\sigma_\varepsilon^2), \tag{22}$$

where

$$(Z'Z/\sigma_\varepsilon^2 + \theta^{-1})^{-1} = \theta - \theta Z'\,\Omega^{-1}Z\theta \tag{23}$$

(see Rao, 1973, p.33). Hence, the Bayesian estimator for ß is

$$\hat{\beta} = \mu + \theta Z'r/\sigma_\varepsilon^2 - \theta Z'\Omega^{-1} Z\theta\,(\theta^{-1}\mu + Z'r/\sigma^2)$$

$$= 1\beta_0 + \theta Z'\Omega^{-1}\,(\Omega\, r/\sigma_\varepsilon^2 - X\beta_0 - Z\theta Z'r/\sigma_\varepsilon^2)$$

$$= 1\beta_0 + \theta Z'\Omega^{-1} v. \tag{24}$$

Rosenberg (1972) and Sarris (1973) prove, in an analogous context, that the Bayesian estimator is the best linear unbiased estimator for the ß vector.

To estimate β_0, σ_ε^2, and σ_u^2, first compute the OLS residuals from (16), $e = R - 1\alpha - R_m\hat{\beta}_o = Mv$, where $M = I - X(X'X)^{-1}X'$, where $X = (1, R_m)$. Noting that $E(ee')$ $= M\Omega M = M(Z\theta Z' + \sigma_\varepsilon^2\,I)M$ and defining $Z\theta Z' = \sigma_u^2 Q = \sigma_u^2\,((\theta_{ts}X_tX_s))$, then

$$\dot{e} = \Gamma\dot{\sigma} + \omega, \tag{25}$$

where $E(\dot{e})$ is the T-vector of diagonal elements of $E(ee')$, $\dot{\sigma} = (\sigma_u^2, \sigma_\varepsilon^2)'$, ω is the T-vector of random disturbances equal to $\dot{e} - E(\dot{e})$, and Γ is the $(T \times 2)$ matrix equal to $[\mathrm{diag}(MQM)\ \mathrm{diag}(M)]$. The restricted least squares estimator, $\hat{\sigma}$ from $\min\,(\dot{e} - \Gamma\hat{\sigma})'\,(\dot{e} - \Gamma\hat{\sigma})$, subject to $\sigma_\varepsilon^2 \geq 0$ and $\sigma_u^2 \geq 0$, is used to obtain consistent (see Hildreth and Houck, 1968) nonnegative estimates of σ_ε^2 and σ_u^2.

The empirical Bayes estimator for the $(T \times 1)$ ß vector is

$$\tilde{\beta} = 1\tilde{\beta}_0 + \tilde{w}. \tag{26}$$

where $(\alpha, \tilde{\beta}_0)' = (X'\hat{\Omega}^{-1}X)^{-1}X'\Omega^{-1}R,\ \tilde{w} = \hat{\theta}Z'\hat{\Omega}^{-1}\tilde{e},\ \tilde{e} = R - 1\tilde{\alpha} - R_m\tilde{\beta}_0$. Because the estimators for σ_ε^2 and σ_u^2 are consistent, the empirical Bayes estimator for ß is asymptotically minimum variance (see Hildreth and Houck, 1968).

Thus, $\tilde{\beta}$ equals its target, $1\tilde{\beta}_o$, plus an estimate of its stochastic component, $\tilde{w} = \hat{\theta}Z\hat{\Omega}^{-1}\tilde{e}$. Note that $\hat{\theta}Z'\hat{\Omega}^{-1}$ is used to allocate or ration the elements of the compound GLS residual $\tilde{e}$ among the elements of $\tilde{w}$.

Factor Analysis of Beta Fluctuations

To test H_1, a principal factor analysis will be performed on the β_{it} estimated for the sample of mutual funds.[7] To ensure the accuracy and computational efficiency of the decomposition of the correlation matrix for $\tilde{\beta}_{it}$, funds will be randomly assigned to groups of thirty (see Roll and Ross, 1980). The existence of common factors in the $\tilde{\beta}_{it}$ will be tested by applying Bartlett's sphericity test (see Green, 1978) on each group.

Horn's (1965) criterion will be applied to determine the minimum number of common factors to retain.[8] To apply Horn's test, the size of each eigenvalue is graphed as a function of the factor number. This set of points is superimposed on the set of eigenvalues generated from simulated independently distributed standardized variables. Thirty samples of size 30 will be simulated from an identity population correlation matrix. For each factor, eigenvalues will be averaged across the 30 simulations. Factors will be retained up to the point where the plot of actual eigenvalues crosses the plot of simulated average eigenvalues. Crawford and Koopman (1973) conduct simulations indicating that Horn's test performs well using principal-component methods.

Methods for Testing H_2

The second proposition states that the common sources of beta variation are related to observable macroeconomic variables. Tests of H_2 will be performed for each group of funds used in tests of H_1.

Canonical Correlation Analysis

Canonical correlation analysis is used to test the strength of the relationship between sets of dependent (criterion) and independent (predictor) variables. Factor scores will form the criterion set (a linear composite of the common factor scores), while the macroeconomic variables (suggested by theory) will comprise the predictor set (a linear composite of RF, DRP, TS, IP, and INF). H_2 is supported if the canonical correlation is statistically significant.[9]

The canonical correlation between the criterion and predictor sets will be tested for significance using Wilks's lambda (see Seber 1984). The redundancy index, a measure of the variance shared by the criterion and predictor sets, will serve as a guideline to evaluate the strength of the canonical relationship. The canonical correlation will be performed on the standardized values of the variables.

Regression

The time series for the most important factors of beta variation will be regressed on the macroeconomic variables. An economic variable (RF, DRP, TS, IP, or INF) is significantly related to the common source of variation if it is significantly related to one of the common factors. A similar test is performed by Chen, Roll, and Ross (1986) to see if asset prices react to changes in hypothesized macroeconomic variables. Appropriate F- and t-tests will be performed for joint and individual testing of the regression coefficients.

Pooling Factor Scores

By testing H_2 on individual groups, information on all the groups is not used simultaneously. Berges (1982), however, has developed a rotation method that pools the factors across groups (also see Chang and Lewellen, 1985). Thus, factors in different groups can be reduced to a common space by rotation with respect to a "basis group." While any group could form the basis, Berges recommends that the group with the maximum explained common variance for a given number of factors be chosen as the basis.

The objective of the Berges method is to estimate F, the unknown true underlying factor score matrix. Let group i be the basis group and define F_i as the factor score matrix estimated for group i. Berges shows that F_j, the factor score matrix for group j, can be brought to congruence with F_i through the transformation, $F_i(j) = F_j(F_j'F_j)^{-1}F_j'F_i$, where $F_i(j)$ is the factor score matrix inferred for the securities in group j after being rotated to congruence with that of group i. F is estimated by pooling (averaging) the $F_i(j)$ matrices across the groups. Thus, the information contained in all funds' beta fluctuations is applied to extract a single set of most representative factor scores. Tests of H_2 will be repeated for the pooled scores.

EMPIRICAL RESULTS

The 374 funds in the sample are randomly divided into 12 groups. Each group contains 30 funds, except for the last group, which contains 44 funds. Monthly estimates of beta are derived for 1978-1986 for each fund in each group using the estimated values of σ_ε^2 and σ_u^2. The resulting 11 (30×108) matrices and 1 (44×108) matrix of beta fluctuations form the basis for subsequent analysis and hypotheses testing.

Results for Tests of H_1

The chi-square values for Bartlett's sphericity test are significant beyond the .01 level for each of the 12 groups. Thus, the null hypothesis (of Bartlett's sphericity test) that the correlation matrix of betas is an identity matrix is rejected. This finding supports H_1, that common factors underlie the intertemporal beta fluctuations.[10]

Table 1 reports the number of factors retained by Horn's criterion. The Horn test indicates that, for the majority of mutual fund groups, three factors should be retained.[11] Table 1 also presents the percentage of variance explained (a) by the number of factors extracted by Horn's test and (b) by three factors. The three factors explain between 90 (group 10) and 95% (group 2) of the variance in mutual fund betas. These results lend further support for the hypothesis (H_1) that common factors underlie beta variability.

Results for Tests of H_2

Canonical Correlation Results

The canonical correlates for each group are tested for significance at the .01 level using Wilks's lambda. Of the 12 individual groups and the pooled group,

Table 1.   Results of Principal Factor Analysis for Mutual Fund Betas

| | Number of Factors Retained | Common Variance Explained | |
Group	by Horn's Criterion[b]	by Horn's Criterion[c]	by Three Factors
1	3	.92	.92
2	3	.95	.95
3	3	.91	.91
4	3-4	.96 (4)	.91
5	3	.93	.93
6	3	.92	.92
7	3	.91	.91
8	3	.94	.94
9	4	.94	.94
10	3	.90	.90
11	3	.91	.91
12	3-4	.93 (4)	.91

Notes: [a]Monthly mutual fund returns for the 108-month period 1978-1986 are used to derive empirical Bayes estimates of monthly fund betas. Monthly betas are derived for a sample of 374 funds. Funds are randomly assigned to 11 groups of 30 and 1 group (group 12) of 44. For each group, a factor analysis on fund betas is performed. For each group, the number of factors extracted and the common variance explained by the extracted factors using Horn's criterion are reported.
[b]When the scree plots of eigenvalues of a group of securities and of average eigenvalues of the simulated group intersect between two factors (e.g., 3 and 4), both factors are reported (e.g., for group 4, 3-4).
[c]Number of factors for which variance is reported is shown in parentheses [e.g., for group 4, (4)] when the scree plot intersects between two factors.

each has two significant canonical correlates.[12] For the first (second) correlate, the canonical correlation coefficient ranges from 0.79 to 0.85 (0.66 to 0.81) across the 12 groups and equals 0.84 (0.75) for the pooled group. These initial results support the models of Galai and Masulis (1976), Turnbull (1977), and Bildersee and Roberts (1981), predicting that beta variability is related to the set of macroeconomic variables RF, DRP, TS, IP, and INF.

Table 2 presents the results of the canonical correlation performed on the pooled scores and the five macroeconomic variables. Factor scores (criterion variables) and macroeconomic variables (predictor variables) with squared loadings that are at least as large as the average squared loading can be considered to be major contributors to the canonical correlation (RF, DRP, TS). The results of the redundancy index indicate that 48% of the variance in the criterion variables is explained by the predictor variables. The data presented in Table 2 suggest that (a) the three factors are major contributors to the canonical relationship and (b) RF, DRP, and TS are major determinants of beta variability.[13] The latter finding lends additional support for the models developed by Galai and Masulis (1976) and Bildersee and Roberts (1981).

Table 2.　Canonical Analysis of the Pooled Factor Scores of Mutual Fund Betas and the Macroeconomic Variables[a]

| | Canonical Function 1 | | Canonical Function 2 | |
	Loading	Squared Loading	Loading	Squared Loading
Criterion variables:				
Factor 1	0.60[b]	0.36	0.19	0.04
Factor 2	0.29	0.08	0.83[b]	0.69
Factor 3	-0.75[b]	0.56	0.42	0.18
Average		0.33		0.30
Predictor variables:				
RF	-0.50[b]	0.25	0.09	0.00
DRP	-0.20	0.04	1.02[b]	1.04
TS	1.01[b]	1.02	0.06	0.00
IP	0.02	0.00	-0.06	0.00
INF	0.04	0.00	0.15	0.02
Average		0.25		0.21
Canonical correlation		0.84	0.78	
Significance level		0.0001	0.0001	
Criterion redundancy index		0.25	0.23	Total = 0.48

Notes:　[a]Empirical Bayes estimates of monthly mutual fund betas for the period 1978-1986 are factor-analyzed to derive factor scores for three common factors for 12 groups of funds. Factor score matrices are pooled across the 12 groups using the Berges (1982) method. Results of a canonical correlation between the set of pooled factor scores (criterion variables) and the set of macroeconomic variables (predictor variables) are reported. The macroeconomic variables are monthly changes in 90-day Treasury bill returns (RF), monthly inflation rate changes (INF), monthly industrial production growth (IP), monthly default risk premia (DRP), and monthly term structure (TS).

[b]Squared loading for the variable is greater than the average squared loading.

Regression Results

A more formal test of the importance of RF, DRP, TS, IP, and INF as common factors of beta variability is provided by a regression of the factor score time series for factor 1, 2, or 3 on the five macroeconomic variables. Findings indicate that RF, DRP, and TS are significant at the 0.05 level (for each of the 12 groups, *t*-statistics for the RF, DRP, and TS are significant using scores for factor 1, 2, or 3 as the dependent variable).[14] Neither INF nor IP is significant in the three regressions for any of the groups. Moreover, the *F*-statistic for joint significance of INF and IP is insignificant in the three respective regressions.

Similar results are found when using the pooled scores. RF, DRP, and TS are statistically significant (at the 0.05 level) when regressed against the pooled scores for factor 1 (*t*-statistics = -2.63, 1.98, and 6.74), factor 2 (*t*-statistics = -1.98, 9.67, and 4.41) or factor 3 (*t*-statistics = 4.51, 7.83, and -9.17). Again, neither INF nor IP is statistically significant in any of the three regressions. The *F*-statistics for joint significance of INF and IP are 0.25, 0.34, and 0.48 in the three respective regressions.

These results indicate that, of the five variables considered, RF, DRP and TS are significantly related to the common factors of beta variation. Thus, support is provided for the theoretical models developed by Galai and Masulis (1976) and Bildersee and Roberts (1981), in which RF, DRP and TS are determinants of beta variability.

SUMMARY

This paper examines the relationship between mutual fund betas and common factors. A model linking systematic risk to a set of factors is derived. An empirical Bayes estimate of the stochastic component of a random-walk beta is developed. The estimated intertemporal fluctuations in beta are factor-analyzed and the extracted factors are tested for statistical significance. The results support the hypothesis that common factors underlie beta variability. From the analysis, three common factors are retained.

This paper also tests the relationship between a set of five macroeconomic variables and the common factors of beta variation. Prior theory is used to select the macroeconomic variables: risk-free rate changes, default risk premium, term structure, industrial production growth, and inflation changes. Of the five variables, risk-free rate changes, default risk premia, and term structure are found to be significantly related to the common factors of beta variation.

ACKNOWLEDGMENTS

Participants in workshops at the University of Texas at Arlington and the University of Missouri—Columbia, especially Dick Pettway and Brad Jordan, are acknowledged for their helpful comments on earlier drafts of this paper. An earlier version of this paper was presented at the 1991 Southern Finance Association Meetings.

NOTES

1.   Fabozzi and Francis (1977, 1979) and Francis and Fabozzi (1979) find that the parameters of the single-index market model estimated for mutual funds are not significantly different between rising and falling markets.

2.   Galai and Masulis (1976) use an option-pricing/capital-asset-pricing model to prove that beta is affected by changes in the risk-free rate and variables relating to the leverage sensitivity of beta such as the default risk premium on corporate bonds and the term structure (also see Hamada, 1972; Lev, 1974; and Boquist, Racette, and Schlarbaum, 1975). Turnbull (1977) derives a solution in which systematic risk depends on macroeconomic variables related to cash flows. Since cash flows generally depend on the state of the economy, changes in variables such as industrial production and inflation (also see Chen, Roll ,and Ross, 1986) can be expected to affect beta.

3.   Also see Oldfield and Rogalski (1981), who factor-analyze Treasury bill returns to identify common factors for stock returns.

4.   Identical testing on 1447 firms was performed. Identical conclusions were reached, namely, that common factors are a source of security beta variability and that these factors are related to changes in

risk-free rate, default risk premia, and term structure variables. Moreover, in addition to the random walk, a purely random coefficient process for ß was also examined. The major conclusions were unchanged.

5.   The multifactor beta model is similar to Rosenberg's (1972) fundamental beta model. Rosenberg uses a factor-analytic model for asset returns and derives a model in which beta is linearly related to firm-unique variables. If part of the variability in the firm-unique variables is captured by common factors, then the fundamental beta model may be recast as the multifactor beta model.

6.   Sunder (1980) provides an intuitive argument for a random-walk beta, contending that a firm is a nexus or portfolio of assets that gradually evolves over time through acquisition, merger, etc. The systematic risk in period t of the evolving portfolio, therefore, is likely to be stochastically related to its value in period t - 1. Sunder finds substantial evidence that betas follow a random-walk process.

7.   Shukla and Trzcinka (1990) provide justification for the use of component analysis versus maximum likelihood factor analysis.

8.   For problems of factor extraction in asset-pricing models see, among others, Brown (1989), Chamberlain and Rothchild (1983), Dhrymes, Friend, and Gultekin (1984), Ehrhardt (1987), and Trzcinka (1986).

9.   For application of canonical correlation analysis to test the relationship of macroeconomic variables to common factors in security returns, see Fogler, John, and Tipton (1981).

10.   Bartlett's extended test (see Green, 1978) also is performed to test the hypothesis that no additional factors, beyond that indicated by Horn's criterion, are needed. The null hypothesis is that the residual matrix, following extraction of the common factors (e.g., as indicated by Horn's criterion), is an identity matrix. The test is performed as a check that Horn's criterion does not overspecify the number of common factors. If the number of common factors is overspecified, noise is introduced into the common factor structure. Results of Bartlett's extended test indicate that the common factors retained in this paper are not overspecified.

11.   The application of the Kaiser (1959) rule (minimum eigenvalue =1) results in the retention of 3 to 5 common factors, whereas Horn's criterion indicates that 3 to 4 factors should be retained. Further, application of the Kaiser rule (Horn's criterion) indicates that the retained factors explain between 92 and 97% (90 and 97%) of the common variance. Green (1978) explains that the Kaiser rule often overstates the number of common factors and, further, that Horn's criterion provides a less ambiguous test.

12.   In applying the pooling technique, Group 2, with 95% of the common variance explained by the three factors retained, is chosen as the basis. The three-factor scores of the remaining groups are rotated with respect to the basis group and are then pooled (averaged) across groups. The pooled factor scores do not exhibit significant correlation and thus are not reorthogonalized.

13.   Similar results are found when the groups are examined individually.

14.   The correlations among the state variables are fairly small, ranging from −0.28 between DRP and RF to 0.26 between TS and RF.

REFERENCES

Berges, Angel (1982). Arbitrage pricing theory: estimation and application. Ph.D. dissertation, Purdue University.

Bildersee, John S, & Roberts, Gordon S. (1981). Beta instability when interest levels change. *Journal of Financial and Quantitative Analysis 16*, 375-380.

Boquist, John A., Racette, George A., & Schlarbaum, Gary G. (1975). Duration and risk assessment for bonds and stocks, *Journal of Finance 30*, 261-263.

Bos, Theodore, & Newbold, Paul (1984). An empirical investigation of the possibility of stochastic systematic risk in the market model, *Journal of Business 57*, 35-41.

Brown, Stephen J. (1989). The number of factors in security returns. *Journal of Finance 44*, 1247-1262.

Chamberlain, Gary, & Rothchild, Michael (1983). Arbitrage and mean variance analysis on large markets. *Econometrica 51*, 1281-1301.

Chang, Eric C., & Lewellen, Wilbur G. (1985). An arbitrage pricing approach to evaluating mutual fund performance. *Journal of Financial Research 1*, 15-30.

Chen, Nai-Fu, Roll, Richard, & Ross, Stephen A. (1986). Economic forces and the stock market. *Journal of Business 59*, 383-403.

Collins, Daniel W., LeDolter, Johannes, & Rayburn, Judy (1987). Some further evidence on the stochastic properties of systematic risk. *Journal of Business 66*, 425-448.

Crawford, Charles B., & Koopman, Paul (1973). A note on Horn's test for the number of factors in factor analysis. *Multivariate Behavioral Research 8*, 117-125.

DeGroot, Morris H. (1975). *Probability and statistics*. Reading, MA: Addison-Wesley.

DeJong, Bradford J., & Collins, Daniel W. (1985). Explanations for the instability of equity beta: Risk-free rate changes and leverage effects. *Journal of Financial and Quantitative Analysis 20*, 73-94.

Dhrymes, Phoebus, J., Friend, Irwin, & Gultekin, N. Bulent (1984). A critical examination of the empirical evidence of the arbitrage pricing theory. *Journal of Finance 39*, 323-346.

Ehrhardt, Michael C. (1987). Arbitrage pricing models: The sufficient number of factors and equilibrium conditions. *Journal of Financial Research 10*, 111-120.

Fabozzi, Frank J., & Francis, Jack Clark (1977). Stability tests for alphas and betas over bull and bear conditions. *Journal of Finance 32*, 1093-1099.

Fabozzi, Frank J., & Francis, Jack Clark (1978). Beta as a random coefficient. *Journal of Financial and Quantitative Analysis 13*, 101-116.

Fabozzi, Frank J., & Francis, Jack Clark (1979). Mutual fund systematic risk for bull and bear markets: An empirical examination. *Journal of Finance 34*, 1243-1250.

Ferson, Wayne, E. (1989). Changes in expected security returns, risk, and the level of interest rates. *Journal of Finance 44*, 1191-1218.

Fogler, H. Russell., John, Kose, & Tipton, James (1981). Three factors, interest rate differentials and stock groups. *Journal of Finance 36*, 323-335.

Francis, Jack Clark, & Fabozzi, Frank. J. (1979). The effects of changing macroeconomic conditions on the parameters of the single index market model. *Journal of Financial and Quantitative Analysis 14*, 351-360.

Galai, Dan, & Masulis, Ronald W. (1976). The option pricing model and the risk factor of stock. *Journal of Financial Economics 3*, 53-81.

Green, Paul E. (1978). *Analyzing multivariate data*. Hinsdale, IL: Holt, Rinehart and Winston.

Hamada, Robert S. (1972). The effects of a firm's capital structure on the systematic risk of common stocks. *Journal of Finance 27*, 383-393.

Hildreth, Clifford, & Houck, James (1968). Some estimators for a linear model with random coefficients. *Journal of the American Statistical Association 63*, 584-595.

Horn, John L. (1965). A rationale and test for the number of factors in factor analysis. *Psychometrika 30*, 179-186.

Jensen, Michael C. (1972). Optimal utilization of market forecasts and the evaluation of investment performance, in G.P. Szego and K. Shell (eds.), *Mathematical methods in investment and finance*. Amsterdam: North Holland.

Kaiser, Harold F. (1959). The application of electronic computers to factor analysis. Paper presented at the symposium on the application of computers to psychological problems, American Psychological Association.

Lee, Cheng F., & Chen, Carl R. (1982). Beta stability and tendency: An application of a variable mean response regression model. *Journal of Business and Economics 34*, 201-206.

Lee, Cheng F., & Chen, Son N. (1980). A random coefficient model for reexamining risk-decomposition method and risk-return relationship test. *Quarterly Review of Economics and Business 20*, 58-69.

Lev, Baruch (1974). On the association between operating leverage and risk. *Journal of Financial and Quantitative Analysis*, 627-641.

Ohlson, James A., & Rosenberg, Barr (1982). Systematic risk of the CRSP equally-weighted common stock index: A history estimated by stochastic parameter regression. *Journal of Business 55*, 121-145.

Oldfield, George, & Rogalski, Richard (1981). Treasury bill factors and common stock returns. *Journal of Finance 36*, 337-354.

Rao, C. Radhakrisna (1973). *Linear statistical inference and its applications*. New York: John Wiley.

Roll, Richard, & Ross, Stephen A. (1980). An empirical investigation of the arbitrage pricing theory. *Journal of Finance 35*, 1073-1103.

Rosenberg, Barr (1972). The estimation of stationary stochastic regression parameters reexamined. *Journal of the American Statistical Association 67*, 650-654.

Sarris, Alexander H. (1973). Kalman filter models: A Bayesian approach to estimations of time-varying regression coefficients. *Annals of Economic and Social Measurement 2*, 501-523.

Seber, G.A.F. (1984). *Multivariate observations*. New York: John Wiley.

Shukla, Ravi, & Trzcinka, Charles A. (1990). Sequential tests of the arbitrage pricing theory: A comparison of principal components and maximum likelihood factors. *Journal of Finance 45*, 1541-1564.

Sunder, Shyam (1980). Stationarity of market risk: random coefficients tests for individual stocks. *Journal of Finance 35*, 883-896.

Trzcinka, Charles (1986). On the number of factors in the arbitrage pricing model. *Journal of Finance 41*, 347-368.

Turnbull, Stuart M. (1977). Market value and systematic risk. *Journal of Finance 32*, 1125-1142.

SPECULATIVE DYNAMICS:
THE CASE OF MASTERSHARES

Samir K. Barua and Jayanth R. Varma

ABSTRACT

The share of a a closed-end mutual fund may be regarded as derived securities because their value depends entirely on the prices of securities that comprise the fund portfolio. Therefore, the net asset value (NAV) of these shares, after adjustments for winding-up costs, can be regarded as their fundamental value. In an efficient market, the prices of these shares would move in line with the changes in their NAV. This paper examines the relationship between the price and the NAV of mastershares, the first closed-end fund in India. The investigations revealed that there is excessive volatility in prices, not justified by the fluctuations in the NAV. The prices also show a mean-reverting behavior. these observations are in line with recent works on irrationality in pricing securities and emphasize the doubts raised about the efficacy of standard tests for market efficiency.

INTRODUCTION

It is well recognized that the usual statistical procedures for testing market efficiency test a joint hypothesis on market efficiency and models for valuation of

Advances in Financial Planning and Forecasting,
Volume 5, pages 17-28.

securities. The procedures are based on the premise that the market rationally values the securities to reflect economic realities. However, works of Shiller (1981a, 1981b, 1990a, 1990b), LeRoy and Porter (1981), Poterba and Summers (1986), Cutler, Poterba, and Summers (1989)), and LeRoy (1989) present mounting evidence that the security prices tend to be far more volatile than what can be justified on the basis of the changes in their fundamental values. This kind of inefficiency in valuation is difficult to detect using the conventional testing procedures for efficiency.

To accommodate observed irrationalities, alternative models for decision-making and valuation of securities have been proposed. Tversky and Kahnman (1981, 1986) have suggested psychological models for individual decision-making, which could explain the behavior of speculative markets. Summers (1986) proposed a "fads" model in which the valuation differs from the fundamental value by a multiplicative factor. This model, which can also capture mean reversion, was subsequently tested by Poterba and Summers (1988). Summers argues in his 1986 paper that the standard procedures for testing the efficient market hypothesis (EHM) would be unable to detect persistent departures from the fundamental values. Therefore, the inability to reject the EHM by conventional methods should not lead to its automatic acceptance, without examining whether the securities are priced irrationally.

This paper reports empirical research done in the same spirit as the works cited above. The setting for the work is the valuation of a closed-end mutual fund in the Indian capital market. The conclusions from the study further establish the universality of the observations and some of the arguments being advanced in these works.

THE SETTING

Despite being a developing economy, India has a mature stock market, established well over a hundred years ago. The first stock exchange in India, established at Bombay in 1885, has more than 6,000 listed companies (*Emerging Stock Markets Factbook 1990*, 1990). This number is exceeded only by the NYSE and is much larger than the number of listed companies in other stock markets in the world. With a market capitalization of about Rs. 1200 billion (Rs., rupees, is the Indian currency) as of early February 1992 and an estimated equity investor base of about 25 million, the Bombay Stock Exchange compares well with the largest stock exchanges in the world.

The Indian stock market, as reported in the works of Rao and Mukherjee (1971), Sharma and Kennedy (1977), Barua (1981), and Ramachandran (1984), to name a few, has been found to be efficient in the weak and the semistrong. This conclusion, arrived at using the conventional methods of testing market efficiency, is in line with similar works in markets in the developed economies. Evidence of inefficiency in some situation, reported in Barua and Raghunathan (1986, 1987), has primarily arises from government regulations in the primary markets. The standard asset-pricing models also apply well in the Indian market, as concluded by Varma (1988) through rigorous testing.

In 1986, after considerable debate on their utility, the government of India finally gave the green light to establishment of mutual funds.[1] Therefore, in September 1986, the Unit Trust of India (UTI) launched Masteshares, the first closed-end mutual fund in the Indian market. The planned size of the fund was half a billion rupees. However, since the issue was oversubscribed, the UTI decided to retain the entire collection of about Rs. 1.50 billion. In March 1989, about another Rs. 0.80 billion was added to the corpus through a rights issue.

Mastershares was conceived as a growth fund. The UTI had made it clear at the time of issue itself that it would be under no obligation to distribute any fixed percentage of income as dividends. The benefits to the shareholders would primarily be in the form of capital appreciation. The UTI also announced that the redemption of Mastershares would commence after October 19, 1993, that is, seven years after the issue, on terms to be specified by the UTI. The redemption price would be based on the net asset value (NAV). In line with the stated objectives, the fund has almost exclusively been invested in equity. To ensure liquidity, Mastershares has been listed in all the major stock exchanges in the country. The UTI computed and announces the NAV of Mastershares periodically, generally once a week, so as to keep the shareholders informed about how the fund is performing.

THE RESEARCH ISSUE

An analysis of performance of Mastershares by Barua and Varma (1991) concluded that while the performance of the fund on the basis of NAV was impressive, its performance in the market, based on prices, could be described as mediocre, because of a much higher systematic risk. The analysis revealed considerable divergence between prices and NAV. Since the NAV, after some adjustments for winding-up costs, may be regarded as the fundamental value of a closed-end mutual fund, the observed divergence has important implications for the process of valuation and market efficiency.

This paper reports a deeper investigation of the nature of the relationship between NAV and prices. The analysis has been done in three distinct stages: (a) estimation of the market model of NAV and prices, (b) assessment of the response of prices to unexpected changes in NAV, (c) examination of the impact of the discount at which Mastershares is quoted below its NAV, on future returns. The details of the methodology used and the empirical results obtained for each stage of analysis are described separately in the following three sections. The concluding section discusses the results by drawing comparisons with similar results obtained in the U.S. capital markets, and offers some plausible explanations in the Indian context.

THE MARKET MODEL FOR NAV AND PRICES

The estimable form of the capital-asset-pricing model (CAPM), the market model, was applied to the NAV and the prices separately:

$$r_t = \alpha + \beta r_{m, t} + e_t, \tag{1}$$

where

r_t is the return in period t,
$r_{m,t}$ is the market return in period t,
e_t is the error term,
α is the constant term, which according to the CAPM should equal $r_f(1 - \beta)$.

The All Industries All India Equity Index computed by the Economic Times (ET index) was used as the market index. The returns were computed assuming continuous compounding:

$$r_{\text{NAV}, t} = \ln(\text{NAV}_t / \text{NAV}_{t-1}), \tag{2}$$
$$r_{\text{MP},t} = \ln(\text{MP}_t / \text{MP}_{t-1}), \tag{3}$$
$$r_{m,t} = \ln(\text{ET}_t / \text{ET}_{t-1}), \tag{4}$$

where

NAV_t is the NAV at the end of period t
MP_t is the price at the end of period t,
ET_t is the ET index at the end of period t.

The ET index, the NAV, and the price of Mastershares were collected for all the dates on which the UTI computed the NAV (hereafter called the *computation dates*). The period of analysis is from July 1987 to September 1990, as the UTI started computing and announcing the NAV, at an average interval of one week form June 1987 onwards. The coefficients estimated for the market model for NAV were as follows:

Period	N	$\alpha*$	$\beta*$	R^2	Test $\alpha = R_f(1 - B)$
Jul 87-	167	0.490%	0.813	0.791	F = 29.065
Sep 90		(5.78)	(24.98)		P = 0.000

Note: *t*-values are in parentheses.

The CAPM specifies that $\alpha = R_f(1 - \beta)$. The result of testing this hypothesis is reported in the last column. The testing was done assuming an R_f of 12% per annum. The *F*-value is the *F*-statistic with $(1, N - 2)$ degrees of freedom for this linear restriction on parameters, and the *P*-value is the probability (significance level) corresponding to the *F*-value. The hypothesis is rejected at a very high level of significance. The value of α $\alpha\tau$ 0.49 is far above the value 0.041% implied by the hypothesis. Thus Mastershares has earned a return that is significantly above the equilibrium return mandated by the CAPM.

The coefficients for the market model based on prices turned out to be as follows:

Period	N	$\alpha*$	$\beta*$	R^2	Test $\alpha = R_f(1 - B)$
Jul 87-	154	0.125%	1.166	0.359	F = 0.255
Sep 90		(0.38)	(9.22)		P = 0.614

The last column contains the result of testing for abnormal returns. The *F*-statistic and *P*-value indicated that the hypothesized value of alpha cannot be rejected. Thus, unlike the case of NAV-based returns, Mastershares has not earned abnormal returns, when returns are based on prices. A similar anomaly is observed in the variability of the returns also: while the standard deviation of returns on NAV is 2.3% per week, the returns on prices show a standard deviation of 5.02%. This is in line with the excess variability observed in the studies cited earlier.

RELATION BETWEEN NAV AND PRICE

Since the NAV is computed using the prices of shares, it represents the current market value of the portfolio held by Mastershares. As mentioned earlier, unlike the book value for an ordinary share, the NAV can, with some adjustments for liquidation costs and management expenses, be regarded as the "fundamental value" of the Mastershares. Hence, one would expect the market price to move in tandem with this fundamental value.

The preceding results, however, indicate that the actual behavior does not conform to this theoretical expectation. As a first step toward understanding the actual relationship, a simple linear regression of market prices on NAV was run. The result was as follows:

$$MP = -1.673 + 0.884\text{NAV}, \qquad R^2 = 0.802$$
$$(-1.81) \quad (21.38)$$

The numbers in parentheses are the *t*-values. The R^2 of 0.802 and a highly significant coefficient of 0.884 indicate a strong influence of NAV on price. However, to confirm that the relationship was not spurious, a simple linear regression of prices on the market index was run. The result was as follows:

$$MP = -5.417 + 0.059ET, \qquad R^2 = 0.867$$
$$(-6.20) \quad (26.86)$$

The high R^2 and significant coefficient of market index indicate a possibility that the relationship between the NAV and the price could be spurious, caused by both being related strongly to the market index. To complete the analysis, a regression was run with both the NAV and the index as independent variables:

$$MP = -6.182 + 0.077ET - 0.293NAV, \qquad R^2 = 0.871$$
$$(-6.43) \quad (7.49) \qquad (-1.81)$$

The regression estimates above indicate that the index provides most of the explanation of variations in prices. The coefficient of NAV is not very significant and is not very significant and is of the wrong sign. However, this result could have arisen from multicollinearity. A more sophisticated methodology based on examining the impact of unanticipated changes in NAV on the prices was used for further investigation.

IMPACT OF UNANTICIPATED CHANGES IN NAV ON PRICES

As mentioned earlier, the NAV is published only at weekly intervals, and even on the date of publication is a few days old. Theoretically, the market should use the latest published NAV to estimate the current NAV and price the Mastershares accordingly. When a new NAV is announced, the market price should be affect only if the announced NAV diverges from the previous estimate. In other words, the market price would respond only to unanticipated changes in NAV. Some notations are introduced to explain the proposed methodology:

$a(n)$ = first trading date after announcement of the nth NAV,
$a'(n)$ = last trading date before announcement of the nth NAV,
$c(n)$ = the date on which the nth NAV is computed.

The behavior of the prices between $a(n)$ and $a'(n)$ is modeled as follows in terms of the of the logarithmic returns:

$$MPRET_1 = b_0 + b_1ETRET_1\, b_2UNEXP, \qquad (5)$$

where

MPRET$_1$ = return on the price = ln[MP$_{a(n)}$]
ETRET$_1$ = return on the market index = ln[ET$_{a(n)}$/ ET$_{a'(n)}$]
UNEXP = unexpected NAV return
　　　　 = ln[NAV$_{c(n)}$/ NAV$_{c(n-1)}$] − (α + β_{NAV} ln[ET$_{c(n)}$/ ET$_{c(n-1)}$])
　　　　　　the second term being the NAV return expected using the market
　　　　　　model.

The model states that the return on prices on the announcement of NAV
depends on two factors: the market return on that day and the unexpected component on the NAV return. This model was estimated using data from July 1988
onwards. The regression results were as follows:

$$\text{MPRET}_1 = 0.042\% + 1.030\text{ETRET}_1 + 0.062\text{UNEXP}, \qquad R^2 = 0.197,$$
$$\qquad\qquad (0.16) \qquad (4.52) \qquad\qquad (0.54)$$

$$\text{MPRET}_1 = 0.015\% + 1.046\text{ETRET}, \qquad\qquad R^2 = 0.194,$$
$$\qquad\qquad (0.06) \qquad (4.68)$$

$$\text{MPRET}_1 = 0.364\% + 0.134\text{UNEXP}, \qquad\qquad R^2 = 0.013$$
$$\qquad\qquad (1.29) \qquad (1.07)$$

(*t*-values are in parentheses).

The results show that the unexpected component of the NAV has no impact on
the market prices. This conclusion is in line with the earlier conclusion suggested
by the simple linear regression of prices on NAV. It now stands confirmed that the
market does not take NAV into account while pricing Mastershares.

This conclusion is inconsistent with the joint hypothesis that Mastershares are
rationally priced in the market and that the NAV represents the intrinsic worth of
the Mastershares. In other words, it can be concluded that either the market price
is irrational or that the NAV does not, for some reason, represent the intrinsic
worth of the Mastershares. Further tests were carried out to determine which of
these alternative conclusions is correct.

AN ALTERNATIVE MODEL FOR RELATIONSHIP
BETWEEN PRICE AND NAV

A preliminary examination of prices and NAV indicated that Mastershares is
always quoted at a discount. At times, the price is at a deep discount from NAV,
and at other times the discount is very narrow. The discount appeared to fluctuate
around a mean value, and whenever the discount moved too far away from the
mean, there was a tendency to return to the mean level. Technically, the discount
appeared to follow a mean-reverting random walk:

$$\text{DIS}_t = (1 - \alpha)\,\text{AVGDIS} + \alpha\text{DIS}_{t-1}v_t, \qquad 0 \leq \alpha \leq 1, \qquad (6)$$

$$\begin{aligned}
\text{DIS}_t &= -\ln(\text{MP}_1/\text{NAV}_t \\
&= -\ln(1 - \text{proportional discount}) \\
&= -(1 - [\text{NAV}_t - \text{MP}_t] / \text{NAV}_t),
\end{aligned} \tag{7}$$

where

DIS_t is the discount at time t,
AVGDIS is the mean value to which discount tends to revert,
α is the parameter determining the speed of reversion, and
v_t is a serially uncorrelated mean zero disturbance.

The above is an autoregressive model. For α close to unity, the mean reversion might not be immediately apparent, and the discount might appear to follow a simple random walk. The model was estimated and the regression result was as follows:

$$\text{DIS}_t = 2.809\% + 0.886\text{DIS}_{t-1} \qquad R^2 = 0.804,$$
$$(3.12) \qquad (24.85)$$

implying $\alpha = 0.886$ and AVGDIS $\approx 24\%$.

The value of α being close to unity would make the process look like a simple random walk. However, the hypothesis that $\alpha = 1$ is convincingly rejected (t-statistic = 3.20). Thus, mean reversion is taking place, implying that either the price or the NAV adjusts to eliminate abnormally high or abnormally low discounts. A further investigation needs to be carried out to determine which of the two does the adjustment.

Subtracting DIS_{t-1} from both sides of Equation (6) and then substituting the definition of discount gives the following:

$$\ln(\text{MP}_t / \text{MP}_{t-1}) - \ln(\text{NAV}_t / \text{NAV}_{t-1}) = (1-\alpha)(\text{DIS}_{t-1} - \text{AVGDIS}) - v_t. \tag{8}$$

This is the same as

$$r_{\text{MP},t} - r_{\text{NAV},t} = (1 - \alpha)(\text{DIS}_{t-1} - \text{AVGDIS}) - v_t. \tag{9}$$

This implies that when there is a deep discount making the right-hand side strongly positive, either there will be a high price return or a low NAV return (or both) to keep the left-hand side also strongly positive. Similarly, a low discount implies that either the price return will be low or the NAV return will be high.

The empirical question now is whether it is the market price or the NAV that does the adjusting. If it is found that tit is the market price that adjusts, then one could conclude that the market price was irrational, and that as investors gradually recognize this they correct the earlier error. The price return and the NAV return were regressed separately on the discount at the beginning of the period. In both cases, the possible impact of the market index as eliminated by including the market return as an additional explanatory variable. The regression results were as follows:

$$\text{MPRET} = -2.505\% + 1.93\text{ETRET} + 0.110\text{DIS}\%, \qquad R^2 = 0.397$$
$$(-2.77) \qquad (9.68) \qquad\qquad (3.10)$$

$$\text{NAVRET} = 0.938\% + 0.814\text{ETRET} - 0.018\text{DIS}\% \qquad R^2 = 0.799,$$
$$(3.90) \qquad (24.68) \qquad\qquad (-1.87)$$

where,

$$\text{MPRET} = \text{return on market price} = \ln[\text{MP}_{c(n+1)} / \text{MP}_{c(n)}],$$
$$\text{NAVRET} = \text{return on NAV} = \ln[\text{NAV}_{c(n+1)} / \text{NAV}_{c(n)}],$$
$$\text{ETRET} = \text{return on market index } \ln[\text{ET}_{c(n+1)} / \text{ET}_{c(n)}],$$
$$\text{DIS}\% = \text{percentage discount beginning of period}$$
$$= -100*\ln[\text{ET}_{c(n)} / \text{NAV}_{c(n)}].$$

The results very clearly show that it is the price that does all the adjustment. The coefficient of discount in the regression equation for the price return is large and significant. In the case of the NAV return, however, the coefficient of the right sign is small and statistically insignificant different from zero. The inference that can be drawn therefore is that the market prices deviate irrationally from the NAV but correct themselves gradually in subsequent periods. The fluctuations in spread are not due to any distortions in NAV.

It would be instructive to link the above model to the fads model proposed by Summers (1986) to capture a situation in which the market prices are irrational and fail to reflect fundamental values. Summers's model is

$$p_t = p_t^* + u_t \qquad u_t = \alpha u_{t-1} + v_t \tag{10}$$

where p is the logarithm of market price, p^* is the logarithm of fundamental value, $0 \le \alpha \le 1$, and v is a serially uncorrelated mean zero disturbance.

Substituting $p = \ln(\text{MP})$, $p^* = \ln(\text{NAV}) - \text{AVGDIS}$, $u = \text{AVGDIS} - \text{DIS}$ reduces equations (6) and (7) to (10).

Thus, the conclusion about the behavior of market price of Mastershares is in line with the mean-reverting behavior of share prices reported by Poterba and Summers (1988) and Cutler, Poterba, and Summers (1991). The method in this paper, however, differs in an important aspect. While these works have assumed that the price fundamental could be noisy, we have empirically examined the possibility that the price fundamental could itself be mean reverting.

CONCLUSION

The conclusions of the current study may be summarized as follows:

1.   On applying the market model to NAV and market prices, it was found that the prices have a sharply higher beta than the NAV. The prices also have a much higher variance. All these indicate that the prices fluctuate far more than what can be justified by fundamentals.

2.   Through the prices are highly correlated with NAV, the correlation is due only to the common influence of the market index. The prices are, in fact, more closely related to the market index than to the NAV indicating that the market does not take the NAV into account in pricing Mastershares.

3.   Lending further support to this conclusion is the sharper result that the information content of the NAV announcement (i.e., the unexpected change in the NAV) has no impact on the market prices.

4.   Deep discount of the market price from NAV is associated with significantly higher returns in future periods, demonstrating that the pricing is irrational and indicating that perhaps a profitable trading rule can be found to exploit this irrationality.

5.   On the other hand, there is no evidence to suggest that the observed discount is a rational adjustment for any accounting or other deficiencies in the NAV computation. There is no significant association between the discount and subsequent changes in the NAV.

The fact that prices do move irrationally only to correct themselves subsequently raises the possibility of a profitable trading rule that would try to buy Mastershares when it is quoting at a deep discount and sell it when the discount narrows. Identification of actual parameters of such a rule would need further research.

Another puzzling issue is the large mean discount of 24% (logarithmic discount), which corresponds to a proportional discount of 21%. Why should the mean discount be so large? Factors like liquidation costs cannot account for such a large value. Of course, there are some situations where holding Mastershares is not a substitute for physical possession of the shares that comprise the Mastershares portfolio. In a takeover struggle, an individual investor may be able to earn a windfall return by selling proxies, while UTI may not wish to get involved in such takeovers and may not exploit such an opportunity; similarly, possession of shares of individual companies allows an individual to engage in "margin" trading in the market. But whether these disadvantages of holding Mastershares justify such a deep discount is an open question.

These conclusions must be seen in light of the considerable literature that exists on the efficiency of the Indian stock markets. Studies, using the standard procedures for testing the EMH, have shown the market to be efficient in the weak form and the semistrong form. However, the conclusions arrived at in this paper are counter to what one would expect in a market dominated by rational investors, and suggest that the market may indeed be governed by irrational considerations. Price movements appear to be divorced from fundamentals and bring into question the methodology that is used for investigating market efficiency. The results are in line with some of the recent work being done on irrationalities in capital markets in developed economies. Since the Indian capital market is on the threshold of major changes that would make it far more international in character than what it is today, these findings would be useful for both policymaking on the operation of mutual funds and for actually setting up mutual funds.

ACKNOWLEDGMENT

This work was partially supported by a research grant from the Indian Institute of Management, Ahmedabad, India.

NOTE

1.   In July 1991, following major government initiative to liberalize the economy, the government decided to allow setting up of private mutual funds. There are also indications that foreign capital would be allowed to invest directly in Indian equities without restrictions.

REFERENCES

Barua, S. K. (1981). The short run price behaviour of securities: Some evidence of efficiency in Indian capital market. *Vikalpa,*

Barua, S. K., & Raghunathan, V. (1986). Inefficiency in the Indian capital market. *Vikalpa,*

Barua, S. K., & Raghunathan, V. (1987). Inefficiency and speculation in the Indian capital market. *Vikalpa, 12*(3), 53-58.

Barua, S. K., & Varma, J. R. (1991). Mastershares: A bonanza for large investors. *Vikalpa, 16*(1), 29-34.

Cutler, D. M., Poterba, J. M., & Summers, L. H. (1989). What moves stock prices? *Journal of portfolio management, 15*(3), 4-12.

Cutler, D. M., Poterba, J. M., & Summers, L. H. (1991). Speculative dynamics. *Review of Economic Studies, 58*(3), 529-546.

Emerging stock markets factbook 1990. (1990). International Finance Corp. Washington, D.C.: Author.

LeRoy, S. F. (1989). Efficient capital markets and martingale. *Journal of Economic Literature, 27* 1583-1621.

LeRoy, S. F., & Porter, R. (1981). The present value relation: Tests based on implied variance. *Econometrica.*

Poterba, J. M., & Summers, L. H. (1986). The persistence of volatility and stock market fluctuations. *American Economic Review, 76*(5), 1142-1151.

Poterba, J. M., & Summers, L. H. (1988). Mean reversion in stock prices: Evidence and implications. *Journal of Financial Economics, 22*(1), 27-59.

Ramachandran, J. (1985), *Behaviour of stock market prices: Information assimilation and market efficiency.* Unpublished dissertation, Indian Institute of Management. Ahmedabad.

Rao, N. K., & Mukherjee, K. (1971). Random walk hypothesis, an empirical study. *Arthaniti, 14*(1&3), 53-59.

Sharma, J. L., & Kennedy, R. E. (1977). A comparative analysis of stock price behaviour on the Bombay, London and New York Stock exchanges. *Journal of Financial and Quantitative Analysis,* (Sept.), 391-413.

Shiller, R. J. (1981a). The use of volatility measure in assessing market efficiency. *Journal of Finance, 36*(2), 291-304.

Shiller, R. J. (1981b). Do stock prices move too much to be justified by subsequent changes in dividends? *American Economic Review, 71*(3), 421-436.

Shiller, R. J. (1990a). A Scott-type regression test of the dividend ratio model. *Review of Economics & Statistics, 72*(2), 356-361.

Shiller, R. J. (1990b). Market volatility and investor behaviour. *American Economic Review, 80*(2), 58-62.

Summers, L. (1986). Does the stock market rationally reflect fundamental values? *Journal of Finance, 41*(3), 591-601.

Tversky, A., & Kahneman, D. (1981). The framing of decisions and the psychology of choice. *Science, 211*(January), 453-458.

Tversky, A., & Kahneman, D. (1986). Rational choice and the framing of decisions. *Journal of Business, 59*(4)l, s251-s278.

Varma, J. R. (1988). *Asset pricing models under parameter nonstationarity.* Unpublished dissertation, Indian Institute of Management, Ahmedabad.

A COST-BENEFIT RULE FOR CORPORATE PENSION ENRICHMENTS

Jihad S. Nader

ABSTRACT

A firm's decision to grant a pension enrichment to its workers entails both incremental costs due to the increased pension obligation, and incremental benefits in the form of wage savings for the firm. Thus an appropriate analytical framework, not applied previously to corporate pension enrichments, is the capital budgeting framework of corporate finance. This article formulates the incremental costs of and benefits from pension enrichments, and develops a cost-benefit (CB) decision rule that integrates the pension enrichment decision into the capital-budgeting framework.

INTRODUCTION

The compensating differentials model (Smith, 1937; Rosen, 1974) has been used as a conceptual framework for economic research on a wide variety of labor

Advances in Financial Planning and Forecasting,
Volume 5, pages 29-34.
Copyright © 1994 by JAI Press Inc.
All rights of reproduction in any form reserved.
ISBN:1-55938-421-2

market phenomena, including the pension-wage trade-off of workers. For example, Ehrenberg (1980), Schiller and Weiss (1980), and Smith (1981) provide empirical evidence that workers' wages incorporate specific differentials for the level, quantity, and other attributes of pension promises made by employers. In particular, this evidence indicates that an enrichment of the pensions promised by a firm to its workers upon retirement would result in a reduction in the workers' current wage demand.

Attesting to the growth and significance of pension enrichments, Ippolito (1986, p. 90) provides evidence of a systematic increase in real benefits offered by the U.S. private pension systems over the entire 30-year period since World War I II. Similarly, McGill and Grubbs (1989, pp. 105-109) state that more and more emphasis is being place on pension enrichments as an integral part of the collective-bargaining process in the private sector. Despite their growing importance, however, pension enrichments have been virtually ignored in the corporate finance literature, which focuses primarily on the pension asset mix, and pays much less attention to pension liability management by the firm (Brigham & Gapenski, 1985 Copeland & Weston, 1988).

A recent article by Arnott and Bernstein (1988) emphasizes the need for a fuller integration of pension liability management issues into the finance literature. Nader (1991) treats one such issue, pension inducements for early retirement, as a capital-budgeting problem. Along the same lines, this article develops a cost-benefit (CB) rule that integrates another issue, the pension enrichment decision, into the firm's capital-budgeting process. The CB rule ultimately permits the firm to make pension enrichment decisions with only a very limited need for decrement-based actuarial projections, which in the finance literature are widely perceived as a potential source of bias in corporate pension policy (Kingsland, 1982). The rule also captures the effect, on the pension enrichment decision, of interactions among the salary growth rate, the discount rate for valuing the pension obligation, and the plan's retirement age provisions.

CB DECISION RULE FORMULATION

Consider a corporate pension plan of the defined-benefit type, which uses a service-related final salary formula.[1] The following notation is used:

p_0, p_1 = initial and enriched pension rate, respectively $(p_1 > p_0)$

s_0, s_1 = current salary demanded by workers, given p_0 and p_1, respectively $(s_1 < s_0)$

ω = salary growth rate assumption[2]

τ = appropriate discount rate for incremental costs and benefits from pension enrichment[3]

N = years remaining until retirement

z = life expectancy upon retirement

Π_N = multiple-decrement probability of surviving in service for the next N years[4]

Π_i = mortality-based probability of surviving for i years in retirement

$a_{t,z}$ = present-value factor for the pension annuity.

Granting a non-retroactive pension enrichment[5] entails incremental pension costs for the firm, whose actuarially adjusted present value is

$$V_c = (p_1 S_1 - p_0 S_0) N \Pi_N \left(\frac{1+\omega}{1+\tau}\right)^N \alpha_{\tau,z}^{-1} \sum_{i=l}^{z} \Pi_i / (i+\tau)^i. \qquad (1)$$

The incremental benefits to the firm from granting the pension enrichment, consists of a stream of wage concessions whose actuarially adjusted present value is

$$v_b = (S_0 - S_1) \Pi_N \sum_{i=0}^{N} \left(\frac{1+\omega}{1+\tau}\right)^i. \qquad (2)$$

As shown in Hummelbrunner (1986), the closed form of Equation (2), for $\tau > \omega$, is

$$v_b = (S_0 - S_1) \Pi_N \left\{ 1 + \left(\frac{1+\omega}{\tau+\omega}\right) \left[1 - \left(\frac{1+\omega}{1+\omega}\right)^N \right] \right\}. \qquad (3)$$

The CB decision criterion prescribes that a rational (shareholder-wealth-maximizing) firm should only grant pension enrichments if $V_c / V_b \leq 1$. From Equations (1) and (3), this requires that

$$\frac{(p_1 S_1 - p_0 S_0) N \Pi_N \left(\frac{1+\omega}{1+\tau}\right)^N \alpha_{\tau,Z}^{-1} \sum_{i=1}^{Z} \Pi_i / (1+\tau)^i}{(S_0 - S_1) \Pi_N \left\{ 1 + \left(\frac{1+\omega}{\tau+\omega}\right) \left[1 - \left(\frac{1+\omega}{1+\omega}\right)^N \right] \right\}} \leq 1. \qquad (4)$$

Rearranging terms and simplifying, it follows that

$$\frac{p_1 S_1 - p_0 S_0}{S_0 - S_1} \leq \frac{1}{N} \left\{ \left(\frac{1+\tau}{1+\omega}\right)^N + \left(\frac{1+\omega}{\tau+\omega}\right) \left[\left(\frac{1+\tau}{1+\omega}\right)^N - 1 \right] \right\} \left[\frac{a_{\tau,Z}}{\sum_{i=1}^{Z} \Pi_i / (1+\tau)^i} \right]. \qquad (5)$$

ANALYSIS

Relation (5) is a CB decision rule for corporate pension enrichments, which could be used for an individual employee or an employee group. In the latter case, average S_0, S_1, ω, and N values for the group should be used. The left-hand side (LHS) is the *instantaneous* CB ratio for the pension enrichment and is totally independent of actuarial decrement factors and of any biases contained therein.[7] The right-hand side (RHS) constitutes a benchmark for the pension enrichment decision and, like the LHS, it simplifies the decision-making process. The simplification is due to the fact that the only actuarial adjustment affecting the RHS is a mortality-based adjustment Π_i, and is confined to the retirement years. For a firm that discharges its pension obligation in lump sum form, even this mortality-based adjustment (and the entire term inside the second set of square brackets) would not apply, and CB rule would be completely independent of any actuarial decrement factors.

The firm can use this benchmark to assess the effects of various factors on pension·enrichment policy. For example, a ceteris paribus change in N, through the introduction of early or late retirement provisions, would imply that the firm can afford more liberal pension enrichments if the RHS of relation (5) increases, and smaller enrichments if the RHS decreases as a result of the change in N. In the same manner, the RHS of relation (5) can be used to analyze the effects of various ω and τ assumptions on pension enrichment policy. In both of the preceding examples, the maximum pension enrichment (expressed as a percentage of salary) that the firm should be willing to grant for a given wage concession by the workers could readily be determined by setting relation (5) as an equation and solving for $P_1 - P_0$. Alternatively, the minimum wage concession the firm should demand in return for granting a given pension enrichment could be determined in like manner by solving for $S_0 - S_1$.

CONCLUDING REMARKS

Two points pertaining to the conceptual basis and formulation of the above CB rule must be noted. First, if labor's total compensation were determined in a perfect-market setting, with information costlessly and equally accessible to all market participants (an idealization widely applied by financial economist to capital markets; e.g., Fama & Miller, 1972, pp. 21-22, 27), then the equilibrium total compensation would be set such that the workers' valuation. Absent any valuation differentials, the costs and benefits of a pension enrichment to the firm would be equal, and relation (5) would always be a strict equality. However, as discussed by Gordon and Hynes (1970), the perfect-market idealization is largely incongruous with the process through which equilibrium compensation contracts are struck in labor market. This process is characterized by informational asymmetry, which might lead the firm and the workers to different valuation of any given component of compensation [as implied by the inequality case in relation (5)]. Such asymmetry may be most pronounced in the case of the pension component, because the firm can exercise a large degree of control over information regarding the extent, quality, firmness, and other attributes of the pension obligation. Thus it is quite possible, and perhaps even probable, that relation (5) will be an inequality.

Second, it is important to note that a pension enrichment may have other, non-wage compensation effects, such as reductions in other fringe benefits, which would be higher without the pension enrichment. Also, a pension enrichment may increase the firm's labor retention rate, especially for workers with unvested benefits, who, after the enrichment, would have to forfeit larger pension benefits if they were to quit the firm. The reduction in other fringe benefits and, with higher work force retention, in search and training costs to the firm constitute incremental savings that must be properly formulated (given the necessary firm-specified information), added to the RHS of Equations (2) and (3), and this included in the CB decision rule [relation (5)].

In like manner, Equation (1) and relation (5) should be expanded (using appropriate firm-specific information) to include secondary costs of the pension enrichment, such as incremental insurance premiums that the firm may have to pay to the Pension Benefit Guaranty Corporation, if the increases in the pension obligation is not fully funded (see VanDerhei, 1990).

NOTES

1.   In the United States and Canada, the vast majority of pension plan members in the private sector are covered by plans of the defined-benefit type. For a detailed discussion of pension plan design, see McGill and Grubbs (1989).

2.   From an economic theory perspective, an argument could be made for defining two salary growth rate, $\omega 0$ and $\omega 1$, with $\omega_1 > \omega_0$ for $S_1 < S_0$. From the actuarial viewpoint, however, the salary growth rate assumption is typically made up of three components (merit, productivity, and inflation; see Winklevoss, 1977, pp. 23-25), which are estimated independently of the workers' current salary level (S_0 or S_1). The use of a single w in the formulation of the CB rule reflects the actuarial perspective, since in the end firms rely on the actuarial assumptions for determining the incremental cost of funding a given pension enrichment.

3.   Since an enrichment of the firm's pension promise is contractually binding, the appropriate discount rate indicated by economic theory (see Treynor, Regan, & Priest, 1976, p. 45; Pesando & Clark, 1982; Nader, 1991, pp. 102-103) is the risk-free rate. Specifically, as shown by Pesando and Clarke (1982), τ should be defined as the nominal risk-free rate if the firm's pension obligation is considered to be a real obligation.

4.   The decrement factors reflected in Π_N are mortality, disability, and termination. See McGill and Grubbs (1989).

5.   For a retroactive enrichment, N must simply be redefined as years of service, from hire to retirement. In this case, a multiple-decrement probability, Π_{N-Y} must be used in place of Π_N, where Y is years of past service. Also, the power of the term $(1 + \omega)/(1 + \tau)$ in Equations (1)-(3) and of this term's reciprocal in relation (5) would go to $N-Y$ instead on N.

6.   Note, in particular, that PN, the actuarial adjustment factor for the remaining active service period, cancels out of the numerator and denominator of relation (4).

7.   Such biases arise because the actual decrement rates affecting the work force may (and usually will) turn out to be different from the decrement rates assumed in the actuarial projects of the pension obligation. In this case, the biases may result either in an "experience gain" or an "experience loss" for the firm, as described in McGill and Grubbs (1989, pp. 270-271).

REFERENCES

Arnott, R. J., & Bernstein, P. L. (1988). The right way to manage your pension fund. *Harvard Business Review* (January/February), 95-102.

Brigham, E. F., & Gapenski, L. C. (1985). *Intermediate financial management.* Dryden.

Copeland, T. E., &Weston, J. F. (1988). *Financial theory and corporate policy,* 3rd ed. Reading, MA: Addison-Wesley.

Ehrenberg, R. (1980). Retirement system characteristics and compensating wage differentials in the public sector. *Industrial and Labor Relations Review, 33,* 470-483.

Fama, E. F., & Miller, M. H. (1972). *The theory of finance.* Dryden.

Gordon, D. F. & Hynes, A. (1970). *The theory of price dynamics.* In E. S. Phelps (ed.), *Microeconomic Formulations of Employment and Inflation Theory* (pp. xx-xx). New York: Norton.

Hummelbrunner, S. A. (1988). *Contemporary business mathematics,* 2nd ed. Prentice-Hall.

Ippolito, R. A. (1986). *Pensions, economics and public policy.* Dow Jones-Irwin.

Kingsland, L. (1982). Projecting the financial condition of a pension plan using simulation analysis. *Journal of Finance, 37,* 577-584.

McGill, D. M., & Grubbs, D. S., J. R. (1989). *Fundamentals of private pensions,* 6th ed. Chicago: Irwin.

Nader, J. S. (1991). Rational decision rules for early retirement inducements contained in corporate pension plans. *Journal of Risk and Insurance, 58*(1), 101-108.

Pesando, J. E., & Clarke, C. K. (1982). Economic models of the labour market: Their implications for pension accounting. Paper presented at the Canadian Academic Accounting Association Conference, Ottawa, May.

Rosen S. (1974). Hedonic prices and implicit markets: Product differentiation in pure competition. *Journal of Political Economy, 82,* 34-55.

Shiller, B., & Weiss, R. (1980). Pensions and wages: A test for equalizing differences. *Review of Economics and Statistics, 62,* 529-538.

Smith, A. (1937). *The wealth of nations.* New York: Random House.

Smith, R. S. (1981). Compensating differentials for pensions and underfunding in the public sector. *Review of Economics and Statistics, 63,* 463-467.

Treynor, J., Regan, P. J., & Priest, W. W., Jr. (1976). *The financial reality of pension funding under ERISA.* Homewood, IL: Dow Jones-Irwin.

VanDerhei, J. L. (1990). An empirical analysis of risk-related insurance premiums for the PBGC. *Journal of Risk and Insurance, 57*(2, June), 240-259.

Winklevoss, H. E. (1977). *Pension Mathematics.* Chicago: Irwin.

CAPITAL GAIN REALIZATION BY INVESTMENT FUNDS AND THE ASSOCIATED TAX COSTS

Michael H. Morris and Kevin Scanlon

ABSTRACT

This study analyzes the tax effects resulting from the realization of capital gains through turnover by mutual fund portfolio managers. Customarily, investors consider risk and return when making investment choices. When considering mutual funds, investors are also concerned with fees such as front-end and back-end loads. This paper documents another significicnat, yet lesser-known cost of mutual funds, the tax cost due to capital gain realization by mutual fund managers. The results of this 11-year study of 88 "growth" mutual funds suggest that the funds have given up a substantial portion of their potential value due to capital gain realization.

Many tests of the performance of mutual funds have been conducted. A general conclusion from these studies is that few mutual funds, on a before-tax basis, are able to outperform the market on a risk-adjusted basis. Rather than perform

Advances in Financial Planning and Forecasting,
Volume 5, pages 35-45.
Copyright © 1994 by JAI Press Inc.
All rights of reproduction in any form reserved.
ISBN:1-55938-421-2

another risk-adjusted test, the purpose of this paper is to examine the performance of mutual funds after considering the capital gain taxes that must be paid by investors. Given the frequent and idiosyncratic portfolio turnover by mutual fund managers in a world with potentially high capital gain tax rates, the difference between commonly reported raw returns and returns calculated net of capital gain taxes can be significant.

On a theoretical level, Constantinides (1983, 1984) and Stiglitz (1983) argue that investors can largely avoid paying capital gain taxes (and a significnat portion of tax on ordinary income) by adopting portfolio strategies such as selling shares with losses and postponing the sale of shares with gains. The tax-minimizing behavior emphasized in these studies suggests that capital gain taxes can be minimized to a level approaching nonexistence.

On a practical level, a number of studies have indicated the importance of capital gain taxes for individual investment decisions. First, prior studies have shown that capital gain taxes influence trading volume of individual stocks (Lakonishok & Smidt, 1986) and purchase and sale of mutual fund shares (Shefrin & Statman, 1985). Second, Poterba (1987) found that only 20% of individual investors reporting capital gains or losses in 1982 followed sophisticated tax-reducing trading strategies. His study suggests that a significant fraction of realized capital gains by individuals are taxed at nonzero marginal tax rates. Also, Lee, Shliefer, and Thaler (1991) provide evidence that closed-end mutual funds are owned primarily by individual investors rather than tax-exempt institutions. Although this study examines open-end funds, open- and closed-end funds are likely to have similar clienteles (individual ownership). It seems likely that institutions would have a hard time explaining to their clients why they are subcontracting a portion of their portfolios (by buying mutual funds) and thus imposing two management fees.

This study analyzes the actual capital gain realization and implied tax effects arising from investment in equity, open-end mutual funds. Using actual mutual fund performance data, this study calculates the returns on a pre- and posttax basis and estimates the costs to investors of losing options associated with capital gain realization. The next section discusses the tax considerations of investment companies followed by a section on the methodological approach of this study. After reporting the cross-sectional descriptive results on return and realization performance and converting the measures to tax costs, the final section contains conclusions and implications.

TAX CONSIDERATIONS

The Tax Reform Act of 1986 eliminated the exclusion for 60% of any long-term capital gain, but retained two preferential tax features of capital gains. First, taxes can be deferred on any unrealized gain; and second, taxpayers retain the ability to time the realization (and the accompanying taxation of gains) when tax rates are lower relative to their current tax rates.[1]

Under special provisions of subchapter M of the federal Internal Revenue Code, investment companies (mutual funds) are not taxable entities provided they meet certain requirements. Investment companies must distribute nearly all (98%) of their realized income to shareholders each year to retain their nontaxable status. That mutual funds are regulated investment companies and not tax entities does not imply that tax considerations are of no importance. On the contrary, mutual funds have unique tax considerations, especially when one expands the tax analysis to encompass all parties to contracts including portfolio managers and shareholders.

One unique tax consideration is that mutual funds are not permitted to distribute net capital losses but are required to distribute realized income. Under these restrictions, taxpayers with investments in mutual funds having realized net capital losses are at a disadvantage relative to investors with direct holdings of the same securities who are permitted to offset other capital gains and up to $3000 of the net loss against ordinary income. In the worst case, which will be discussed subsequently, investors can have the price of their fund fall during the year, yet have a tax liability due to the fund's net realization of capital gains during the same year.

Capital gain realization takes on importance for two related reasons. First, it determines the degree of control that an investor has over recognition (timing) of capital gains and losses. Only if the portfolio manager chooses to have no realization does the investor have approximately the same degree of control over the investment (by being able to sell shares in the mutual fund) as that maintained by an investor holding securities directly.[2] Investors facing a comparatively low (or zero) capital gain tax rate because of large losses during a given year have the option to sell the mutual fund shares and pay a low (or zero) tax on the capital gain. This feature is called the timing option. Second, realization at early stages of an investment program and the accompanying tax payment can have a large negative impact on the future value of the investment in the mutual fund. This second factor is called the deferral option.[3] The deferral option arises because capital gains are taxed at the point of realization rather than accrual, making the instantaneous rate of return increase with the length of time the asset is held. The next sections discuss the sample selection and cost estimation techniques associated with these two options, which are lost through turnover of investments by mutual fund managers.

METHODOLOGY

To measure the cost of options lost, this study utilizes actual performance data for 88 funds with complete return data for the 11-year period 1978-1988. The funds were selected from Weisenberger's (1977-1988) "growth" categorization and includes "maximum capital gains," "long-term growth, income secondary," and "growth and current income" descriptions. Growth funds were selected due to their emphasis on capital appreciation, making them more sensitive to capital gain realization, which may accent the difference between pre- and posttax returns.

For comparative purposes, this study reports the returns of 88 growth funds with the return of a benchmark fund, the Vanguard Index Trust, which attempts to mirror the S&P 500. This benchmark is chosen since the index should roughly track "the market." More importantly, however, the index fund serves as a realization proxy. The index fund does not attempt to time the market or seek value-enhancing trades but rather attempts a buy-and-hold strategy with turnover only to match changes in the S&P 500. Although this matching process and normal inflow and outflow of funds cause turnover to be higher than a diversified portfolio with a strict buy-and-hold strategy, the index fund represents a realization policy a step closer to the Constantinides ideal. Since this index had its first full year of trading in 1978, an 11-year data set ending in 1988 is used in the analysis.

To capture the cost of captial gain realization or turnover by portfolio managers, this study isolates the realized and unrealized portion of capital appreciation or return, for each year and each mutual fund. Utilizing actual return and actual realization histories over the 11-year period and assuming the investor falls in the highest statutory federal tax bracket, this study estimates the 1988 after-tax fund value of $100 invested in 1978 for each of the 88 mutual funds. As a means of comparison, this study also calculates the fund value if the portfolio manager followed an optimal tax strategy for the mutual fund. Brickley et. al (1991) define the optimum tax strategy for a mutual fund as one that postpones all capital gains indefinitely, unless they can be offset by capital losses. The methodological approach of this study is to measure the value lost by not deferring all capital gain realization until the end of the 11-year period (deferral option cost). In addition, this study measures the incremental value lost by not timing the realization of all capital gains to a year when the capital gain tax rate is zero (timing option cost). The options lost (or cost to the investor) are estimated as follows:

$$\text{deferral option cost} = \frac{\text{ATFV}_D - \text{ATFV}}{\text{ATFV}} \times 100\% \tag{1}$$

$$\text{timing option cost} = \frac{\text{ATFV}_{D+T} - \text{ATFV}_D}{\text{ATFV}} \times 100\% \tag{2}$$

where

ATFV = the 1988 year end-fund value after paying all capital gain and dividend taxes in accordance with actual return and realization histories, assuming maximum statutory tax rates

ATFV_D = the 1988 after-tax fund value if all capital gain taxes are deferred (not realized) until the end of the holding period.

ATFV_{D+T} = the 1988 after-tax fund value if all capital gain taxes are deferred (not realized) until the end of the holding period and are timed to coincide with a capital gain tax rate of zero.

As defined in this fashion, the total value lost through capital gain realization is the sum of the two options, or

$$\text{total value lost} = \text{deferral option cost} + \text{timing option cost}$$

$$= \frac{\text{ATFV}_{D+T} - \text{ATFV}}{\text{ATFV}} \times 100\%. \tag{3}$$

Having presented the formulas for the after-tax fund value lost through turnover, it is important to mention a few caveats at this point. Equation (3) incorporates the highest statutory federal tax rates in the denominator, while the numerator measures deviation from complete deferral and liquidation when the capital gain tax rate is zero. Such assumptions overstate the cost of turnover by portfolio managers for those investors who do not seek complete deferral and optimal timing. However, the formulas might be considered conservative cost estimates for several reasons. First, this study ignores transaction costs. Second, this study understates marginal tax rates by ignoring state and local taxes, and circumstances that can raise the marginal federal tax brackets. And finally, no estimate of the offset option (see note 3) is quantified in this study.

In addition, this paper quantifies the cost of capital gain realization by mutual fund managers. Even though a portion of the observed realization may be forced on mutual fund portfolio managers by growth or contraction of a mutual fund, this study quantifies these tax-related costs as if all realization activity were controllable by the fund manager.

RESULTS

After estimating returns for these funds on a before-tax basis, the next step in the analysis is to estimate the after-tax value of the fund. This study assumes an investor in the highest statutory marginal tax bracket. Prior to 1982, maximum statutory personal tax rates were 0.7 with accompanying maximum capital gain tax rates of 0.28. For 1982 through 1987, maximum statutory personal tax rates were 50%, with capital gains rates at 40% of the applicable personal rate (maximum 0.20). For 1987, top personal-tax rates were 38.5% with capital gains equal to the personal rate but no larger than 28%. For 1987 and 1988, the maximum personal and capital gains tax rates are equivalent at 28% (ignoring the

Table 1.   Mutual Fund Return Compostion (%) 1978-1988

	Index Fund	Mean	Growth Funds (n=88)	
			Range[a]	
Average annual capital gain realization (capital gain distributed$_t$/P_{t-1})[b]	3.08	6.92	0	13.8
Average annual dividend yield (dividend paid$_t$/P_{t-1})	4.65	3.29	0	6.0
Average annual unrealized capital gain $(P_t - P) / P_{t-1}$	6.93	4.42	(2.1)	12.6
Annual average total return over 1978-1988 holding period	14.66	14.63	6.5	21.1

Notes: [a] The range reports extreme values of annual return for the 88 funds. The average annual return is computed using the geometric mean of the 11-year period for each mutual fund.

[b] P_t = price at end of year t.

33% bubble) depending on taxable income levels. Maximum capital gain tax rates increased 40% in 1987, substantially increasing the cost of realization in the late 1980s.

As displayed in Table 1 the annual geometric mean return for the 11-year period 1978-1988 for the sample of 88 growth funds is 14.63%. The index fund returned a similar before-tax rate of return of 14.66%. While the mean returns are nearly identical, the composition of returns differs. For the growth funds, the average composition of the return is 6.92% as realized (taxable) capital gain, 3.29% in the form of dividend yield, and 4.42% as unrealized (and therefore untaxed) capital gains. In contrast, the index fund had smaller realized capital gain (3.08%), but higher dividend yield (4.65%) and unrealized capital gain (6.93%).

Since the variable of interest in this study is the realized capital gain, closer examination of this component is provided in Tables 2 and 3. Any capital gain distribution causes tax-paying investors to incur a tax cost on their investment in a mutual fund.[4] Optimal portfolio management (in a tax sense) would suggest that no capital gains be distributed. This implies no turnover or just enough turnover of shares with gains to offset the loss from turnover of shares with losses. As the total (last) column of Table 2 indicates, only 261 of 968 observations (88 funds × 11 years) for growth funds distributed no capital gains.

Adding one further element to the analysis provides some surprising results concerning the capital gain distribution. The change in net asset value of each fund is analyzed for the year of each capital gain distribution and the breakdown is also provided in Table 2. The total row at the bottom of Table 2 indicates that 77.9% of the fund-years analyzed had net asset value increases (prior to making the capital gain distribution). Of the funds experiencing an increase in net asset value (quadrants I and II), less than one-third (quadrant II) adopted what might be considered an optimal turnover policy for tax purposes of no capital gain distribu-

Table 2.　Capital Gain Distributions (1978-1988)[a]

	Mutual fund net asset value[b]		Total
Capital gain distribution	Increase	Decrease	Total
Positive	I　535　55.3%	IV　172　17.8%	707　73.0%
Zero	II　219　22.6%	III　42　4.3%	261　27.0%
Total	754　77.9%	214　22.1%	968　100%

Notes:　[a] The observations reflect the number of firm-years with the characteristics of each quadrant. Eighty-eight firms analyzed over 11 years provides 968 observations.

[b] The mutual fund net asset value is prior to the capital gain distribution.

Table 3.　Capital Gain Realization (Turnover)

	Turnover[a] (%)	
	Index fund	Growth funds (N = 88)
Highest	–	144.7
Top quartile	–	84.0
Median	30.8	65.4
Bottom quartile	–	42.9
Lowest	–	0 (N=1)

Notes:　[a] Turnover is computed as the average annual capital gain realization (defined in Table 1) divided by the average annual capital gain both realized and unrealized (also defined in Table 1). This represents a long-term average realization policy over the 11-year period for each fund.

tion. Even more surprising, for funds experiencing a decrease in net asset value (quadrants III and IV, 172 of 214 (or about 80%) had positive capital gain distributions (quadrant IV). In these cases, tax-paying mutual fund investors were required to pay taxes on capital gains while their investments had declined in value for the year. Portfolio managers apparently chose not to offset the realized gains with realized losses, even though the potential to do so clearly existed.

Since Table 2 dichotomizes the results and pools the fund-year observations, the realization history of individual mutual funds is lost. Table 3 provides distributional characteristics on the gain realization or turnover policy of growth mutual funds for the 11-year period.

While the SEC has its prescribed measure of turnover (defined as the lesser of purchases or sales of portfolio securities for the fiscal year divided by the monthly average of the portfolio securities owned by institutions during that fiscal-year),

Table 4.   Mutual Fund Values and Tax Costs

Value at the end of 1988 of $100 invested at the beginning of 1978 assuming:	Index fund		Growth funds[a]	
	Value ($)	*As percentage of after-tax value*	*Value ($)*	*As percentage of after-tax value*
Shareholder is not subject to any tax	450.37	160.4	448.92	156.0
Shareholder subject to ordinary dividend tax only	349.30	124.4	378.97	131.7
Shareholder subject to dividend and capital gains tax	280.74	100.0	287.79	100.0

Notes: [a] Figures presented are means of the 88 funds, using actual average return and actual distributions for each fund. The analysis also assumes the investor was in the maximum tax bracket throughout the 11-year period.

its purpose is not to indicate the tax implications of turnover. One can create a turnover proxy more meaningful in a tax sense by defining distributed net capital gains on an annual basis as a proportion of total net gains, realized and unrealized.

Table 3 reveals that, through turnover, the index fund realized 30.8% of the total net gain availabe during the period 1978-1988. By contrast, the 88 growth funds turned over at a median rate more than twice as high (65.4%). While one fund distributed no capital gains during the 11-year period and apparently maximized after-tax growth with zero turnover, 12 funds maintained average annual turnover in excess of 100%, with the highest at 144.7%, as displayed in Table 3. It appears that the emphasis on capital gain appreciation as implied in the title "growth funds" must be on a before-tax basis, since high turnover suggests high capital gain realization, which means higher tax payments.[5]

The important statistic in this analysis is not the capital gain distributed or the turnover of the funds, but rather how much fund value is lost through capital gain tax payments. Table 4 compares the accumulated value of 11-year investments in the index fund and the average of the growth funds in the sample, assuming a $100 investment in each at the beginning of 1978 and compounding by the actual annual retunrs. In a world without taxes, the accumulated values of $450.37 for the index fund and $448.92 for the average growth fund are virtually indistinguishable. For purposes of comparision with the Constantinides ideal of no net realization of capital gains, the middle row of this table calculates mutual fund value where the shareholder is subject to tax on ordinary dividends only. Row 2 of Table 4 is analagous to a taxpayer holding equity directly and being subject to tax on any ordinary dividends received but choosing to defer the realization of capital gains and timing such realization when the capital gain tax rate is zero.[6] The large companies in the index have a far higher dividend yield and taxes on dividends remove over $100 of fund value (the difference between row 1 and row 2 in Table 4), while the smaller growth companies have a yield resulting in only a $70 loss of value to dividend taxes.

Table 5. Cost of Capital Gain Realization[a]

	Index fund			Growth funds (N = 88)		
	Deferral option lost	*Timing option lost*	*Total Value Lost*	*Deferral option lost[b]*	*Timing option lost[c]*	*Total Value Lost[d]*
Highest	—	—	—	18.85	37.42	55.99
Top quartile	—	—	—	7.38	26.92	34.75
Median	2.09	22.33	24.42	4.89	24.68	29.47
Low quartile	—	—	—	3.27	21.49	24.48
Lowest	—	—	—	−.19	13.97	13.97

Notes: [a] The numbers in this table represent the percentage of fund value lost through capital gain realization and taxation over the 11-year period.

[b] The deferral option lost is the decline in fund value from not deferring the capital gain distributions until the end of the 11-year period. The decline is expressed as a percentage of the after-tax fund value when all taxes are assumed to be at the maximum statutory rate on actual distributions.

[c] The timing option is the decline in fund value from not deferring all capital gains to a time when the investor's capital gain tax rate is zero. The decline is expressed as a percentage of the same value as that for the deferral option.

[d] The total value lost is the sum of the timing and deferral option values lost. Since each column represents seperate distributional statististics, the sum of the deferral and timing option percertages may not equal the total value lost percertage.

The most telling statistic comes from examining the difference in accumulated value between rows 2 and 3 of Table 4. After allowing for the maximum tax on ordinary dividends and capital gains, $100 invested in the index grows to $280.74 while the growth fund value is $287.79. The shareholder of the average growth fund did not have access to the discretionary increment to after-tax fund value of 31.7% because of the fund realization of capital gains, compared to 24.4% lost by the index fund investor. In sum, the average growth fund in the sample performed similarly to the index over the period of rising equity value on both a pre-and post-tax basis. However, the majority of value lost to taxes for the index fund was due to dividend yield, whereas the majority of value lost for the average growth fund was through capital gain realization. That is, due to the nature of an index fund, the lower realization of capital gains preserves a greater portion of the deferral and timing options, which are examined in more detail in Table 5.

The total cost for the mutual funds is split between the deferral and timing options in Table 5. Distributional characteristics for the total cost (right column of Table 5) reveal that mutual funds lost between 13.97 and 55.99% of their after-tax value as a result of capital gain realization. The major portion of the total is the lost timing option, which varies between 13.97 and 37.42%. The deferral option lost is smaller due to the relatively short period examined (11 years) and would be quite significant if the compounding process were able to proceed for longer holding periods. Nonetheless, the deferral option lost ranged from −0.19 to 18.85% of the after-tax fund value.[7] The two option values are highly correlated, since each arises as a result of capital gain realization which precludes investors from obtaining the incremental values from either option. The option values lost are also widely varying and quite significant in many mutual funds.

CONCLUSIONS AND IMPLICATIONS

This study points out the tax implications caused by the realization of capital gains by mutual funds. In a rising equity market, fund turnover accelerates the payment of capital gain taxes by fund investors. This acceleration has two important implications. First, it takes a portion of the value of the option of timing the recognition of capital gains from individual investors. Second, current realization increases the present value of the tax liability faced by mutual fund investors, reducing the value of the deferral option. An empirical investigation of open-end equity growth funds (those most likely to realize capital gains) finds that the tax-related costs can be substantial.

One may ask, Why aren't professional managers more sensitive to the tax cost of investors? Lakonishok and Smidt (1986) speculate that although mutual funds are not tax exempt, they might behave as if they were because of their pretax performance evaluation. They also suggest that professional managers, who are compensated based on performance, may tend to realize gains and restructure their portfolios to ensure that the gains are not lost by subsequent market downturns.

Mutual funds provide many advantages to investors including diversification obtainable for a low initial investment, professional record keeping, and management at relatively modest expense. The choice of which fund to invest in is a choice left to individual investors. Previously, the advice was to make this choice on a risk-return basis with consideration also being given to management and load fees. This paper adds another potential member to this choice set: the investment value lost to taxes due to fund capital gain realization.

NOTES

1. An individual's tax rate could be lower in the future because of legislative changes, lower taxable income, or the possibility of facing a year with large losses, which could be used for offset purposes. With large enough capital losses in a future year, the marginal capital gain tax rate could approach zero.

2. Investors holding a diversified portfolio directly actually have more degrees of freedom than an investor in a mutual fund, since the former can sell *individual* shares to realize losses to offset gains while the latter must sell mutual fund shares that reflect average values across the entire mutual fund.

3. A related feature of high turnover by the portfolio manager is that it does not preserve unrealized gains for offset against net losses (which cannot be distributed) in future years. This offset option, although minor relative to the timing and deferral option, is also lost through turnover by the portfolio manager.

4. This assumes, consistent with the findings of Poterba (1987), that the investor does not offset the capital gain distribution with capital losses from other investment holdings.

5.　A legitimate argument from growth fund managers may be that the pursuit of "undervalued" firms and the sale of "overvalued" firms is their job. Although previous studies have questioned the ability of mutual funds to outperform the market, we have no quarrel with this line of reasoning. Our purpose is only to point out the approximate cost of such turnover.

6.　Maximum deferral and a minimum capital gain tax rate are consistent with the Constantinides ideal for maximizing after-tax fund value. For alternative realization policies and different assumptions regarding marginal tax rates, a valuation formula is provided in Ferris and Reichenstein (1988).

7.　The negative deferral option is the result of a decline in fund value. Deferral of fund value decline can result in a lower after-tax value or a negative deferral option cost.

REFERENCES

Brickley, J. Manaster, S., and Shallheim, J. (1991). The tax-timing option and the discounts on closed-end investment companies. *Journal of Business, 64,* 287-312.

Constantinides, G. M. (1983). Capital market equilibrium with personal tax. *Econometrica, 51, 611-636.*

Constantinides, G. M. (1984). Optimal stock trading with personal taxes: Implications for prices and the abnormal January returns. *Journal of Financial Economics, 12,* 65-89.

Ferris, K. R., & Reichenstein, W. R. (1988). A note on the tax-reduced clientele effects and tax reform. *National Tax Journal* (March), 131-137.

Lakonishok, Josof, & Smidt, Seymour. (1986). Volume for winners and losers: Taxation and other motives for stock trading. *Journal of Finance* (September), 951-974.

Lee, C. M. C., Shleifer, A., & Thaler, R. H. (1991). Investor sentiment and the closed-end fund puzzle. *Journal of Finance* (March), 75-109.

Poterba, James M. (1987). How burdensome are capital gains taxes? *Journal of Public Economics,* 157-172.

Shefrin, Hersh, & Stateman, Meir. (1985). The disposition to sell winners too early and ride losers too long: Theory and evidence. *Journal of Finance* (July), 777-792.

Stiglitz, Joseph E. (1983). Some aspects of the taxation of capital gains. *Journal of Public Economis,* 257-294.

Weisenberger, Arthur. (1977-1988). *Investment Company Survey.* New York.

A UNIVERSAL PERFORMANCE MEASURE:
AN EMPIRICAL INVESTIGATION

C. J. Frohlich

ABSTRACT

This study examines whether a single conventional performance measure can be used on all types of funds. The results indicate that the same performance measure is *not* an adequate measure for all types of funds. The Lehmann-Modest (1987) results are not only reinforced, but their premise that benchmarks make a difference in the rankings of funds is extended. Not only are conventional measures of excess mutual fund performance sensitive to the benchmark chosen, thus affecting the relative and absolute rankings, but in addition some types of funds do not have a benchmark that is a valid measure. Results indicate that conventional performance measures work well for stock funds but are *not* valid performance measures for bond funds. It may be that when mutual funds are segregated by type and the appropriate model is found to measure a fund's performance some types of mutual funds outperform their respective markets.

Advances in Financial Planning and Forecasting,
Volume 5, pages 47-58.

INTRODUCTION

Generally, a conventional performance measure using the capital asset-pricing model (CAPM) or an arbitrage pricing theory (APT) model has been applied to a pool of mutual funds without consideration of the unique characteristics of the funds. The performance measure on the sample of bond, balanced, and stock and specialty funds provides initial empirical evidence that neither the CAPM nor the APT performance measure adequately captures the performance of all types of funds.

The validity of the performance measurement when the same measure is used for all types of funds is determined by examining the goodness of fit for performance measurement. In examining the possibility of misspecification in the performance measures, some possible macroeconomic factors relating to interest rates are added to the measures. Their effect upon the goodness of fit is examined for any evidence of misspecification of the model by type of fund. This article is organized as follows: the following section deals with the problems associated with both the CAPM and the APT model followed by information on the data. The fourth section is the methodology followed by the empirical results and any concluding remarks.

CAPM VERSUS APT

Previous studies that have examined the most appropriate model of the return-generating function have yielded mixed results. These studies have essentially been in the public utility industry, where the estimation of the required return on equity capital is an important determinant of the allowed return for these firms. Bower, Bower, and Logue (1984) suggests that the APT is superior to the CAPM. Pettaway and Jordan (1987) expanding upon Bower et al.'s work found that the CAPM is too conservative and underestimates the actual returns when compared to an APT model. Bubnys (1990) found that the estimates of a utility's expected return are quite sensitive to the type of asset-pricing model used. His work, however, found no clear evidence of one model's superiority over the other. Both models have weaknesses.

One criticism of the CAPM has dealt with the possible error in choosing the appropriate benchmark proxy for the market. As often noted in the literature, "strictly speaking, the market portfolio consists of all available investment opportunities, weighted according to their proportion of the total market value" (Lee, Finnerty, & Wort, 1990, p. 168). Since the majority of the performance studies have dealt with stock portfolios, the benchmark used has been a variation of a stock index. Although many of the stock indexes are value weighted, they include only common-stock investments, which are only a small proportion of the "true" market. The index-proxy error is a serious matter since many financial analysts and portfolio managers are evaluated using CAPM-based performance measurement models.

An alternative to the CAPM-based performance measurement is the APT, which mitigates the problem associated with the selection of the correct broader-based market index. However, the APT-based models are not without their own weakness. The major criticisms of the APT model have centered around the factor analysis procedure (Dhyrmes, Friend, & Gultekin, 1984; Shanken, 1982). Although Dybvig and Ross (1985) and Roll and Ross (1980) have addressed many APT weaknesses, some problems still remain with the factor analysis procedure. To avoid many of the concerns raised by factor analysis, this study will use the Connor-Korajczyk asymptotic principal-component technique.[1] The factors being used are derived from a data base of stock, government bonds, and corporate bonds. These factors provide the base for a Jensen-like performance measure on a sample of mutual funds during the period January 1977 to March 1984.[2]

The Jensen-like performance measure's alpha can be a reasonable measure of its stock selection ability (discounting benchmark error) if the fund's risk level is constant. Fabozzi, Francis, and Lee (1980) found that the use of monthly returns allows the beta coefficient of the fund to remain fairly constant. If follows that the risk level of the fund under consideration should, likewise, remain fairly constant. This approach mitigates problems associated with market-timing techniques that cause shifting in the risk level of the fund.

DATA

The data cover the period from January 1977 through March 1984 (87 periods). Three databases are constructed of annualized monthly returns. First, the APT database is used to derive the factors in the APT model. These data sources are form the CRSP stock tapes, CRSP government bond tapes, *Moody's Bond Guide,* and *Standard and Poor's Bond Guide.* Second, the marcroeconomic database from the Data Resources, Inc. (DRI), tapes is used in the construction of the interest rate proxies. Last, the base of 92 mutual funds that are segregated by type (objective) is from Weisenberger's Investment Companies.[3]

In order to simulate a closer "true" market portfolio, both bond and stock returns are included in the APT factor database. U.S. government securities account for 35%, corporate bonds for 15%, and equities for the remaining 50% of the 1984 year-end outstanding bond and equity market value.[4] These percentages determine the data mix of 254 randomly selected stock and bond returns.

The returns on the 87 government notes and bonds are the adjusted returns, which represent the price equivalent of the total return on a common stock. The adjusted returns minimize the variability in the bond returns due to the differences in the time between quotation dates. If during this period a government note or bond with less than 87 periods to maturity leaves the data sample, a similar issue (note to note, bond to bond) takes its place to ensure a continuous flow of returns. This special construction of the returns on the government notes and bonds provides a continuous flow of returns occurring during this period for the 87 data points.

METHODOLOGY

Each of the 254 (n) randomly selected stock and bond securities for the APT factor data returns has nonmissing returns for each 87 (T) time period. Therefore, the data matrix has a 254 × 87 dimension. From this matrix, subtract the appropriate period's annualized seasoned one-month Treasury bill return as the proxy for the risk-free rate to evaluate excess return of the security. In matrix notation:

$$R_{(n \times T)} = r_{(n \times T)} - e_{(n \times 1)} r'_{F(1 \times T)}, \tag{1}$$

where

$R = n \times T$ matrix of annualized excess monthly return on securities
$r = n \times T$ matrix of security annualized monthly returns;
r'_F = transportation of the row vector on the annualized one-month Treasury bill with $1 \times T$ dimension;
e = column vector of ones with $n \times 1$ dimension.

The Connor-Korajczyk (C-K) asymptotic principal-component procedure for the APT model is used in deriving the factors.[5] The component analysis procedure uses the APT data base of annualized excess monthly returns. This technique generates the principal components that serve as a proxy for the varying true market factors influencing the market returns.

This procedure does avoid many of the criticisms of the factor analysis procedure used in the APT model. The approximate factor structure is unique and therefore the C-K APT method does not depend upon an exact factor structure.[6] The C-K procedure is a direct application of the competitive equilibrium version of Ross's APT.

The appropriate number of eigenvalues that will be treated as negligible may be determined by a graphic method known as the scree test (Tatsuoka, 1971, Chapter 5). Using the scree test, after the fifth principal component the curve becomes almost a straight line. At this point the addition of further factors does not add any significant insight to the model. Thus, this study's APT performance measure centers around a five-factor model.

A Jensen-like APT performance measure is developed using a time-series analysis:

$$R_{it} = \beta_0 + \sum_{j=1}^{k} [\beta_{ij} G_{jt}] + \mu_{it}, \tag{2-A}$$

where

R_{it} = the ith mutual fund's annualized monthly excess return;

β_0 = intercept term allowing for a return different from the normal risk premium; this intercept is the APT analog to Jensen's measure of abnormal performance;

G_{jt} = the jth eigenvector as a proxy for a factor that influences the returns;

β_{ij} = sensitivity of fund i's returns to movement in G_{jt};

μ_{it} = a finite-variance residual error team, the covariance between μ_{it} and G_{jt} is assumed to be zero.

If the goodness of fit test for the bond funds is poor in comparison to stock funds (Frohlich, 1989), it might be that the APT measure is missing the effect of interest rates upon a security's return. If this is an accurate assumption, then by adding a proxy for interest rates to the performance measure, the adjusted R^2 should increase significantly.

Interest rate proxies should include variables that capture the effects of short-term and long-term interest rates and their changes. The difference between the returns on corporate Baa and corporate Aaa bonds (RP), the difference between the long-term government bonds and one-month Treasury bills (UTS), and the difference between the corporate Baa return and the one-month Treasury-bill returns (UPR) are proxies for the interest rate effect. In addition, the change in long-term government bond returns (DLGB) and the change in the one-month Treasury bill returns (DTB) also serves as proxies. Each one of the proxies is added individually to the APT Jensen-like five-factor model (CAPM), and the resulting adjusted R^2s are compared to the adjusted R^2s of the original five-factor model.

Derive an APT Jensen-like model [Equation (2-A)] with interest rate proxies added as an additional independent variable as follows:

$$R_{it} = \beta_0 + \sum_{j=1}^{k} [\beta_{ij}G_{jt}] + IP + \mu_{it}, \qquad (2\text{-}A')$$

where

R_{it} = the ith mutual fund's annualized monthly excess return;

β_0 = intercept term allowing for a return different from the normal risk premium; this intercept is the APT analog to Jensen's measure of abnormal performance;

G_{jt} = the jth eigenvector as a proxy for a factor that influences the returns;

β_{ij} = sensitivity of fund i's returns to movement in G_{jt};

IP = interest rate proxy;

μ_{it} = a finite-variance residual error term, the covariance between μ_{it} and G_{jt} is assumed to be zero.

A similar process is applied to the Jensen CAPM performance measure. The benchmark used in the CAPM is the value-weighed New York Stock Index for the balanced and the stock and specialty funds and the Dow Jones Bond Average (DJBA) for the bonds funds. The traditional CAPM Jensen performance measure is developed using the same time series analysis:[7]

$$R_{it} = \beta_0 + \beta_i (R_{mt} - R_{ft}) + \mu_{it}, \qquad (2\text{-}B)$$

$$R_{it} = \beta_0 + \beta_i (R_{mt} - R_{ft}) + IP + \mu_{it}, \qquad (2\text{-}B')$$

where

R_{it} = the ith mutual fund's annualized monthly excess return;

β_0 = intercept term allowing for a return different from the normal risk premium; this intercept is the traditional Jensen's measure of abnormal performance;

R_{mt} = return on value-weighed New York Stock Index for balanced and stock and specialty funds or the Dow Jones Bond Average for bond funds in time period t;

R_{ft} = one-month Treasury bill rate;

β_i = sensitivity of fund i's returns to movement in the market;

IP = interest rate proxy;

μ_{it} = a finite-variance residual error term, the covariance between μ_{it} and G_{jt} the market is assumed to be zero.

Allow for superior (inferior) ability by simply permitting the estimating regression to pass through the origin. That is, the possibility of non-zero constant in Equation (2-A) or (2-B) [(2-A)' or (2-B)'] exists. A naive random selection buy-and-hold policy yields a zero intercept. With more than a random chance, a superior forecaster will realize $\beta_0 > 0$ in Equation (2-A) and (2-B) [(2-A)' and (2-B)']. Thus, if the portfolio manager has superior (inferior) ability, the intercept β_0 in Equation (2-A) or (2-B) [(2-A)' or (2-B)'] will be positive (negative). The intercept represents the average incremental rate of return on the portfolio per unit of time. This incremental rate of return is due solely to the manager's ability to forecast future security prices.

To make statistically significant inferences regarding the fund manager's ability, the sampling distribution of the estimate β_0, the Student t distribution with the appropriate degrees of freedom, is used. One can test whether β_0 is significantly different from zero using the t test with appropriate degrees of freedom for the sample.

The goodness of fit test is examined for each interest rate proxy in the reformulated models (2-A)' and (2-B)'. The interest rate proxies are substituted for each other in the reformulated models. If the APT model and the CAPM model are missing some exclusive interest rate factor in their specification, then the goodness of fit test (adjusted R^2) for the reformulated models should increase.

EMPIRICAL RESULTS

The original results from Equations (2-A) and (2-B) are examined for the validity of one performance measure on all types of funds. Neither model has significant intercepts (β_0s) for bond funds. Both models' balanced funds have one fund, which is the same fund with a significant intercept at the 90% confidence level. The APT model has 14 stock funds at the 90% confidence level and 9 stock funds at the 95% confidence level with significant intercepts. The CAPM model has stronger statistical results. It has 17 stock funds at the 90% confidence level and 12 stock funds at the 95% confidence level with significant intercepts.

The Lehman and Modest (1987) work found the CAPM Jensen alphas to be much less negative (which is supported by the results of this study), but less statistically significant than their APT Jensen-like alphas. This latter result is where the two studies vary. In this work, the traditional CAPM Jensen alphas have greater statistical significance than the APT version.

The fund's net returns include all commissions and administrative expenses. Comparing the fund's net returns with the market return, which is void of these expenses, more than half of β_0s are negative. Unlike other studies (Jensen, 1968; and Sharpe, 1966), most of the intercepts are not significant, which is especially true for the bond and balanced funds. Of the significant intercepts, four under the APT Jensen measure and eight under the CAPM Jensen measure are positive. A positive intercept indicates performance superior to the market. Positive intercepts occur especially in the stock funds. These results lend support for Ippolito's (1989) work, which found a significantly positive industry alpha (unlike the first-generation studies).

The models imply that with a random selection buy-and-hold policy one should expect, on average, to do no worse than $\beta_0 = 0$. However, since the mutual fund data consist of net returns, it is not surprising that the average intercepts (β_0) for the APT Jensen model are less than zero. As Jensen (1968) has pointed out, it is easy to lower a fund's returns by spending resources in an unsuccessful attempt to forecast security prices. The normal costs of liquidity involving occasional money withdrawals, dividend payment, and coupon reinvestment create some transaction costs. Therefore, some small negative alphas are consistent with an efficient mutual fund. Similar results occur with the CAPM Jensen model.

In comparing the β_0s, a negative intercept is not the case in all the funds. The results indicate that stock and specialty funds are more successful in forecasting security prices than the balanced or bond funds. The exact explanation of this is not known. One reason may be that as a fund's characteristics become similar to a bond fund, the investment strategy becomes more of a buy-and-hold strategy. Another reason may be that the performance measure is inadequate or, at least, misspecified for bond funds.

Table 1-A.   Average Adjusted R^2 by the Type of Fund on the APT Five-Factor Model and APT Five-Factor Model with Interest Rate Proxy

Type (no.)	PRIN 5	UPR	UTS	DLGB	DTB	RP
Bond (6)	0.1356	0.1983	0.3146	0.5578	0.1780	0.3489
Balanced (17)	0.5787	0.6160	0.6401	0.7419	0.5833	0.6593
Stock (69)	0.7330	0.7428	0.7455	0.7725	0.7360	0.7543

Table 1-B.   Average Adjusted R^2 by the Type of Fund on the CAPM and the CAPM with Interest Rate Proxy

Type (no.)	CAPM	UPR	UTS	DLGB	DTB	RP
Bond (6)	0.0457	0.0903	0.1999	0.5222	0.0891	0.2344
Balanced (17)	0.7187	0.7290	0.7525	0.8161	0.7291	0.7291
Stock (69)	0.7947	0.7970	0.7977	0.8149	0.8000	0.8029

The latter reason constitutes the major research concern of this study. Namely, are the conventional performance measures misspecified? How do we determine whether a model adequately explains the dependent variable?

The traditional procedure is to examine the model's goodness of fit. Although the t test measures the significance of the individual point estimate, it neither signifies the goodness of fit for the model, nor the existence of a linear relationship between the independent and dependent variables. To validate the model look at the F test and the adjusted R^2 for the individual funds.

The F statistic, with, $K - 1$ and $N - K$ degrees of freedom, tests the joint hypothesis that $\beta_2 = \beta_3 \cdots = \beta_K = 0$. If the null hypothesis is true, then we would expect the adjusted R^2, and therefore F, to be close to 0.

Of the 92 mutual funds in the APT model, in 89 cases the null hypothesis was rejected at the 99% confidence level, and in 2 more at the 95% confidence level. Only in 1 case could the null hypothesis not be reject at a 95% or above confidence level. Similar results appear in the CAPM model. Therefore, the F test validates the fund's adjusted R^2. Tables 1-A and 1-B present the average adjusted R^2 of the funds by type.

It is interesting to note that for either model the adjusted R^2 for bond funds is very low. Only an average of 13.6% (4.57% for the CAPM model) of the total variation in the bond fund's net excess returns is explained by the regression of the net excess returns on the component factors. The balanced and the stock and speciality funds average adjusted R^2 is much higher.

Even in using the mixed data of bonds and stocks to more closely represent the true market in deriving the factors for the APT model, a misspecification in the model appears to exist for some types of funds. In deriving the component factors, some important factor(s) is missing in the performance measure when

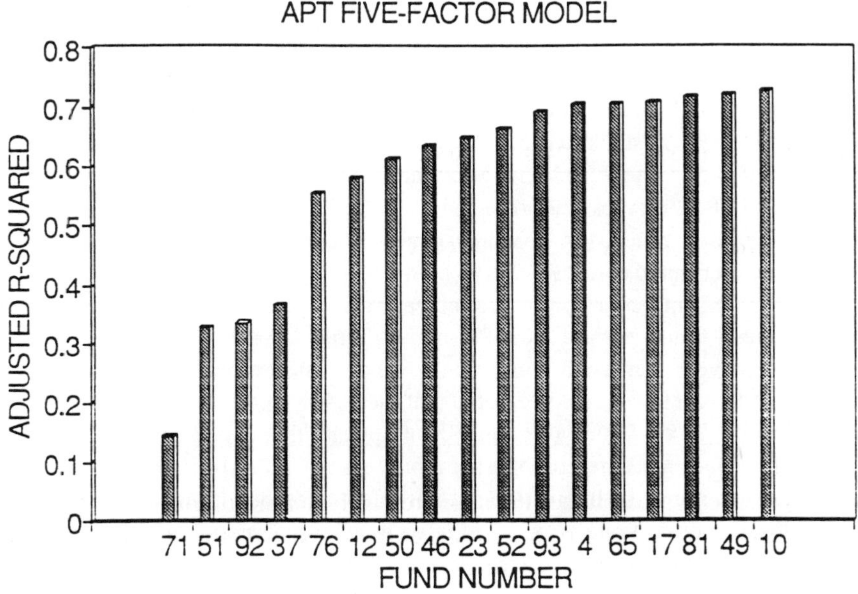

Figure 1.   Balanced Fund's Adjusted R^2

Table 2-A.   Average Adjusted R^2 on All Funds
by Quartiles on the APT Five-Factor Model
and the APT Five-Factor Model with Interest Proxy

Range (no.)	PRIN 5	UPR	UTS	DLGB	DTB	RP
0 < .25 (11)	0.1462	0.1899	0.2907	0.4906	0.1745	0.3146
.25 < .50 (7)	0.3293	0.3612	0.3952	0.5216	0.3404	0.4138
.50 < .75 (41)	0.6552	0.6719	0.6738	0.7080	0.6563	0.6851
.75 < 1.00 (33)	0.8118	0.8193	0.8149	0.8281	0.8145	0.8224

Table 2-B.   Average Adjusted R^2 on All Funds
byQuartiles on the CAPM and the
CAPM with Interest Rate Proxy

Range (no.)	PRIN 5	UPR	UTS	DLGB	DTB	RP
0 < .25 (10)	0.0828	0.1097	0.1935	0.4173	0.1171	0.2040
.25 < .50 (8)	0.4100	0.4116	0.4616	0.5816	0.4286	0.4532
.50 < .75 (41)	0.6607	0.6761	0.6739	0.6882	0.6779	0.6801
.75 < 1.00 (33)	0.8565	0.8585	0.8588	0.8706	0.8600	0.8591

applied to bonds. In reviewing the balanced fund's adjusted R^2 (Figure 1), it appears that as the fund's composition changes to stock, the adjusted R^2 of the regression line increases. For example, in the APT model, the adjusted R^2 of fund 71 (composed of 14% stock and 86% bond) is 14.3%, the adjusted R^2 of fund 92 (composed of 40% stock and 60% bond is 33.7%, the adjusted R^2 of fund 50 (composed of 48% stock and 52% bond) is 61.3%, the adjusted R^2 of fund 81 (composed of 57% stock and 43% bond) is 71.7%, and the adjusted R^2 of fund 10 (composed of 52% stock and 48% bond) is 72.7%. Therefore, the performance results for bond funds and, to some degree, balanced funds for either model should be interpreted carefully.

Although all interest rate proxies increase the adjusted R^2s for both the bond and balanced funds in the C-K APT model (Table 1-A), it is the change in the long-term government bond return that has the greatest effect upon the fit of the regression line. It should also be noted that the CAPM model's results in Table 1-B are similar. From Tables 1-A and 1-B, it appears that neither the APT Jensen-like performance measure nor the traditional Jensen CAPM performance measure adequately captures the interest-rate factor effect upon bond funds. In examining the tables, the interest rate proxies' addition to the initial models add little explanatory value when applied to the stock and specialty funds (unlike the bond and balanced funds results). This result indicates that a single performance measure for all types of mutual funds is not appropriate.

Table 2-A segregates the funds by quartiles using the original C-K APT model's average adjusted R2. Of the 11 funds in the lowest quartile, all 6 bond funds are represented. The remaining 5 funds are composed of 1 balanced fund and 4 stock and specialty funds. Table 2-B presents similar results in the CAPM model. Of the 9 funds in the lowest quartile, 5 of the 6 bond funds are represented. The remaining 4 funds are composed of 1 balanced fund and 3 stock and specialty funds. These findings reinforce the hypothesis that of the conventional performance measures used neither model produces statistically valid measurements for all types of funds, in particular bond funds.

From a practitioner's point of view, this result may have some very interesting ramifications. If bond managers are compensated for performance using the same performance model used on stock funds, they will not be compensated correctly.

CONCLUSION

The evidence on mutual fund performance discussed above further validates previous work (Jensen, 1968; Sharpe, 1966; among others) when applied to stock funds. Previous work indicated that funds are, *on the average, not* able to predict security prices well enough to *outperform* a buy-and-hold policy. Unlike the previous empirical work, the overwhelming evidence from this study indicates that fund managers do *perform as well* the market. In addition, observing those funds with excess returns, 4 under the APT Jensen measure and 8 under the CAPM Jensen measure, are positive. Therefore, *some* fund managers to *outperform* the market.

When the stock and specialty funds were examined for a goodness of fit test on both performance measures, on an average, at least 70% of their return was explained by the measurement. The results tend to indicate that both the APT Jensen-like performance measure and the CAPM measure work well for stock and specialty funds.

When the goodness of fit was considered on the APT Jensen-like performance measure, bonds were found to have on average only 13.6% (4.57% CAPM model) of their return explained by the measurement. Speculating that the models were not adequately capturing the interest rate effect, interest rate proxies were added to the two models as explanatory variables. After adding proxies for the interest rate effect, it appears that neither the APT model nor the CAPM model captured this factor adequately. Therefore, neither model is an appropriate measure for the performance of bond funds. Thus, one performance measure is not valid for all types of mutual funds.

These results may be due to the inefficiency of the bond market or an inappropriate measure for bond funds. Given the size of the adjusted R^2 increase when interest rate proxies are added to the conventional measures, a more appropriate measuring technique seems to be the more likely cause of these results. The authors's next attempt in this area will be to find a more appropriate bond performance measurement technique.

ACKNOWLEDGMENTS

This paper has greatly benefited from the helpful comments of C. F. Lee, Morgan Lynge, Ken Jennings, Dilip Kare, and particularly Louis Scott. I am solely responsible for all remaining errors.

NOTES

1. For a more complete discussion of the principal-component analysis as an alternative to the factor analysis procedure in the APT model, see Chamberlain (1983), Chamberlain and Rothschild (1983), and Connor and Korajczyk (1986).

2. Refer to Section III for complete description.

3. A listing of the mutual funds in the data is available from the author.

4. Municipal bonds are excluded due to their distinct tax treatment.

5. For complete details on the Connor-Korajczyk methodology, see Connor and Korajczyk (1986, pp. 380-382). Further sources include Chamberlain (1983) and Chamberlain and Rothschild (1983).

6. See Chamberlain (1983) and Chamberlain and Rothschild (1983), for more complete differences between the factor analysis and C-K procedures.

7. For complete details on Jensen's CAPM performance measure, see Jensen (1968).

REFERENCES

Bower, D. H., Bower, R. S., & Logue, D. E. (1984). Arbitrage pricing theory and utility stock returns. *Journal of Finance, 39* (September), 1041-1054.

Bubnys, Edward L. (1990). Simulating and forecasting utility stock returns: Arbitrage pricing theory vs. capital asset pricing model. *Financial Review, 25* (February), 1-23.

Chamberlain, Gary (1983). Funds, factors, and diversification in arbitrage pricing models. *Econometrica, 51* (September), 1305-1323.

Chamberlain, Gary, & Rothschild, Michael (1983). Arbitrage factor structure and mean-variance analysis on large asset markets. *Econmetrica, 51* (September), 1281-1304.

Connor, Gregory, & Korajczyk, Robert A. (1988). Performance measurement with the arbitrage pricing theory: A new framework for analysis. *Journal of financial economics, 15* (March), 373-394.

Dyrymes, Phoebus, J., Friend, Irwin, & Gultekin, N. Bukent (1984). A critical reexamination of the empirical evidence on the arbitrage pricing theory. *Journal of Finance, 39* (June), 323, 346.

Dybvig, Phillip H., & Ross, Stephen A. (1985). Yes, the APT is testable. *Journal of Finance, 40* (June) 1172-1188.

Fabozzi, Frank J., Francis, Jack C., & Lee, Cheng F. (1980). Generalized functional form for mutual fund returns. *Journal of Financial and Quantitative Analysis, 15* (December), 1107-1119.

Frohlich, C. J. (1989). Comparative performance measures: Using APT and CAPM as benchmarks. Working paper.

Ippolito, Richard A. (1989). Efficiency with costly information: A study of mutual fund performance, 1965-1984. *Quarterly Journal of Economics, 105* (February), 1-23.

Jensen, Michael C. (1988). The performance of mutual funds in the period 1945-1964. *Journal of Finance, 39* (May), 389-416.

Lee, Cheng F., Finnerty, Joseph E., & Wort, Donald H. (1990). *Security analysis and portfolio management*. Glenview, IL: Scott, Foresman / Little, Brown Higher Education.

Lehmann, Bruce H., & Modest, David M. (1987). Mutual fund performance evaluation: A comparison of benchmarks and benchmark comparisons. *Journal of Finance, 42* (June), 233-265.

Pettway, Richard H., & Jordan, Bradford D. (1987). APT vs. CAPM estimates of the return-generating function parameters for regulated public utilities. *Journal of Financial Research, 10* (Fall), 227-238.

Roll, Richard, & Ross, Stephen A. (1980). Empirical investigation of the arbitrage pricing theory. *Journal of Finance, 35* (December) 1073-1103.

Shanken, Jay (1982). The arbitrage pricing theory: Is it testable? *Journal of Finance, 37* (December), 1129-1140.

Sharpe, William F. (1966). Mutual Fund Performance. *Journal of Finance, 39* (January), 119-138.

Tatsuoka, Maurice M. (1971). *Multivariate analysis: Techniques for educational and psychological research*. New York: John Wiley.

A NEW MEASURE OF PORTFOLIO PERFORMANCE

Ladd Kochman and Ravija Badarinathi

ABSTRACT

The main purpose of this paper is to develop a new major of portfolio performance. Some empirical study is also used to test the new major. The very real prospect of finding under-rated mutual funds has efficient-market implications for researchers and profit potential for investors. Equally intriguing is the rankings of our funds. The Fidelity Magellan emerged as the top-ranked fund tends to validate our semistandard deviation approach, while lesser-known names such as Lindner, Sequoia, and Nicholas may only now be receiving the kind of recognition accorded Magellan.

There is something inconsistent about requiring portfolio managers to beat the market and at the same time eliminate unsystematic risk. The uniqueness necessary to outperform the average can create the very kind of risk that managers are expected to nullify.

Advances in Financial Planning and Forecasting,
Volume 5, pages 59-64.
Copyright © 1994 by JAI Press Inc.
All rights of reproduction in any form reserved.
ISBN:1-55938-421-2

Of course, a novel approach does not necessarily introduce unique risk to a portfolio. Relying on special insights to buy underpriced stocks, for example, does not preclude a high portfolio R^2. However, for managers who resort to specialization by industry, geographic region, or anything else, nonmarket risk is an inescapable reality.

To the extent that mounting pressure to perform acts to diminish the correlation between portfolios and the market, evaluation models based on market risk will underestimate required rates and, in turn, overrate portfolio performance. While a total-risk approach can lead to overstated required returns and underrated performances, erring on the conservative side in matters of finance has always been the lesser evil. One such comprehensive measure is Fama's (1972) *net selectivity.*

If *selectivity* can be defined as the difference between a portfolio's actual and beta-based required returns, it follows that net selectivity represents a second hurdle in the form of a premium for insufficient diversification. Above-average portfolios in Fama's scheme would have to beat

$$RFR + b_p(k_m - RFR) \qquad (1)$$

and

$$[SD_p / SD_m(k_m - RFR)] - [b_p(k_m - RFR)] \qquad (2)$$

or

$$RFR + SD_p(k_m - RFR) / SD_m, \qquad (3)$$

where

$$RFR = \text{risk-free return,}$$
$$b_p = \text{portfolio beta,}$$
$$k_m = \text{market return,}$$
$$SD_p = \text{portfolio standard deviation}$$
$$SD_m = \text{market standard deviation.}$$

For portfolios that are completely diversified, Equation (3) and (2) reduce to Equation (1) and zero, respectively.

For portfolios with symmetrical return distributions, then

$$RFR + SSD_p(k_m - RFR) / SSD_m, \qquad (3)$$

where

SSD_p = portfolio semistandard deviation,
SSD_m = market semistandard deviation,

should be equivalent to Equation (3). The benefit of replacing standard deviations with semistandard deviations is the ability to discriminate between above- and below-average downside risk and to assign required rates accordingly. The common practice of measuring how far above and below an expected value the actual return will be conflicts with the equally popular habit of thinking of risk as the chance of earning a return below expectations only.

Markowitz (1959) dismissed the semistandard deviation as an expensive duplication of the more familiar and intuitive standard deviation, but subsequent research has suggested that the two total-risk measures may not be as interchangeable as Markowitz argued. Klemkosky (1973) reported that his excess-return-to-semistandard-deviation ratio was less biased than portfolio performance measures based on betas and standard deviations to the extent that low-risk portfolios were not favored over their high-risk counterparts. In tests between variances and semi-variances, Kochman and Badarinathi (1990) and Kochman (1983) demonstrated that the latter was superior to the former in their ability to reproduce the rankings of several market indices based on their respective returns.

METHODOLOGY

The purpose of this study is to evaluate a sample of mutual funds using the required rates from both Equations (3) and (4). Donoghue (1990) furnished the returns from the 155 funds that satisfied the conditions of a *growth* objective and a 10-year return history beginning in 1980.

The funds were assigned one of four possible ratings based on the rules in Table 1 as well as on the propositions that conventional total-risk analysis considers only the standard deviation but that any conflicts between Equations (3) and (4) necessitate a recognition of and a preference for the measure, which discriminates between upside and downside deviations (see Table 1).

RESULTS

On the basis of simple selectivity, 56.8% of our funds emerged as above average. That is to say, in the absence of any premium for risk in excess of market risk, 88 out of 155 funds produced returns greater than their respective beta-based hurdle rates. When a diversification premium in the standard deviation sense was additionally required, only 46 funds (or 29.7%) proved to be above average. Finally, when the diversification premium was included and

Table 1.   Possible Fund Ratings[a]

Rating	Criteria
Above average	SD-based net selectivity > 0
	SSD-based net selectivity > 0
Below average	SD-based net selectivity < 0
	SSD-based net selectivity < 0
Underrated	SD-based net selectivity < 0
	SSD-based net selectivity > 0
Overrated	SD-based net selectivity > 0
	SSD-based net selectivity < 0

Notes: [a] SD, standard deviation; SSD, semistandard deviation.

Table 2.   Underrated Mutual Funds (1980-1989)

Fund	SD = based net selectivity (%)	SSD = based net selectivity (5)
AMEV Special	−0.57	+0.77
Alliance Quasar	−0.01	+0.66
Country Capital Growth	−0.16	+0.18
Dreyfus Leverage	−0.12	+0.12
Evergreen	−0.17	+0.82
IDS Growth	−1.39	+0.82
MidAmerica Mutual	−0.03	+0.44
Sentinel Growth	−0.58	+0.02
Sigma Capital Shares	−0.04	+1.03
State Farm Growth	−0.38	+0.09
Twentieth Century Growth	−2.17	+0.45
Valley Forge	−0.20	+1.08

linked to the semistandard deviation, the number of above-average funds was 58—or 37.4%

Those 58 funds judged above average per Equation (4) decompose into46 funds that generated positive net selectivity values regardless of how the diversification premium was defined and 12 funds that enjoyed positive net selectivity only when the premium was based on semistandard deviation—i.e., *underrated* funds. No *overrated* funds were found. Those underrated funds appear in Table 2.

If Equation (4) is useful in rating funds, it should also be valuable for ranking them. The fund with the largest positive semistandard deviation-based net selectivity would be ranked last. Table 3 displays the top 10 and bottom 10 for our 155 funds.

CONCLUSIONS

It seems fair to conclude that evaluating portfolio performance relative to beta-based required returns is too lenient and that adding a premium for diversification

Table 3.   Ten Best and Ten Worst Performing Mutual Funds
(1980-1989) from a SSD-Net Selectivity Perspective

Rank	Fund	N.S. (%)
	Top 10	
1	Fidelity Magellan	−10.87
2	Lindner	8.50
3	Sequoia	6.63
4	Fidelity Destiny I	5.64
5	Phoenix Growth	5.45
6	Phoenix Stock	5.42
7	Guardian Park Avenue	5.11
8	Nicholas	4.49
9	Neuberger & Berman Partners	4.39
10	American Capital Pace	4.21
	Bottom 10	
155	44 Wall Street	−31.11
154	Sherman Dean	−12.00
153	American Investors Growth	−11.83
152	Afuture	−9.98
151	ML Special Value	−8.74
150	Keystone S-4	−8.71
149	Value Line Special Situations	−8.38
148	Vance Sanders Special	−7.32
147	Security Ultra	−7.00
146	Lord Abbet Developing Growth	−7.00

based on standard deviations is too harsh. The large dropoff in the number of above average funds (88 to 46) when Equation (3) replaced Equation (1) as the hurdle rate suggests that fund managers have not eliminated unsystematic risk. Further proof that beta may not fully capture portfolio risk is the failure of 80 of our 155 funds to achieve an R^2 value above 0.70.

The increase in the number of above-average funds (46 to 58) when Equation (4) was substituted for Equation (3) as the rate to beat would seem to indicate that fund managers possess some talent for limiting downside deviations. Such a skill translates into a lower required return, which in turn can either strengthen an above-average rating assigned by Fama's conventional net selectivity measure or reverse a below-average judgement from the same (deviation-indifferent) model.

The very real prospect of finding underrated mutual funds has efficient-market implications for researchers and profit potential for investors. Equally intriguing is the rankings of our funds. The Fidelity Magellan emerged as the top-ranked fund tends to validate our semistandard deviation approach, while lesser-known names such as Lindner, Sequoia, and Nicholas may only now be receiving the kind of recognition accorded Magellan.

REFERENCES

Donoghue, W. E. (1990) *Mutual funds almanac*. Holliston, MA: Donoghue.

Fama, E. F. (1972). Components of Investment Performance. *Journal of Finance* (June),

Klemkosky, R. C. (1973). The bias in composite performance measures. *Journal of Financial and Quantitative Analysis* (June),

Kochman, Ladd (1983). A direct comparison of two measures of risk. *American Business Review* (June),

Kochman, Ladd, & Badarinathi, Ravija (1990). Comparing two ways to measure risk. *Central Business Review* (Winter),

Markowitz, H. M. (1959). *Portfolio selection*. New Haven, CT: Yale University Press.

RULE 12b-1: AN SEC GIFT TO MUTUAL FUND MANAGERS

William P. Dukes and James B. Wilcox

ABSTRACT

This paper analyzes the effect of SEC Rule 12b-1 on expense ratios, returns, and risk-adjusted returns of mutual funds over 1-, 5-, and 10-year time periods. The empirical evidence demonstrates very strongly that performance of those funds electing 12b-1 is inferior, by substantial amounts, to those funds not using the 12b-1 authority. It may be that, contrary to the intent of the SEC, 12b-1 has become a shelter for ineffectiveness rather than one that facilitates efficiency.

The Investment Company Act 1940 (ICA; Release No. 11414, Oct. 28, 1980) was changed rather dramatically by the Securities and Exchange Commission (SEC) in 1980. The change, commonly known as the SEC Rule 12b-1, permits "open-end management investment companies to bear expenses associated with the distribution of their shares" (p. 324). Under the SEC rule, mutual funds electing to do so may force their shareholders to pay the equivalent of a load charge every year for as long as the investors retain their shares. Mutual funds do this by

Advances in Financial Planning and Forecasting,
Volume 5, pages 65-78.
Copyright © 1994 by JAI Press Inc.
All rights of reproduction in any form reserved.
ISBN:1-55938-421-2

retaining and using part of the income that otherwise would be distributed as dividends. The dollars retained are used by a fund primarily to pay distributors/ salesmen a fee to encourage them to sell their mutual fund shares to new investors. In other words, the old shareholders foot the bill to get others to join them in footing the bill for others. Therefore, no-load (no sales charge) funds participating in the 12b-1 rule are really no longer no-load funds.

The SEC was reluctant to reverse "its traditional view that is generally improper under the Act for mutual funds to bear direct or indirect expenses related to the distribution of their shares" but did so after public comments were received that supported the proposal. Those opposing the 12b-1 proposal cited "irreconcilable conflicts of interest of fund advisors and because the shareholder benefits would not be as discernible as that of advisors, since advisers clearly benefit from increased sales of funds shares." Others were of the opinion that the "rule would destroy the entrepreneurial incentives provided by the Act." In adopting the rule the SEC said that "in light of their fiduciary duties under state law and under the Act, that their is a reasonable likelihood that a plan will benefit the fund and its shareholders" (ICA, pp. 325-327). The SEC intent of the rule appears to be for shareholders to receive a benefit in the form of efficiency and/or higher returns.

Haskell (1987) has said much about the directors' "fiduciary duties under state law and under the Act," and especially as these duties apply to "disinterested/ independent directors who have a duty to serve as 'watchdogs' for shareholders" (pp. 454-477). Burgunder and Hartman (1988) put the issue into perspective in such a way that even strong proponents of 12b-1 can understand the issue:

> It is often argued that the board of directors and officers of a mutual funds are essentially captive to the investment advisor. The advisor creates the fund and selects its initial board of directors. Thereafter, as "management" to the fund, the advisor nominates all subsequent board personnel for shareholder approval. Since the shares of mutual funds are so widely held, approval of these nominees is an empty ritual. Thus, the mutual funds' board of director members, who theoretically guard the interest of the shareholders, are handpicked by the same advisor with whom the funds should have an arm's-length arrangement and from whom the shareholders need protection. Therefore, board approval of an advisor's use of fund assets for distribution may not guarantee the propriety of such action....[B]ecause the fund generally, is created, controlled, and managed day-to-day by its advisor, it is an entirely dependent shell in a virtually captive relationship to its advisor. (p. 375)

The entire investment community experienced hard times in the decade of the 1970s. Mutual funds were hit with net redemption in seven of eight years 1972-1979.1 In addition to the net redemptions, fund managers pointed to an inability to achieve economies of scale necessary to minimize fund expenses.

Burgunder and Hartman (pp. 391-392) report that "the historical circumstances surrounding its preparation [the 12b-1 rule] as well as its legislative history strongly infer that the rule is aimed at the possible problems associated with periods of stagnant growth or net redemptions, especially for relatively small mutual funds." Burgunder and Hartman noted further that "the extent of benefits from

Table 1. Portfolio Cash and Asset Size

Year (December)	Non-2b-1		12b-1	
	Cash (%)	*Asset size ($ millions)*[a]	*Cash (%)*	*Asset size ($millions)*[a]
1986	9.90	334.37 (304)	12.38	163.58 (177)
1987	10.95	325.11 (451	12.77	140.00 (253)
1988	11.19	315.21 (452)	13.98	184.75 (315)
1989	10.00	363.54 (464)	10.92	222.15 (378)
1990	13.85	290.95 (474)	16.27	193.22 (451)

Source: Business Week.
Notes: [a] Number of funds in parentheses

scale economics will diminish until the fund reaches the net asset level at which scale economies are zero. Growth above this size will result in diseconomies of scale" (p.392).

In 1980, "The SEC announced that it remained strongly concerned about the serious potential for fiduciary breaches when advisers use fund assets to sell shares, and thus it would stand prepared to adjust the rule if it were employed other than to rectify appropriate problems in a responsible fashion" (p. 392).[2]

The last year for net redemptions in general for equity, bond, and income funds was 1979. The average annual growth from 1981 through 1989 for these funds was an astounding 33.4% (Investment Company Institute, 1990, p. 24). In the year 1989 at least four funds each with assets over a billion dollars and average asset size of $1,760,000,000 were permitted to elect 12b-1 and thereby increase their expense ratios. The SEC allowed the election of 12b-1 even though there were no net redemptions, no low or stagnant growth, and no "appropriate problem" to be rectified.

The number of funds electing 12b-1 increased at more than a 25% compound annual rate from 1986 through 1990, with average asset size ranging from $140 million to over $222 million, as shown in Table 1. The net redemption problem means that funds would have to hold more cash to meet the redemptions. In theory the 12b-1 election would permit funds to avoid net redemptions, hold less cash, and thereby increase returns. Table 1 shows that in every year from 1986 to 1990, 12b-1 funds held more cash than non-12b-1 funds, and Table 2 shows an inability to obtain better return than non-12b-1 funds, to this point in time.

Ferris and Chance (1987) researched the effect of 12b-1 plans on mutual fund expense ratios. They reasoned that the 12b-1 election would not affect management of the fund and therefore, the only impact possible would be on the expense ratio. If the 12b-1 plan offers the benefit of economies of scale as proponents suggest, the economic benefits, which would outweigh the cost, would result in a decreased expense ratio. Rather than reducing the expense ratio Ferris and Chance found increases in the expense ratio for 12b-1 funds of 0.083 to 0.085% in 1984

Table 2.   Annualized Average Return Ending December[a]

Year (December)	Non-12b-1 (%)	12b-1 (%)[b]	Difference (%)	p-value
One Year				
1986	16.36 (389)	16.22 (159)	0.14	0.195
1987	3.24 (434)	2.12 (208)	1.12	0.004
1988	14.53 (450)	13.04 (317)	1.49	0.0007
1989	24.21 (466)	23.04 (378)	1.17	0.004
1990	−6.75 (507)	−7.16 (442)	0.41	0.20
Five Year				
1986	17.03 (267)	13.98 (70)	3.05	<0.0001
1987	12.24 (292)	10.91 (96)	1.33	0.01
1988	10.48 (315)	9.91 (133)	0.57	0.16
1989	15.82 (325)	15.95 (171)	−0.13	0.39
1990	9.04 (364)	9.11 (226)	−0.07	0.44
Ten Year				
1986	15.86 (218)	12.67 (59)	3.19	<0.0001
1987	15.59 (236)	12.96 (65)	2.63	0.0002
1988	15.55 (230)	13.97 (87)	1.58	0.014
1989	15.04 (219)	14.30 (101)	0.74	0.145
1990	11.12 (210)	10.71 (122)	0.41	0.177

Notes: [a] Number of funds shown in parentheses.

[b] Funds listed as having elected 12b-1 on or before December of the year indicated.

and 0.157 to 0.159% in 1985. Therefore, Ferris and Chance concluded that "the plan is only a dead-weight cost" (p. 1082).

Ferris and Chance found load funds to have a slightly lower expense ratio than no-load funds (0.92% versus 0.99% for 1984). Therefore, they tested the impact of the difference in expense ratios on the investors' return over time. They found that it would take "almost 127 years for the return from a load fund to exceed that of an otherwise equivalent no-load fund using the 1984 expense ratios and 88 years using the 1985 expense ratios" (1987, p. 1082).

Trzcinka and Zweig (1990) found "that a 12b-1 plan increased the expense ratio of a 12b-1 funds by 26.9 basis points in 1986, 35.4 basis points in 1987, and 32.5 basis point in 1988." The coefficients were statistically significant, and therefore Trzcinka and Zweig join Ferris and Chance in rejecting "the industry claims that the existence of a 12b-1 plan reduces expense ratios" (p. 23).

Chance and Ferris (1991) repeated the findings of Ferris and Chance (1987) that load funds have lower expense ratios than no-load funds. However, when 12b-1

Table 3. Expense Ratios

Year	No Sales Fee[a]	Sales Charge and/or 12b-1	Differences	p-value
1986	1.14 (154)	1.29 (425)	−0.15	0.0001
1987	1.13 (170)	1.40 (542)	−0.27	0.0001
1988	1.18 (185)	1.50 (563)	−0.32	0.0001
1989	1.17 (212)	1.63 (621)	−0.46	0.0001
1990	1.20 (251)	1.64 (694)	−0.44	0.0001

Source: Business Week.
Notes: [a] No load and no 12b-1 fee.

Table 4. Sales Charge and Expense Ratios with and without 12b-1[a,b]

Year (December)	Non-12b-1 Expense Ratio (%)	12b-1 Expense Ratio (%)	Difference (%)	p-value
A. No Sales Charge				
1986	1.14 (154)	1.76 (57)	−0.62	0.0001
1987	1.13 (170)	1.89 (65)	−0.76	0.0001
1988	1.18 (185)	1.84 (57)	−0.66	0.0001
1989	1.17 (212)	2.11 (60)	−0.94	0.0001
1990	1.20 (251)	2.06 (74)	−0.86	0.0001
B. With Sales Charge				
1986	1.08 [6.79] (248)	1.49 [5.37] (120)	−0.41	0.0001
1987	1.10 [6.02] (282)	1.66 [4.94] (195)	−0.56	0.0001
1988	1.24 [5.82] (258)	1.69 [4.85] (248)	−0.45	0.0001
1989	1.35 [5.50] (250)	1.76 [4.87] (311)	−0.41	0.0001
1990	1.37 [5.29] (253)	1.75 [4.89] (367)	−0.38	0.0001

Source: Business Week.
Notes: [a] Number of firm in parenthesis
[b] Percentage sales charge in brackets.

funds are included in the load category as indicated by Chance and Ferris (1991) we find just the reverse to be true, as shown in Table 3. A straight comparison of no-load, no-12b-1 funds and load funds without 12b-1 shows the load funds with lower expense ratios for the years 1986 and 1987, but higher for the years 1988 through 1990. In addition, the expense ratios for no-load funds with the 12b-1 fee are higher than load funds with 12b-1, as shown in Table 4. Further, Ferris and Chance found that 12b-1 plans increased the expense ratio by 8 basis points in 1984 to over 30 basis points in 1987. Depending on the comparisons made, the basis points increase is 62-94 for firms with no sales charge and 38-56 for those with sales charge for the years 1986 through 1990, as shown in Table 4. All comparisons are statistically significant at the 1% level.

Further, Ferris and Chance note, "Since 12b-1 plans are only sales incentives, they would be expected to have no effect on the management of a fund; thus gross returns and risk should be unaffected. Unless the plan produces an offsetting benefit through economies of scale, the net effect on shareholders should be to lower net returns at the same level of risk" (1987, p. 1077). We hypothesize that a 12b-1 election would impact managerial performance via a diminished incentive to perform. That is, given that funds without a source of sales support in the form of a load or 12b-1 status, must "sell themselves" by means of their performance, it would seem that there is potential for an effect on management.[3] Following this line of reasoning, a load or the presence of a 12b-1 election provides an insulating barrier for funds with inferior performance, perhaps resulting in a reduced incentive for management to perform, as suggested in one of the SEC comments.

Haskell takes a philosophical rather than an analytical approach to 12b-1 plans. He states that "shareholders benefit not only from economies of scale under 12b-1 plans, but also from the opportunity to have more of their money invested immediately" (1987, p. 488). He proceeds to show (Table IV, p. 489) that it would take 15 years for an 8.5% load fund to have a value greater than a spread-load (12b-1 plan on an otherwise no-load) fund. The author assumes an 8% return on both funds, an 8.5% load on one fund, and a 1% 12b-1 fee, on the other. He fails to point out that even with the maximum sales charge (load) the investor would be better off at an increasing rate from the 15th year on. Further, he omits consideration of the fact that no-load, no-12b-1 funds would provide superior results from the very beginning. In addition he does not recognize that a large number of investors paid their 8.5% maximum load to get into the fund, which later elects 12b-1 and then the investor has to pay the fee for as long as he or she holds the fund. The average sales charge for 972 equity funds in December 1990 (*Business Week*) was 3.31%, but slightly higher (4.06%) for 458 funds that elected 12b-1 status. If we expand the comparison to include the average sales charge of 3.31%, the load is preferable in the fourth year of life to the 1% 12b-1 fee. Further, the expanded comparison, as shown in Table 5, shows the no-load, no-12b-1 funds to be superior from the initiation of the purchase.

Haskell concludes that 12b-1 plans "reduce the individual shareholder's overall expense ratio, allow the advisor to retain greater profits, ...and create a potential for greater total return on investment" (1987, p. 490). As shown in Table 4 for the five years December 1986-December 1990, the expense ratios for 12b-1 funds were on average about 36% higher than non-12b-1 funds for those with sales charges and 66% higher for those without sales charges. The statement that the rule "allows the advisor to retain greater profits" is supported by Ruth Simon (1991), who reports "Why Good Brokers Sell Bad Funds." "The answer, simply put, is annual fees. Chief among them is the investment management fee, typically 0.4% to 1% of fund assets a year," and "the marketing or distribution charges

Table 5. Accumulated Wealth Position per $10,000 Invested for Average Load Charge, Spread-Load, and No-load, Non-12b-1

Year	Sales Charge 3.31%	Spread-load: 12b-1 fee for No-load Fund	No Load/Non-12b-1
0	$ 9,669	$10,000	$10,000
1	10,442.52	10,700	10,800
2	11,277.92	11,449	11,664
3	12,180.15	12,250.43	12,597.12
4	13,154.56	13,107.96	13,604.88
5	14,206.93	14,025.51	14,693.28
6	15,343.48	15,007.30	15,868.74
7	16,570.96	16,057.81	17,138.24
8	17,896.64	17,181.86	18,509.30
9	19,328.37	18,384.59	19,990.04
10	20,874.64	19,671.51	21,589.24
11	22,544.61	21,048.51	23,316.38
12	24,348.18	22,521.91	25,181.70
13	26,296.04	24,098.45	27,196.23
14	28,399.72	25,785.34	29,371.93
15	30,671.70	27,590.31	31,721.69
16	33,125.43	29,521.63	34,259.42
17	35,775.47	31,588.15	37,000.18
18	38,637.51	33,799.32	39,960.19
19	41,728.51	36,165.27	43,157.01
20	45,066.79	38,696.84	46,609.57
21	48,672.13	41,405.62	50,338.33
22	52,565.90	44,304.01	54,365.40
23	56,771.18	47,405.29	58,714.63
24	61,312.87	50,723.66	63,411.80
25	66,217.90	54,274.32	68,484.75

known as 12b-1 fees, common on brokerage funds, bring in as much as 1% of fund assets a year; the brokerage generally keeps 90%." Table 2 shows performance of non-12b-1 funds to be superior to 12b-1 funds. On each occasion that returns are statistically different, the difference favors non-12b-1 funds.

Chance and Ferris (1991) show that differences in growth of assets are not significant for the most part. Only three of ten comparisons made for growth of assets between non-12b-1 funds and 12b-1 funds were found to be significant, and in each of the three comparisons non-12b-1 funds grew at a greater rate.

The point is made "that if investors do not approve of distribution plans, they will not invest money in mutual funds that have them" (p. 29). Many investors who are opposed to distribution plans and paid an 8.5% load during an accumulation over many years are now faced with a dilemma: redeem their shares, pay an inflation-related capital gains tax (lock in effect), and thereby have a much smaller investment to move to a fund without such a plan, or continue to permit the fund to use their assets in a way that was prohibited for a large number of years. It would appear that a "grandfathering" for this category of investor would be appropriate. The benefit to be received by the fund and/or the fund manager is clear. If the fund can transfer part of its responsibility to a salesperson or distributor or "come up with a product their brokers can easily sell rather than one suited to their customers' risk tolerance (Simon, 1991, p. 98) and the fund becomes larger, the management fee will increase in dollar amount even when the rate remains the same.[4] The shareholder benefits must come in the form of increased return or a decrease in the expense ratio, if available, which in turn will increase returns. This agency cost conflict is quite obvious.

Ferris and Chance (1987) found a negative and highly significant relationship between log of size and expense ratios, suggesting potential substantial benefits from economies of scale. Proponents would point to this factor as sufficient justification for participating in 12b-1 plans. In view of the often repeated statement that "mutual funds are not brought—they are sold.," the 12b-1 election should create additional selling pressure, which would increase size and thereby the economies of scale proponents expect. However, in a sample of 789 mutual funds, those electing 12b-1 decreased in size by 0.32%, while those without 12b-1 increased in size by 9.4% for the 12-month time period from April 1988 through March 1989 as shown in Table 6. (For a comparison of asset size of 12b-1 funds and non-12b-1 funds see Table 1.) The public appears willing to bear the additional cost of the load funds, but the willingness may be decreasing in view of the increasing number of funds reducing the amount of the load charge. The expense preference behavior of a significant proportion of mutual funds could find that this agency cost type of expenditure might well backfire. When mutual fund buyers understand the impact of the 12b-1 fee structure, mutual funds will drop the 12b-1 election to avoid the agency type cost that is causing the conflict between mutual fund investors and managers.

Ferris and Chance have performed a significant public service by their analysis of the expense ratio. During the period of their study, their "evidence suggest that the plan is only a dead weight cost" (1991, p. 1082). Trzcinka and Zweig join Ferris and Chance in the public service when they "find conclusively that expenses of 12b-1 are higher than expenses on non 12b-1funds" (1990, p. 67). Our research is an extension to that of Ferris and Chance and Trzcinka and Zweig in that what investors are really concerned with is the performance of mutual funds. In our opinion, the expense ratio is of secondary importance to investment performance. If the 12b-1 expenditure can improve investment performance and/or reduce the

Table 6. Twelve-Month Change (%)
in Assets, from April 1988-March 1989

	Non-12b-1	*12b-1*
Overall		
12-month Change	9.4	−0.32
By Objective		
Growth	9.77	-0.24
Growth and income	7.28	-3.84
Income and balance	10.77	6.9

expense ratio, thereby improving performance in terms of rate of return to share-holders, it could be justified. Therefore, the thrust of our research is on perfor-mance of those funds electing/not electing 12b-1.

Mutual fund performance has been studied from several different points of view over the last three decades, to include risk-adjusted performance based on the cap-ital asset-pricing theory, asset size, expense ratio, and market timing. Only a few papers have attempted to evaluate the effects of SEC Rule 12b-1 as shown above. The factors of greatest concern appear to be risk-adjusted performance, expense ratio, and asset size, and the relationship between them. The single-parameter per-formance measures derived from portfolio theory and the capital asset-pricing model (CAPM) by Treynor (1985), Sharpe (1966), and Jensen (1968) are applied to one degree or another in much of the literature.

The primary objective of this research is to address the issue of management performance. Specifically, it addresses the question: Do funds without the 12b-1 provision provide higher risk-adjusted returns than funds with 12b-1? The remainder of the paper is organized as follows: Part I contains a description of data and the methodology employed. Part II presents our findings and a summary and concluding remarks are contained in Part III.

DATA AND METHODOLOGY

Data

The mutual fund data used herein were obtained from Business Week Mutual Fund Scoreboard Disks[5] from December 1986 through December 1990, Wiesen-berger Investment Service (various issues), and Morningstar's *Mutual Fund Val-ues*. Statistical data for all funds for which complete data were available for 10-, 5-, and 1-year periods were collected for each year ending in December, for 1986 through 1990. The number of funds in each set varied, depending on the availabil-ity of data, and are shown in each set. It should be noted that the time periods beyond 12-month data do not necessarily correspond to the length of a time a fund

Table 7.   Number of 12-1 Plans by Funds Objectives

Fund Objective	Non-12b-1	12b-1	Total
1-year Time Period			
Growth	144	82	226
Growth and income	53	43	96
Income and balanced	47	20	67
Total	244	145	389
5-year Time Period			
Growth	129	55	184
Growth and income	45	29	74
Income and balanced	47	15	62
Total	221	99	320
10-year Time Period			
Growth	103	33	136
Growth and income	38	21	59
Income and balanced	41	13	54
Total	182	67	249

had elected the 12b-1 plan. Therefore, a fund that had elected the 12b-1 option in 1989 or 1990 but had been in existence for 10 years would be considered to be a 12b-1 fund in any time period ending in the year 1989 or 1990.

Although information was available for mutual funds with a variety of objectives, sample size considerations narrowed the set considered to objective of growth, growth and income, and a pooling of funds with income and balanced objectives. Thus, only three types were considered when objectives were part of the test. Funds were also coded by whether or not they were 12b-1 funds. This resulted in a six cell classification: three levels of objectives and two for 12b-1 provision. This design reduced the sample size for 1-, 5-, and 10-year periods to 389, 320, and 249 respectively. The number of funds classified by objective and presence or absence of 12b-1 for each of the time periods is presented in Table 7. Information for each fund included total return for the appropriate period, total assets, and beta.

Methodology

The primary research question was addressed by first computing risk-adjusted performance for the 1-, 5-, and 10-year periods by using the Treynor (1985) index.[6] These performance figures were then submitted to three separate regression analyses with the performance levels for each of the three time periods as the dependent variable. Dummy variables were created to represent the funds objectives and the presence or absence of 12b-1. In addition, asset size of each fund was included in the regression both by itself and in interaction with the 12b-1 variable. We reasoned that this procedure would account for any differences in performance resulting from economies of scale—the rationale for 12b-1. That is, all of the factors that could account for differential performance resulting from 12b-1 were considered. The proposed regression model is:

$$\begin{aligned} RARR = a &+ b_1 ASSETS + b_2(ASSETS \times 12B1) \\ &+ b_3(ASSETS \times GROWTH) + b_4(ASSETS \times GROINC) \\ &+ b_5 GROWTH + b_6 GROINC + b_7 12b1 + e. \end{aligned} \tag{1}$$

The variables are defined as:

> RARR = risk-adjusted rate of return;
> ASSETS = end-of-year net assets or average end-of-year net assets for the period;
> GROWTH = a dummy variable equal to 1 if the fund had a growth-only objective and 0 if not;
> GROINC = a dummy variable equal to 1 if the fund had a growth and income objective and 0 if not; firms with an income or balanced objective represent the omitted class;
> 12B1 = a dummy variable equal to 1 if a 12b-1 plan was in effect and zero if not.

Data from each of the time periods were used to examine this model. In addition, since nonlinear economies of scale have been demonstrated (Ferris & Chance, 1987), a separate set of analyses using the logarithm of assets in the above equation was conducted.

EMPIRICAL RESULTS

Before reporting the results of the analyses described above, some simple descriptive results are presented. The key variable in the research is risk-adjusted rate of return, the mean values for which are presented by fund objective and presence or absence of 12b-1 in Table 8. It is obvious that in every case, risk-adjusted returns of 12b-1 funds were inferior to those of comparable funds without 12b-1, although these differences vary by fund objective. The question remains. Are the differences in management performance as measured by risk-adjusted rate of return significantly different between 12b-1 and non-12b-1 funds for reasons other than asset size?

Table 8.   Average Risk-Adjusted Performance for 1, 5, and 10 Years

Fund Objective	Non-12b1	12b-1	Difference	p-value
1-year Performance (%)				
Growth	7.33 (144)	6.24 (82)	1.09	0.34
Growth and income	10.82 (53)	7.36 (43)	3.46	0.03
Income and balanced	9.17 (47)	3.22 (20)	5.95	0.02
5-year Performance (%)				
Growth	7.48 (129)	6.06 (55)	1.42	0.07
Growth and income	10.50 (45)	7.43 (29)	3.07	0.05
Income and balanced	14.91 (47)	10.94 (15)	3.97	0.10
10-year Performance (%)				
Growth	8.01 (103)	6.02 (33)	1.99	0.02
Growth and income	8.15 (38)	4.97 (21)	3.18	0.03
Income and balanced	10.72 (41)	8.37 (13)	2.35	0.06

Table 9.   Regressions of Risk-Adjusted Return[a]

| | Time Period | | | | | |
Variable	1 Year		5 Years		10 Years	
Intercept	9.68	5.96	17.18	18.10	12.70	9.59
	(5.98)	(1.53)	(12.54)	(5.51)	(11.04)	(3.41)
ASSETS	0.001		−0.002		0.0001	
	(0.85)		(−1.24)		(0.13)	
ASSETS × 12B1	0.00		0.003		0.001	
	(0.00)		(2.24)		(1.46)	
$\log_e$ASSETS		0.79		−0.40		0.59
		(1.03)		(−0.64)		(1.11)
$\log_e$ASSETS × 12B1		0.23		1.27		0.59
		(0.43)		(2.81)***		(1.49)
GROWTH	−0.089	0.09	−6.65	-6.52	−2.49	−2.56
	(−0.08)	(0.09)	(−7.11)***	(−7.28)***	(−3.31)***	(−3.59)***
GROINC	2.04	2.03	−4.80	−4.85	−3.38	−3.36
	(1.55)	(1.57)	(−4.33)***	(−4.58)***	(−3.80)***	(−4.00)***
12B1	−2.24	−2.94	−3.01	−7.90	−2.65	−4.77
	(−2.33)**	(−1.16)	(−3.46)***	(−3.48)***	(−3.50)***	(−2.37)***
R^2	0.05	0.08	0.20	0.26	0.19	0.27
Obs.	389	389	320	320	249	249

Notes: a t-statistics are in parentheses.
      **Significant at the 5% level or better.
      ***Significant at the 1% level or better.

The results of the regressions on risk-adjusted fund performance are reported in Table 9. All six of the models (three each using ASSETS and $\log_e$ ASSETS) achieve significance, although they explain substantially different proportions of the variance in performance. In every case the 12b-1 coefficient is negative and in every case but one (1 year, $\log_e$ASSETS) the coefficient for 12b-1 is significant as well as negative, even after fund objectives and the impact of asset size have been accounted for. (In the 1-year, $\log_e$ASSETS equation, the coefficient is similar, but does not research significance). And, although ASSETS are not significant predictors of performance in any of the six equations, the equations for the 5-year time period indicate significant interaction between asset size and the presence of 12b-1. We also considered the possibility that the presence or absence of 12b-1 acted as a surrogate for higher or lower expense ratios, since previous research has demonstrated a relationship (Ferris & Chance, 1987). We thus added expense ratios to the various rates of returns as suggested by Sharpe (1986) and Jensen (1968), and reanalyzed the models. The results (not shown) were essentially the same as those presented in Table 9. It would appear that management performance of 12b-1 funds is, on average, significantly inferior to other funds, but not as a result of a lesser asset base, nor higher expense ratios.

SUMMARY AND CONCLUDING REMARKS

Justification or rationalization given to the SEC for permitting funds to adopt distribution plans that had been prohibited for something like 40 years included net redemptions, stagnant growth, the ability to hold less cash, and the chance to rectify appropriate problems. On average there has been no net redemption since 1979, the rate of growth in fund assets has exceeded 33% from 1981 through 1989, and by choice, 12b-1 funds have continued to hold more cash than non-12b-1 funds. The expense ratios of 12b-1 funds increased and the number of funds electing 12b-1 increased at more than a 25% compounded rate from 1986 through 1990. Expense ratios were 38-94 basis points higher for 12b-1 funds, depending on the year and whether the traditional sales charge was being applied.

In order to evaluate the management of 12b-1 funds, risk-adjusted performance of 12b-1 funds was compared with that of non-12b-1 funds. The empirical evidence demonstrates very strongly that 12b-1 fund performance is inferior and, as indicated in Tables 2, 8, and 9, by substantial amounts. This was true irrespective of the time period over which the funds were compared, which suggests an interesting hypothesis. Recall that many of the funds classified as 12b-1 in the 10-year period would have adopted the 12b-1 plan at various points across the 10 years. Thus, some portion of the data represent their performance prior to shifting to 12b-1. Nonetheless, the performance of 12b-1 funds is uniformly inferior across all three time periods. There are two possible reasons. Either, contrary to the intent of the SEC 12b-1 has become a shelter for ineffectiveness rather than one that facilitates efficiency, or effectiveness decreases after the election of the 12b-1 plan. While, given the nature of the data used in this study, such conjecture must remain purely speculative, it does suggest an avenue for future research, not to demonstrate inferior performance on the part of 12b-1 funds, but rather to understand why this is so.

ACKNOWLEDGMENTS

We acknowledge partial support for this research from the College of Business Administration, Texas Tech University, Merrill Lynch Pierce Fenner and Smith, Inc., and Business Week Mutual Fund Scoreboard.

NOTES

1.   Investment Company Institute (1989, p. 24)

2.   Investment Company Act of 1940, Release No. 11414. Fed. Reg. 73898, 73901 (Oct. 28, 1980)

3.   See for example, "Now There's More to Fees Than Meets the Eye," *Business Week*, February 23, 1987; "Bark, Watchdog!" *Forbes*, June 16, 1986; "The Long Trail," *Forbes*, September 21, 1987; "Watch Out for the Fee Grabbers!" *Money*, May 1990.

4.   Trzcinka and Zweig state, "It is also possible that 12b-1 expenses may pay for agents whose purpose is to convince investors to place their money in more expensive funds when identical, less expensive alternatives exist" (1990, p. 67).

5.   Several of the disks were provided by Business Week Mutual Fund Scoreboard.

6.   The Treynor index for a risk-adjusted return is $(R_i - R_f)/b$, where R_i is the return on security i; R_f the risk-free rate proxied by 1-, 5-, 10-year yields on constant-maturity Treasury securities obtained from various issues of *Federal Revenue Bulletins*; and b the beta: slope of the regression line between returns on security i, regressed against returns on the market, proxied by the S&P 500 index of common stocks. The beta used is that reported by the Mutual Fund Scoreboard Disk and calculated using 5 years of monthly data (*Business Week*).

REFERENCES

Burgunder, Lee B., & Harman, Karl O. (1988). The mutual fund industry and rule 12b-1 plans: An assessment. *Securities Regulation Law Journal, 15*.

Chance, Don M, & Ferris, Stephen P. (1991). Mutual fund distribution fees: An empirical analysis on the impact of deregulation. *Journal of Financial Services Research, 5*, 25-42.

Ferris, Stephen P., & Chance, Don M. (1987). The effect of 12b-1 plans on mutual fund expense ratios: A note. *Journal of Finance, 32*(4, September), 1077-1082.

Haskell, Derwood (1987). Mutual fund distribution expenses: Shareholder investment costs and the propriety of 12b-1 plan. *New England Law Review, 22*.

Investment Company Institute (1990). *Mutual fund fact book*. Washington, DC.

Jensen, Michael C. (1968). Performance of mutual funds in the period 1945-1964. *Journal of Finance, 23* (May), 389-416.

Sharpe, William F. (1966). Mutual fund performance. *Journal of Business, 39* (January, Supp.), 119-138.

Simon, Ruth (1991). Why good brokers sell bad funds. *Money* (July), 95-99.

Treynor, Jack L. (1965). How to rate management of investment funds. *Harvard Business Review, 43* (January-February), 63-75.

Trzcinka, Charles, & Zweig, Robert (1990). *An economic analysis of the cost and benefits of SEC Rule 12b-1*. Monograph Series in Finance and Economies, Leonard N. Stern School of Business of New York University.

INVESTMENT HORIZON AND MUTUAL FUND PERFORMANCE: A THEORETICAL ANALYSIS AND EMPIRICAL INVESTIGATION

Cheng-few Lee and Jack Clark Francis

ABSTRACT

Chen and Lee (1981, 1986) have theoretically analyzed the effects of the sample size and the investment horizon on the validity of composite investment performance measures. This paper empirically investigates Chen and Lee's theoretical and statistical propositions. Our findings indicate that the Sharpe measure is probably more desirable than the Treynor and Jensen performance measures. This suggestion is consistent with theoretical results of Chen and Lee (1981, 1986) that considered the properties of the statistical distribution. The problem with the Treynor and the Jensen performance measures is that the underlying average-return-beta relationship is not stable and not consistently either linear or log-linear. This statistical ambiguity argues against using either of the beta-based performance measures for empirical work.

Advances in Financial Planning and Forecasting,
Volume 5, pages 79-102.
Copyright © 1994 by JAI Press Inc.
All rights of reproduction in any form reserved.
ISBN:1-55938-421-2

INTRODUCTION

Treynor (1965), Sharpe (1966), Treynor and Mazuy (1966), and Jensen (1969) have introduced single-parameter portfolio performance measures. The possibility of biases in the Treynor, Sharpe, and, Jensen portfolio performance measures were reported by Friend and Blume (1970) in an empirical study using monthly returns. Klemkosky (1973) used quarterly mutual fund data and found similar biases in these measures. These studies did not investigate deeply the causes for the biases they reported.

It was suggested by Levy (1972) that Sharpe's measure will be biased unless the investment horizon used in empirical work corresponds to the investor's true investment horizon. Levhari and Levy (1977) have also shown that Treynor's measure gives biased empirical performance rankings unless the true investment horizon is employed. Lee (1976) has shown that the risk-return relationship measured empirically will be nonlinear unless the true investment horizon is used. Since the Treynor, Sharpe, and Jensen models are all based on linear relationships, Lee's evidence on non-inear results further pinpoints the nature of possible biases in these models. Lee (1977) investigated the functional form relationship between return and risk; however, he does not consider the impact of investment horizon on the functional form determination. More recently, Chen and Lee (1979, 1981, 1986) analyzed the sampling relationship between these alternative performance measures and their risk proxies. However, they do not explicitly consider the issue of the functional relationship between risk and return.

Stone (1973) developed a theoretical three-parameter model. Stone was able to show that the standard deviation, variance, semivariance, mean absolute deviation, and probability of an outcome worse than some prespecified level are all special cases of this more general risk measure. Then, Stone went on to show (1976) that the risk-return relationship is expected to be linear when the standard deviation is used as a risk proxy. But Stone's analysis suggested a nonlinear relationship when the variance, semivariance, or mean absolute deviation were used to measure risk. Stone's theory ignored the empirical question of the appropriate differencing interval over which to measure the assets' returns.

Empirical evidence suggesting that financial risk statistics vary with the length of the differencing interval used to measure returns has been provided by Hawawini (1977), Schwartz and Whitcomb (1977), Smith (1978), and Cohen et al. (1983). For example, a given risk-return relationship may be linear using monthly returns but nonlinear using quarterly returns.

This paper employs empirical data and econometric theory to discern the impact of using different investment horizons (or differencing intervals) with the Sharpe, Treynor, Treynor and Mazuy, and Jensen portfolio performance measures. A generalized transformation technique derived by Box and Cox (1964) is applied to the financial models in an effort to identify the appropriate investment horizon, the most realistic risk proxy, and the most robust portfolio performance measure to use in ranking mutual funds' desirability. The functional relationship between return and alternative risk measuring is also carefully examined.

A simple linear regression model called the characteristic line is introduced in Section II. The Treynor-Mazuy portfolio performance measure, which is based on a quadratic formulation of the characteristic line, is the topic of Section III. Section IV presents empirical estimates of the characteristic line that were prepared with the Box-Cox procedure. After the return-generating process for mutual fund returns has been analyzed, the remainder of the paper turns to the investment performance measures themselves. The Treynor, Sharpe, and Jensen performance measures are defined in Section V. Section VI presents empirical evidence about these three performance measures that was estimated from a sample of 93 mutual funds. Bias is shown to exist in all three of the performance measures. The Box-Cox generalized transformation technique is used to estimate nonlinearities in the risk-return relationships in Section VII. Monthly, quarterly, semiannual and annual data from 93 mutual funds observed over an 84-month sample period are used for the empirical tests. The impact of using the monthly, quarterly, and annual differencing intervals on the linearity of the various risk-return trade-offs is also examined. The results of this are summarized in Section VIII.

THE CHARACTERISTIC LINE

The Treynor (1965) and the Jensen (1969) performance measures both presume that the portfolio's one-period rates of return are generated by the simple linear regression model shown.

$$r_{it} - R_t = J_i + B_i (r_{mt} - R_t) + u_{it} \qquad \text{for } E(u_{it}) = 0 \qquad (1)$$

Treynor called this model the *characteristic line*. Equation (1) is a time series ordinary least squares (OLS) regression. The dependent variable, r_{it}, is a single-period rate of return in period t for the ith portfolio. The symbol R_t denotes the three month T-bill yield in month t, a measure of the riskless rate of return. The tth time period's *risk premium* for the ith fund, $r_{it} - R_t$, is regressed onto the simultaneous risk premium for the market portfolio, $r_{mt} - R_t$. The ith portfolio's undiversifiable risk is measured by the slope coefficient B_i.

THE TREYNOR-MAZUY
NONLINEAR CHARACTERISTIC LINE

Treynor and Mazuy (1966) extended the classic characteristic line by proposing a quadratic time series regression model of the following form to measure the market timing ability of an investment manager.

$$r_{it} - R_t = J_i + B_{1i}(r_{mt} - R_t) + B_{2i}(r_{mt} - R_t)^2 + u_{it} \qquad \text{for } E(u_{it}) = 0. \qquad (2)$$

Equation (2) is a time-series ordinary least squares (OLS) quadratic regression model.

If the portfolio manager adeptly invested in rapidly appreciating assets during bull markets and then liquidated and shifted into defensive assets during bear markets, the excess returns earned should cause the coefficient on the second-order term to be statistically significant. If the B_{2i} term is statistically insignificant, this is evidence that the ith portfolio's manager demonstrated no ability to "time the market."

Empirical Estimates Of The Treynor-Mazuy Model

Equation (2) was estimated over 84 months for each of the 93 mutual funds comprising the sample. The B_{1i} was positive and highly statistically significant for every portfolio regardless of whether 1-month or 6-month rates of return were drawn from the sample period. The left-hand side of Table 1 shows that when using monthly rates of return 31% (23%) of the B_{2i} coefficients were significant at the .95 (.975) level of significance. Since the number of significant B_{2i} coefficients in Equation (2) is more than should occur because of random sampling error, these statistics suggest that Equation (2) is a valid description of reality for a statistically significant minority of the mutual funds.

In order to delineate the effect of changing the differencing interval, 6 monthly rates of return were compounded together to create semiannual returns from the data for the same 93 mutual funds over the identical sample period. Equation (2) was estimated a second time using the 6-month returns and the results are reported in the right-hand side of Table 1. The number of significant B_{2i} coefficients is approximately what would be expected as a result of normal sampling error if the true underlying parameter were zero.

Interestingly, not a single one of the mutual funds that had a significant B_{2i} coefficient when estimated with the monthly returns also had a significant B_{2i} coefficient when estimated with the semiannual returns. The fact that these two sets of significant B_{2i} coefficients have no common elements suggests that the significant minority of B_{2i} coefficients that were calculated with the monthly returns were spurious. Stated differently, the second-order term in Equation (2) appears to

Table 1.   Significant Coefficients on the Second Order Term
in Equation (2), B_{2i}, at different Levels of Significance

	Differencing interval	
Level of significance	*Monthly*	*Six months*
At .95 level: $t = 1.645$	$29/93 = .31$	$6/93 = .06$
At .975 level: $t = 1.96$	$21/93 = .23$	$4/93 = .04$

be superfluous. The quadratic model of Equation (2) appears to be a misspecification of the linear regression model of Equation (1).

Looking Beyond the Treynor-Mazuy Model

In their original study, Treynor and Mazuy (1966) concluded that an insignificant number of the B_{2i} coefficients that they estimated were nonzero. Their finding corroborates the conclusion suggested by the statistics in Table 1. It appears that mutual fund returns are generated by some form of a linear or log-linear process rather than a quadratic process.

BOX-COX ESTIMATES OF
THE CHARACTERISTIC LINE

In order to discern if Equation (1) is linear, log-linear, or some similar transformation of Equation (1) the Box-Cox (1964) technique is used to derive a generalized time series relationship suitable for estimation.

The Box-Cox Transformation of the Characteristic Line

Following Box and Cox (1964), Zarembka (1974), and Lee (1976b), the following generalized time series relationship is defined:

$$RP_{it} = a_i + b_i RP_{mt} + e_{it}, \tag{3}$$

where the ith portfolio's risk premium (RP) in time period t is represented by the convention $RP_{it} = (r_{it} - R_{it})$ and RP_{mt}, is the simultaneous risk premium on the market portfolio. Equation (3) is simply a concise but equivalent restatement of Equation (1).

We define λ as a functional form parameter to be estimated across the ith mutual fund's time series rates of return for a sample of $t = 1,2,....., T$ time periods. Equation (3) reduces to a linear from when λ equals positive unity. Or if λ approaches zero, Equation (3) approaches log-linear. That is, the Equation (3) includes both the linear and log-linear forms as special cases, and therefore it is a generalized functional form to be used to test the observed time series relationship. Lambda was added to Equation (3) to obtain Equation (4) for testing the functional relationship between RP_{it} and RP_{mt}:[1]

$$RP_{it}(\lambda) = a_i(\lambda) + b_i RP_{mt}(\lambda) + e_{it}, \tag{4}$$

where

$$RP_{it}(\lambda) = \frac{RP_{it}^{\lambda-1}}{\lambda} \tag{4a}$$

$$RP_{mt}(\lambda) = \frac{RP_{mt}^{\lambda-1}}{\lambda} \tag{4b}$$

$$a_i = \frac{(a+b)-1}{\lambda} \tag{4c}$$

$$e_i \sim N(0, \sigma_e^2) \tag{4d}$$

Box and Cox (1964) have derived the maximum logarithmic likelihood value denoted L-Max in equation (5) by using the maximum likelihood method to determine the functional form parameter.

$$L\text{-max}(\lambda) = -T\log[\sigma_e(\lambda)] + (\lambda-1)\sum_{t=1}^{T}\log(RP_{it}) + \text{constant} \tag{5}$$

where T is the sample size ($T = 84$ months, for example) and $\sigma_e(\lambda)$ is the estimated regression residual standard error of equation (4). (*L*-Max equals log max.) Note that $\sigma_e(\lambda)$ is a function of the functional form parameter. After Equation (5) is estimated over a range of values for λ, Equation (5) is used to determine the optimum value for λ. The optimal value of λ is the value that maximizes the logarithmic likelihood, Equation (5), over the parameter space.

The likelihood ratio method derived by Box and Cox (1964) indicates the 95% confidence limits λ for shown in Equation (6).

$$L\text{-max}(\lambda) - TL\log(\lambda) < .5x_1^2(.05) = 1.92 \tag{6}$$

where $x_1^2(.05)$ indicated the chi-square critical value with one degree of freedom and 5% significant level. The factor 1/2 associated with $x_1^2(.05)$ results from the fact that $2L\text{-max}(\lambda)$, $-2L\text{-Max}(\lambda)$, and $-2[L\text{-Max}(\lambda) - L\text{-max}(\lambda)]$ are x^2 distributions. Now $[L\text{-max}(\lambda) - L\text{-max}(\lambda)]$ is used instead of $2[L\text{-max}(\lambda) - L\text{-max}(\lambda)]$ to perform the significant test. Therefore, one-half of the critical value instead of the whole critical value for x^2 distribution is used to do the significance test. The 95% confidence region for λ is used to determine the true functional form. If the maximum likelihood value of λ is significantly different from zero, for example, this implies that the log-linear from is not descriptive of the empirically observed risk-return relationship.

Empirical Estimates of the Box-Cox Transformation

One-month and six-month differencing intervals were used to calculate monthly returns and semi-annual returns, respectively, for each mutual fund; then the transformed characteristic line regressions were estimated with both sets of returns. The dependent variable RP_{it} and the independent variable RP_{mt} used to estimate the true functional form were transformed in accordance with equations (4a) and (4b) for values of λ ranging from -5.0 up to $+5.0$ at intervals of .1. Thus, 101 regressions were estimated for each differencing interval and every mutual fund that was estimated. The maximum logarithm likelihood (L-Max) value of λ was calculated with Equation (5) to determine the optimal value of λ for every regression. The statistics that had the highest values for L-Max, measured with Equation (5), are listed in Tables 2 and 3.

Tables 2 and 3 illustrate a lack of consistency in the statistics for the 93 different mutual funds. The lack of any pattern in the λ statistics for the same mutual fund's statistics when they are calculated with 1-month and 6-month returns is noteworthy. The differences between the beta slope coefficients reported in Tables 2 and 3 for the same mutual fund are also disconcerting. As suggested by McDonald and Lee (1988), heteroscedasticity, skewness in the residuals, and/or residuals that are not normally distributed can account for the variations in the λ and beta statistics for any given mutual fund. It appears that the return-generating function for mutual funds is not easily characterized as being linear-additive, log-linear, or any other fixed form because of troublesome residuals.

Table 2. Maximum Logarithmic Likelihood Estimates of
Each Mutual Fund's Characteristic Line Using 1-Month Returns

Mutual Fund	λ	L_{max}	R^2	D-W	α (t)	$\beta(t)$
1	$-.6$	318.08	.59	1.86	.009 (3.19)	.72 (11.25)
2	-1.8	233.95	.06	1.64	.02 (3.37)	.39 (2.50)
3	2.4	382.89	.89	1.85	.008 (5.74)	.82 (26.44)
4	.8	384.35	.86	1.59	.003 (2.48)	.69 (22.72)
5	$-.7$	279.24	.52	2.21	.008 (1.79)	.96 (9.62)
6	1.7	333.35	.70	1.97	.007 (2.85)	.78 (14.30)
7	$-.2$	276.12	.27	1.96	.009 (2.08)	.59 (5.67)
8	2.1	275.33	.33	1.86	.01 (2.10)	.70 (6.51)
9	2.4	319.27	.69	1.98	.006 (2.23)	.88 (13.76)
10	.3	336.10	.56	1.81	.007 (3.44)	.55 (10.43)
11				No optimum found		
12	-2.5	344.64	.73	1.93	.002 (.85)	.70 (15.16)
13	.6	286.71	.28	1.81	.02 (3.81)	.55 (5.89)

(continued)

Table 2. (Continued)

Mutual Fund	λ	L_{max}	R^2	D-W	α (t)	$\beta(t)$
14				No optimum found		
15	1.2	299.17	.50	1.88	.006 (1.67)	.76 (9.37)
16	−.1	294.80	.46	2.21	.009 (2.61)	.72 (8.62)
17	2.0	404.02	.91	1.69	.004 (3.65)	.72 (29.70)
18	.1	297.80	.38	1.94	.01 (3.89)	.59 (7.30)
19	−4.7	372.73	.80	1.92	.005 (3.87)	.59 (18.30)
20	−1.5	374.87	.85	1.91	.006 (4.27)	.73 (22.01)
21	.4	292.65	.37	1.65	.01 (3.56)	.62 (7.21)
22	4.3	315.12	.66	1.98	.006 (2.11)	.88 (13.05)
23	1.7	350.56	.70	2.45	.007 (3.64)	.64 (14.32)
24	−1.9	293.66	.30	1.81	.01 (2.99)	.51 (6.19)
25	−1.3	304.40	.56	2.06	.002 (.75)	.79 (10.52)
26	2.5	301.34	.61	2.01	.01 (3.35)	.93 (11.62)
27	−2.4	287.00	.34	1.94	.01 (3.93)	.59 (6.75)
28	−2.1	278.76	.29	1.95	.006 (1.52)	.59 (5.96)
29	−1.9	212.27	.03	1.75	.04 (5.55)	.35 (1.90)
30	.8	317.60	.62	2.00	.009 (3.34)	.78 (11.96)
31	2.4	356.73	.88	1.68	.002 (1.00)	1.03 (24.66)
32	−2.5	232.35	.08	2.26	.03 (4.18)	.46 (2.98)
33	1.0	332.60	.75	1.89	.004 (1.89)	.88 (16.04)
34				No optimum found		
35	−1.3	316.11	.18	2.41	.004 (1.26)	.29 (4.48)
36	−3.6	306.44	.21	2.49	.005 (1.67)	.35 (4.91)
37	−1.6	341.19	.56	2.29	.004 (2.12)	.52 (10.58)
38				No optimum found		
39	.3	294.33	.42	2.19	.005 (1.33)	.68 (8.03)
40	−3.0	251.17	.16	1.91	.02 (3.52)	.53 (4.21)
41	−2.5	230.51	.19	1.71	.03 (3.96)	.72 (4.62)
42	−.6	313.38	.48	2.00	.007 (2.44)	.60 (8.89)
43	3.7	270.36	.48	2.24	.02 (4.16)	1.03 (8.83)
44	−2.5	326.58	.35	1.50	.004 (1.76)	.40 (6.90)
45	−1.6	260.05	.05	1.70	.009 (1.74)	.28 (2.29)
46	−1.9	301.66	.20	1.89	.02 (5.93)	.36 (4.83)
47	.8	306.11	.42	2.16	.01 (3.18)	.59 (7.99)
48	1.5	293.95	.55	2.16	.007 (1.77)	.89 (10.32)
49	1.8	307.32	.38	1.97	.01 (4.13)	.54 (7.32)
50	−4.2	366.03	.79	1.92	.007 (4.34)	.62 (17.83)
51				No optimum found		
51	−1.9	372.63	.82	1.48	.004 (3.09)	.67 (19.87)
52	−3.9	330.40	.26	1.58	.003 (1.46)	.30 (5.53)

(continued)

Table 2. (Continued)

Mutual Fund	λ	L_{max}	R^2	D-W	α (t)		$\beta(t)$	
54	−2.1	331.93	.40	1.39	.001	(.47)	.42	(7.70)
55	−4.5	317.99	.21	1.52	.001	(.41)	.30	4.87)
56				No optimum found				
57	3.6	326.44	.70	1.93	.01	(3.73)	.85	(14.22)
58	−.9	265.62	.28	1.78	.01	(2.58)	.68	(5.93)
59	−.3	318.29	.43	1.71	.01	(3.72)	.52	(8.12)
60	1.9	368.74	.89	1.86	.004	(2.65)	.96	(26.35)
61	−1.0	345.49	.85	1.61	.005	(2.69)	1.02	(21.94)
62	3.4	358.54	.85	2.16	.0009	(.51)	.88	(21.73)
63	.3	381.68	.93	1.91	.006	(4.24)	1.02	(32.71)
64	1.3	360.07	.89	1.94	.000005	(.003)	1.03	(26.28)
65	1.2	352.58	.78	1.57	.003	(1.51)	.76	(17.46)
66	−3.1	396.70	.93	2.16	.006	(5.17)	.83	(33.60)
67	−.5	312.41	.59	2.18	.005	(1.76)	.77	(11.22)
68	4.8	346.37	.21	1.42	−.009	(−4.93)	.22	(4.92)
69	−.5	361.16	.88	2.00	.004	(2.37)	1.00	(25.65)
70				No optimum found				
71	−.5	322.02	.21	1.60	.003	(−1.06)	.31	(4.95)
72	1.7	292.09	.26	2.13	.005	(1.26)	.49	(5.54)
73	3.0	390.63	.93	1.92	.004	(3.65)	.93	(32.78)
74	−.6	338.18	.86	2.09	.003	(1.48)	1.18	(23.31)
75	-3.9	387.84	.91	2.26	.003	(2.62)	.81	(29.78)
76				No optimum found				
77	1.8	373.13	.84	1.92	.003	(1.81)	.75	(21.61)
78				No optimum found				
79	2.0	328.77	.76	2.01	−.002	(−.93)	.96	(16.71)
80	2.3	310.14	.76	2.18	.006	(1.87)	1.18	(16.52)
81	2.1	354.78	.82	2.58	.007	(.36)	.85	(19.93)
82	1.7	349.24	.82	1.61	.007	(3.79)	.90	(19.69)
83	1.5	218.78	.42	2.00	.02	(1.76)	1.62	(7.94)
84	−2.5	374.89	.86	1.95	.002	(1.32)	.75	(22.84)
85	.5	185.04	.12	2.00	.02	(1.70)	1.08	(3.63)
86	3.4	301.13	.69	1.69	.01	(2.91)	1.11	(13.86)
87	3.0	331.06	.72	1.93	.006	(2.70)	.85	(15.06)
88	2.7	298.11	.77	1.98	.01	(4.22)	1.41	(16.99)
89				No optimum found				
90	.9	357.68	.87	1.95	.001	(.63)	.98	(23.89)
91	1.3	370.00	.88	1.63	.005	(3.49)	.88	(24.70)
92	1.2	341.72	.48	1.73	.005	(.22)	.44	(8.86)
93				No optimum found				

Table 3.   Maximum Logarithmic Likelihood Estimates of
Each Mutual Fund's Characterisitic Line Using 6-Month Returns

Mutual Fund	λ	L_{max}	R^2	D-W	α (t)		$\beta(t)$	
1				No optimum found				
2	−4.3	19.13	.06	1.54	.15	(2.54)	.72	(3.33)
3	1.6	52.12	.93	2.20	.04	(6.10)	.79	(13.24)
4	.6	46.86	.82	2.00	.008	(.89)	.68	(7.81)
5	−.7	35.77	.84	1.98	.04	(2.26)	1.51	(8.08)
6				No optimum found				
7	−1.3	27.90	.53	2.84	.04	(1.18)	1.26	(3.95)
8	−1.9	33.24	.33	2.13	.03	(1.20)	.59	(2.71)
9	−2.5	37.24	.74	1.64	.02	(1.57)	.99	(6.09)
10				No optimum found				
11	0.9	38.40	.52	2.66	.007	(.43)	.62	(3.91)
12	−4.3	41.43	.55	2.95	−.005	(−.34)	.54	(4.12)
13	−4.1	31.94	.53	1.89	.06	(2.95)	.70	(3.98)
14	−4.4	31.44	.67	1.40	.07	(3.40)	.88	(5.29)
15	−3.2	36.04	.73	1.64	.02	(1.22)	1.04	(6.04)
16	.7	34.66	.59	2.22	.05	(2.43)	.92	(4.44)
17	1.2	51.18	.90	1.98	.01	(1.47)	.67	(10.62)
18				No optimum found				
19				No optimum found				
20				No optimum found				
21	−3.1	30.67	.62	1.53	.05	(1.99)	1.08	(4.72)
22				No optimum found				
23	−1.4	45.42	.71	2.21	.03	(2.73)	.54	(5.69)
24	−.5	31.18	.39	2.30	.05	(2.01)	.77	(3.03)
25				No optimum found				
26	−.6	32.77	.63	1.59	.06	(2.67)	1.08	(4.83)
27	−4.6	35.25	.73	1.85	.06	(3.85)	.78	(6.02)
28	−.9	31.32	.43	2.37	.03	(1.15)	.85	(3.30)
29	0.0	17.19	.45	1.89	.31	(5.20)	1.87	(3.38)
30	−4.3	37.92	.60	2.02	.39	(2.51)	.59	(4.55)
31	1.7	40.27	.85	2.39	.02	(1.31)	1.21	(8.93)
32	.1	25.11	.34	1.82	.20	(5.28)	.97	(2.75)
33	−1.0	41.14	.81	.85	.02	(1.42)	.10	(7.57)
34	−3.7	37.67	−.04	1.83	−.02	(−.894)	.13	(.729)
35	−1.4	37.32	.16	2.15	−.008	(−.41)	.34	(1.89)
36	2.9	39.52	.42	1.97	.008	(.496)	.44	(3.21)
37	−2.3	47.32	.72	1.68	.007	(.766)	.51	(5.89)
38	−4.5	35.19	.72	1.03	.03	(1.66)	.93	(5.88)
39	−1.4	34.71	.62	2.12	.02	(.803)	.97	(4.69)

(continued)

Table 3. (Continued)

Mutual Fund	λ	L_{max}	R^2	D-W	α (t)		$\beta(t)$
40	−2.1	27.05	.47	2.38	.1	(3.99)	.89 (3.55)
41	1.8	24.55	.25	2.45	.3	(5.00)	1.11 (2.29)
42	−2.1	36.46	.65	1.91	.03	(1.36)	.88 (5.00)
43	.5	29.00	.58	2.00	.12	(3.80)	1.30 (4.37)
44	.1	37.05	.12	1.93	−.0007	(−.036)	.30 (1.67)
45	.4	25.97	.04	1.89	.03	(.815)	.47 (1.24)
46				No optimum found			
47				No optimum found			
48	.7	35.19	.75	1.34	.03	(1.49)	1.25 (6.25)
49	−4.5	37.25	.70	2.56	.05	(3.66)	.69 (5.65)
50	−3.2	46.33	.63	2.38	.02	(2.30)	.41 (4.81)
51	4.1	36.24	.37	2.80	.002	(.119)	.46 (2.92)
52				No optimum found			
53	−1.8	37.27	.07	1.85	−.01	(−.58)	.26 (1.40)
54	−4.1	39.67	.04	1.71	−.03	(−1.57)	.20 (1.24)
55	1.2	35.40	.09	2.05	−.02	(−.89)	.29 (1.51)
56	0.0	34.92	.02	2.04	−.01	(−.43)	.24 (1.13)
56	0.0	34.92	.02	2.04	−.01	(−.43)	.24 (1.13)
57				No optimum found			
58	−2.3	27.71	.55	1.93	.06	(2.11)	1.12 (4.08)
59	−3.1	35.58	.70	1.98	.06	(3.59)	.85 (5.56)
60	2.6	46.81	.90	2.98	.02	(2.37)	.89 (10.72)
61	−1.2	40.96	.77	2.02	.03	(2.51)	.85 (6.62)
62	−.5	45.27	.86	2.19	.007	(.649)	.91 (9.03)
63	4.5	54.45	.97	1.32	.04	(5.67)	1.09 (20.58)
64	−.6	47.71	.92	1.53	.003	(.328)	1.03 (12.03)
65				No optimum found			
66	2.6	54.06	.96	2.21	.03	(5.75)	.87 (17.14)
67	4.3	42.62	.79	1.67	.03	(2.28)	.76 (7.09)
68	−1.6	39.97	.09	1.46	−.07	(−3.50)	.26 (1.52)
69	3.0	46.42	.88	1.68	.03	(2.54)	.85 (10.04)
70	2.5	45.06	.91	2.25	.02	(1.50)	1.08 (11.55)
71	−1.9	37.71	.01	1.56	−.02	(−1.08)	.20 (1.09)
72	3.2	40.39	.63	1.48	.02	(1.45)	.62 (4.78)
73	.5	55.33	.97	2.27	.03	(6.64)	1.04 (21.84)
74	1.7	45.42	.94	2.14	.03	(3.21)	1.36 (14.39)
75				No optimum found			
76	−1.6	49.03	.76	1.53	.009	(1.13)	.50 (6.51)
77	.6	49.49	.80	2.37	.02	(1.99)	.52 (7.21)
78	−1.4	39.53	.49	.91	−.03	(−1.79)	.61 (3.68)

(continued)

Table 3.   (Continued)

Mutual Fund	λ	L_{max}	R^2	D-W	α (t)		$\beta(t)$
79	−1.3	40.58	.69	2.18	−.02	(−1.16)	.82 (5.48)
80	1.0	36.63	.84	2.30	.04	(2.18)	1.50 (8.31)
81	3.7	52.29	.96	1.80	.006	(.935)	.96 (18.58)
82	4.4	39.58	.78	.94	.05	(2.96)	.96 (6.93)
83	1.8	71.02	.51	2.14	.01	(2.03)	1.95 (11.35)
84	−1.6	22.41	.42	2.86	.03	(.628)	1.47 (3.23)
85	−2.2	54.48	.95	2.30	.02	(2.76)	.88 (17.33)
86	0.0	16.94	.46	2.16	.12	(1.59)	2.37 (3.45)
87	1.0	33.71	.53	1.64	.05	(2.22)	.87 (3.92)
88				No optimum found			
89	.9	34.01	.74	2.17	.08	(3.39)	1.34 (6.18)
90	1.3	53.07	.96	2.24	.005	(.82)	.95 (17.33)
91	1.1	45.63	.92	1.88	.01	(1.13)	1.18 (12.54)
92	2.5	45.24	.87	1.85	.03	(2.98)	.88 (9.23)
93	−4.0	43.31	.40	2.43	.003	(.25)	.34 (3.09)

The natural question that arises next is, Are the Treynor, Sharpe, and Jensen portfolio performance measures statistically related in a linear manner to the risk surrogates on which each one of them is based, as the underlying financial theory says they should be? Or, are they too plagued by statistical problems that create slight nonlinearities?

THE TREYNOR SHARPE, AND JENSEN PERFORMANCE MEASURES

Equations (7), (8), and (9) define the Treynor, Sharpe, and Jensen portfolio performance measures, respectively, for the *i*th mutual fund.

$$T_i = \frac{\overline{r_i - R}}{b_i}. \tag{7}$$

The symbol r_i denotes the arithmetic average single-period rate of return for the *i*th portfolio.

$$\bar{r}_i = \frac{l}{n} \sum_{t=1}^{n} r_{it} \qquad \bar{R} = \frac{l}{n} \sum_{t=1}^{n} R_t. \tag{7a}$$

The average difference, $\overline{r_i - R}$, measures the arithmetic average risk premium for ith portfolio. Here b_i is the beta systematic risk coefficient for fund i, and T_i denotes Treynor's performance index for the ith portfolio:

$$S_i = \frac{\overline{r_i - R}}{\sigma_i} \tag{8}$$

where S_i is Sharpe's performance measure for fund i and σ_i is the fund's standard deviation of returns:

$$r_{it} - R_t = J_i + B_i\,(r_{mt} - R_t) + u_{it} \qquad \text{for } E_{it}(u) = 0 \tag{9}$$

Equation (9) is a time series OLS regression in which the tth time period's risk premium for fund i, $r_{it} - R_t$, is regressed onto the simultaneous risk premium for the market portfolio, $r_{mt} - R_t$. Equation (9) is entirely analogous to Equation (1). Jensen's performance measure is the OLS intercept coefficient J_i, a measure of unusual (or excess) returns. If the intercept term is positive (negative) this is evidence of above- (below-) average performance by the portfolio.

BIAS ESTIMATES FOR THE PERFORMANCE MEASURES

Bias in the Treynor, Sharpe, and Jensen portfolio performance measures was first documented by Friend and Blume (FB) (1970). FB used continuously compounded and also noncompounded monthly returns from hypothetical portfolios they created with samples of New York Stock Exchange stocks. FB estimated cross-sectional regressions like the following to evaluate possible relationships between the performance measures and their associated risk statistics.

$$T_i = c_o^a + c_{1i}^a \beta_i + z_i^a, \tag{10}$$

$$S_i = c_0^b + c_{1i}^b \sigma_i + z_i^b, \tag{11}$$

$$J_i = c_0^c + c_{1i}^c \beta + z_i^c \tag{12}$$

where c_0 is the regression intercept, c_1 is a slope coefficient, and z_i is the unexplained residual for the ith portfolio, $E(z) = 0$.

The FB findings were substantiated by Klemkosky using noncompounded quarterly returns from a sample of 40 mutual funds. Both the FB and Klemkosky studies reported positive and significant bias in all the portfolio performance measures they examined. These biases were documented by regression slope coefficients c_1 that were significantly greater than zero. Both the FB and Klemkosky studies mentioned the borrowing rate exceeding the lending rate, $R_B > R_L$, as being the most likely cause of the nonlinearities they documented.

Table 4.   Estimates of Equations (10)-(12)[a]

A. Estimates of Equation (10) for Treynor		
Months	c_1(t value)	c_1(t value)	R^2
---	---	---	---
1	−.004923 (−2.210)	.008471 (3.432)	.1049
2	−.013213 (−3.543)	.020072 (5.015)	.2079
3	−.017021 (−3.149)	.025319 (4.973)	.2050
4	−.017880 (−2.627)	.030475 (4.292)	.1592
5	−.014715 (−1.649)	.030163 (3.225)	.0927
6	−.028460 (−3.049)	.044942 (4.831)	.1954
9	−.064164 (−3.317)	.083719 (4.288)	.1590
12	−.031969 (−1.446)	.072211 (3.230)	.0930

B. Estimates of Equation (11) for Sharpe		
Months	c_0(t value)	c_1(t value)	R^2
---	---	---	---
1	−.053445 (−2.095)	2.1298 (4.115)	.1476
2	−.072029 (−2.131)	1.9071 (4.247)	.1563
3	−.052872 (−1.354)	1.5530 (3.615)	.1160
4	−.084982 (−1.872)	1.5674 (4.021)	.1416
5	−.057590 (−1.358)	1.2013 (3.814)	.1283
6	−.085643 (−1.705)	1.3758 (4.052)	.1435
9	−.123010 (−2.243)	1.2585 (4.430)	.1684
12	−.105230 (−1.462)	1.1580 (3.786)	.1266

C. Estimates of Equation (12) for Jensen		
Months	c_0 (t value)	c_1 (t value)	R^2
---	---	---	---
1	−.003085 (−2.354)	.007574 (5.216)	.2217
2	−.010448 (−3.819)	.019536 (6.650)	.3198
3	−.018194 (−4.511)	.031047 (7.287)	.3769
4	−.019031 (−4.143)	.036687 (7.656)	.3881
5	−.018883 (−3.663)	.042398 (7.848)	.3971
6	−.032468 (−4.168)	.057321 (7.383)	.3677
9	−.022483 (−2.296)	.061745 (6.246)	.2924
12	−.044574 (−2.458)	.096356 (5.256)	.2244

Notes: [a] T_i, Treynor's measure for the ith fund; S_i, Sharpe's measure, J_i, Jensen's measure; c_0, intercept term, c_1, slope of coefficient of linear risk variable; R^2, adjusted coefficient of determination.

Empirical Estimates

The possibility of nonlinear relationships was tested with empirical return data measured over different investment horizons. Table 4 shows the estimates of equations (10) through (12) in panels 4A, B, and C for the Treynor, Sharpe, and Jensen measures, respectively. Each panel contains statistics obtained using 84 monthly, 42 bimonthly, 28 quarterly, 21 four-month, 16 five-month, 14 six-month,

9 nine-month, and 7 annual noncompounded rates of return from 93 mutual funds. Standard & Poor's 500 composite stocks market index is used to calculate the market rates of return, and the monthly Treasury bill rate is used as a proxy of risk-free rates of return. The sample data included 84 monthly returns from January 1978 through December 1984.[2] The statistics from Equations (10)-(12) indicated the presence of a statistically significant positive linear relationship between the three performance measures and their associated risk statistics.

The coefficients of determination (R^2) for 24 alternative measures in Table 4 are generally smaller than those found by FB. It is also interesting to note that the values of R^2 are not independent of the investment horizon. The R^2 values for the 2-, 3- or 4-month returns all tended to be larger than those obtained from either the monthly or the annual return data.

Further Investigation Needed

Note that in Table 4 most of the intercept coefficients are significantly negative and the slope coefficients positive and significantly different from zero. These statistics indicate that all three performance measures are biased. In the following section, Box and Cox's (1964) generalized transformation technique is used to explore the nature of the bias. In particular, the linearity of the risk-return relationship is investigated.

THE LINEARITY OF THE RISK-RETURN RELATIONSHIP

Stone (1976) has shown theoretical evidence that the risk-return relationship should be linear for the standard deviation but nonlinear for the variance. To test Stone's findings, and also to test the linearity assumptions on which the Treynor, Sharpe, and Jensen portfolio performance measures are based, the Box-Cox transformation technique is used to derive a generalized risk-return relationship suitable for estimation.

The Box-Cox Transformation for Risk-Return Relationships

Following Box and Cox (1964), Zarembka (1974), and Lee (1976b), the following generalized risk-return relationship was developed.

$$R_i^{-\lambda} = a + by_i^{\lambda}, \tag{13}$$

where unity plus the ith portfolio's arithmetic average rate of return is represented by the convention $R_i = (1 + r_i)$. λ is a functional form parameter that will be estimated. Y_i represents some risk surrogate that is being used to explain the ith mutual fund's arithmetic average return for a cross-sectional sample of $i = 1,2,...,$ 93 funds; it represents either the standard deviation of returns, the variance, or the beta coefficient. Equation (13) reduces to a linear when λ equals positive unity, or Equation (13) approaches log-linear as λ approaches zero. That is, Equation (13) includes both the linear and log-linear forms as special cases, and therefore it is a generalized functional form to be fit to the observed risk-return relationship. In order to estimate the functional form of the risk-return trade-off empirically, a stochastic error term (e_i) may be added to Equation (13) to obtain[3]

$$R_i(\lambda) = A(\lambda) + bY_i(\lambda) + e_i, \tag{14}$$

where

$$\bar{R}_i(\lambda) = \frac{\bar{R}_i - 1}{\lambda}, \tag{14a}$$

$$Y_i(\lambda) = \frac{Y_i - 1}{\lambda}, \tag{14b}$$

$$A(\lambda) = \frac{(a+b) - 1}{\lambda}, \tag{14c}$$

$$e_i \sim N(0, \sigma_e^2). \tag{14d}$$

As explained above, Box and Cox (1964) have shown how to employ the maximum likelihood method to determine the functional form parameter. To compute the maximum logarithmic likelihood values, Equation (5) is used with $n = 93$ funds substituted in place of $T = 84$ months. Furthermore, the regression residual standard error should be taken from Equation (14) instead of Equation (4). As before, $\sigma_e(\lambda)$ is a function of the functional form parameter. After Equation (14) is estimated over a range of values for λ, the appropriately modified Equation (5) is used to determine the optimum value for λ. The optimal value of λ is the value that maximizes the appropriately modified L-Max function, Equation (5), over the parameter space. The 95% confidence limits for λ should be calculated as shown in Equation (6).

Empirical Findings About Linearity

The dependent variable R_i and whichever risk surrogate was being used to estimate the true functional form were transformed in accordance with Equations (14a) and (14b) for values of ranging from −5.0 up to +5.0 at intervals of .1. Thus, 101 regressions were estimated for each combination of a differencing interval

Table 5. L-Max for 93 Mutual Funds
[Equation (13)] with Beta As the Risk Measure

Month	λ	L_{max}	R^2	D-W	$\alpha\ (t)$	$\beta(t)$
1	*0.0	508.576	.1934	2.026	−.004106 (−8.130)	.004943 (4.801)
	1.0	507.837	.1866	2.045	−.004250 (−8.642)	.006825 (4.701)
2	0.0	448.805	.2982	1.996	.000338 (.362)	.014498 (6.332)
	1.0	447.511	.2898	2.015	−.000206 (−.227)	.018233 (6.209)
	*−0.1	448.818	.2973	1.996	.000358 (.383)	.014489 (6.319)
3	0.0	413.496	.3393	1.952	.003470 (2.669)	.026382 (6.945)
	1.0	412.225	.3373	1.960	.002338 (1.848)	.028522 (6.915)
	*−0.1	413.498	.3377	1.953	.003545 (2.716)	.025800 (6.922)
4	0.0	387.148	.3385	1.914	.008763 (5.055)	.028977 (6.934)
	1.0	387.088	.3563	1.916	.007510 (4.449)	.034532 (7.206)
	*0.5	387.268	.3494	1.908	.008380 (4.845)	.032699 (7.099)
5	0.0	359.198	.2728	1.937	.012722 (5.264)	.025401 (5.960)
	1.0	362.506	.3509	1.893	.011613 (5.242)	.038485 (7.124)
	*1.9	363.501	.3909	1.896	.009064 (4.295)	.040153 (7.749)
6	0.0	348.152	.3487	1.954	.015334 (6.005)	.050247 (7.089)
	1.0	344.953	.3354	1.953	.013013 (5.060)	.053471 (6.851)
	*−1.0	349.204	.3356	1.983	.016214 (6.282)	.036893 (6.890)
9	0.0	301.011	.2811	1.965	.027009 (6.145)	.041035 (6.080)
	1.0	294.745	.2373	1.953	.023329 (5.186)	.053801 (5.443)
	*−0.7	301.943	.2638	2.001	.025968 (5.993)	.022581 (5.828)
12	0.0	274.772	.2404	1.993	.040659 (7.310)	.085393 (5.489)
	1.0	268.807	.2040	1.978	.038319 (6.525)	.090882 (4.957)
	*−3.4	282.146	.2733	1.972	.034860 (7.381)	.018003 (5.966)

and a risk proxy. The maximum likelihood value of λ for every risk-return relation at the 1-, 2-, 3-, 4-, 5-, 6-month, 9-month, and annual differencing intervals were calculated with Equation (5)—after the equation was modified to represent $n = 93$ funds instead of $T = 84$ months. The L_{max} values that were calculated are listed in Tables 5, 6 and 7.

For illustration purposes, the $L_{max}(\lambda)$ values for the average return and β relation that were computed with 4-month returns are plotted in Figure 1. The linear model (namely, when $\lambda = 1.0$) has the global peak maximum likelihood value. The vertical bars at −0.2 and 1.3 in Figure 1 indicate the 95% confidence region for the maximum likelihood estimates of λ. Note that the global peak of the maximum likelihood value for $\lambda = 1.0$ is not significantly different from log-linear (namely, when $\lambda = 0$). The maximum likelihood values that maximized Equation (14) were similarly calculated for all three risk-return relationships being examined here at each of the eight different investment horizons being tested. These results are summarized in Tables 5, 6, and 7.

Table 6.   L-Max for 93 Mutual Funds
[Equation (13)] with Variance As the Risk Measure

Month	λ	L_{max}	R^2	D-W	$\alpha\ (t)$	$\beta(t)$
1	0.0	526.062	.4462	1.969	.025587 (7.144)	.004925 (8.662)
	1.0	528.707	.4807	2.032	1.355198 (9.247)	1.363785 (9.083)
	*0.7	529.102	.4839	2.016	.386596 (9.216)	.278187 (9.842)
2	0.0	461.459	.4654	1.980	.056331 (8.594)	.010853 (9.005)
	1.0	464.512	.5073	2.035	1.262113 (9.767)	1.271581 (9.784)
	*0.8	464.724	.5080	2.029	.643161 (9.761)	.524350 (9.797)
3	0.0	421.952	.4491	1.991	.081494 (8.685)	.016096 (8.718)
	1.0	424.457	.4906	2.032	1.131405 (9.468)	1.140458 (9.465)
	*0.7	424.914	.4918	2.022	.482601 (9.492)	.348983 (9.488)
4	0.0	392.887	.4153	1.931	.094278 (8.408)	.019988 (8.145)
	1.0	393.640	.4409	2.016	1.049210 (8.609)	1.059615 (8.577)
	*0.6	394.328	.4426	1.983	.372526 (8.691)	.238157 (8.606)ʳ
5	0.0	371.623	.4433	1.952	.107608 (9.040)	.238167 (8.618)
	1.0	377.502	.5299	2.015	.885569 (10.307)	.895134 (10.232)
	*0.9	377.658	.5293	2.008	.713168 (10.314)	.652989 (10.221)
6	0.0	355.607	.4451	1.994	.137947 (9.203)	.031580 (8.648)
	1.0	358.804	.5066	2.011	.987200 (9.871)	.998790 (9.771)
	*0.9	358.852	.5046	2.008	.799832 (9.853)	.733572 (9.731)
9	0.0	310.858	.4183	1.939	.151358 (8.956)	.037131 (8.195)
	1.0	310.085	.4516	1.929	.824865 (8.942)	.838864 (8.762)
	*0.4	311.890	.4470	1.930	.289277 (9.148)	.144616 (8.681)
12	0.0	273.564	.3713	2.029	.216621 (8.502)	.060110 (7.439)
	1.0	284.786	.4355	2.017	.920762 (83786)	.940140 (8.483)
	*0.8	284.882	.4263	2.023	.672389 (8.731)	.566062 (8.329)

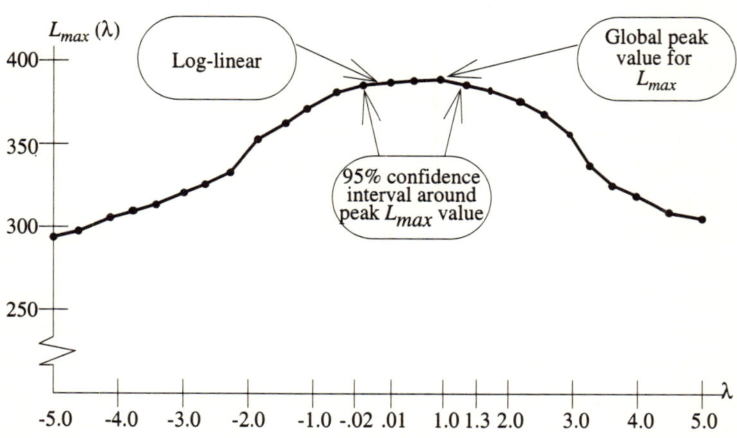

Note: The values of L_{max} (λ) were plotted at λ intervals of 0.4.

Figure 1. L_{max} values as a function of λ for standard deviation versus 4-month average return estimates of Equation (13)

Table 7. L_{max} for 93 Mutual Funds
[Equation (13)] with Standard Deviation as the Risk Measure

Month	λ	L_{max}	R^2	D-W	α (t)	$\beta(t)$
1	0.0	526.068	.4462	1.969	.025588 (7.144)	.009850 (8.668)
	1.0	528.709	.4808	2.001	.170792 (9.004)	.184555 (9.283)
	*1.4	528.980	.4853	2.016	.384673 (9.242)	.556586 (9.388)
2	0.0	461.460	.4654	1.980	.056332 (8.595)	.021706 (9.005)
	1.0	464.085	.5028	2.013	.242191 (9.602)	.263024 (9.699)
	*1.6	464.484	.5119	2.030	.648700 (9.838)	1.057636 (9.871)
3	0.0	421.952	.4491	1.991	.081493 (8.685)	.032192 (2.118)
	1.0	424.359	.4895	2.014	.281006 (9.451)	.306560 (9.445)
	*1.4	424.586	.4971	2.023	.489610 (9.594)	.708005 (9.581)
4	0.0	392.887	.4153	1.931	.094277 (8.408)	.039975 (8.145)
	*1.0	393.799	.4428	1.974	.293871 (8.719)	.325543 (8.609)
5	0.0	371.623	.4433	1.952	.107608 (9.040)	.046929 (8.618)
	1.0	375.826	.5126	1.972	.303825 (10.090)	.339111 (9.887)
	*1.7	377.033	.5403	2.003	.663039 (10.551)	1.151824 (10.446)
6	0.0	355.607	.4451	1.994	.137946 (9.204)	.063099 (8.648)
	1.0	357.443	.4920	2.000	.357573 (9.754)	.403081 (9.491)
	*1.8	358.006	.5195	2.012	.838716 (10.149)	1.538562 (10.024)
9	0.0	310.859	.4183	1.939	.151359 (8.956)	.074263 (8.195)
	1.0	310.213	.4531	1.935	.354008 (9.196)	.408686 (8.788)
	*0.3	310.933	.4313	1.935	.192762 (9.066)	.126920 (8.413)
12	0.0	283.564	.3713	2.039	.216622 (8.502)	.120221 (7.439)
	1.0	283.133	.4180	2.035	.446046 (8.743)	.531890 (8.141)
	*0.1	283.569	.3758	2.039	.231390 (8.501)	.140283 (7.509)

The results in Table 5 show that if the β measured over any differencing interval from monthly to annual is used as a risk proxy the functional form parameter λ with the maximum likelihood is significantly different from positive unity in every case that was estimated. The log-linear model ($\lambda = 0$) yields the best empirical fit when 1-, 2-, and 3-month returns are used, however.

In contrast to Table 5, Table 6 shows evidence suggesting that if the variance model is estimated with anything from monthly to annual returns the maximum likelihood value of λ is near positive unity in almost every case. The optimal values of λ are all within the range from 0.4 to 0.9 and tend to cluster about the value of 0.8 in Table 6. This is the most stable and most nearly linear risk-return relationship examined in this study. The desirable statistical properties of this relationship suggest that it would be appropriate to do further work aimed at the development of a variance based performance measure.

Table 7 suggests that if the standard deviation is used to explain average returns the linear values of λ are within the acceptance region when returns measured

Table 8.   The Maximum Likelihood Estimates
of λ and Their 95% Confidence Regions

Horizon	L_{max} Values For		Best λ^*	L-Max of λ^*	95% Confidence Interval For λ^*	
	$\lambda = 0$	$\lambda = 1$			Low	High
A. $R = a_1 + b_1(\beta_i)$						
1	508.576	507.837	0.0	508.576	506.656	510.496
2	448.805	447.511	−0.1	448.818	446.898	450.738
3	413.496	412.225	−0.1	413.498	411.578	415.418
4	387.148	387.088	0.5	387.268	385.348	389.188
5	359.198	362.506	1.9	363.501	361.581	365.421
6	348.152	344.953	−1.0	349.204	347.284	351.124
9	301.011	294.745	−0.7	301.943	300.023	303.863
12	274.772	268.807	−3.4	282.146	208.226	284.066
B. $R_i = a_2 + b_2 \mathrm{Var}(R_i)$						
1	526.062	528.707	0.7	529.102	527.182	531.022
2	461.459	464.512	0.8	464.724	462.804	466.64?
3	421.952	424.457	0.7	424.914	422.994	426.83?
4	392.887	393.640	0.6	394.328	392.408	396.248
5	371.623	377.502	0.9	377.658	375.738	379.57?
6	355.607	358.804	0.9	358.852	356.932	360.772
9	310.858	310.085	0.4	311.890	309.970	313.810
12	273.564	284.786	0.8	284.882	282.962	286.802
C. $R_i = a_3 + b_3(\text{std. dev.})$						
1	526.068	528.709	1.4	528.980	527.060	530.900
2	461.460	464.085	1.6	464.484	462.564	466.404
3	421.952	424.359	1.4	424.586	422.666	426.506
4	392.887	393.799	1.0	393.799	391.879	395.719
5	371.623	375.826	1.7	377.033	375.113	378.953
6	355.607	357.443	1.8	358.006	356.086	359.926
9	310.859	310.213	0.3	310.933	309.13	312.853
12	283.564	283.133	0.1	283.569	281.649	285.489

over 1, 2, 3, or 4 months. However, the functional form parameter tends to be log-linear ($\lambda = 0$) if the 9-month or annual return data are used.

If the existence of a linear risk-return relationship is used as a criterion for selecting a performance measure, then a performance measure using the mutual funds' variance statistics as a risk proxy appears to be the most desirable. Unfortunately, none of the received theoretical models are cast in terms of the variance. However, if the standard deviation is used to gauge the riskiness of mutual funds, a linear model appears to be appropriate when using 1-, 2-, 3-, or 4-month return data. Table 7 shows that the log-linear model tends to reduce the bias better if 9- or 12-month returns are employed.

Table 8 contains summary statistics comparing the linear and log-linear models with whatever model had the highest over-all L_{max} value, λ^*. The statistics in Panel A suggest that perhaps the log-linear model had a little more explanatory power with the β risk measure. However, since the L_{max} values for $\lambda = 0$ and $\lambda = 1$ both lie within the confidence limits for every value of λ that had the best fit overall, λ^*, except one (namely, the 5-month horizon, which is so far out of line with the others that the possibility of a sampling error arises) we must conclude that neither model is significantly different.

The data in Panel B of Table 8 indicate that over all of the horizons that were estimated most of the λ^* values are not far removed from $\lambda = 1.0$. All of the statistics in Panel 8B provide fairly compelling evidence that the return-variance relationship is closer to being linear than it is to being log-linear. The fact that most of the L_{max} values for $\lambda = 0$ lie below the lower confidence limit for the λ^* comprises a statistically significant rejection of the log-linear hypothesis.

Panel C suggests conclusions that differ from both Panels A and B. The data in Panel C show that when the standard deviation is used as a risk measure λ^* tends to vary inversely with the length of the horizon over which the returns are measured. Thus, a nearly log-linear model, namely, $\lambda^* = .1$, is suggested for annual returns. In contrast, $\lambda^* = 1.4$ for monthly returns.

SUMMARY

In this paper, econometric analysis is employed to empirically estimate the characteristic line and various risk-return relationships. Then the statistics obtained are used as a basis for selecting the appropriate investment performance measure with which to evaluate mutual fund performance.

First, the characteristic line was empirically estimated. It was tested as a quadratic model and also using the Box-Cox functional form model, which includes linear and log-linear as special cases. The characteristic line model was found to be unstable in all the formulations that were explored. Various causes for this statistical instability have been suggested; for example, see Friend and Blume (1970), Fabozzi and Francis (1978), Chen and Lee (1981, 1986), and others. The investigation then turned away from the time-series model to the cross-sectional risk-return relationship.

Intuitively, it might seem like the investment horizon should not be an important factor that affects the Sharpe, Treynor, and/or Jensen measures for ranking mutual fund performance. However, if the generalized transformation technique is used to test the linearity of the risk-return relationship, it is found that both the investment horizon and risk proxy are factors that should be considered when choosing the appropriate investment performance measure. Our findings indicate that the Sharpe measure is probably more desirable than the Treynor and Jensen performance measures. This suggestion is consistent with theoretical results of Chen and Lee (1981, 1986), which considered the properties of the statistical distribution. The problem with the Treynor and the Jensen performance measures is that the underlying average-return-beta relationship is not stable and not consistently either linear or log-linear. This statistical ambiguity argues against using either of the beta-based performance measures for empirical work.

NOTES

1.   The quarterly returns qr_t were calculated by multiplying three monthly link relatives $(1 + mr_t)$ as follows:

$$qr_t = [(1 + mr_{t-2})(1 + mr_{t-1})(1 + mr_t)] - 1.0.$$

The annual returns were likewise prepared by multiplying 12 monthly link relatives. This procedure minimizes the measurement error and bias analyzed in some detail by Mains (1977).

2.   It should be noted that the sample size associated with Equations (10)-(12) is all 93 no matter whether annual, quarterly, or monthly, or what mutual fund data are used. Therefore, the R^2 values of these cross-sectional regressions have the same degrees of freedom.

3.   Equation (14) is a modification of equation (13).

$$\frac{R_i - 1}{\lambda} = \frac{a + b - 1}{\lambda} + b\left(\frac{Y_i - 1}{\lambda}\right) + e_i.$$

Note that $R_i(\lambda)$ and $Y_i(\lambda)$, instead of $R^\lambda i$ and $Y^\lambda i$, are continuous as λ approaches zero.

REFERENCES

Anderson, T. W. (1958). *An introduction to multivariate statistical analysis.* New York: Wiley.

Bey, R.P., & Pinches, G.E. (1980). Additional evidence of heteroskedasticity in the market model. *Journal of Financial and Quantitative Analysis, 15,* 299-322.

Box, G.E.P., & Cox, D.R. (1964). An analysis of transformations. *Journal of the Royal Statistical Society, 26,* 211-243.

Box, G.E.P., & Tidwell, P.W. (1962). Transformation of the independent variables. *Technometrics, 4,* 531-550.

Clark, P.K. (1973). A subordinated stochastic process model with finite variance for speculative prices. *Econometrica, 41,* 135-159.

Chen, S. N., & Lee, Cheng F. (1979). Sampling properties of composite performance measures and their implications. Working paper 541, University of Illinois at Urbana-Champaign.

Chen, S. N., & Lee, Cheng Few (1981). The sampling relationship between Sharpe's performance measure and its risk proxy: Sample size, investment horizon and market condition. *Management Science, 27,* pp. 607-618.

Chen, S. N., & Lee, Cheng Few (1986). The effects of the sample size, the investment horizon, and market conditions on the validity of composite pereformance measures: A generalization. *Management Science, 32*, 1410-1421.

Cohen, K.J., Hawawini, G.A., Maier, S.F., Schwartz, R.A., & Whitcomb, David K. (1983). Estimating and adjusting for the intervaling-effect bias in beta. Management Science, *29*, 135-148.

Elton, J. E., Gruber, M. G., & Padberg, M. W.(1976). Simple criteria for optimal portfolio selection. *Journal of Finance, 31*(5), 1341-1357.

Fabozzi, Frank J., & Francis, J. C. (1978). Beta as a random coefficient. *Journal of Financial and Quantitative Analysis* (March), 101-115.

Francis, Jack Clark, & Lee, Cheng Few (1983). Investment horizon, risk, and mutual fund performance. *Research in Finance, 4*, 1-19.

Friend, I., & Blume, M. E., Measurement of portfolio performance under uncertainty. *American Economic Review, 60*(September), 561-575.

Giaccotto, C., & Ali, M. (1982). Optimum distribution-free tests and further evidence of heteroscedasticity in the market model. *Journal of Finance, 37*, 1247-1258.

Goldfeld, S.M., & Quandt, R.E. (1976). *Nonlinear methods in econometrics*, Amsterdam. North-Holland.

Hawawini, Gabriel A. (1977). On the time behavior of financial parameters: An investigation of the intervaling effect. Unpublished Ph.D. dissertation, New York University.

Hinkley, D.V., & Runger, G. (1984). The analysis of transformed data. *Journal of the American Statistical Association, 79*, 302-312.

Jensen, M. C. (1969). Risk, the pricing of capital assets and the evaluation of investment portfolios. *Journal of Business, 42*(April), 167-247.

Klemkosky, R. C. (1973). The bias in composite performance measure. *Journal of Financial and Quantitative Analysis* (June), 505-514.

Lahiri, K., & Egy, D. (1981). Joint estimation and testing for functional form and heteroskedasticity. *Journal of Econometrics, 15*, 299-307.

Lee, C.F. (1976a). Functional form and the dividend effect in the electric utility industry, *Journal of Finance, 31*, 1481-1486.

Lee, C.F. (1976b). Investment horizon and the functional form of the capital asset pricing model. *Review of Economics and Statistics, 58*, 356-363.

Lee, C. F. (1976c). On the relationship between the systemic risk and the investment horizon. *Journal of Financial and Quantitative Analysis, 11*(December), 803-815.

Lee, C. F. (1977). Functional form, skewness effect, and the risk-return relationship," *Journal of Financial and Quantitative Analysis, 12*(March). 55-72.

Levhari, D., & Levy, H. (1977) The capital asset pricing model and the investment horizon. *Review of Economics and Statistics, 49*, 92-104.

Levy, H. (1972). Portfolio performance and investment horizon. *Management Science* (August), 645-653.

Mains, Norman E. (1977). Risk, the pricing of capital assets, and the evaluation of investment portfolios: Comment. *Journal of Business* (July).

Markowitz, Harry M. (1957). *Portfolio Selection.* Cowles Foundation Monograph 16. New York: John Wiley.

Mayers, D., & Rixe, E. (1979). Portfolio performance, residual analysis and capital asset pricing tests. *Journal of Financial Economics* (June), 3-28.

McDonald, B. (1983). Functional forms and the capital asset pricing model, *The Journal of Financial and Quantitative Analysis, 18*, 319-329.

McDonald, Bill, & Lee, C.F. (1988). An analysis of non-linearities, heteroscedasticity, and functional form in the market model. *Journal Of Business And Economic Statistics.*

McDonald, B., & Morris, M. (1983). "The existence of heteroscedasticity and its effects on estimates of the market model parameters. *The Journal of Financial Research, 6*, 115-126.

McDonald, J. G. "Objectives and performance of mutual funds, 1960-1969," *Journal of Financial and Quantitative Analysis* (June).

Roll, R. (1977). A critique of the asset pricing theory's tests; Part 1: On past and potential testability of the theory. *Journal of Financial Economics, 4,* 129-175.

Roll, R. (1978). Ambiguity when performance is measured by the securities market line. *Journal of Finance* (September), 1051-1069.

Rosenberg, B., & Marathe, V. (1979). Tests of Capital Asset Pricing Hypotheses In H. Levy (Ed.), *Research in Finance* (pp. 115-223). Greenwich, CT: JAI Press.

Schwartz, R. A., & Whitcomb, D. K. (1977). The time-variance relationship: evidence of autocorrelation in common stock returns. *Journal of Finance, 32*(March), 41-45.

Sharpe, William F. (1964). Capital asset prices: A theory of market equilibrium under conditions of risk. *Journal of Finance* (September), 425-442.

Sharpe, William F. (1966). Mutual fund performance. *Journal of Business* (January), 119-138.

Smith, K. V. (1978). The effect of intervaling on estimating parameters of the capital asset pricing model. *Journal of Financial and Quantitative Analysis* (June).

Spitzer, J. J. (1984). Variance estimates in models with the Box-Cox transformation: Implications for estimation and hypothesis testing. *The Review of Economics and Statistics, 66,* 645-652.

Stone, Bernell (1973). A general class of three parameter risk measures. *Journal of Finance* (June), 675-685.

Stone, Bernell (1971). Linearity of Risk-Return Curve. Unpublished paper.

Theil, H. (1971). *Principle of Econometrics.* New York: Wiley.

Treynor, J. L. (1965). How to rate management of investment funds. *Harvard Business Review* (January-February), 63-75.

Treynor, Jack L., & Mazuy, Kay K. (1966). Can mutual funds outguess the market? *Harvard Business Review, 44*(4, July-August), 131-136.

Zarembka, P. (1968). Functional form and the demand for money. *Journal of The American Statistical Association, 63,* 502-511.

Zarembka, P. (1974). Transformation of variables in econometrics. In P. Zarembka (Ed.), *Frontiers in Econometrics* (pp. 81-104), New York: Academic Press.

REVIEW, INTEGRATION, AND CRITIQUE OF MUTUAL FUND PERFORMANCE STUDIES DURING 1965-1991

Cheng-few Lee and Shafiqur Rahman

ABSTRACT

This paper surveys the works of several authors over the last 26 years (1965-1991) on the problem of evaluating the portfolio performance of the managers of mutual funds. The traditional measures of Sharpe, Treynor, and Jensen are critically discussed and their pitfalls pointed out. Alternative measures developed to resolve the problems of traditional measures are discussed in greater detail and in an integrated fashion. Their relative strengths and weaknesses are also presented. Suggestions for further research are provided.

Advances in Financial Planning and Forecasting,
Volume 5, pages 103-128.
Copyright © 1994 by JAI Press Inc.
All rights of reproduction in any form reserved.
ISBN:1-55938-421-2

INTRODUCTION

The investment performance of mutual fund managers has been extensively examined in the finance literature over the last 26 years. Beginning with the works of Sharpe (1966), Treynor (1965), and Jensen (1968, 1969), all these studies have been concerned with measuring performance in two dimensions: return and risk. In other words, these studies seek a measure that would adjust raw returns for risk in some manner. The evaluation of academic research on performance measurement of mutual fund managers is the topic of this paper. The paper is organized as follows: Section 2 discusses three traditional measures. Section 3 presents critique of the traditional measures. Section 4 examines new measures developed to date to resolve problems of traditional measures, and Section 5 concludes the paper.

TRADITIONAL PERFORMANCE MEASURES

This section examines three risk-adjusted performance measures that are in widespread use. All three are based on the capital asset-pricing model (CAPM). These measures develop a number that reflects both risk and return in order to measure the performance of each portfolio. They all a set of portfolios to be ranked and compared to a naive market standard. They are the Sharpe index, they Treynor index, and the Jensen index.

The Sharpe Index

The Sharpe (1966) index uses the capital market line as a benchmark. The index in computed by dividing the average excess (net of risk-free rate) return for the portfolio by its standard deviation. This is called the *reward-to-variability ratio*. It is simply the ratio of reward (which is good) to variability (which is bad). It is simply the risk premium earned per unit of risk exposure. The reward-to-variability ratio provides an absolute measure of the performance of a portfolio. Two or more portfolios can be compared using it. The larger the ratio, the better is the performance. To determine the quality of performance, the Sharpe index for the portfolio is compared with that for the market portfolio. A higher Sharpe index would indicate that the portfolio manager has outperformed the market, while a lower Sharpe index would indicate underperformance.[1]

Sharpe (1966) analyzed 34 mutual funds' performance over the period 1954-1963. The average ratio for the 34 funds was .633, which is below the .677 for the Dow-Jones Industrial Average (DJIA), a proxy for the market portfolio. Of the 34 funds, only 11 outperformed the market.

The Treynor Index

Treynor (1965) developed an index of portfolio performance that is based on systematic risk, as measured by portfolio beta coefficient. The Treynor index uses security market line (SML) as a benchmark. The index is computed by dividing the average excess return for the portfolio by its beta. This is called the *reward-to-volatility ratio.* It measures the risk premium earned per unit of systematic risk. For comparison with other portfolios, higher ratio is better. Relative performance is measured with reference to reward-to-volatility ratio for the market. A Treynor index higher (lower) than that of market portfolio would be indicative of superior (inferior) performance.

The Jensen Index

Jensen (1969) developed a one-parameter portfolio performance measure that differs from Sharpe's and Treynor's indices. Like Treynor's index, Jensen's index is based on the asset pricing implications of the CAPM. The Jensen index uses the security market line as a benchmark. Jensen (1969) wrote the excess return on a portfolio as

$$R_{pt} = \beta_p R_{mt} + e_{pt},\tag{1}$$

where R_{pt} is the excess return on the pth portfolio, βp measures the sensitivity of the portfolio return to the market return, R_{mt} is the excess return on the market portfolio, and e_{pt} is a random error that has an expected value of zero. A portfolio manager who is a superior forecaster will tend to select securities that realize $e_{pt} > 0$. Such a portfolio will earn more than the "normal" risk premium for its level of risk. Equation (1) can be modified to measure such forecasting ability by adding a constant:

$$R_{pt} = \alpha_p + \beta_p R_{mt} + u_{pt}.\tag{2}$$

The new error term u_{pt} will now have an expected value of zero. If the portfolio manager has an ability to forecast security prices, the intercept α_p in Equation (2) will be positive. A passive strategy (random buy-and-hold policy) can be expected to yield a zero intercept. If the manager is not doing as well a a random-selection buy-and-hold policy, α_p will be negative. Such results might be attributable to generation of excess in unsuccessful forecasting attempts.

Grinblatt and Titman (1989b) examined the Jensen measure for a sample of 274 funds during December 1974 to December 1984. Samples of fund returns were constructed by employing data on their quarterly portfolio holdings. Results indicate that superior performance may in fact exist, particularly among aggressive growth funds and those funds with the smallest net asset values.

Comparison of Alternative Measures

McDonald (1974) estimates the Sharpe, Treynor, and Jensen indices for 123 mutual funds using monthly data for 1960-1969. The majority of the funds did not perform as well as the NYSE index, which is the market-weighted average of the returns of NYSE-listed stocks. He also examined the relationship between actual portfolio risk and stated objectives of mutual funds. The results indicate that, on average, the mutual funds' stated willingness to assume risk corresponded with their actual levels of both systematic and total risk.

Haugen (1990) examined the relative strength of the Sharpe, Treynor, and Jensen indices. We can think of a portfolio manager's performance in terms of depth and breadth. The depth relates to the magnitude of the excess returns captured by the manager. Bredth relates to the number of different securities for which a manager can capture excess returns. Haugen (1990) argues that the Jensen and Treynor indices focus on the depth of performance and ignore the breadth of performance. The Treynor index recognizes the opportunity for portfolio investors to lever excess returns. It is in that sense a better measure. However, it measures risk in terms of the beta factor. Since a portfolio's beta is a weighted average of the betas of its securities, there is no propensity for the portfolio beta to become smaller as the number of securities in the portfolio increases. So there is no propensity for the Treynor index to grow larger as we increase the number of securities in the portfolio, given a fixed value for the excess return. The Treynor index, therefore, is insensitive to the breadth dimension of portfolio performance. The Sharpe index is a composite measure of the depth and bredth of performance. As the number of securities in the portfolio increases, the portfolio's standard deviation would become smaller because the residual variance of the portfolio becomes small with diversification. the portfolio's position moves to the west in the risk-return space and the Sharpe index increases. Since the Treynor index cannot capture the portion of variability that is due to lack of diversification, it is an inferior measure of performance. However, for a perfectly diversified portfolio, the Sharpe and Treynor indices will be the same. For relatively undiversified funds (or, more likely, privately held portfolios), the latter will generally be smaller. The difference can be considered the decline in performance resulting from lack of diversification.

CRITIQUE OF TRADITIONAL MEASURES

The measures discussed in the previous section have been subject to criticisms on two grounds. First, these measures assume that risk level of the portfolio is stationary through time. Second, there may be error in specifying the market portfolio. These criticisms will be discussed in greater detail next.

Misspecification of the Market Portfolio

Roll (1977) argued that for all practical purposes the CAPM was not empirically testable because of its inability to measure accurately the true market portfolio's return and the problem associated with the use of a proxy. Roll (1978) also criticized the Jensen (and implicitly the Treynor) index. He concluded that performance evaluation using SML analysis is very sensitive to the choice of the benchmark and leads to ambiguous conclusions. It can be argued that the assessment of performance under these measures is more related to the character of the chosen market index and its position relative to the efficient set than it is to the quality of the managers running the portfolios. Lee and Jen (1978) showed that measurement error on the market index will cause significant biases in both the risk measures (β_p) and performance measures (α_p). Moreover, the direction of the bias depends on whether the true beta is smaller or larger than one. In general, the estimated risk measure will be downward (upward) biased when the true beta is larger (smaller) than one. In addition, α_p and β_p will be biased in opposite directions.

In order to rank the portfolios with wither the Treynor or Jensen index, a market portfolio needs to be identified. Roll showed that if a mean-variance-efficient portfolio is used, then all the portfolios lie on the SML and there is no ability to discriminate among portfolios. On the other hand, if the benchmark portfolio lies off the efficient frontier, some portfolios lie above SML and other lie below. Depending on the composition of the benchmark portfolio, also not on the efficient frontier, could virtually reverse the ranking. Hence, performance evaluations with the SML is more an artifact of the evaluator's choice of a benchmark portfolio than a valid tool for measuring investment skill. The logic behind Roll's argument lies in the relationship between market proxies and the estimation of beta. In particular, a mean-variance-inefficient proxy for the market portfolio can be found that will produce a beta for a portfolio of any desired magnitude, and hence any desired measure of performance can be produced. Since the problem arises from the sensitivity of beta to the choice of a market index, rankings under the Sharpe index (which uses standard deviation as opposed to beta) are immune from this problem. However, the problem works its way in through the back door, when a market proxy is selected as a basis of comparison.[2]

Dybvig and Ross (1985b) examined Roll's assertion to determine whether SML analysis is valid in several plausible theoretical frameworks, that is, whether theory justifies intuition. In particular, they found some support for using SML analysis in the presence of a riskless asset. They concluded that when there is a riskless asset, Roll's assertion that for any inefficient index another can be found that reverses the ranking of all portfolios, is false. When there is no riskless asset, similar to Roll, they found that, in general, any ranking is possible. However, Dybvig and Ross (1985b) ignored possible measurement error in the risk-free rate. Lee and Jen (1978) showed that measurement errors in the risk-free (and the market return) generally bias the estimated performance measure and the estimated systematic risk.

Green (1986) further examined the validity of SML analysis from a theoretical perspective. Green (1986) showed that the Jensen index or the deviation of a portfolio from SML is given by the following expression:

$$\frac{\overset{\text{portfolio risk premium}}{[E(r_p) - E(r_z)]\, \sigma^2(\varepsilon_M)} - \overset{\text{market index risk premium}}{[E(r_M) - E(r_z)]\, \text{Cov}(\varepsilon_M, \varepsilon_p)}}{\sigma^2(r_M)},$$

where r_p, r_m, and r_z are the portfolio return, market return and zero-beta return, respectively, and $E(\ )$ is the expected value operator. If the risk premium on the portfolio is greater than the risk premium on the market index, there is propensity for the propensity for the portfolio to be positioned above the SML. Much depends, however, on the risk characteristics of the index. If the index is highly inefficient, its residual variance $\sigma^2(\varepsilon_M)$ is likely to be large. This by itself increases the expected size of the first term in the numerator, but it also increases the expected size of the covariance between the residuals on the portfolio and the index, $\text{Cov}(\varepsilon_p, \varepsilon_M)$, in the second term. The sign of the Jensen index will depend on the relative magnitudes of the risk premiums, the residual variance of the index, and the covariance between the residuals on the portfolio and the index. Green concluded that for any given inefficient proxy portfolio, there exist another proxy arbitrarily close in mean-variance space and associated zero-beta rates that are arbitrarily close to each other, such that the relative rankings provided by the two proxies exactly reverse each other. This result is stronger than similar results in Roll (1978) and Dybvig and Ross (1985b). The former argues that there is always a proxy that exactly reverses the benchmark errors. The reversing portfolio, however, will in general be very far away from the original proxy, and in many cases one must choose a zero-beta rate that reverses the market price of risk. Dybvig and Ross (1985) point out these problems and also illustrate a degenerate case where no reversal is possible. They suggest that an affine reversal of the benchmark errors is always possible, but again the reversing portfolio may be very far away from the original proxy.

Mayers and Rice (1979) countered Roll's criticism of SML analysis. They argued that in order to be able to detect superior information, the possibility of such must be allowed. Misspecification is the only source of deviation from SML in Roll's model. Superior performance based on superior information is ruled a priori. Mayers and Rice (1979) postulated the existence of two classes of investors. The uninformed, due to their numbers, determine market prices, while the informed have access to inside information. They assumed that the benchmark portfolio used to compute beta is on the mean-variance-efficient frontier from the perspective of uninformed managers and that the informed managers are unable to forecast the return of the benchmark portfolio. Mayers and Rice proved that when uninformed investors use this market portfolio to compute betas, they will observe that the portfolios of the informed plot above the SML. In particular, the efficient frontier of informed managers always lies to the left of that of uninformed managers. Hence, the slope of the line connecting the risk-free rate the benchmark portfolio will always be less than the slope of the line connecting the risk-free rate and tangent portfolio on the efficient frontier on the informed managers. Their analysis assumes that the informed manager's superior information is "security specific." They are unable to show superior designation by SML analysis when the informed managers have superior information about individual securities and the market return. Therefore, in their model, with completely general information the possibility of incorrect designation by SML remains.

Dybvig and Ross (1985a) explored in detail SML deviations caused by superior performance based on superior information. They concluded that an uninformed observer using the tools of mean variance and SML analysis to measure the performance of a portfolio manager who has superior information is unlikely to be able to make any reliable inferences. While some positive results of a very limited nature are possible, for example, when there is a riskless asset or when information is restricted to be security specific, in general anything is possible. In particular, a manager with superior information can appear to the observer to be below or above the SML and inside or outside the mean-variance-efficient frontier, and any combination of these is possible.

Nonstationarity of Risk Level

The Treynor, Jensen, and Sharpe indices assume that the risk level of the portfolio under consideration is stationary through time. Jensen (1968) acknowledged the ability of the fund managers to change the risk level of their portfolios in anticipation of broad market movements. Fama (1972) and Jensen (1972) addressed this issue and suggested a somewhat finer breakdown of performance. Fama (1972) suggested that portfolio manager's forecasting skills could be partitioned into two distinct components: (1) forecasts of price movements os selected individual stocks (i.e., microforecasting); and (2) forecasts of price movements of the general stock market as a whole (i.e., macroforecasting). The former is known as *security analysis,* while the latter is called *market timing.* This partitioning of forecasting skills is also evident in Treynor and Black (1973), who have shown that portfolio managers can effectively separate actions related to security analysis from those related to market timing.

The various aspects of Fama's decomposition of overall performance are shown in Figure 1. Overall performance of the chosen portfolio is the difference between the return on the chosen portfolio, r_p, and the return on the riskless asset, r_f. The overall performance is divided into two parts: return from selectivity and return from risk. The former measures how well the chosen portfolio did relative to a

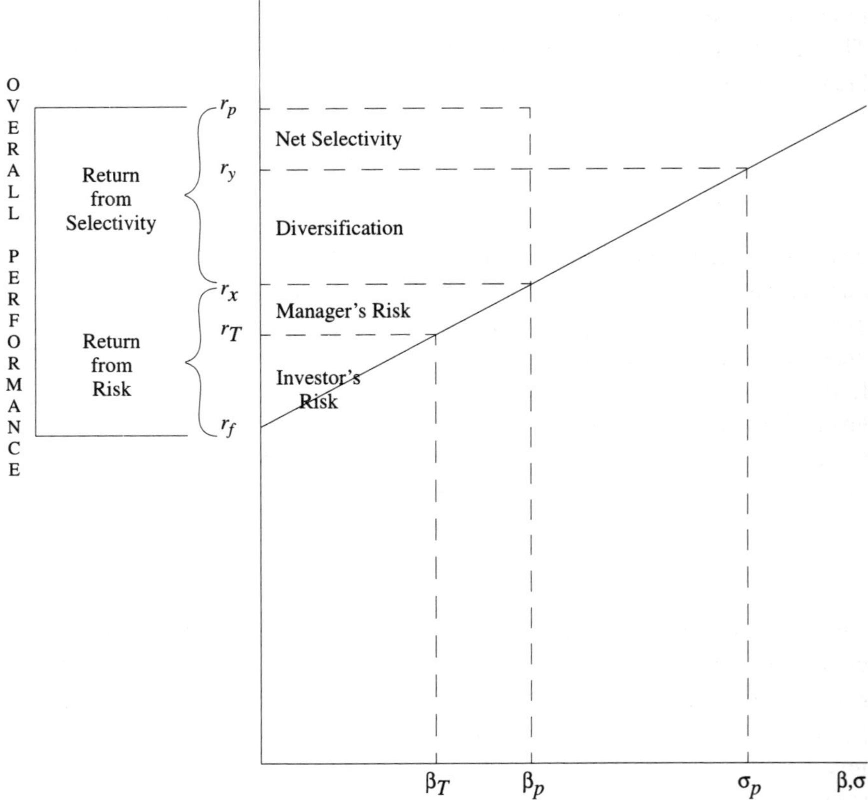

Figure 1.   Decomposition of investment performance

naively selected portfolio with the same level of risk. The latter measures the extra return from the decision to take on a positive amount of risk. One benchmark against which r_p is compared is r_x, the return on the combination of the riskless asset and market portfolio that has same systematic risk (β_p) as r_p. Thus[3]

$$\underset{\substack{\text{overall}\\\text{performance}}}{r_p - r_f} = \underset{\substack{\text{return from}\\\text{selectivity}}}{(r_p - r_x)} + \underset{\substack{\text{return from}\\\text{risk}}}{(r_x - r_f)}.$$

Selectivity, or some slight variant thereof, is the sole measure of performance in the traditional measures. The total risk of the chosen portfolio may exceed its diversifiable risk. In other words, the portfolio manager decided to take on some positive portfolio dispersion that could have been diversified away because he thought he had some securities in which it would pay to concentrate resources. The results of such a decision can be evaluated in terms of the following breakdown of selectivity:

$$\underset{\text{selectivity}}{r_p - r_x} = \underset{\text{net selectivity}}{(r_p - r_y)} + \underset{\text{diversification}}{(r_y - r_x)},$$

where r_y is the return on the combination of riskless asset and market portfolio that has same total risk (σ_p) as r_p. Thus return from diversification measures the extra return that the manager's chosen securities ("winners") have to produce in order to make concentration of resources in them worthwhile. Fama (1972) further decomposed the return from risk, that is, $r_x - r_f$. If the investor has a target level of systematic risk, β_T, for his portfolio, the part of overall performance due to risk can be allocated to the investor and to the manager as follows:

$$\underset{\text{risk}}{r_x - r_f} = \underset{\text{manager's risk}}{(r_x - r_T)} + \underset{\text{investor's risk}}{(r_T - r_f)},$$

where r_T is the return on the combination of the riskless asset and market portfolio with the target beta of β_T. Thus manager's return from risk is the result of his or her decision to take on a level of risk, β_p, different from the investor's target level, β_T, while investor's return from risk is the return that results from the fact that the investor's target level of risk is positive. Manager's return from risk might in part result from a timing decision. That is, in part at least the manager might have chosen a portfolio with a level of risk higher (lower) than the target level because he or she felt risky portfolios in general would do abnormally well (poorly) during the period under consideration. We can subdivide manager's risk into:

$$\underset{\text{manager's risk}}{r_x - r_T} = \underset{\text{total timing}}{\{\,[r_x - E(r_x)] - \underset{\text{market conditions}}{[r_T - E(r_T)]}\,\}} + \underset{\text{manager's expected risk}}{E(r_x) - E(r_T)}$$

where $E(\ )$ is the expected return. Manager's expected risk is the incremental expected return from the manager's decision to take on a nontarget level of risk. Market conditions is the difference between the return on the naively selected portfolio with the target level of risk and the expected return of this portfolio. Total timing is the difference between the ex post return on the naively selected portfolio with risk β_p, and the ex ante expected return. Manager's timing is the difference between total timing and market conditions. It measures the excess of total timing over timing performance that could have been generated by choosing the naively selected portfolio with the target level of risk.

Admati and Ross (1985) further examined the inability of traditional measures when changing risk level and information asymmetries exist. In the presence of information asymmetries, the composition of the portfolio changes in response to the private information the manager obtains. For each informative signal received, the manager forms his or her posterior distribution of assets' returns, which is unknown to others and varies over time (depending on what the information happens to be). The "true" and relevant risk actually borne by the manager now change over time even of other parameters are fixed or stationary. since the private information itself is usually not available to an outsider, the observed returns come from a complicated distribution (from the observer's point of view) involving the joint prior distribution over the possible private signals and assets' returns. It is not clear, therefore, that there exists a single parameter, estimable from the data, that would serve as an appropriate measure of risk in a risk-return analysis.

Another way to explain the failure of the SML analysis to evaluate fund mánager is to note that the conditional expectation of the manager's return given those on the benchmark portfolio becomes a nonlinear function of the benchmark return. This is in part because the unconditional returns are not normally distributed if the manager has private information. Since SML is based on the residuals in a linear regression of the manager's returns on those of the benchmark, it becomes inappropriate. Also, the calculated beta of the portfolio is not appropriate as a measure of risk since the true beta, which depends on the private information, is changing over time. Indeed, it should be viewed by an uninformed agent as a random variable, and part of the problem is that it is correlated with the benchmark returns. What is done in the traditional method is to estimate this regression coefficient as if it were constant.

Admati and Ross showed that the negative results concerning the SML analysis, which is based on the beta of a portfolio as a measure of risk, is also applicable to Sharp's reward-to-variability ratio. Intuitively, although better information implies higher expected returns, it also leads to a larger variance (unconditional and also given only prices). This is because the informed manager reacts to private information signals that are unavailable to the uninformed by making changes in the composition of his or her portfolio. Indeed, the changes are sharper the more accurate the information is. As a result, the observed returns appear to have relatively high variability when, in fact, the informed agent is choosing optimal (mean-variance efficient portfolios relative to the parameters implied by his or her information. This results in a lower reward-to-variability ratio for the better-informed manager. The difficulty is that the uniformed observer does not know these parameters and cannot estimate them directly, since they depend on information he or she does not possess.

It appears that fund managers be evaluated by both selection ability and market-timing skill. Accordingly, it is necessary to model timing and selectivity simultaneously. Jensen (1968) demonstrated that, in the presence of market-timing ability, the estimated risk parameter β_p in Equation (2) will be biased downward and the estimated performance measure α_p will be biased upward. Grant (1978) explained how market-timing actions will affect the results of empirical tests that focus only on microforecasting skills. He showed that market-timing ability will cause the regression estimate of α_p in Equation (2) to be downward biased. Grant (1978) showed that, given Jensen's (1968) assumptions, the least-squares estimator of β_p, and therefore his performance measure represents downward-biased, not upward-biased, estimates of performance. See Grant (1978, p 843) for details.

NEW PERFORMANCE MEASURES

The mounting evidence against the validity of the traditional measures presented a tremendous challenge to financial researchers. Several lines of research originated from it. Some researchers attempted to identify alternative measures of performance that were not based on SML analysis and were not sensitive to the choice of a benchmark portfolio. These measures employ data on asset holdings of the portfolio. Another attempt was to develop a measure that did not use portfolio holdings data, and to better understand the relation between the choice of a benchmark portfolio, the nature of superior information, and performance measurement with the SML. Other researchers attempted to recognize the importance of explicitly modeling information asymmetries in the analysis of performance evaluation. These efforts led to the development of a number of measures based on quadratic regression analysis, arbitrage pricing theory, and the option pricing model.

Measures That Use Portfolio Holding Data[4]

Cornell (1979) developed a measure that did not require the computation of beta or the selection of a benchmark portfolio. It did, however, require the observation of the historical sequence of portfolio weights (i.e., the investment choices) for the investment strategy being evaluated. Cornell's idea was very simple. A successful portfolio manager holds securities only during periods when their returns are higher than usual. Thus, observing the returns of a security when it is held in the portfolio of a manager and comparing it to the return on the same security when it is not held by the manager indicates whether the manager is purchasing the security at the right time.

Cornell's measure is calculated as follows:

1. Using a sample period outside the evaluation period, estimate the mean return on each security included in the portfolio during the evaluation period. These mean returns represent security benchmark returns for corresponding observation interval of the evaluation period

2. Compute the portfolio expected return for each interval of evaluation period by employing actual portfolio weights during evaluation period and security benchmark returns from sample period.
3. The difference between actual and expected portfolio returns during evaluation periods, when averaged across observation intervals, gives Cornell's measure.

Cornell suggested that benchmark returns for securities be computed in prior periods. Copeland and Mayers (1982) and Grinblatt (1986/1987) pointed out that the Cornell measure should be modified by using securities benchmark returns in periods after they were held by fund managers, rather than before, because trading strategies may be based on past returns. This, however, introduces survivorship bias. If a particular stock fails to exist shortly after it is included in an evaluated portfolio, the investor's holding of that stock cannot be used to assess the portfolio's performance. This creates a critical problem for evaluating portfolio managers who specialize either in near bankrupt stocks or in takeover plays. Grinblatt and Titman (1990) developed a refined Cornell measure, which for each time period applies current and past portfolio weights to current returns. This new measure, unlike the measure used by Copeland and Mayers, cannot have survivorship bias by construction. It also has some computational advantage for statistical inference.

Grinblatt and Titman (1989) developed two measures called the *selective measure* and the *timing measure*. In contrast to the Cornell measure, which does not require an index portfolio, the selectivity and timing measures may be sensitive to the choice of the index portfolio. They are not a sensitive, however, to problems associated with the risk and expected returns of assets changing over time, which is technically referred to as *nonstationarity*. These measures are computed as follows: first, the betas of individual securities are computed by running the usual time series regressions (one for each security) against a mean-variance-efficient index portfolio. The portfolio-weighted average of these betas yields the portfolio's beta at any instant in time. In each holding period, subtract the product of the beta of the portfolio being evaluated and the excess return of the index portfolio from the actual excess return of the portfolio being evaluated. Average these differences over all holding periods to get the selectivity measure. The counterpart of the selectivity measure, the timing measure, is defined as the sample covariance between the time series of portfolio betas and the time series of excess returns of the index portfolio.

A variant of the Cornell measure, developed by Copeland and Mayers (1982), was used to study the recommendations of the Value Line Investment Survey. This measure subtracts a benchmark period's selectivity measure from the actual selectivity measure. In contrast to the selectivity measure of Grinblatt and Titman (1989a), for which an approximately mean-variance-efficient index portfolio is required, the Copeland-Mayers measure is valid for any index portfolio. This is because errors in actual and benchmark alphas that stem from the index portfolio lying inside the efficient frontier cancel out in the subtraction of the two selectivity measures. Grinblatt and Titman (1989a) showed that under relatively mild assumptions, these measures have the following desirable properties: on average, they are positive for active investment strategies based on superior information and zero for passive investment strategies or strategies based on public information.

Measures That Do Not Use Portfolio Data

All the measures discussed above require information about the security holdings of the evaluated portfolio. Unfortunately, data on portfolio holdings are very costly and time consuming to acquire, and often are not available.

Grinblatt and Titman (1989a) developed a new measure, called the *positive period weighting measure,* that has the same data requirements as the Jensen index but correctly designates informed investors as positive performers. This measure finds a time series of weights that sum to one and have two properties:

1. They are nonnegative.
2. They make the weighted average of the time series of excess returns on a portfolio on the mean-variance-efficient frontier zero.

Once having found such weights, apply them to the excess returns of the portfolio being evaluated. That is, the positive period weighted measure is

$$w_1(r_{p1} - r_{f1}) + w_2(r_{p2} - r_{f2}) + \ldots w_T(r_{pT} - r_{fT}),$$

where

w_t = weighted for period t,
r_{pt} = period t return of the portfolio being evaluated, and
r_n = period t risk-free return

The authors showed that, on average, the measure is zero for uniformed managers and positive for informed managers, even when there is timing ability. The positive period weighting measure has been implemented on hypothetical data in Grinblatt (1986/1987) and on the 1975-1984 monthly returns of 279 mutual funds in Grinblatt and Titman (1988). One weakness of this measure is that there may be more than one set of weights with the properties mentioned above. Additional assumption is made to select a set of weights. This makes results sensitive to the weights chosen.

Measures Based on APT

Connor and Korajczyk (1986) developed a performance measure based on arbitrage pricing theory (APT). It is analogous to the Jensen index. They extended

Connor's (1984) equilibrium version of APT to include a small set of investors with superior information. Since the number of investors is very small relative to the total number, these investors have no impact on equilibrium prices. They argued that this simplified the analysis by eliminating the rational inferences that uninformed investors would try to make about the information set of informed investors by observing equilibrium prices. The model places restrictions on the special information of informed investors. Informed investors have superior information about marketwide events. This precludes information about the realizations of the k factors. Hence market timing or factor timing activities are not included in the model. The model is

$$R_{pt} = \alpha_p + \beta_{p1}f_1 + \dots + \beta_{pk}f_k + \varepsilon_p,$$

where

j_t = excess return on a portfolio with unit correlation to the factor j,
β_{pj} = period t risk-free return

and α_p is the performance measure. An investor's portfolio will have a positive α_p if and only if he or she has superior information.

Connor and Korajczyk (1991) employed the APT model of Connor and Korajczyk (1986) in examining the performance of 130 mutual funds during the period January 1968–December 1982. They developed and applied an instrumental-variables procedure to transform the factor betas of the APT into "economically meaningful" categories of risk in capital markets such as inflation risk, term structure risk, and industrial output risk. They argued that one the problems in using the APT to measure risk lies in the rotational indeterminacy in the definition of the factor model. This implies that estimated betas are specific to the particular rotation used in identifying the factors. Hence, the beta estimates have little, if any economic meaning, since they depend on an arbitrary rotation. Also, beta estimates from different time periods will not be comparable, since the factors will have a different rotation. Chen, Roll, and Ross (1986) developed a model that eliminates the rotational indeterminacy of the APT. They propose a set of economic variables whose unexpected shocks can be used in place of the derived factors. This provides a specific rotation (the same across different time periods) and allows one to interpret the factor betas in terms of meaningful macroeconomic risks. Connor and Korajczyk (1991) follow Chen et al. (1986) in their choice of economic shocks with some modifications. They employed a five-factor version of APT. Four macroeconomic shocks are used: the shock to the term structure, the shock to the junk bond premium, the shock to unemployment, and the shock to inflation. The final factor is a market residual factor, that is, the part of the value-weighted market index excess return that is not explained by the other four factors. This approach is motivated by the work of McElroy and Burmeister (1988) and Wei (1988). Connor and Korajczyk (1991) found no statistically significant selection skill by mutual fund managers.

Chang and Lewellen (1985) used a test procedure, derived from APT, to measure security selection performance of mutual fund managers. They used monthly data for January 1971-December 1979 on 67 funds. At the .05 level, 2 funds had significant positive selection ability while 11 had significant negative performance.

Measures Based on the Option-Pricing Model

Using the option-pricing model, Merton (1981) and Henriksson and Merton (1981) developed a measure that permits identification and separation of selectivity and timing skills of portfolio managers. In their model, the portfolio manager forecasts that the stock market will provide a higher (lower) return than the riskless assets, that is $r_{mt} > r_{ft}$ ($r_{mt} < r_{ft}$). The forecaster does not attempt or is not able to predict by how much stocks will outperform (underperform) riskless assets. Based on his or her forecast, the portfolio manager will adjust the relative proportions of the market portfolio and the riskless assets that are held in the fund. Merton (1981) demonstrated that the returns on the portfolio using the indicated market timing rule are same as those that would be generated by a strategy of investing in the market portfolio and riskless assets and acquiring free put options on the market portfolio having an exercise price equal to the riskless rate.

Henriksson and Merton (1981) arrived at a regression model to estimate empirically the separate contributions of selectivity and timing of the form

$$R_{pt} = \alpha_p + \beta_p R_{mt} + \gamma \; \text{put}\,(R_{mt}) + \varepsilon_{pt},$$

where

$$R_{mt} = r_{mt} - r_{ft}, \qquad \text{put}(x) = \max(-x,0).$$

They show that $\gamma > O$ if and only if the manager possesses superior market timing ability and $\alpha_p > 0$ if the manager has superior selection skill. Chang and Lewellen (1984) and Henriksson (1984) employed the Henriksson-Merton model in evaluating mutual fund performance and found no evidence of market timing by fund managers.

One weakness of the Henriksson-Merton model is that information is measured but there is no test of whether information is being used correctly. The forecasters in this model are less sophisticated than those of Jensen (1972), where they do forecast how much better the superior investment will perform. They assume that managers have a coarse information structure in which dichotomous signals are only predictive of the sigh of the excess return of he market relative to the risk-free rate. In their model, the probability of receiving an "up" or a "down" signal in no way depends upon how far the market will be "up" or "down."

In their empirical analysis of the Henriksson-Merton model, both Cheng and Lewellen (1984) and Henriksson (1984) found a large number of negative timing coefficients. Such negative coefficients imply irrational behavior on the part of fund managers. In order to produce a negative timing coefficient, the fund manager must possess superior information and employ it irrationally, that is, raise (lower) market risk when he or she receives a signal that the market will fall (rise). Connor and Korajczyk (1991) call this behavior *perverse timing.* Jahanathan and Korajczyk (1986) argued that such results could arise from artificial market timing due to the differential leverage of the firms in the indices and those invested in by the mutual funds. They theoretically and empirically demonstrated how to create a portfolio that would exhibit negative timing performance when no true timing exists. Connor and Korajczyk (1991) identified two sources of artificial timing or noninformation-based variation in the market risk of the portfolio under consideration. The information advantage in the Henriksson-Merton model is equivalent to the ownership of a free put option on the market portfolio. Connor and Korajczyk (1991) showed that there are two ways besides true market timing that a mutual fund manager could include put option-like payoffs in its return. First, it could follow a dynamic trading strategy that replicates a put option. If fund managers trade more frequently than we observe returns, then their dynamic trading decisions (without any superior information) can create false evidence of timing. Second, the underlying return process driving assets could have beta non-linearities that give rise to false evidence of timing or putlike structure to returns even in the absence of true market-timing skill. The authors developed a new version of the Henriksson-Merton model that allows for superior-information-based true selectivity and timing skill on the part of fund managers as well as noninformation-based variation in the market risk of the portfolio caused by dynamic trading and asset beta nonlinearities. Their model is of the form

$$R_p = \alpha^* + \beta \, (R_m) + \gamma \; \text{Nput} + \varepsilon,$$

where Nput = put $- (1 + r_f)P_0$ and P_0 is the time-zero market value of the put option on the market index. This model introduces a new variable called net put (Nput), which is the payoff to a put option on the market index minus the risk-free rate necessary to pay the market price of the put. This new instrument is similar to portfolio insurance. A fund that holds this instrument and the market portfolio is guaranteed the risk-free return minus the future value (at the risk-free rate) of the put price.

The above model is consistent with the original Henriksson-Merton model and the dynamic trading and asset beta nonlinearities hypotheses. Under the null hypothesis of no selection and timing ability, even when the manager is trading optionlike securities, α^* should be zero. If the manager has true selection or timing ability (of the type hypothesized in the original Henriksson-Merton model), then α^* should be positive. Given zero selection and timing ability, the original Henriksson-Merton model predicts $\alpha^* = \gamma(1 + r_r)P_0$. In a model with only dynamic trading and asset beta nonlinearities, $\alpha^* = 0$ if no true selectivity and timing exist.

The new model has the advantage over the original Henriksson-Merton model in that it still gives a consistent measure of performance when mutual funds buy or sell costly put options. However, it has several limitations. First unlike the original Henriksson-Merton model that allows timing skill and selectivity skill to be separately identified, in the new specification, only the sum of timing and selectivity skills can be measured. Second, it only allows for one-month-ahead European options, whereas the return of the fund could correspond to an infinite variety of optionlike patterns.[5] Third, it requires data on the put option in addition to observed returns on the portfolio, market index, and riskless asset. Additional data requirement increases the potential measurement error in the model.

An alternative version of the Henriksson-Merton model was developed by Kon and Jen (1978, 1979), who assume that the portfolio manager sets the portfolio beta at one of the two alternative levels based on his or her forecast. Furthermore, they assume that there is an unknown probability that the portfolio manager will choose one of the alternative beta regimes in a given period. Alexander and Francis (1986) pointed out that this leads to the key distinction between the Henriksson-Merton and Kon-Jen models. The former tests to see if there is a correspondence between the observed value of R_{mt} and the beta chosen by the manager, whereas the latter does not test for such a correspondence. Accordingly, the Henriksson-Merton model can be viewed as testing for timing ability, while the Kon-Jen model can be viewed as testing for the existence of timing activities that may or may not be successful. In this respect, the Kon-Jen model falls short of the Henriksson-Merton model. Using a sample of 49 mutual funds and their net monthly returns from January 1960 to December 1971, Kon and Jen (1979) found the existence of multiple levels of beta for 37 funds, suggesting that a large number of funds engage in timing activities. Alexander and Francis (1986) criticized Kon and Jen's (1979) analysis. Alexander, Benson, and Eger (1982) show that if common stock betas approximately follow a random walk process and mutual funds do not engage in timing decisions, then mutual fund betas will themselves approximately follow a random walk process. Thus, a potential problem in drawing conclusions from Kon and Jen's test results is that some funds may have actually had random walk betas, yet Kon and Jen's test may have indicated they had two or three betas, thereby leading too the false conclusion that they did engage in timing activities. Subsequently, Kon (1983) extended the Kon-Jen model to examine both timing and selectivity. His sample consisted of monthly returns over the period January 1960-JUne 1976 for 37 mutual funds. Fourteen funds had overall timing skill that were positive but none were statistically significant at a reasonable level. Twenty-three funds had overall selectivity measure, 5 of which were statistically significant.[6]

Measures Based on Quadratic Regression Models

Several studies have begun to recognize the importance of explicitly modeling information asymmetries in the analysis of performance evaluation. Admati and Ross (1985) pointed out that in the presence of information asymmetries, the conditional expectation of portfolio return given those on the benchmark portfolio becomes a nonlinear function of the benchmark return. This nonlinearity makes the inference problem more complicated. This can be partially overcome by using quadratic terms in a linear regression. Treynor and Mazuy (1966) suggested such a model.

Treynor and Mazuy (1966) added a quadratic term to Equation (2) to test for market-timing ability. In the standard CAPM regression equation, a portfolio's return is a linear function of the market return. Treynor and Mazuy argue that managers who can forecast market returns will hold a greater proportion when the return on the market is high and a smaller proportion when the return on the market is low. Thus, the portfolio return will be a nonlinear function of the market return as follows:

$$R_{pt} = \alpha_p + \beta_p R_{mt} + \gamma (R_{mt})^2 + \varepsilon_{pt}.$$

A positive value of γ would suggest that portfolio returns are more sensitive to large positive market returns than to large negative market returns. This, of course, would be indicative of good market timing. Using annual returns for 57 open-end mutual funds, Treynor and Mazuy find that for only one of the funds can the hypothesis of no market-timing ability by rejected with 95% confidence.

Jensen (1972) developed a similar model to detect selectivity and timing skill of managers. Jensen's measure of market-timing performance calls for the fund manager to forecast the deviation of the market portfolio return from its consensus expected return. Jensen assumed that the forecasted return and the actual return on the market have a joint normal distribution. Jensen shows that, under this assumption, a market timer's forecasting ability can be measured by the correlation between the market timer's forecast and the realized return on the market (see Jensen 1972, pp. 317-318; Treynor and Black 1973). Jensen defined market factor (π_t) as $R_{mt} - E(R_m)$, where $E(R_m)$ is the consensus expected return on the market portfolio perceived by the market participants, and π^* is the optimal forecast of he market factor based on the fund manager's information. The fund manager receives information (not available to others in the market about the returns to be earned on the market portfolio next period. On the basis of this information, the manager's optimal forecast of the market factor is

$$\pi^* = \pi_t + \upsilon_t$$

where υ_t is a normally distributed random error unrelated to π_t.

Whenever the fund manager's expectations concerning the market factor (π_t) are identical to the consensus of all market participants, a target risk level β_T will be selected. Whenever the manager's information is different from the consensus, the portfolio risk level β_t will be adjusted in anticipation of market movement to earn abnormal returns. This allows us to decompose the systematic risk of a mutual fund (β_t) as follows:

$$\beta_t = \beta_T + \theta\pi^*.$$

The first term is the target beta in the absence of market timing. The second term reflects a fund manager's timing decision and indicates the risk-level deviation from the find's target risk level depending on the optimal forecast of the market factor (π^*) and the manager's response to the information (θ).

Jensen shows that the target risk level will equal consensus expected return on the market, $E(R_m)$, times the manager's response to the information:

$$\beta_T = \theta E(R_m).$$

He then writes Equation (2) as

$$R_{pt} = \alpha_p + [\beta_t + \theta(\pi_t + v_t)][E(R_m) + \pi_t] + u_{pt}.$$

Consider the regression of R_{pt} on a constant π_t and $(\pi_t)^2$:

$$R_{pt} = \eta_0 + \eta_1\pi_t + \eta_2(\pi_t)^2 + u_{pt}.$$

Jensen (1972) claims that

$$\text{plim } \widehat{\eta}_0 = \alpha_p + \beta_T E(R_m) + \theta(\rho^2 - 1)(\sigma_\pi)^2,$$

$$\text{plim } \widehat{\eta}_1 = \rho^2 \theta E(R_m)\beta_T,$$

$$\text{plim } \widehat{\eta}_2 = \theta,$$

where ρ is the correlation between the prediction and the realization of π_t and $(\sigma_\pi)2$ is the variance of π_t. This system has more unknowns than number of equations.j Jensen concluded that, under the above structure, separate contributions of micro- and macroforecasting can not be identified unless, for each period, the market timing forecast and $E(R_m)$ are known.

Bhattacharya and Pfleiderer (1983) extended the work of Jensen (1972). By correcting an error made in Jensen (1972), they show that one can use a simple regression technique to obtain accurate measures of timing and selection ability. The authors assume that the manager observes at the beginning of period t a signal $\pi_t + \varepsilon_t$, where ε_t is a mean-zero normal deviate that is independent of π_t. Jensen assumes that the manager uses the unadjusted forecast of market factor in the timing decision. Bhattacharya-Pfleiderer assume that the manager adjusts forecasts to minimize the variance of the forecast error. The manager's optimal forecast[7] is

$$\pi^* = \Psi(\pi_t + \varepsilon_t), \tag{3}$$

and the adjustment factor Ψ will be equal to $(\sigma_\pi)^2/[\sigma_\pi)^2 + (\sigma_\varepsilon)^2]$, which is the coefficient of determination between the manager's forecast and the excess return on the market and $(\sigma_\varepsilon)^2$ is the variance of ε_t.

Using Equation (3) and the relationships mentioned earlier, $\beta_T = \theta E(R_m)$ and $\pi_t = R_{mt} - E(R_m)$, we can rewrite Equation (2) as

$$R_{pt} = \alpha_p + \theta \{ E(R_m) + \Psi [R_{mt} - E(R_m) + \varepsilon_t] \} (R_{mt}) + u_{pt}.$$

Rearranging, we get

$$R_{pt} = \alpha_p + \theta E(R_m)(1 - \Psi) R_{mt} + \Psi\theta (R_{mt})^2 + \theta\Psi\varepsilon_t R_{mt} + u_{pt}$$

and

$$R_{pt} = \eta_0 + \eta_1 R_{mt} + \eta_2 (R_{mt})^2 + \omega_t. \tag{4}$$

The relationship is similar to one suggested by Treynor and Mazuy (1966) and is in terms of observable variables. If we run the quadratic regression given by Equation (4), the large-sample coefficient estimates are

$$\text{plim } \eta_0 = \alpha_p,$$

$$\text{plim } \eta_1 = \theta E(R_m)(1 - \Psi),$$

$$\text{plim } \eta_2 = \theta\Psi.$$

The above regression allows us to detect the existence of stock selection ability as revealed by α_p. Now consider the disturbance term in Equation (4):

$$\omega_t = \theta\Psi\varepsilon_t R_{mt} + u_{pt}.$$

The first term in ω_t contains the information needed to quantify the manager's timing ability. We can extract this information by regressing $(\omega_t)^2$ on $(R_{mt})^2$:

$$(\omega_t)^2 = \theta^2\Psi^2(\sigma_\varepsilon)^2(R_{mt})^2 + \varsigma_t,$$

where

$$\varsigma_t = \theta^2\Psi^2(R_{mt})^2[(\varepsilon_t)^2 - (\sigma_\varepsilon)^2 + 2\theta\Psi R_{mt}\varepsilon_t u_{pt}.$$

The proposed regression produces a consistent estimator of $\theta^2\Psi^2\sigma_\varepsilon^2$. Using the consistent estimator of $\theta\Psi$, which we recover from Equation (4), we obtain $(\sigma_\varepsilon)^2$. This, coupled with knowledge about $(\sigma_\pi)^2$, allows us to estimate $\Psi = (\sigma_\pi)^2/[(\sigma_\pi)^2 + (\sigma_\varepsilon)^2] = \rho^2$. Finally, we calculate ρ, which truly measures the quality of the manager's timing information.

Bhattacharya and Pfleiderer (1983) showed that α_p is an accurate measure of security selection ability. A manager having no security specific information will register $\alpha_p = 0$. An informed manager who acts appropriately and optimally will record a positive α_p. In this model, managers who have security specific information may also have information that permits them to time the market. This model is a refinement of the Treynor and Mazuy (1966) model, which focuses on the coefficient of the squared excess market return to detect timing skill. It is the first model to-date that analyzes the error term to identify a manager's forecasting skill. Such a refinement should make the model more powerful than previous ones.

Lee and Rahman (1990) discussed conceptual and econometric issues associated with the Bhattacharya-Pfleiderer model. They applied the model to monthly return data for the period January 1977-March 1984 for a sample of 93 mutual funds. The empirical results indicate that there is some evidence of superior selectivity and timing on the part of fund managers. Out of 93 funds, 24 funds (25.81%) have α_p significantly different from zero at the .05 level. Fourteen of these funds (15.05%) have positive α_p. Sixteen funds (17.2%) have ρ significantly different from zero at the .05 level. The correlation between α_p and ρ is .47. This implies that the funds do not exhibit a considerable degree of specialization in one forecasting skill. Ten funds have both significant selection and timing skills. Four funds have significant selection skill with no timing skill while five funds have significant timing skill with no selection skill.

Admati, Bhattacharya, Pfleiderer, and Ross (1986) extended the work of Bhattacharya and Pfleiderer (1983). They offer two basic modeling approaches to identify timing and selectivity: the factor approach and the portfolio approach. The portfolio approach is simply a generalization of the Bhattacharya and

Pfleiderer (1983) model. In the factor approach, a factor-generating process is postulated for asset returns, and timing and selectivity information are interpreted in terms of their statistical relation to the factors and to the idiosyncratic terms in the generating process, respectively. It is possible to recover the appropriate measures of the quality of both the timing and selectivity information. In this approach, it is not necessary to assume any particular asset-pricing model to identify the information quality of a manager. However, because of the larger number of interactions between information signals and asset returns, this approach requires an extremely large number of regressors in the estimation and, most likely, this exceeds the number of time series observations obtainable for any fund. For this reason, estimation of the quality parameters of the timing and selectivity information seems to be possible only when the number of time series observations is impracticably large. Although the factor approach has conceptual advantages over the portfolio approach, identification of information quality is easier under the portfolio approach than it is under the factor approach.

The work of Bhattacharya and Pfleiderer (1983) has been conducted in the context of a model with private information where equilibrium is determined according to the CAPM that assumes homogeneous beliefs. Such analysis implicitly assumes that fund managers, who might not share these homogenous beliefs. Such analysis implicitly assumes that fund managers, who might not share these homogeneous beliefs, do not effect equilibrium. Admati and Ross (1985) argued that this is somewhat disturbing since there is no reason to believe either that the bulk of the market has the same beliefs or that the combined effect of managed portfolios on equilibrium is zero. In contrast, they developed a model that includes many agents with heterogeneous belief and asymmetric information. These agents are perfectly rational and optionally use all the information available to them, including prices. Their model is a noisy rational-expectations equilibrium CAPM. Under some conditions, the Bhattacharya and Pfleiderer (1983) model can be treated as a special case of the Admati and Ross (1985) specification. However, that analysis is still preliminary. To develop a complete statistical model that is consistent with observation of a time series, a multiperiod model is required, from which the properties of such time series can be derived. This is a difficult task, especially in the context of rational-expectations equilibrium models.

Integration of APT Measures with Timing Models

One weakness of Connor and Korajczyk's (1986) APT measure is that it ignores any potential timing by managers. There have been two attempts to integrate APT measure with other models to resolve this problem. One involves combining APT with a quadratic regression model and the other involves combining APT with the Henriksson-Merton model.

Lehmann and Modest (1987) combined the APT performance evaluation method with the Treynor and Mazuy (1966) quadratic regression technique. They found statistically significant measured abnormal timing and selectivity performance by mutual funds. They also examined the impact of alternative (CAPM and a variety of APT) benchmarks on the performance of mutual funds. They found that performance measures are quite sensitive to the benchmark chosen. The authors found a large number of negative selectivity measures.

One criticism of Lehmann and Modest's (1987) integration of APT and quadratic regression is that unlike the Bhattacharya and Pfleiderer (1983) model, it incorporates timing and selectivity in a model on an ad hoc basis. Bhattacharya and Pfleiderer (1983) refined the Treynor and Mazuy (1966) model by analyzing the error term of the quadratic regression to identify the manager's forecasting skill. No such refinement is achieved in the Lehmann and Modest (1987) model.

Connor and Korajczyk (1991) integrated the Henriksson-Merton model with the APT model as follows:

$$R_p = \alpha_p + \beta_{p1}f_1 + \dots + \beta_{pk}f_k + \gamma_1 \text{put}\,(f_1) + \dots + \gamma_k \text{put}\,(f_k) + \varepsilon,$$

where $\gamma_j > 0$ if and only if the manager has superior information about factor j. The term α_p is included to measure selection ability; $\alpha_p > 0$ implies superior selectivity. In the empirical work reported in the paper, they simplified the above equation to include only the put on the market portfolio (which is a linear combination of the factor portfolios). In the empirical work, Connor and Korajczyk (1991) found little evidence of superior timing ability.

CONCLUDING REMARKS

Over the 25 years (1965-1991), a large number of authors have considered the problem of evaluating the portfolio performance of the managers of mutual funds and developed a number of alternative measures. A critical examination of these alternative performance measures is the subject matter of this paper. We started with the detailed discussion of traditional measures of Sharpe, Treynor, and Jensen and pointed out their pitfalls. The mounting evidence against the validity of traditional measures led to the development of a number of alternative measures. We discussed these measures in an integrated way and focused on their relative strengths and weaknesses.

We conclude this paper with recommendations for further work in the area of performance evaluation. Although much progress has been made on this issue, it seems clear that certain areas are still unexplored and underexplored. In our view, models examining measurement and specification errors, the impact of macroeconomic factors and business cycles, and performance evaluation of pension managers are the most promising. It seems to us that the first two issues have not been adequately investigated. It is likely that further efforts on these topics will lead to significant new insights.

While investment performance of mutual fund managers has been extensively examined in the finance literature, the performance of other institutional investors has not received such attention. For example, corporate pension plans currently control assets that have a market value of more than $1 trillion (Berkowitz, Finney, & Logue 1988). Ippolito (1986) estimates that by the year 2000, the total value of corporate pension plans will approximate $2.2 trillion in 1984 dollars, and by that time these plans can own as much as 50% or more of all outstanding corporate stocks and bonds. Yet little has been done to examine investment performance of corporate pension funds. Tests of market efficiency have relied on studies of mutual funds, not those of corporate pension funds. A closer examination of these group of investment managers is therefore needed.

NOTES

1. Arditti (1971) extended Sharpe's reward-to-variability index and suggested a three-parameter performance index that also takes into account the portfolio skewness. Francis (1975) argued that although skewness was theoretically relevant, it could not be measured empirically with sufficient reliability to justify considering it. Martin (1978) supported Francis's contention.

2. See Chen and Lee (1984) for a discussion of trade-off between using the Sharpe measure and the Treynor measure in the presence of measurement error in the market index.

3. Fama (1972 uses *selectivity* and *risk* to indicate return from selectivity and return from bearing risk, respectively.

4. This subsection draws on Grinblatt (1986/1987), which contains numerical examples on alternative measures discussed here.

5. Glosten and Jaganathan (1988) developed a contingent-claim approach to performance evaluation for portfolio managers who trade a variety of options on optionlike securities.

6. Alternative versions of the Henriksson-Merton model have also been tested by Alexander and Stover (1980) and Fabozzi and Francis (1979), with results consistent with Henriksson's (1984) results.

7. See Lee and Rahman (1990, p. 266) for a proof of this.

REFERENCES

Admati, A., Bhattacharya, S., Pfleiderer, P.C., & Ross, S.A. (1986). On timing and selectivity. *Journal of Finance, 41*, 715-730.

Admati, A., & Ross, S.A. (1985). Measuring investment performance in a rational expectations model. *Journal of Business, 58*, 1-26.

Alexander, G.J., Benson, G.P., & Eger, C.E. (1982). Timing decisions and the behavior of mutual fund systematic risk. *Journal of Financial and Quantitative Analysis, 17*, 579-602.

Alexander, G.J., & Francis, J.C. (1986). *Portfolio Analysis*. New Jersey: Prentice-Hall.

Alexander, G.J., & Stover, R.D. (1980). Consistency of mutual fund performance during varying market conditions. *Journal of Economics and Business, 32*, 219-226.

Arditti, F.A. (1971). Another look at mutual fund performance. *Journal of Financial and Quantitative Analysis, 6*, 909-912.

Berkowitz, S.A., Finney, L.D., & Logue, D.E. (1988). *The Investment Performance of Corporate Pension Plans*. New York: Quorum.

Bhattacharya, S., Pfleiderer, P.C. (1983). A note on performance evaluation. Technical Report 714, Graduate School of Business, Stanford University, October.

Chang, E., & Lewellen, W. (1984). Market timing and mutual fund investment performance. *Journal of Business, 57,* 57-72.

Chang, E., & Lewellen, W. (1985). An arbitrage pricing approach to evaluating mutual fund performance. *Journal of Financial Research, 8,* 15-30.

Chen, N., Roll, R., & Ross, S.A. (1986). Economic forces and stock market. *Journal of Business, 59,* 383-403.

Chen, S., and Lee, C.F. (1984). On the measurement errors and ranking of three alternative composite performance measures. *Quarterly Review of Economics and Business, 24,* 6-17.

Connor, G. (1984). A unified beta pricing theory. *Journal of Economic Theory, 41,* 13-31.

Connor, G., & Korajczyk, R. (1986). Performance measurement with the arbitrage pricing theory: A new framework for analysis. *Journal of Financial Economics, 15,* 373-394.

Connor, G., & Korajczyk, R. (1991). The attributes, behavior, and performance of U.S. mutual funds. *Review of Quantitative Finance and Accounting, 1,* 5-26.

Copeland, T., & Mayers, D. (1982). The value line enigma (1965-1978): A case study of performance evaluation issues. *Journal of Financial Economics, 10,* 289-322.

Cornell, B. (1979). Asymmetric information and portfolio performance measurement. *Journal of Financial Economics, 7,* 381-390.

Dybvig, P.H., & Ross, S.A. (1985a). Differential information and performance measurement using a security market line. *Journal of Finance, 40,* 383-399.

Dybvig, P.H., & Ross, S.A. (1985b). The analytics of performance measurement using a security market line. *Journal of Finance, 40,* 401-416.

Fabozzi, F.J., & Francis, J.C. (1979). Mutual fund systematic risk for bull and bear markets: An empirical investigation. *Journal of Finance, 34,* 1234-1250.

Fama, E.F. (1972). Components of investment performance. *Journal of Finance, 27,* 551-567.

Francis, J.C. (1975). Skewness and investors' decisions. *Journal of Financial Quantitative Analysis, 10,* 163-172,

Glosten, L.R., & Jaganathan, R. (1988). A contingent claim approach to performance evaluation. Working paper, Kellogg Graduate School of Management, Northwestern University.

Grant, D. (1978). Market timing and portfolio management. *Journal of Finance, 33,* 1119-1131.

Green, R.C. (1986). Benchmark portfolio inefficiency and deviations from the security market line. *Journal of Finance, 41,* 295-312.

Grinblatt, M. (1986/1987). How to evaluate a portfolio manager. *Financial Markets and Portfolio Management, 1,* 97-112 (1986/1987).

Grinblatt, M., & Titman, S. (1988). The evaluation of mutual fund performance: An analysis of monthly returns. Working paper, Graduate School of Management, UCLA.

Grinblatt, M., & Titman, S. (1989a). Portfolio performance evaluation: Old issues and new insights. *Review of Financial Studies, 2,* 393-421.

Grinblatt, M., & Titman, S. (1989b). Mutual fund performance: An analysis of quarterly portfolio holdings. *Journal of Business, 61,* 393-416.

Grinblatt, M., & Titman, S. (1990). Performance measurement without benchmarks: An examination of mutual fund returns. Working paper, Graduate School of Management, UCLA.

Haugen, R.A. (1990). *Modern Investment Theory.* Englewood Cliffs, New Jersey: Prentice-Hall.

Henriksson, R.D. (1984). Market timing and mutual fund performance: An empirical investigation. *Journal of Business, 57,* 73-96.

Henriksson, R.D., & Merton, R.C. (1981). On market timing and investment performance II: Statistical procedures for evaluating forecasting skills. *Journal of Business, 54,* 513-533.

Ippolito, R.A. (1986). *Pensions, Economics, and Public Policy.* Homewood, IL: Dow Jones-Irwin.

Jaganathan, R., & Korajczyk, R. (1986). Assessing the market timing performance of managed portfolios. *Journal of Business, 42,* 217-235.

Jensen, M.C. (1986). The performance of mutual funds in the period 1945-64. *Journal of Finance, 23,* 389-416.

Jensen, M.C. (1969). Risk, the pricing of capital assets and the evaluations investment portfolios. *Journal of Business, 42,* 167-247.

Jensen, M.C. (1972). Optimal utilization of market forecasts and the evaluation of investment performance. In G.P. Szego and K. Shell (Eds.), *Mathematical Methods in Investment and Finance.* Amsterdam: Elsevier.

Kon, S.J. (1983). The market-timing performance of mutual fund managers. *Journal of Business, 56,* 323-347.

Kon, S.J., & Jen, F.C. (1978). Estimation of time-varying systematic risk and performance for mutual fund portfolios: An application of switching regression. *Journal of Finance, 33,* 457-475.

Kon, S.L., & Jen, F.C. (1979). The investment performance of mutual funds: An empirical investigation of timing, selectivity, and market efficiency. *Journal of Business, 52,* 263-289.

Lee, C.G., and Jen, F.C. (1978). Effects of measurement errors on systematic risk and performance measure of a portfolio. *Journal of Financial and Quantitative Analysis, 13,* 299-312.

Lee, C.F., & Rahman, S. (1990). Market timing, selectivity, and mutual fund performance: An empirical investigation. *Journal of Business, 63,* 261-278.

Lehman, B.N., & Modest, D.M. (1987). Mutual fund performance evaluation: A comparison of benchmarks and benchmark comparisons. *Journal of Finance, 42,* 233-265.

Martin, C.G. (1978). Ridge regression estimates of ex post risk-return trade-off on common stock. *Review of Business and Economic Research,* 1-15.

Mayers, D., & Rice, E.M. (1979). Measuring portfolio performance and the empirical content of asset pricing models. *Journal of Financial Economics, 7,* 3-28.

McDonald, J.G. (1974). Objectives and performance of mutual funds. *Journal of Financial and Quantitative Analysis, 9,* 311-333.

McElroy, M., & Burmeister, E. (1989). Arbitrage pricing theory as a restricted nonlinear multivariate regression model. *Journal of Business and Economic Statistics, 6,* 29-42.

Merton, R.C. (1981). On market timing and investment performance I: An equilibrium theory of value for market forecasts. *Journal of Business, 54,* 363-406.

Roll, R. (1977). A critique of the asset pricing theory's tests, part I: On past and potential testability of the theory. *Journal of Financial Economics, 4,* 126-176.

Roll, R. (1978). Ambiguity when performance is measured by the securities market line. *Journal of Finance, 33,* 1031-1069.

Sharpe, W.F. (1966). Mutual fund performance. *Journal of Business, 39,* 119-138.

Treynor, J.L. (1965). How to rate management of investment funds. *Harvard Business Review, 13,* 63-75.

Treynor, J.L., & Black, R. (1973). How to use security analysis to improve portfolio selection. *Journal of Business, 46,* 66-86.

Treynor, J.L., & Mazuy, K.K. (1966). Can mutual funds outguess the market? *Harvard Business Review, 44,* 131-136.

Wei, K.C. (1988). An asset pricing theory unifying the CAPM and APT. *Journal of Finance, 43,* 881-892

MODEL SPECIFICATION, INFORMATION ASYMMETRY, AND ANTITAKEOVER DEFENSES

Beni Lauterbach, Ileen B. Malitz, and
Michael S. Long

ABSTRACT

This study provides two possible explanations for conflicting results of studies investigating the effect of antitakeover amendments on shareholders' wealth: model specification and the information component inherent in the proposal of antitakeover defenses. We find that results of some event studies may be dependent on the discretionary choices of individual researchers. Specifically, we show that results cited in the Jarrell and Poulsen (1987) study of antitakeover amendments are particularly sensitive to model choices. When we used alternative specifications, our results change both quantitatively and qualitatively; we are unable to document shareholder losses. A second possible reason for inconclusive results is the information content of antitakeover amendments. The proposal itself alerts the market that the firm may become a takeover target. We find that the information effect is empirically important. Firms that become takeover targets after the

Advances in Financial Planning and Forecasting,
Volume 5, pages 129-148.

amendment proposal exhibit large positive stock price reactions. Firms that do not become takeover targets, and therefore convey little information, show no response to the proposals. Because information effects unrelated to the defense may dominate the market reaction, we suggest that care be taken in interpreting all studies of stock price reactions to any antitakeover defense.

During the past decade there was a continuous debate about the purpose, merit, and effect on shareholder wealth of hostile takeovers. At the same time, there emerged a series of innovative and creative tactics intentionally designed to thwart them. The tactics, which include antitakeover amendments to the corporate charter, became a fruitful area for academic research.[1] Most studies conclude that antitakeover activity reduces shareholder wealth by entrenching management and shielding them from outside competition for corporate control. However, a minority view (Harris, 1990) contends that by enabling management to negotiate a better price for the firm, antitakeover defenses benefit stockholders. Despite the extensive research, it is still unclear if, when and why antitakeover amendments affect firm value.

In this paper, we suggest two explanations for the inconclusive empirical results: model specification and information content of the defenses. First, we believe event studies are sensitive to discretionary choices of individual researchers: the market index, the number of days over which the parameters are estimated, and the test period. We do not criticize the statistical methodology of event studies, but rather suggest that results of some studies may be extremely sensitive to such specifications. Ever since Brown and Warner's papers (1980, 1985), event studies have become the norm for empirical research.[2] Particularly in recent years, many studies have found statistically insignificant, or marginally significant, excess returns and have drawn conclusions about the importance of the event. By changing various parameters, we demonstrate that the results, and the conclusions inferred, might change. We consider a set of nonarbitrary, generalized specifications and use them to test the effect on shareholder wealth of a particular antitakeover defense: the proposal of amendments to the corporate charter.

We also examine a second possible reason for inconclusive test results first suggest by Brickley, Lease, and Smith (1988): the mere presence of takeover related actions signals a possible change in the probability of takeover. In a world characterized by asymmetric information, antitakeover defenses proposed before a takeover attempt may be a low-cost way for firms to put themselves "in play." Thus a second reason why results of existing work are contradictory may be the presence of an information signal that obscures any underlying change in economic value due to takeover opposition. By alerting the market to a possible increased likelihood of takeover, the proposal of an antitakeover amendment (ATM), or any other antitakeover defense serves as low-cost signal of new information.

The remainder of the paper is organized as follows. Section I develops a model incorporating information effects under symmetric and asymmetric information and outlines the research design. Section II presents results using alternative model specifications. Section III documents the "information effects," while Section IV offers a summary and conclusions.

THE EFFECT OF ASYMMETRIC INFORMATION

In this section, we model the market's reaction to ATM proposals. Consider a firm whose stock price consists of the current value per share if there is no takeover, V, and an additional component representing the present value of expected takeover premiums, Π, that is,

$$S = V + \Pi \tag{1}$$

Increasing the present value of expected future takeover premiums increases stock price. The elements that affect the expected takeover premium depend on the assumption made concerning the availability of information.

In the absence of information asymmetry, the magnitude of the takeover component depends on E, the expected premium stockholders receive if there is a takeover, and on p_t, the probability of a successful bid. The probability of a successful bid is a joint probability of receiving a bid, p_b, and the probability of success given a bid is received, $p_{s|b}$:

$$\Pi = \Pi(p_t E), \tag{2}$$

$$p_t = p_b p_{s|b}, \tag{3}$$

$$\partial \Pi / \partial p_t > 0, \qquad \partial p_t / \partial E < 0$$

The expected takeover premium increases with the probability of a successful bid. If the probability of a takeover were not affected by changes in the required bid premium, increasing the bid would increase the takeover component of stock price. However, as the acquisition price increases, marginal bidders are discouraged, and the probability of receiving a bid declines, leaving the net effect unclear.

Antitakeover defenses, D affect both the takeover premium and the probability of a successful bid. It seems plausible to assume that

$$E = E(D), \tag{4}$$

$$p_t = p_t(D), \tag{5}$$

$$\partial E / \partial D > 0, \qquad \partial p_t / \partial D < 0.$$

With symmetric information, an antitakeover amendment affects the expected premium in two ways. First, the more defenses the firm has in place, the higher the required bid premium, which increases the expected takeover component of stock price. At the same time, because the bid is more costly, the firm becomes less attractive to potential bidders than it might otherwise be, and the probability of receiving a bid decreases. Thus the pure economic content of antitakeover amendments is unclear and depends on the relative magnitude of the two offsetting effects. Predictions of the expected effect are based on which of the two prevailing theories is correct. DeAngelo and Rice (1983) and Jarrell and Poulsen (1987) suggest that by hampering takeover threats, ATMs entrench incumbent management and reduce shareholder wealth. The alternative theory, suggested by Linn and McConnell (1983) and Harris (1990), argues that ATMs increase stockholder wealth because they enable management to negotiate a better price for the firm. Proponents of the management entrenchment hypothesis view the reduction in the probability of takeover as more important than the increase in the premium a bidder must pay. Proponents of the bargaining power hypothesis assume the opposite.

Empirical evidence is mixed. In 1983 back-to-back articles, DeAngelo and Rice present weak evidence supportive of the management entrenchment hypothesis, while Linn and McConnell present evidence indicating positive effects of antitakeover amendments. In a study of 649 firms proposing antitakeover amendments, Jarrell and Poulsen (1987) report a significantly negative stock market reaction. Jarrell and Poulsen's results are strong, and suggest that even modest defenses are detrimental to the firm. In more recent papers, Agrawal and Mandelker (1990) and Lauterbach, Malitz, and Vu (1991), using the Jarrell and Poulsen database, find no stock price response to antitakeover amendments in general, but positive reactions to specific subsamples of firms proposing antitakeover defenses.

Attributing excess returns to the market's reaction to the economic content of antitakeover defenses ignores the important real-world element suggested by Brickley et al. (1988): information seldom is equally available to all interested parties. In a world of asymmetric information, where insiders know more about the firm than outsiders, the proposal of an ATM alerts the market that the firm is in play. In this context, antitakeover amendments signal the market to reexamine the firm as a potential takeover target, causing an increased perception that the firm will receive a bid and an increase in stock price.

The partial derivatives

$$\partial p_b/\partial D > 0, \qquad \partial \Pi/\partial D > 0,$$

indicate that the information effect may offset the impact of the antitakeover amendment per se. Even though without new information defenses decrease the probability of receiving a bid, with an information effect, the perceived probability of takeover increases. The information effect offsets the content effect and may transform a negative response to the ATM into an observed nonnegative stock price reaction. In this context, failure to detect a decline in stock price neither proves nor disproves the management entrenchment hypothesis. Without isolating the information component, little can be said about the net economic effect of ATMs.

To provide empirical evidence evaluating the magnitude of the asymmetric information effect, we develop a research design that facilitates a test for the presence of an information effect. Our methodology is based on the selection of firms that have never been takeover targets. We exploit ex post knowledge of whether each firm became a takeover target after proposing the ATM. We jointly test for the presence of an information effect and the ability of the market to distinguish between likely and unlikely target firms, by accurately identifying future targets. Our methodology (similar to Lauterbach et al., 1991) creates two subsamples: firms that do not become takeover targets in the future and those which do. If the stock price response differs, we have evidence supporting the joint hypothesis that the market can distinguish between the two groups and that information is conveyed by the antitakeover defense. If there is an information effect, the stock price of likely future targets will increase significantly more than that of nontargets. Further, the signal requires a reexamination of each firm's characteristics. The information production process, consisting of information search, acquisition, and evaluation, is normally a time-consuming task, taking place during a postevent period. Thus the information component will be detected during the postevent period, when the market distinguishes between likely and unlikely future takeover targets. Firms experiencing the greatest upward reassessment of the probability of becoming a target will experience a large long-run increase in stock price.[3] The increase will occur gradually, as the market, and particularly arbitrageurs, assimilates the relevant information and reassesses the likelihood of takeover. Conversely, since the probability of a takeover has increased only slightly, unlikely future targets should show insignificant stock prices movements during the postevent period.

MODEL SPECIFICATION

In this section, we analyze the effect of model specification on event study results. The specifications we address are not strictly statistical in nature (as was Brown and Warner's) but rather relate to measurement and proxy choices made by individual researchers. We limit our investigation to the proposal of antitakeover defenses, and recognize that our results cannot be generalized in the same way as Brown and Warner's. However, we believe we have identified a significant aspect of the event study methodology. For at least some studies, the choice of model specifications affects the results in both a quantitative and qualitative manner.

We use the Jarrell and Poulsen (1987) sample as a basis for our tests. Because we use data available on the CRSP tapes, we limit our analysis to the 372 firms listed on the NYSE or ASE for which Jarrell and Poulsen could obtain sufficient data on the ISL tapes. We investigate the effect of four specific choices of model specification: the source of data, the market index, the parameter estimation period, and the length of the event window.

In their study, Jarrell and Poulsen use a market model with a 150-day preevent estimation period, the Standard and Poor's (S&P) value-weighted index, and an event window extending from day −20 through day 10.[4] By way of comparison, DeAngelo and Rice (1983), Linn and McConnell (1983), and Lauterbach et al. (1991) use CRSP data and the CRSP equal-weighted index. All three studies estimate market model parameters over a 200-day period ($t = -220$ through $t = -21$). DeAngelo and Rice focus on the 2-day (0 and 1) stock price response. Linn and McConnell distinguish between a preevent period (days −90 through −1) an event period (days 0 and 1), and a postevent period (days 2 through 90) to separate various significant dates associated with the ATM proposal and adoption process.

The Sources of Measurement Error

To determine the possible impact of the measurement differences between Jarrell and Poulsen (JP hereafter) and other studies, we conduct a series of sensitivity tests using their sample of 372 exchange-listed firms. In all cases, we use CRSP data rather than the ISL and parameters are estimated using OLS. Results are offered for three different proxies of the market index: the equal-weighted, the value-weighted, and the S&P indices. Six alternative estimation periods are used: 150 and 200 days preevent, 150 and 200 days postevent, days −400 to −200 preevent and 200 to 400 days postevent.[5] Finally, we vary the event window and report results using windows of −20 through 20, −10 through 10, and −60 through 60, as well as Jarrell and Poulsen's −20 through 10 window. Table 1 summarizes the results of these tests.

Panel A of the Table indicates that for the 372 events, the cumulative excess return declines from −1.01% (t-statistic −1.63) to −0.79% ($t = 0.80$) using the CRSP data. While neither return is statistically significant, it does indicate that using a more accurate database changes the results slightly. We also verify that CRSP data are more complete than the ISL data: JP identified only 372 ATMs proposed by exchange-listed firms, while we obtain data for 404 of the events included in the JP sample list. The addition of 32 firms further reduces the CAR to −0.53. Therefore, the use of CRSP data cuts the negative response documented by JP in half. For some studies, this could make an important quantitative and qualitative difference. Therefore, we suggest that the benefits of using the CRSP data may outweigh the gains from obtaining the slightly expanded sample possible with the more current ISL data.

We next examine the effect of the choice of market index proxy. On Panel B of Table 1 and on Figure 1, we present results using CRSP data and 150-day prepe-

Table 1. The Effect of Alternative Model Specifications on the Cumulative Average Excess Returns for Periods Surrounding the Proxy Signing Date: 372 Firms Proposing ATMs in the Period 1979-1985

	Mean CAR	t-statistic
A. The effect of data source. S&P index, 150-day preevent estimation		
CAR(−20,10) ISL data, 372 firms[a]	−1.01	−1.63
CAR(−20, 10) CRSP data, 372 firms	−0.79	−0.80
CAR(−20,10) CRSP data, 404 firms	−0.53	−0.87
B. The effect of market index, CRSP data, 150-day preevent estimation, 372 firms		
CAR(−20,10) CRSP S&P index[a]	−0.79	−0.80
CAR(−20,10) CRSP value-weighted index	−0.50	−0.30
CAR(−20,10) CRSP equal-weighted index	0.51	1.42
CAR(−20,10) best-fit index	0.15	0.71
C. The effect of alternative estimation periods, CRSP data, S&P index, 372 firms		
CAR(−20,10) 150 day preevent estimation[a]	−0.79	−0.80
CAR(−20,10) 200 day preevent estimation	−0.46	−0.48
CAR(−20,10) -400 to -200 preevent estimation	−0.35	−0.06
CAR(−20,10) 150 day postevent estimation	0.24	0.44
CAR(−20,10) 200 day postevent estimation	0.23	0.31
CAR(−20,10) 200 to 400 postevent estimation	0.87	1.39
D. The effect of the choice of event window, S&P index, CRSP data, and 150-day preevent estimation period		
CAR(−20,10)[a]	−0.79	−0.80
CAR(−10,10)	0.02	0.26
CAR(−20,20)	−0.65	−0.34
CAR(−60,60)	0.96	0.85

Source: [a]Jarrell and Poulsen specifications.

riod estimation and the S&P, CRSP value-weighted, and CRSP equal-weighted indices respectively.

The choice of index affects the results. The S&P index gives the lowest CARs, −0.79% (*t*-statistic −0.80). Using the CRSP value-weighted index generates an estimate of −0.5% (*t*-statistic −0.30), while the CRSP equal-weighted index produces a CAR(−20,10) of 0.51% (*t*-statistic 1.42). Again, none of the estimates are statistically significant. However, comparing the CAR with the S&P to the CAR with the equal-weighted index shows a statistically significant (*t*-value of 3.73) change from −0.79 to 0.51%. This increase of 1.3% could easily affect the results in other, more marginal studies.

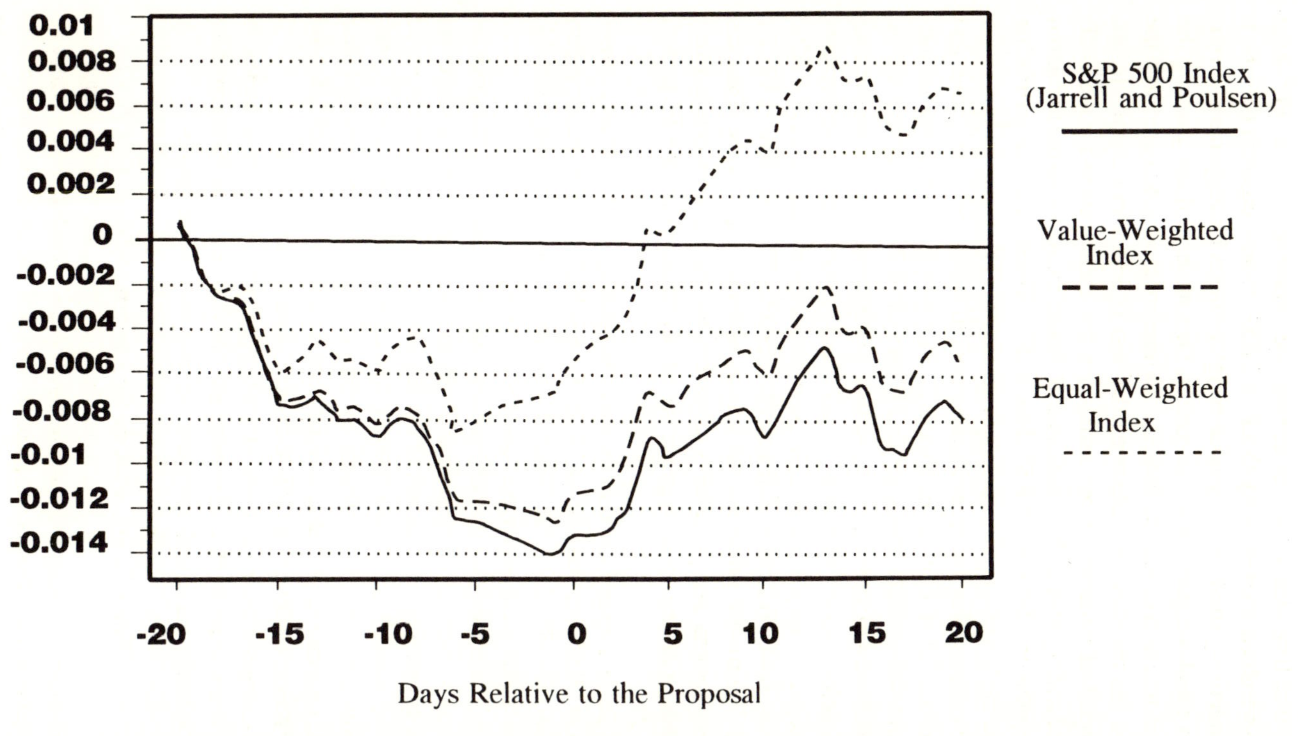

Notes: 372 firms; 150 days preevent estimation period.

Figure 1.   The sensitivity to the choice of market index:
Cumulative average excess returns during 41 days surrounding proposal of ATMs

We suggest that firm size should determine the appropriate index. For large firms, a value-weighted market proxy (S&P or CRSP value-weighted) is correct. However, for relatively small firms, a value-weighted index biases parameter estimation and an equal-weighted index is correct. One method of determining the correct index is to use size-related indices. Another method is to determine the index that best fits the data. To determine the best fit index in our sample, we examine the residual variance of our estimation for each firm using the S&P, value-weighted and equal-weighted indices and choose the one with the minimum variance. Using the best fit index, CRSP data, and a 150-day preevent estimation period, we find the CAR(–20,10) is 0.15% (*t*-statistic 0.71%).

We next investigate alternative estimation periods using the S&P index and CRSP data on Panel C of Table 1 and Figure 2. With preevent estimation periods of 150, 200, and –400 to –200 days, we find CARS of –0.79% (*t*-statistic –0.80), –0.46% (*t*-statistic–0.48), and –0.35% (*t*-statistic –0.06), respectively. As the estimation period before the event increases (goes back in time), the excess returns become less negative. In postevent estimation periods, we find positive CARs: 0.24% (*t*-statistic 0.44), 0.23% (*t*-statistic 0.31), and 0.87% (*t*-statistic 1.39) for 150, 200, and 200 to 400 postevent estimation periods, respectively. Thus the negative excess returns are observed only when estimating parameters using preevent periods, with the most negative result occurring using the JP period: days –170 to –21.

Panel D of Table 1 examines various event windows used by JP and shows excess returns of –0.65% (*t*-statistic –0.34) for CAR(–20,20) and an excess return of 0.96% (*t*-statistic 0.85) for CAR (-60,60). In contrast, the nonsymmetric CAR (-20,10) generates the most negative excess return, –0.79%.

The results in Table 1 suggest that the true response of exchange-listed stocks is considerably less negative than reported in JP. While the specifications addressed in this section do not alter the statistical significance of the results, the reported CARs change by as much as 2%, and some of the changes are statistically significant. The weakening of the JP results for exchange-listed firms implies that their overall sample response might be less significant than noted.[6] Thus, JP's dataset does not offer robust evidence that ATMs reduce shareholder wealth.

Our analysis suggests the importance of verifying results of all event studies. In many studies, where wealth effects are marginal, the choice of specifications may change both the statistical significance and the interpretation of results.

The Choice of Mode Specifications

For the remainder of this paper, and in testing for an information effect of ATMs, we select event study specifications that we believe lead to the most reliable results. Our sample is taken from Jarrell and Poulsen (1987). JP identify 649 ATM proposals in the period January 1979-May 1985. We exclude 225 proposals by OTC firms, 35 proposals by firms reacting to previous takeover attempts, and

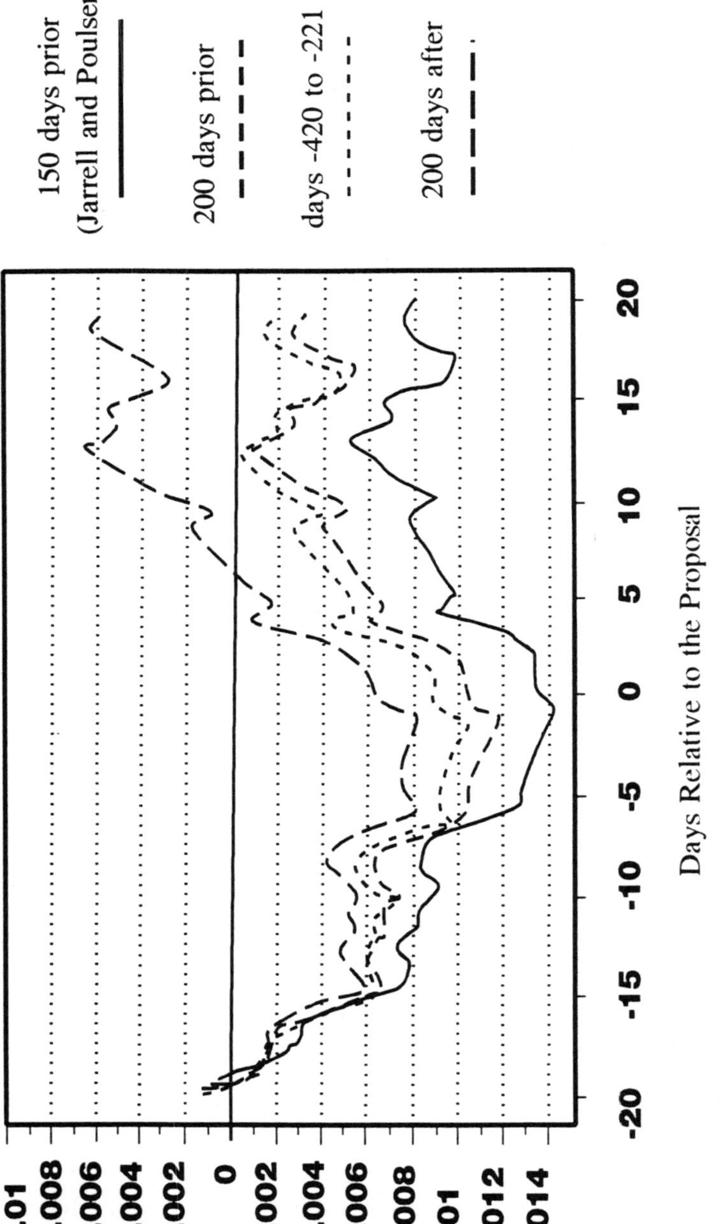

Figure 2. The sensitivity to parameter estimation period:
Cumulative average excess returns during 41 days surrounding the proposal of ATMs

Notes: 372 firms; S&P 500 index.

138

20 firms for which stock returns for the period extending from one year before to one month after the signing date are not available on the CRSP Daily Returns File. This reduces the sample to 369 ATMs. The event date is the proxy signing date, which is the same day or the day before the proxy mailing date. We then search the *Wall Street Journal Index* for firms that are takeover targets during the four years surrounding the ATM proposal. The 369 events include 302 proposals by firms that were not and did not become takeover targets and 67 firms that did.[7] Finally, searching the *Wall Street Journal Index* identifies 79 significant events unrelated to takeover activity, occurring during the 41 days surrounding signing. The final sample consists of 290 firms: 241 nontarget firms and 49 future target firms.[8] Cumulative average excess returns are computed applying standard event study methodology, based on the market model.

We choose the market index that best fits the data of each firm. For 65% of the firms, the equal-weighted index provides a "better" fit (lower residual variance) than either value-weighted index. An estimation period of 200 days had the lowest residual variance, whether the estimation was preevent or postevent. Since firms that are takeover targets are known to experience positive abnormal performance, we estimate the parameters for all firms using a preevent period.[9]

We choose the appropriate event window by examining the cumulative average excess returns over the 121 days surrounding the proxy mailing using CRSP data, the best fit index, and a 200-day preevent estimation period.

Figure 3 shows that the CAR becomes negative 28 days before the proposal, declines until day –4, and then increases until approximately day 20. We believe that the use of symmetric event windows is less arbitrary and therefore more appropriate than a nonsymmetric window.[10] Because our primary interest is the direct effect of the amendment and its role as a signal, we concentrate on the postevent period and choose a 41-day window: –20 through 20. The observed pattern of response suggests a division of event time into three periods: preevent, immediate, and postevent. CAR(–20,–1), the cumulative average excess return in the preevent period, indicates the firm's relative performance before the proposal. CAR(0,1), the average excess return on days 0 and 1, measures the immediate reaction to an ATM on the days it presumably becomes public information, and is expected to be the same for both subsamples. CAR(2,20), the cumulative average excess return after the event, measures the reaction during the period the market is reevaluating the probability of takeover for each firm that has not been a previous target and is expected to uncover the information effect of ATMs.

To summarize, tests of the information effect are conducted using CRSP data for 290 firms with no confounding events during the 41 days surrounding the proxy mailing date. We specify a 200 day preevent estimation period and use the index that best fits the data: equal- or value-weighted market index. Statistical inferences are drawn from average abnormal performance measures computed using the Patell (1976) "standardized residual" methodology. The Appendix outlines the test statistics for average and cumulative average prediction errors.

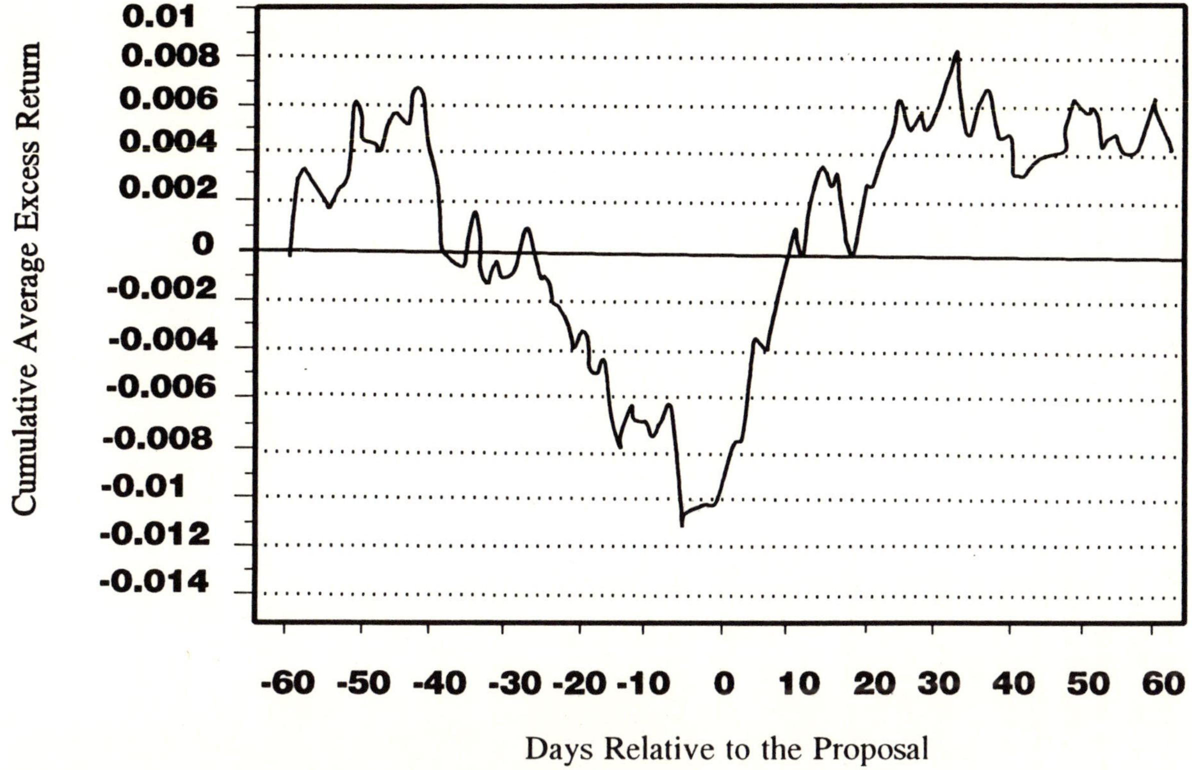

Figure 3. The choice of event window: Cumulative average excess returns during 121 days surrounding the proposal of ATMs

THE STOCK PRICE REACTION
TO ANTITAKEOVER AMENDMENTS

Our model predicts that the market will react strongly to any new information provided by an ATM. Initially, because the market has no way to differentiate between true and false signals, we expect no price reaction. However, the market engages in a time-consuming information production process whereby it searches out and assimilates the relevant firm-specific information necessary to distinguish between likely and unlikely future targets. The stock price adjusts gradually, and the response measured by CAR(2,20) becomes evident over time. Thus, while the initial response of targets and nontargets should be similar, the postproposal response of future targets should significantly exceed that of nontargets.

The Response of Firms That Do Not Become Takeover Targets

The 241 firms that do not become threatened by takeover within two years after proposing an ATM should experience a positive immediate stock price response, followed by a nonpositive postevent response.

Table 2. Cumulative Excess Returns and Fraction of Positive Cumulative Excess Returns for 290 Firms That Were Not Takeover Targets Prior to Proposing Antitakeover Amendments. 241 Firms That Were Not and Did Not Become Takeover Targets, and 49 Firms That Became Targets After Proposing an ATM[a]

	Mean	*Fraction Positive*	*Median*
A. The effect ATM proposals on stock price of 241 firms that were not takeover targets during the four-year period surrounding the ATM proposal			
CAR(−20,−1)	−0.89	45.6	−1.0
	(−1.12)	(−1.37)	
CAR(0,1)	0.21	52.7	0.1
	(0.99)	(0.84)	
CAR(2,20)	0.23	51.9	0.3
	(0.31)	(0.59)	
B. The effect of ATM proposals on stock price of 49 firms that became takeover targets during the two years after the ATM proposal			
CAR(−20,−1)	−0.90	51.0	1.0
	(−0.45)	(0.14)	
CAR(0,1)	0.42	61.2	0.4
	(1.88)	(1.61)	
CAR(2,20)	3.28	63.3	2.6
	(2.20)	(1.93)	

Notes: [a]*T*-statistics in parentheses. The *t*-statistic for the difference between CAR(0,1) for nontargets and future targets is 0.46. The *t*-statistic for the difference between CAR(2,20) for nontargets and future targets is 2.21, which is statistically significant at the 0.05 level.

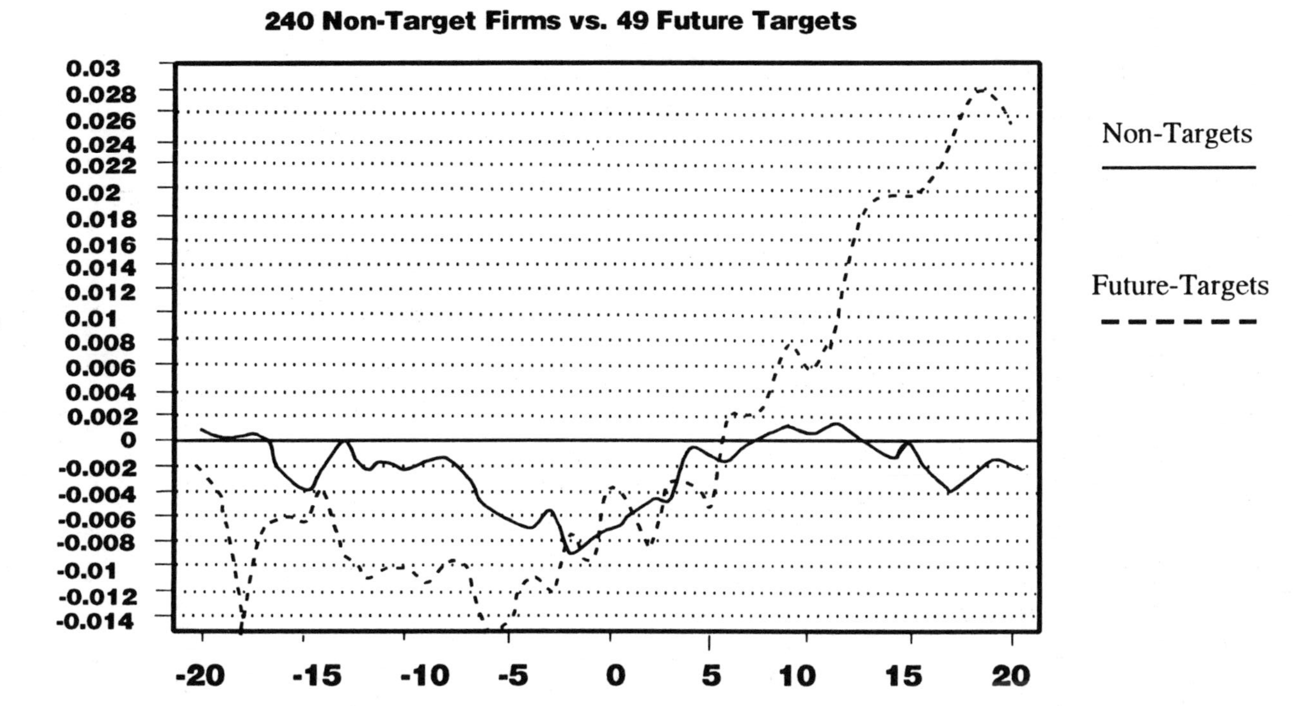

Figure 4. The information component of ATM proposals: Cumulative average excess returns during 41 days surrounding the proposal of ATMs

Panel A of Table 2 examines the stock price response for nontarget firms. During the 20 days before the amendment proposal, the average excess return is –0.89%, with 55% of the firms exhibiting poor performance. In the immediate two-day period, the average excess return is 0.21%, and 53% of the firms have a positive stock price reaction. This reaction is similar to the postproposal response, where 52% of the firms exhibit a positive response, with the average firm gaining 0.23% ($t = 0.31$). Since there is at most a slight information effect, the stock price response should represent the true market reaction to ATMs. Thus the evidence indicates ATMs neither reduce nor increase shareholder wealth.

The Response of Firms That Become Subsequent Takeover Targets

If there is a significant information component, it should be reflected in the postevent period. As the market assimilates information, the probability of take-over of likely targets should adjust upward. This adjustment is expected to produce a significantly positive postproposal response. Alternatively, if there is no information conveyed by ATMs, then we expect a similar postevent stock price response to that found for nontarget firms.

Panel B of Table 2 documents that future targets do not earn significant excess returns before or during the time of the proxy signing. The immediate stock price response is similar to that of the unlikely future targets. However, the postpro-posal reaction, CAR(2,20), is 3.3%, which is statistically different from that of nontargets. Sixty-three percent of the firms exhibit a positive postproposal response.[11] Figure 4 reinforces the numerical evidence and shows the difference between the postevent responses of the two subsample.

The difference is striking. During the five days following proxy signing, excess returns are almost identical. Over the next three weeks, they differ remarkably. It is during this period that the arbitrageurs digest the information content of the ATM and distinguish between likely and unlikely targets.[12] The evidence is con-sistent with a strong information component in the proposal of an ATM. While the probability of a takeover bid is reevaluated upward for all firms proposing ATMs, the adjustment and the resulting increase in stock price are greatest for firms iden-tified as likely future takeover targets.

SUMMARY AND CONCLUSIONS

This paper provided two explanations for conflicting results of previous studies of antitakeover amendments and shareholder wealth: model specification and the information component inherent in the proposal of antitakeover defenses.

Regarding the importance of model specification, we found that results of some event studies may be dependent on the market index proxy, the parameter estima-tion period, and the event window, specifications left to the discretion of individ-ual researchers. Specifically, we look at one example of inconclusive and contradictory evidence in various studies: antitakeover amendments.Using the Jarrell and Poulsen (1987) sample, we vary specifications. While we do not find significant results, we do find significant differences between various subsets of specifications. Results are particularly sensitive to the market index and the estimation period. We conclude that while we are unable to document significant losses or gains in this study, at least some studies are likely to be more sensitive to discretionary choices. We recommend that researchers be extremely conscientious in designing their studies, and take care to check their results for sensitivity to alternative specifications.

We analyzed a second reason for inconclusive results: the presence of an information component inherent in antitakeover activity. Proposals of antitakeover defenses increase the market's perception of the probability of takeover. The information signal offsets and negates any economic content of antitakeover amendments, so that previous studies may not have measured the effect of antitakeover amendments at all. We isolate the information from the content components of the amendment. In a subsample of firms that become takeover targets after the antitakeover amendment proposal, we document relatively large positive stock price revelations following the amendment proposal. In the sample of stocks that did not become takeover targets so that there is, at most, a slight information effect, the reaction to the antitakeover amendment proposal is positive but insignificant. The results suggest that antitakeover amendments are neither harmful nor helpful to shareholders.

The evidence supports the existence of a strong information component to the proposal of antitakeover amendments. Apparently, some managers use antitakeover amendments to signal the market that their firms have become more likely takeover targets than previously assumed. Because similar information may be conveyed by other types of defenses, we suggest that care be taken when interpreting results of studies measuring the stock price reactions to any antitakeover defense.

APPENDIX: AVERAGE EXCESS RETURNS, CUMULATIVE AVERAGE EXCESS RETURNS, AND TEST STATISTICS

We use the standard event study methodology to compute excess and cumulative excess returns and assume that stock returns follow the market model:

$$r_{i,t} = a_i + b_i r_{m,t} + e_i, \tag{A1}$$

where

$r_{i,t}$ = return of stock i in day t,

$r_{m,t}$ = return on the minimum variance index of NYSE and ASE stocks on day t,

$e_{i,t}$ = a random-error term with a mean of zero and which is orthogonal to $r_{m,t}$,
a_i, b_i = intercept and slope coefficients.

The excess returns $AR_{i,t}$ for each firm's stock in each day of the period $t = -20$ through $t = +20$ are calculated as:

$$AR_{i,t} = r_{i,t} - (\hat{a}_i + \hat{b}_i r_{m,t}) . \tag{A2}$$

Individual excess returns of the N firms traded on day t are aggregated into the average excess return on day t, AR_t:

$$AR_t = \sum_{i=1}^{N} AR_{i,t} / N. \tag{A3}$$

Finally, cumulative average excess returns are computed as follows:

$$CAR(E, B) = \sum_{t=B}^{E} AR_t. \tag{A4}$$

The statistical significance of the abnormal performance measures is assessed using the Patell (1976) "standardized residual" methodology delineated below. We test the statistical significance of each daily excess return by first standardizing the return of firm i in day t by the residual standard error from the regression of stock i in the estimation period, S_i, inflated by $C_{i,t}$, which allows for prediction outside the period:

$$SAR_{i,t} = AR_{i,t} / S_i (C_{i,t})^{1/2} . \tag{A5}$$

Patell (1976) shows that under the null hypothesis of no excess returns in day t, the appropriate test statistic is:

$$Z_t = \sum_{i=1}^{M} SAR_{i,t} / \left(\sum_{i=1}^{M} \frac{N_i - 2}{N_i - 4} \right)^{1/2} , \tag{A6}$$

where M is the number of stocks for which excess returns in day t can be calculated and N is the number of nonmissing returns of stock i in the parameter estimation period. Under the null hypothesis, Z_t is distributed $N(0,1)$ in samples of reasonable size.

A.   Tests of the Cumulative Mean Excess Return

The statistical significance of the cumulative mean excess return from day B through day E, CAR(B,E), is tested by the statistic Z_L:

$$Z_L = \sum_{L=B}^{E} Z_t / (E - B + 1)^{1/2}. \tag{A7}$$

Under the null hypothesis, Z_L is distributed $N(0,1)$ in samples of reasonable size.

B.   Tests of the Fraction of Positive Returns

A test statistic for the proportion of positive excess returns, P_t, is distributed $N(0,1)$ for samples with at least 10 observations:[13]

$$P_t = \frac{p^* - p}{[p(1-p)/n]^{1/2}} \tag{A8}$$

where p^* is the fraction of positive excess returns as calculated in the sample and p is the hypothesized proportion.

ACKNOWLEDGMENTS

The authors wish to thank Anup Agrawal, Espen Eckbo, Ed Rice, and Kristian Rydqvist for their comments.

NOTES

1. See Jarrell, Brickley, and Netter (1988) for a survey of these studies.

2. Brown and Warner concentrate on the statistical aspects of event study methodologies. Specifically, they examined the effects of the two-parameter model, relative to the market model, as well as various corrections for cross-correlation and nonindependence. They concluded that, with few exceptions, the simplest methodology was the best: the one-parameter market model using ordinary least squares regression. Brown and Warner judged that the market model is quite robust to conditions they tested. However, they did not test the nonstatistical specifications that are the topic of this study.

3. Thus results for the sample of future targets may actually be biased in that the market might have considered some of them to be likely targets even before the proposal.

4. Jarrell and Poulsen used the ISL data and S&P index in order to include more recent ATMs. We do not mean to criticize them on this basis, but rather to point out differences in results.

5. In the experiments using 200-400 days after the proposal, the sample is reduced from 372 events to 288 events. Thus, results using this specification may be biased.

6. For example, JP find a -1.25% loss for all firms (t-statistic -2.27). We document a difference of 1.30 and 0.84% when switching from the S&P to the equal-weighted index or best fit index, respectively. Numerically, changes of this magnitude reduce their CAR to 0.05% or -0.41%, neither of which is likely to be significant.

7.   ATMs do not seem to reduce the frequency of future takeover attempts. In the first year after proposing ATMs, 27 of the 319 firms (8.5%) came under a threat, which is greater at the 0.05 level of significance from the 5.2% found in a random sample of 250 firms reported by Maletesta and Walkling (1988). In studies of poison pills, Ryngaert (1988) and Malatesta and Walking find similar results and suggest that pills also convey information about the firm's likelihood as a takeover candidate. Of course, the main premise of this paper is that ATMs convey similar information.

8.   Our results are virtually identical when we use the full sample of 369 firms. Nevertheless, it seems more appropriate to exclude firms with confounding events during the test period.

9.   Throughout our empirical investigation, we tried numerous methods of estimation suggested in the literature, none of which affected our results. For example, using the Scholes-Williams method, we find a CAR of −0.90 with a t-statistic of −0.94. We also use a best fit estimation period: 200 days before or 200 days after the event date. For 69% of the firms residual variance was minimized using a postevent estimation period. All of our results are virtually identical to those reported. Following the suggestion of Brown and Warner (1985), and since we have few statistical problems (e.g., there is little, if any nonsynchronous trading in our sample) we choose to report results using the simplest methodology.

10.   Virtually all event studies with other than a 2-day event period use a symmetric widow.

11.   The analysis of future targets in Panel B includes 7 firms that became takeover targets within one month after proposing an ATM. To determine whether inclusion of these firms biases our results, we eliminate these firms and find similar, but less dramatic results. The postevent average excess return, CAR(2,20), declines to 1.78%, which is statistically significant at the 0.10 level, and 61.9% of the firms respond positively. While not as dramatic as with the 49 firms, the postevent response remains slightly larger ($t = 1.65$) than that of nontargets and is still indicative of a strong information effect.

12.   The full response may take three weeks because the "arbs" reach their conclusions independently and move into the market on different dates. They also are careful not to affect the price noticeably during the period when they are purchasing the stock.

13.   Brown and Warner (1980, 1985) note that the cross-sectional distribution of excess returns is skewed to the right so that the true expected proportion of positive excess returns is less than 0.5. This biases nonparametric tests toward accepting the null that the proportion of positive excess returns is not higher than normal. It is unknown how the bias can be corrected; hence we follow the custom of earlier research (e.g., JP, 1987; Ryngaert, 1988) and report the biased statistics.

REFERENCES

Agrawal, A., & Mandelker, G. (1990). Large shareholders and the monitoring of managers: The case of antitakeover amendments. *Journal of Financial and Quantitative Analysis, 25,* 143-161.

Brickley, J., Lease, R., & Smith, C. (1988). Ownership structure and voting on antitakeover amendments. *Journal of Financial Economics, 20,* 264-294.

Brown, S., & Warner, J. (1980). Measuring security price performance. *Journal of Financial Economics, 8,* 205-258.

Brown, S., & Warner, J. (1985). Using daily stock returns: The case of event studies. *Journal of Financial Economics, 14,* 3-17.

DeAngelo, H., & Rice, E. (1983). Antitakeover charter amendments and stockholder wealth. *Journal of Financial Economics, 11,* 329-360.

Harris, E. (1990). Antitakeover measures, golden parachutes and target firm shareholder welfare. *Rand Journal of Economics, 21,* 614-625.

Jarrell, G., & Poulsen, A. (1987). Shark repellents and stock prices: The effects of antitakeover amendments since 1980. *Journal of Financial Economics, 19,* 127-168.

Jarrell, G., Brickley, J., & Netter, J. (1988). The market for corporate control: The empirical evidence since 1980. *Journal of Economic Perspectives, 2,* 49-68.

Lauterbach, B., Malitz, I., and Vu, J. (1991). Takeover threats, antitakeover amendments, and stock price reaction. *Managerial and Decision Economics, 12,* 499-510.

Linn, S., & McConnell, J. (1983). An empirical investigation of the impact of antitakeover amendments on common stock prices. *Journal of Financial Economics, 11,* 361-399.

Malatesta, P, & Walkling, R. (1988). Poison pill securities: Stockholder wealth, profitability, and ownership structure. *Journal of Financial Economics, 20,* 347-376.

Patell, J. (1976). Corporate forecast of earnings per share and stock price behavior: Empirical Tests. *Journal of Accounting Research, 14,* 246-276.

Ryngaert, M. (1988). The effect of poison pill securities on shareholder wealth. *Journal of Financial Economics, 20,* 377-417.

THE ROLE OF CORPORATE PENSION ASSETS AND LIABILITIES IN DETERMINING THE MARKET VALUE OF EQUITY

V. Gopalakrishnan and Timothy F. Sugrue

ABSTRACT

If the pension liabilities of a firm are merely "legal liabilities," with property rights of assets lying with the pension trust, then the magnitude of pension assets and liabilities should have no role in determining the value of common equity. If, on the other hand, pension benefit obligations constitute an "economic liability," with property rights held by the firm itself, then pension assets and liabilities should be important determinants of market value. Using an accounting identity valuation model and a cross-sectional sample of firms with defined benefit pension plans, we investigate the role of both accumulated and projected pension benefit obligations as well as pension assets in the determination of equity value. This study differs from prior research in that we offer evidence on the stock market perception of the equivalency of nonpension assets and liabilities vis-à-vis pension assets and liabilities. Our findings suggest that investors regard pension assets as similar to

Advances in Financial Planning and Forecasting,
Volume 5, pages 149-164.
Copyright © 1994 by JAI Press Inc.
All rights of reproduction in any form reserved.
ISBN:1-55938-421-2

nonpension assets and pension liabilities as similar to nonpension liabilities in assessing the market value of a firm.

INTRODUCTION

One need only make a cursory examination of the balance sheet of any major U.S. corporation to understand the potential significance of pension liabilities. Though pension liabilities are important features on the financial landscape, the finance literature has dedicated considerably more effort to the examination of debt, perhaps because pension assets and liabilities are thought by some to be within the province of a separate pension trust. Most pension studies have looked primarily at accumulated pension liabilities, even though projected pension benefits have been disclosed since 1987, and are deemed to be more reflective of the actual obligations of the firm.

The purpose of this paper is twofold. First, like others before us, we provide evidence of the impact of funding level of pension liabilities upon stock price. In this, however, our research extends the extant literature, not only by utilizing a much larger sample of firms and more recent data but also by using the newly available projected measures of pension liability. Second, and more importantly, this paper goes beyond providing evidence concerning the impact of pension liabilities upon equity value: it statistically tests the *equivalence*, in value determination, of pension assets and liabilities vis-á-vis their nonpension counterparts. The issue of equivalence of pension/nonpension liabilities is particularly important in light of the customary exclusion of pension liabilities from studies of capital structure and leverage.

In the next section we review the literature concerning pension liabilities/assets and market values. Then we develop our hypotheses and outline our methodology. Results are presented in the next section, followed by summary and conclusions in the final section.

PRIOR RESEARCH

There have been three approaches to examining the linkage of pension costs and equity value: earnings-based valuation models, asset-based models, and event studies. A summary of the prior research using earnings and asset-based models appears in Table 1.

The four major studies utilizing the earnings based approach are Oldfield (1977), Feldstein and Seligman (FS; 1981), Feldstein and Morck (FM; 1983), and Daley (1984). Both Oldfield and FS, utilizing a Miller and Modigliani (MM; 1966) cross-sectional valuation approach, explored the impact of unfunded vested benefits (UVB) on equity value. Both concluded that unfunded vested benefits are, in fact, capitalized by the equity markets but that they are underestimated. The MM model predicts a coefficient of $-(1 - t_c)$ for UVB, where t_c is the marginal corporate tax rate. Their estimates were significantly lower (in absolute terms), though neither study explicitly incorporates a tax adjustment of the theoretical value into its analysis. In a similar study, FM report a like result but also observe that market capitalization appears to be more sensitive to underfunding than to overfunding. Daley (1984) used the expected coefficient for UVB on the valuation model of Litzenberger and Rao (LR; 1971), which decomposes earnings into pension and nonpension components. Daley finds little difference between capitalization of pension and nonpension assets and liabilities. Daley was unable to demonstrate any significant relationship between the interest rates used for actuarial calculations and equity prices, implying that the market capitalizes projected pension expenses via the reported expenses.

As the principal proponent of the asset-based approach, Landsman (1986) studied the impact of pension assets and liabilities on the firm's equity value. This study differs from all of the above in that the theoretical basis for Landsman is the Miller (1977) capital market equilibrium model. In this approach the separate effects of pension assets and pension liabilities are accounted for, as opposed to the net pension liability measures used in the previous studies. The model predictions derived from the Miller model are coefficients of -1 and 1 for pension assets and pension liabilities, respectively. Landsman utilizes ABO (accumulated benefit obligations) as a liability measure, though the superiority of a projected measure is argued. Landsman observes different capitalization rates between pension assets (liabilities) and nonpension assets (liabilities).

Bulow, Morck, and Summers (1987) dispute the value of the approaches taken above. Because of instability of coefficients (when the sample is expanded) and the difficulty in interpretation of the coefficients within a "mixed" (i.e., having regressors from both income statement and balance sheet) model such as that used by FM, they advocate using a model based exclusively on balance sheet information. Theirs, however, is not an identity model (utilizing pension and nonpension assets and liabilities), such as Landsman's and they encountered a "weak-firm" effect, confounding the effects of financial strength with those of funding status. To remedy this problem, rather than adopting an identity model, they utilize an event study methodology to assess the sensitivity of pension and nonpension liabilities to changes in interest rates. The results of both sets of tests are consistent with the notion that the market, in fact, capitalizes pension liabilities.

The results of the Landsman study may be interpreted as evidence in support of the "economic liability" view of pensions, since both pension assets and liabilities are strong determinants of the market value of equity. Thies and Sturrock (1988) provide similar evidence disputing the assumption of "disinterested management" in determining the funding levels of these plans. Managers can, on one hand, shelter excess earnings by modifying actuarial assumptions and prefunding plans and can, on the other hand, effectively borrow by reducing payments through liberal-

Table 1. Comparison of Regression Models for Studies Linking Equity Prices and Pension Liabilities

Study	Model	Sample Years	Estimation Techniques	R^2 Range	Liability Measure	Test for Debt Equivalency
Oldfield (1977)	$\frac{MVE}{A} = \delta_0 + \delta_1 \frac{x(1-t)}{A} + \delta_2 \frac{R(1-t)}{A} + \delta_3 \frac{PSD}{A} + \delta_4 \frac{VBO}{A} + \delta_5 \frac{\Delta A}{A} + \varepsilon$	1972-1974	OLS	.15-.76	VBO	No
Feldstein & Seligman (1981)	$\frac{V}{A} = \delta_0 + \delta_1 \frac{E}{A} + \delta_2 GROW + \delta_3 \frac{RD}{A} + \delta_4 BETA + \delta_5 DEBT + \delta_6 \frac{VBO}{A} \varepsilon$	1976-1977	OLS	.49-.80	VBO	No
Feldstein & Morch (1983)	$\frac{V}{A} = \delta_0 + \delta_1 \frac{E}{A} + \delta_2 GROW + \delta_3 \frac{RD}{A} + \delta_4 BETA + \delta_5 DEBT + \delta_6 \frac{VBO}{A} \varepsilon$	1979	OLS	.05-.78	VBO	No
Daley (1984)	$\frac{V}{A} = \delta_0 \frac{1}{A} + \delta_1 \frac{EBPC}{A} + \delta_2 \frac{PC}{A} + \delta_3 \frac{r_m S_E}{A} + \delta_4 \frac{G}{A} + \varepsilon$	1971-1979	WLS	.46-.62	VBO	No
Landsman (1986)	$\frac{MVE}{S} = \delta_0 + \delta_1 \frac{ASSET}{S} + \delta_2 \frac{LIABY}{S} + \delta_3 \frac{PASSET}{S} + \delta_4 \frac{ABO}{S} + \varepsilon$	1979-1981	OLS	.25-.56	ABO	No

152

Bulow, Morch, & Summers (1987)	$\dfrac{V}{A} = \delta_0 + \delta_1 \dfrac{UVB}{A} + \delta_2 \dfrac{DEBT}{A} + \delta_3 \dfrac{RD}{A} + \delta_4 BETA + \sum \gamma_i D_i + \varepsilon$	1979-1981	OLS	.39-.53	VBO	No
This Study	$\dfrac{MVE}{S} = \delta_0 + \delta_1 \dfrac{ASSET}{S} + \delta_2 \dfrac{LIABY}{S} + \delta_3 \dfrac{PASSET}{S} + \delta_4 \dfrac{PBO}{S} + \varepsilon$	1987-1988	OLS	.74-.91	ABO, PBO	Yes

Notes:

MVE: market value of equity	R: payment to debt	VBO: vested benefit obligations
E: after-tax earnings	RD: expenditure for R&D	BETA: systematic risk
PSD: perferred stock dividends	UVB: unfunded vested benefits	EBPC: earnings before pension cash flow
ASSET: book value of nonpension assets	ABO: accumulated benefit obligations	X: normalized cash flow-depreciation
LIABY: book value of nonpension liabilities	D_i: two-diget SIC dummies	G: growth in assets
PASSET: market value of pension assets	PC: after tax pension cost	DEBT: book value of debt
$r_m S_E$: market return times standard deviation of earnings	GROW: 10-year growth in profits	PBO: projected benefit obligations
DA: 5-year growth in assets	t: marginal tax rate	S: sales

izing these assumptions. At the extreme, the plan amounts to a put option for the firm, where the Pension Benefit Guarantee Corporation (PBGC) has written the put and can be forced to assume the stewardship of underfunded plans. However, as Alderson (1990) observes, this environment was dramatically altered by the Omnibus Budget Reconciliation Act 1987 (OBRA). This act, in effect, reduced the put value of the defined benefit pension plan by sharply limiting the ability of the firm to use the plan as a "captive finance unit." In such a changed environment, the questions answered, in part, by the Landsman study (analyzed years 1979-1981) would appear to be again open.

Three recent studies utilize the standard event study methodology to link pension liabilities and stock prices. Durkee, Groff, and Boatsman (DGB; 1988) measure the market reaction to disclosure of pension liability data in Department of Labor (DOL) and Internal Revenue Service (IRS) documents (costly) versus disclosure through post-SFAS 36 (FASB, 1985) financial statements (costless). DGB find that market reaction to financial statement disclosure is negative and significantly more negative than for the previously costly (DOL/IRS) disclosure. They infer that the FASB endorsement of pension liability is *itself* stimulating a response. In a similar study, Gopalakrishnan and Sugrue (1992), in studying the market reaction to SFAS 87, investigated the hypothesis that explicit pension liability recognition would have a negative impact on the debt covenants of the affected firms. Although 75% of the firms had negatively affected debt covenants, they observed no significant market reaction. Hsieh, Ferris, and Chen (HFC; 1990) examined the market reaction to pension plan terminations. Consistent with the findings of the two previous studies, they find significant and positive market reactions to plan termination. They, like Landsman, find evidence that both pension fund assets and liabilities are capitalized by the market.

Dhaliwal (1986) examined the debt equivalency of unfunded vested pension liabilities and found that market participants treat unfunded vested pension liabilities similarly to debt in assessing the firm's systematic risk. Using Dhaliwal's model, Gopalakrishnan and Sugrue (1990) examined the debt equivalency of unfunded accumulated and projected pension liabilities. Their evidence indicates that investors regard unfunded vested, accumulated, and projected pension liabilities as similar to debt in assessing the systematic risk of a firm. However, neither of these studies addresses the debt equivalency issue in the context of the valuation of stockholders' equity.

While there is no empirical investigation of the impact of projected pension liabilities on stock prices in the extant literature, Pesando (1985) attempted to improve upon pension liability measures via a wind-up measure (capital required to discharge the firm's legal obligations if the pension loan were terminated). Due to empirical problems he faced, Pesando concluded that even the wind-up measure might understate pension liabilities. He therefore advocated the use of a projected benefit measure employing assumptions concerning salary progression.

HYPOTHESES AND METHODOLOGY

Model Development

Utilizing Miller's (1977) capital market equilibrium approach, Landsman (1986) developed and tested a valuation model to investigate the property rights of pension assets and liabilities (accumulated benefits). Based on this model, we develop the following models to examine the association between the market value of equity and PBO (projected benefit obligations):

$$MVE_i = \beta_0 + \beta_1 ASSET_i + \beta_2 LIABY_i + \beta_3 PASSET_i + \beta_4 ABO_i + \varepsilon_i \qquad (1)$$

$$MVE_i = \beta 0 + \beta_1 ASSET_i + \beta_2 LIABY_i + \beta_3 PASSET_i + \beta_4 PBO_i + \varepsilon_i \qquad (2)$$

where

MVE_i = market value of shareholder equity, firm i,
$ASSET_i$ = historical cost book value of nonpension assets, firm i,
$LIABY_i$ = historical cost book value of nonpension liabilities, firm i,
$PASSET_i$ = market value of pension assets, firm i,
ABO_i = accumulated pension benefit obligation, firm i.
PBO_i = projected pension benefit obligation, firm i.

Even though the primary focus of this research is on projected benefit obligations, we examine the association between MVE and both ABO and PBO. Equations (1) and (2) differ only in terms of the measure of pension obligation examined. In Equation (1) the measure of pension obligation examined is the accumulated benefit obligation, whereas in Equation (2) it is the projected benefit obligation. The other three regressors that are common in Equations (1) and (2) are defined as follows: ASSET and LIABY represent the book value of total nonpension assets and liabilities, respectively. PASSET is the market value of pension plan assets. To separate pension assets and liabilities from nonpension assets and liabilities, if a firm reported prepaid pension cost (accrued), it was subtracted from total assets (total liabilities) to calculate total nonpension assets and liabilities.

Use of Deflator to Control for Heteroscedasticity

Since heteroscedasticity is endemic to cross-sectional analyses such as this, like Landsman, we attempt to control for heteroscedasticity by deflating the regressors in Equation (1) by SALES using a procedure developed by Park (1966) to estimate the power of the deflator instead of assuming it to be 2. Consistent with Landsman, the following steps were taken to determine the size of the deflator: first, model (1) was run in undeflated form to estimate the residuals, $\hat{e}_i$.[7] second, the following model was run to estimate the transform of the deflator:

$$ln(\hat{e}_i^2) = \Gamma_0 + \Gamma_1 ln\ SALES_i + \Gamma_2(ln\ SALES_i)^2 + \upsilon_i. \tag{3}$$

In the above model, the dependent variable, the natural log of the residual variance, was obtained from the undeflated form of model (1). After estimating the Γs, the deflator (SALES) is estimated as follows:

$$SALES(\Gamma_1 + \Gamma_2 ln\ SALES)/2 \tag{4}$$

Each of the regressors in Equation (1) was deflated using a value obtained through Equation (4). Since there are two measures of pension liabilities (accumulated and projected), the above steps were repeated to estimate the deflator for model (2).

Debt Equivalency of Pension Obligations

Models (1) and (2) attempt to offer evidence on the property rights of pension assets and liabilities with PBO as the measure of pension liability. However, they do not address the debt equivalency issue of nonpension liabilities and pension liabilities. In this section we develop the necessary hypotheses to answer the following questions: (1) Are pension assets perceived as equivalent to nonpension assets by investors in valuing the stock price of a firm? (2) Similarly, are pension liabilities perceived as equivalent to nonpension liabilities in the context of security valuation by investors? The debt equivalency of PBO is of particular interest. The "minimum liability" disclosure mandated by SFAS No. 87 (FS, 1985) is based on ABO, not PBO. If market participants regard PBO of a firm as no different than any other corporate liability, then it is justifiable to recognize and report it on the balance sheet. Similarly, SFAS No. 87 does not allow for the recognition of PASSET or a net pension asset (when PASSET exceeds ABO) on the face of the balance sheet. If investors treat PASSET of a firm as an equivalent to nonpension assets, then it is justifiable to recognize and report the total pension plan assets. The equivalence of pension liabilities (assets) to nonpension liabilities (assets) will be assessed by statistical comparison of the coefficients derived in the regression of models (1) and (2).

Sample Selection

Since mandatory disclosure of projected pension benefit obligations was initiated in 1987, we chose 1987 and 1988 as relevant time periods for this analysis. All data used to estimate models (1) and (2) were obtained from COMPUSTAT PC-Plus. Our sample consists of those firms, with defined benefit plans in place, in compliance with SFAS 87, and with complete data on COMPUSTAT. The sample is comprised of 1398 observations, 659 for 1987 and 739 for 1988. Descriptive statistics for the sample are contained in Table 2.

Table 2. Descriptive Statistics (Dollar Values in millions)

Variable	Full Sample		No-growth Sample	
	Mean	*SD*	*Mean*	*SD*
MVE				
1987	939.78	2969.10	1475.95	4871.65
1988	1039.77	3375.13	746.42	2832.62
ASSET				
1987	2431.42	8679.29	3042.24	8278.18
1988	2681.10	11438.06	1555.40	4292.12
LIABY				
1987	1643.60	5776.86	2109.85	5612.84
1988	1563.54	5582.64	1192.47	3525.32
PASSET				
1987	323.58	2098.66	498.99	2347.25
1988	303.82	1994.65	305.67	2253.93
ABO				
1987	248.53	1562.96	337.34	1476.04
1988	243.27	1638.88	189.90	1221.87
PBO				
1987	284.63	1676.73	426.27	1822.92
1988	278.56	1759.59	232.79	1467.61

A comparison of the sample means for our sample with Landsman's sample reveals some interesting findings. The range for the mean of the market value variable in Landsman's sample is $49-106 million over a 3-year period as compared to $940-1040 million for our sample. Similarly, the mean values of the pension assets and pension liabilities (ABO) are greater for our sample by nearly 10 times. This suggests either that our samples consist of firms that are larger compared to firms included in his sample, or that the differences in sample means can be attributable to time-based phenomena such as inflation or growth. The other implication of the differences between the two samples is that a meaningful comparison of coefficients obtained by Landsman with those of models (1) and (2) may not be possible given the underlying differences between the two samples. Pearson correlation coefficients are presented in Table 3. We address the multicollinearity issue later.

While the predicted value for the intercept term in our estimated models is zero, Landsman (1986) reported a significantly higher value. He argued that the theoretical values of the pension coefficients are a function of the firm-specific growth rates and suggested that an analysis of zero growth firms might control for this anomaly. We consequently identified a subsample of no-growth firms, defined as those with a 5-year compound growth rate in revenue of less than or equal to zero. We identified 193 such firms for 1987 and 169 for 1988.

Table 3.   Pearson Correlation Coefficient Matrix

	MVE	ASSET	LIABY	PASSET	ABO	PBO
A: Full sample (N = 1,398 observations)						
MVE	1.00	0.54	0.37	0.62	0.61	0.63
ASSET		1.0	0.98	0.47	0.50	0.98
LIABY			1.00	0.28	0.29	0.31
PASSET				1.00	0.98	0.98
ABO					1.00	0.99
PBO						1.00
B: No-growth sample (N = 362 observations)						
MVE	1.00	0.84	0.73	0.72	0.77	0.79
ASSET		1.00	0.97	0.61	0.68	0.69
LIABY			1.00	0.55	0.60	0.62
PASSET				1.00	0.99	0.98
ABO					1.00	0.99
PBO						1.00

RESULTS

Basic Models

The results of the basic models (1) and (2) are contained in Tables 4 and 5. Table 4 reports the summary statistics for model (1) representing ABO, and Table 5 reports the statistics corresponding to model (2) representing PBO. Both tables present the summary statistics for the no-growth sample in panel B.

The results indicate that the nonpension variables, ASSET and LIABY in both models (1) and (2), have coefficients that are both highly significant and have the correct sign. This is consistent with the findings of Landsman (1986). Similarly, the coefficient values for all the pension variables—PASSET, ABO, and PBO—are highly significant and have the correct sign. Also, the R^2 values consistently exceed values reported in prior studies. Landsman establishes that the benchmark coefficient for nonpension and pension assets (β1 and β3) should be 1 whereas for nonpension liabilities and pension liabilities (β2 and β4) it should be −1. Our estimates of the nonpension assets and pension assets range from 1.01 to 1.97. For nonpension liabilities and pension liabilities, the range is −2.06 to −1.05. The coefficient value for ABO exceeds 2 in absolute value in one of the four models run. Thus the magnitudes of the coefficients are near the theoretical values only in few cases. This suggests possible measurement error in the regressors. During model development we substituted book value measures for the unobservable market values for three of the four regressors in models (1) and (2). Only PASSET is measured on a market value basis. It is possible that these surrogates systematically understate the true values of nonpension assets, nonpension liabilities and

Table 4. Results of Regression Analysis
(Accumulated Benefit Obligations, Model 1)

	β_0	β_1	β_2	β_3	β_4	R^2	DFE^a
			A. Full Sample				
1987							
Estimate	189.62	1.56	−1.60	1.21	−2.06	0.77	654
t-ratio	4.59***	32.60***	−30.28***	5.44***	−6.53***		
1988							
Estimate	88.33	1.54	−1.56	1.14	−1.05	0.77	734
t-ratio	2.88***	30.36***	−28.55	4.04***	−2.36***		
			B. No-growth Sample				
1987							
Estimate	59.28	1.56	−1.59	1.16	−1.50	0.86	188
t-ratio	1.14	18.02***	−15.82	3.14***	−2.57***		
1988							
Estimate	17.36	1.77	−1.80	1.33	−1.43	0.86	164
t-ratio	0.48	13.84***	−12.88	2.53**	−1.70*		

Notes: ^{a}DFE = degrees of freedom of regression error.
; *Significant at the .10 level in a two-tailed test.
**Significant at the .05 level in a two-tailed test.
***Significant at the .01 level in a two-tailed test.

Table 5. Results of Regression Analysis
(Projected Benefit Obligations, Model 2)

	β_0	β_1	β_2	β_3	β_4	R^2	DFE^a
			A. Full Sample				
1987							
Estimate	219.67	1.63	−1.67	1.13	−1.84	0.77	654
t-ratio	4.80***	30.16***	−28.35***	4.87***	−5.82***		
1988							
Estimate	204.68	1.29	−1.31	1.37	−1.18	0.74	734
t-ratio	5.41***	26.44***	−24.92***	6.44***	−3.83***		
			B. No-growth Sample				
1987							
Estimate	56.15	1.64	−1.66	1.01	−1.30	0.91	188
t-ratio	1.14	18.02***	−15.82***	3.14***	−2.57***		
1988							
Estimate	20.81	1.97	−2.01	1.49	−1.68	0.90	164
t-ratio	0.27	14.38***	−13.35***	3.81**	−2.70*		

Notes: ^{a}DFE = degrees of freedom of regression error.
*Significant at the .10 level in a two-tailed test.
**Significant at the .05 level in a two-tailed test.
***Significant at the .01 level in a two-tailed test.

pension liabilities and could introduce measurement error in their corresponding regressors.

A disturbing feature of the results contained in Panel A of Tables 4 and 5 deals with the presence of a large and significant intercept term. The intercept terms range from 88.33 to 219.67 and are consistently significant across the sample years. This suggests that models (1) and (2) may have been misspecified. Landsman's intercept term ranges from 12.66 to 41.61 for the PLU regressions, but for other models his intercept terms are much higher. We believe that the increase in the intercept term in our models compared to Landsman's models is mainly attributable to time factor, inflation, growth, bullish stock market, etc. We also conducted analyses on the sample of no-growth firms previously described. For the no-growth sample, the estimate of the asset coefficients was 1.01 to 1.97 and the liability range was -2.01 to -1.30. These results are thus consistent with those of the full sample, but in each of the no-growth sample regressions, the intercept term is not significantly different from zero at the .01 level.

Debt Equivalency of Pension Obligations

This section presents the test results of the debt equivalency hypotheses discussed previously. These results are contained in Table 6. Panel A of Table 6 presents the results of the equivalency tests of assets for models (1) and (2); the results of the equivalency tests of liabilities for both models (1) and (2) are displayed in panel B. Of the eight cases examined, we failed to reject the null hypothesis that pension assets are treated as similar to nonpension assets in at least seven cases at a significance level higher than 10%. The results based on model (2) representing PBO are rather mixed with the asset null hypothesis not being rejected only during 1987. On the other hand, we failed to reject the null hypothesis that pension liabilities are regarded as similar to nonpension liabilities in all eight cases at significance levels higher than 13%. Thus, it appears that the results of equivalency tests are much stronger for pension liabilities compared to pension assets.

One may argue that since PBO and PASSET are disclosed in the footnotes to the financial statements, market participants are capable of using the footnote disclosure in their assessment of market value. Therefore, if the stock market is efficient with respect to publicly available information, it does not matter how the information is reported. However, Harper, Mister, and Strawser (1987) found that bankers and students, acting as surrogates for naive investors, perceived the pension liability to be debt more often when it was included in the balance sheet rather than disclosed in a footnote. Similarly, SFAC No. 5, (FASB, 1984) makes it clear that footnote disclosure is not a substitute for recognition in financial statements, and this viewpoint is also reiterated in paragraph 116 of SFAS No. 87 (FASB, 1985). Therefore, we believe that the present practice of the FASB not to fully recognize PBO and PASSET on the balance of sheet of the employer is inconsistent with SFAC No. 5.

Table 6.   Debt Equivalency of Accumulated and Projected Obligations

	Full Sample		No-growth Sample	
	1987	*1988*	*1987*	*1988*
A. H_o: $\beta_1 = \beta_3$				
Model (1)				
F-statistic	2.71	2.28	1.37	0.70
Prob > *F*	0.10	0.13	0.24	0.40
Model (2)				
F-Statistic	5.46	0.15	6.03	1.63
Prob > *F*	0.02	0.70	0.02	0.20
B: H_o: $\beta_2 = \beta_4$				
Model (1)				
F-Statistic	2.32	1.51	0.03	0.18
Prob > *F*	0.13	0.22	0.87	0.67
Model (2)				
F-Statistic	0.33	0.20	0.78	0.32
Prob> *F*	0.56	0.65	0.38	0.57

Use of Net Asset Regression Models to Control Multicollinearity

The correlation matrix contained in Table 3 suggests possible ill-conditioning (multicollinearity) among some regressors, particularly between pension assets and pension liabilities and between nonpension assets and nonpension liabilities. It might be useful to examine the condition number in order to understand the severity of the ill-conditioning. Belsley, Kuh, and Welsch (1980) show that condition numbers with values around 5 or 10 signify weak dependencies, whereas moderate to strong relations are associated with condition numbers 30 to 100. The highest condition numbers for models (1) and (2) were 21.55 and 23.47, respectively. This suggests that the degree of dependency among the regressors is not strong.

We examined the following net asset regression model to control for multicollinearity between nonpension asset and nonpension liability on one hand and pension asset and pension liabilities on the other:

$$\text{MVE}_i = \beta_0 + \beta_1\text{NETASSET}_i + \beta_2\text{NETPASSET}_i + \varepsilon_i \qquad (5)$$

In model (5) NETASSET is the difference between ASSET and LIABY and NETPASSET is the difference between PASSET and ABO. A similar model was run to estimate β_2 where NETPASSET is defined as the difference between PASSET and PBO. The results of these models are contained in Table 7.

Even though these models were examined for each one of the sample years, for the sake of brevity we report only the summary statistics pertaining to the pooled models. Panels A and B in Table 7 present the estimates of $\beta1$ and $\beta2$ for the two

Table 7.   Net Asset Regression Results (Model 5)

	β_0	β_1	β_2	R^2	DEF^a
A. Accumulated Benefit Obligations					
Full Sample					
Estimate	88.85	1.45	0.91	0.77	1,388
t-ratio	4.45*	55.88*	10.17		
No-growth Sample					
Estimate	45.39	1.43	1.06	0.86	352
t-ratio	1.34	36.33*	9.46*		
B. Projected Benefit Obligations					
Full Sample					
Estimate	89.84	1.49	1.04	0.77	1,388
t-ratio	4.48*	61.99*	10.67*		
No-growth Sample					
Estimate	46.71	1.48	1.12	0.86	352
t-ratio	1.37	39.67*	9.25		

C.   Correlation Coefficients ofNet Asset Regression Variables

	NETASSET	*NETPASSET (Accumulated*	*NETPASSET (Projected)*
NETASSET	1.00	0.45	0.29

Notes: ^{a}DFE = degrees of freedom of regression error, NETASSET = (ASSET − LIABY), NETPASSET = (PASSET − ABO) in panel A and (PASSET − PBO) in panel B.
     *Significant at the .01 level in a two-tailed test.

definitions of the NETPASSET variable. Panel C reports the correlation coefficients of the variables included in model (5). Table 7 indicates that the highest correlation among the variables included in model (5) is only 0.45 (recall from Table 3 that the correlation between PASSET and ABO or PBO was 0.98). The estimates of $\beta1$ and $\beta2$ are highly significant and positive. Thus, it appears that the netting of nonpension assets and liabilities and pension assets and liabilities has helped in reducing the severity of the multicollinearity problem.

SUMMARY AND CONCLUSIONS

A few studies in the extant literature have examined the relationship between shareholder equity and pension liability using earnings-based cross-sectional models. Some, as we do here, have used a balance sheet-based identity model. This research, unlike similar prior studies makes use of the newly available projected pension liability information mandated by SFAS No. 87. In addition, we conducted statistical tests to examine the equivalency of nonpension assets and liabilities vis-á-vis pension assets and liabilities.

We found that both corporate liabilities and assets as well as pension liabilities and assets are important determinants of the market value of equity. Furthermore, we have presented evidence that investors perceive pensions assets and liabilities, both accumulated and projected, to be equivalent to corporate assets and liabilities.

Consistent with the findings of Landsman (1987), we find that pension property rights lie fully with the firm as opposed to the pension trust. Our evidence sheds light on the controversial issue concerning the appropriate measure of pension liability to be used for financial reporting purposes. The concept of "legal liability" is consistent with the viewpoint that, in a legal sense, property rights of pension assets and liabilities lie with the trust, and therefore pension assets and liabilities should not be reported on the balance sheet. On the other hand, the concept of "economic liability" is consistent with the view that the employer is ultimately liable to the employees and not only the pension trust. Under this notion the property rights of plan assets and liabilities lie fully with the employer, and not with the trust. By issuing SFAS No. 87, the FASB *implicitly* supports the economic liability notion and offers PBO as an important measure of pension liability. Our results provide strong evidence that the market concurs.

REFERENCES

Alderson, Michael J. (1990). Corporate pension policy under OBRA 1987. *Financial Management,* 79(4, Winter), 87-97.

Belsley, David A., Kuh, Edwin, & Welsch, Roy E. (1980). *Regression diagnostics: Identifying influential data and sources of collinearity.* New York: Wiley.

Bulow, J.I., Morck, R., & Summers, L. (1987). How does the market value unfunded pension liabilities? In Z. Bodie, J.B. Shoven, and D.A. Wise (Eds.), *Issues in Pension Economics.* Chicago: University of Chicago Press.

Daley, Lane (1984). The valuation of reported pension measures of firms sponsoring defined benefit plans. *Accounting Review, 59*(2, April), 177-198.

Dhaliwal, D. (1986). Measurement of financial leverage in the presence of unfunded pension obligations. *Accounting Review, 61*(4, October), 651-661.

Durkee, David, Groff, James, & Boastsman, James (1988). The effect of costly versus costless pension disclosure on common share prices: The case of SFAS 36. *Journal of Accounting Literature, 7,* 180-196.

Feldstein, Martin, & Morck, Randall (1983). Pension funding decisions, interest rate assumptions and share prices. In Zri Bodie and John B. Shoven (Eds.), *Financial Aspects of the United States Pension System.* Chicago: University of Chicago Press.

Feldstein, M., & Seligman, S. (1981). Pension funding, share prices and national savings. *Journal of Finance, 36*(4, September), 801-824.

Financial Accounting Standards Board (1982). *Preliminary views on major issues related to employers' accounting for pensions and other portemployment benefits.* New York: Author.

Financial Accounting Standards Board (1984). *Statement of financial accounting concepts No. 5, "Recognition and measurement in financial statements of business enterprises."* New York: Author.

Financial Accounting Standards Board (1985). *Statement of financial accounting standards No. 87, "Employers' accounting for pensions."* New York: Author.

Gopalakrishnan, V., & Sugrue, Timothy (1990). The debt equivalency of unfunded accumulated and projected pension obligations. *Advances in Accounting, 8,* 113-129.

Gopalakrishnan, V., & Sugrue, Timothy (1992). Economic consequences of pension policy deliberations (SFAS No. 87): An Empirical assessment of the debt-covenant hypothesis. *Journal of Business Finance and Accounting, 19(*5, September), 751-775.

Harper, Robert M., Mister, William G., Strawser, Jerry R. (1987). The impact of new pension disclosure rules on perceptions of debt. *Journal of Accounting Research, 25*(2, Autumn), 327-330.

Hsieh, Su-Jane, Ferris, Ken, & Chen, Andrew (1990). Securities market response to pension fund termination. *Contemporary Accounting Reseach, 6*(2, Spring), 550-572.

Landsman, Wayne (1986). An empirical investigation of pension fund property rights. *Accounting Review, 61*(4, October), 662-691.

Litzenberger, Robert, & Rao, Cherukun (1971). Estimates of the marginal rate of time preference and average risk aversion of investors in electric utility shares: 1960-1966. *Bell Journal of Economics and Management Scie*nce, 2(1, Spring), 265-277.

Miller, Merton (1977). Debt and taxes. *Journal of Finance, 32*(2, May), 261-275.

Miller, Merton, & Modigliani, Franco (1966). Some estimates of the cost of capital to the electric utility industry: 1954-1957. *American Economic Review, 56,*(1, June), 333-391.

Oldfield, George (1977). Financial aspects of the private pension system. *Journal of Money, Credit and Banking, 9*(1, February), 48-55.

Park, R.E. (1966). Estimation with heteroscedastic error terms. *Econometrica, 34*(4, October), 888.

Pesando, James (1985). The usefulness of the wind-up measure of pension liability: A labor market perspective. *Journal of Finance, 40*(3, July), 927-940.

Thies, Clifford F., & Sturrock, Thomas (1988). The pension-augmented balance sheet. *Journal of Risk and Insurance, 55*(3, September), 467-480.

ON THE EXISTENCE OF ALTERNATIVE DYNAMIC MARKET MODELS

Chung Chen, Cheng-few Lee, Paul Newbold, and Chunchi Wu

ABSTRACT

In this paper, we have considered the possibility of departure from the simple static market model for individual rates of return, contemplating the existence of leads and lags in the system. Two approaches, (a) the lagged regression and (b) the VARMA modeling, are employed. In addition to testing for the existence of a dynamic daily market model, we also attempt (1) to measure the strength of the relationship in terms of gains in forecasting rates of return and (2) to examine the stability of the relationship. Using long series of daily data, we have found statistical evidence indicating that the simple market model is often misspecified against alternatives involving a market lead. This evidence is particularly strong for the lightly traded stocks. A multiple-hypotheses testing procedure and the VARMA test are employed to investigate the intertemporal relationship between market and individual stock returns. We find that the structure of the dynamic relations changes over time.

Advances in Financial Planning and Forecasting,
Volume 5, pages 165-180.
Copyright © 1994 by JAI Press Inc.
All rights of reproduction in any form reserved.
ISBN:1-55938-421-2

Consequently, applying any fixed order lead-lag structure to a dynamic market model over different time periods might result in improper estimation of security betas. To obtain more accurate estimates of the systematic risk, researchers should carefully scrutinize return series and examine the stability of the fitted model.

INTRODUCTION

In the traditional asset pricing theory, the market risk, or beta, of a security or portfolio of securities, is generally estimated by fitting through least squares of the market model

$$R_{jt} = \alpha_j + \beta_j R_{mt} + \varepsilon_{jt}, \tag{1}$$

where R_{jt} is the rate of return on the jth security, R_{mt} the market rate of return, and ε_{jt} a random disturbance. In a system with potential dynamic relationship between R_{jt} and R_{mt}, an essentially static formulation such as (1) will be inadequate. Dimson (1979) and Reinganum (1982) have considered an elaboration of the model (1), including on the right-hand side terms in $R_{m,t-k}$ for both positive and negative k, for portfolios of stocks. Using the methodology of the econometric causality literature, this formulation, which resembles one employed by Sims (1972), suggests the possibility of testing for leads and lags between individual rates of return and market rates. As Reinganum shows, the existence of strong leads or lags in the market model would lead to alternative definitions of beta. Moreover, if the rate of return on an individual security depends to some extent on previous market rates, this implies some predictability of future individual returns, and hence market inefficiency.

The advantage of applying the regression method to determine the lead or lag structure for the dynamic market model is the ready availability of computational algorithm and test statistics. However, this procedure may produce less powerful results due to a possibly misspecified lead or lag structure in which the number of leads or lags, K, is somewhat arbitrarily chosen. In a Monte Carlo study on a vector autoregressive model of order 1, VAR(1), Nelson and Schwert (1982) have shown that the likelihood ratio test based on a VAR(1) model is more powerful than the two-sided regression F-test. Furthermore, there is no natural alternative for the possible direction of dynamic relationship between R_{jt} and R_{mt} when the null hypothesis of contemporaneous relation between them as in (1) is rejected. In a dynamic framework, the possibilities are (a) R_{jt} and Rmt are independent ($R_{jt} \wedge R_{mt}$), (b) R_{jt} causes R_{mt} ($R_{jt} \Rightarrow R_{mt}$), (c) R_{mt} causes R_{jt} ($R_{mt} \Rightarrow R_{jt}$), and (d) a feedback relationship exists between R_{mt} and R_{jt} ($R_{mt} \Leftrightarrow R_{jt}$). Since there is no established theory to support any of the above hypotheses, the determination of the dynamic relation between R_{mt} and R_{jt} is an empirical issue of multiple-hypotheses. A test procedure that systematically examines all possible alternatives is required.

In this paper, we apply two approaches to investigate the dynamic relationship between market returns and individual stock returns, using daily rate of return series on samples of both heavily traded and lightly traded common stocks. The first approach follows the traditional line of causality testing examining the null hypothesis of no relationship versus $R_{jt} \Rightarrow R_{mt}$ and $R_{mt} \Rightarrow R_{jt}$ separately. The lag regression test is employed in this part. The second approach treats the issue as a multiple-hypotheses testing problem. A vector ARMA model is taken as the underlying structure for the return series $\{R_{mt}, R_{jt}\}$ and a procedure based on a decision tree approach is used to examine all possible relationships systematically. The vector ARMA test is employed for this purpose. In addition to testing for the existence of a dynamic daily market model, we also attempt (1) to measure the strength of the relationship in terms of gains in forecasting rates of return and (2) to examine the stability of the relationship.

The remainder of this paper is divided into four sections. Section 2 presents the method of the Granger test and the corresponding empirical results. Section 3 discusses the vetor ARMA test and examines the intertemporal relationship between the market and individual stock returns. Section 4 explores the implications of these results. Finally, Section 5 summarizes our findings.

THE TRADITIONAL GRANGER
TEST OF DYNAMIC RELATION

Let $R_{j,t}$ and $R_{m,t}$ denote two time series of returns, and consider the problem of forecasting $R_{j,n+1}$, based on two sets of information $I_0 = \{R_{j,n-k}; k \geq 0\}$ and $I_1 = \{R_{j,n-k}R_{m,n-k}; k \geq 0\}$. In practical implementation, attention is restricted to predictors that are linear functions of members of the information sets. Then, if $R_{j,n+1}$ is better predicted, in the expected-squared-error sense, using information set I_1, rather than I_0, R_m is said to "cause" R_j ($R_m \Rightarrow R_j$), in the sense of Granger (1969). In an analogous fashion we can define the event "R_j causes R_m" ($R_j \Rightarrow R_m$). If as can be the case, causality runs in both directions, the pair of time series is said to exhibit "feedback" ($R_m \Leftrightarrow R_j$).

Granger proposes a test of causal direction based on the fitting of vector autoregressive models to a pair of time series. Assume that the vector process $\widetilde{R}^{i}_{t} = (R_{j,t}, R_{m,t})$ admits a stationary infinite-order autoregressive representation

$$\underset{\sim}{R}_t = \underset{\sim}{\alpha} + \sum_{k=1}^{\infty} \Phi_k \underset{\sim}{R}_{t-k} + \underset{\sim}{\varepsilon}_t, \qquad (2)$$

where $\underset{\sim}{\alpha}$ is a vector, Φ_k are 2×2 matrices of parameters, and $\underset{\sim}{\varepsilon}$ is zero-mean-vector white noise,[1] so that

$$E(\underset{\sim}{\varepsilon}_t \underset{\sim}{\varepsilon}'_t) = \Sigma \quad \text{and} \quad E(\underset{\sim}{\varepsilon}_t \underset{\sim}{\varepsilon}'_{t-k}) = \underset{\sim}{0} \qquad (k \neq 0).$$

Then, R_m causes R_j if and only if the (1,2) elements of the Φ_k are not all zero. Similarly, R_j does not cause R_m if and only if the (2,1) elements of these matrices are all zero. In practice, of course, it is not possible to estimate an infinite number of free parameters, so that the autoregression is truncated at some maximum lag K, chosen (often arbitrarily) to be sufficient high to allow adequate description of any dynamic relationship. To implement the test then, consider the model

$$R_{j,t} = \alpha_1 + \sum_{k=1}^{K} \Phi_{11,k} R_{j,t-k} + \sum_{k=1}^{K} \Phi_{12,k} R_{m,t-k} + \varepsilon_{1,t}, \qquad (3)$$

where $\varepsilon_{1,t}$ is a randon-error term. The null hypothesis that R_m does not cause R_j is then checked by testing $\Phi_{12,k} = 0$ $(k = 1,\ldots,K)$ using the usual F-test based on the ordinary least squares fitting of (3). Similarly, to test the null hypothesis that R_j does not cause R_m, we can fit

$$R_{m,t} = \alpha_2 + \sum_{k=1}^{K} \Phi_{21,k} R_{j,t-k} + \sum_{k=1}^{K} \Phi_{22,k} R_{m,t-k} + \varepsilon_{2,t}, \qquad (4)$$

where $\varepsilon_{2,t}$ is a random-error term, and test $\Phi_{21,k} = 0$ $(k = 1, \ldots, K)$.

Now, the use of the term causality in connection with these tests is certainly controversial. However, for our present purposes, we do not need to get involved in this philosophical debate. Rather, we simply require tests of predictability in our search for possible leads and lags. For example, if the rate of return for an individual stock is better predicted when information on past market rates is added to the information on past individual rates, we will say that the market rate *leads* the individual rate.

The empirical tests we report in the next section are based on relatively long series of daily data on rates of return. Given such an abundance of data, the tests of our null hypotheses will be very powerful. We will therefore want to distinguish between statistical significance and practical significance. For instance, it may be that the null hypothesis $\Phi_{12,k} = 0$ $(k = 1, \ldots, K)$, following from the fitting of (2), can be rejected at, say, the 1% significance level. In order to assess the magnitude of the effect found, we would want to measure the extent of the gains in predictability resulting from the addition of previous market rates of return to the information set. To do this we find the ratio of the degrees-of-freedom corrected, mean-squared error for the full model to that of the model where the $\Phi_{12,k}$ are restricted to be zero. The restricted model, of course, corresponds to the case where the individual rate of return is predicted on the basis of its past history alone. In this way we obtain a direct measure of the strength of any leads or lags found.

Empirical Results of the Granger Test

The data analyzed in this study are daily rates of return on 27 heavily traded and 22 lightly traded corporate stocks.[2] Table 1 provides a listing of the stocks used. For the heavily traded stocks our sample consists of 1,515 observations from January 3, 1975, to December 31, 1980. Our series for lightly traded stocks contain 1,010 observations for the period beginning January 3, 1977, and ending Decem-

Table 1.   Corporate Stocks Used in the Study

Heavily Traded Stocks

1.	Allied Chemical	15.	International Harvester
2.	Aluminum Corporation of America	16.	International Paper
3.	American Brands	17.	Merk and Co.
4.	American Can Corporation	18.	3M Corporation
5.	A.T.T.	19.	Owens Illinois
6.	Bethleham Steel	20.	Protor and Gamble
7.	DuPont	21.	Sears
8.	Eastman Kodak	22.	Standard Oil of California
9.	Exxon	23.	Texaco
10.	General Electric	24.	Union Carbide
11.	General Foods	25.	U.S. Steel
12.	General Motors	26.	Westinghouse
13.	Goodyear	27.	Woolworth
14.	INCO, Ltd.		

Lightly Traded Stocks

1.	Aro Corporation	12.	Great Northern Iron Ore
2.	Bethlehem Corporation	13.	Hastings Manufacturing Co.
3.	Breeze Corps. Inc.	14.	Holiday Inns Inc., Spl. Stk. A
4.	Carries and General Corp.	15.	Indiana Gas Inc.
5.	Community Public Service Co.	16.	Jaclyn Inc.
6.	Continental Metals Corp.	17.	O'Okeip Copper Company
7.	Equifax Inc.	18.	Pacific Tin Consolidated
8.	Fidelity Union Bancorporation	19.	Shopwell Inc.
9.	First Connecticut Small Business Investment	20.	South Jersey Industries
10.	First National State Corp.	21.	Wies Markets Inc.
11.	GATX Corporation	22.	Winn-Dixie Stores Inc. B

ber 31, 1980. Data are taken from the CRSP tape. Our market rate is the CRSP value-weighted index of NYSE and AMEX stocks.

We estimate Equations (3) and (4), and test the respective null hypotheses $\Phi_{12,k} = 0$ ($k = 1, ..., K$) and $\Phi_{21,k} = 0$ ($k = 1, ..., K$). For the maximum permitted lag K, we use values of both 5 and 10. We verify that this is adequate by examining the multivariate partial autocorrelations, as discussed, for example, in Ansley and Newbold (1979). A high-order autoregression is intended to provide an adequate, computationally convenient representation on the underlying stochastic generating process. A value of K that is "too low" will invalidate the assumed significance levels of the tests, while a value that is "too high" will lower the power of the tests. Since our sample sizes are large, we feel that the second of these considerations is less important than the first. Time series analysts generally take one of two approaches to order determination in autoregressive models. One possibility is to employ one of the order estimation criteria, whose theoretical properties are discussed in the context of univariate time series models by Hannan (1980). Alternatively, model selection can be based on the sample partial autocorrelations. For our data these sample partial autocorrelations invariably indicate that an autoregressive order of at most 5 would be adequate. However, to be conservative with regard to the adequacy of the autoregressive approximation, we also emply $K = 10$. As already indicated, for samples of this size, the effect of this more elaborate formulation on the power of the tests should be minimal.

Table 2 shows the results of our F-tests for the 27 heavily traded stocks. As can be seen from this table, we frequently find strong statistical evidence of the market rate leading the individual rate. This pattern of findings is fairly consistent whichever maximum lag length is used. On the other hand, there is much less strong evidence of the market rate lagging the individual rates. This is perhaps not surprising as, a priori, we would not expect a great deal of success when employing movements in a single stock rate of return to predict the overall market rate.

Turning now to Table 3, we can put these results in perspective. We note there that, although the statistical evidence indicating lagged relationships is very strong, our analyses suggest that the relationships themselves do not seem to improve the prediction performance. The estimated prediction mean squared error for the individual rate, when market rates are included in the information set, is never reduced to less than 97.5% of the prediction mean squared error resulting from the use of past individual rates alone. For the majority of these series, the reduction in mean squared error from the use of the addittional information is less than 1%. The relationships in the other direction are even weaker. The best that can be achieved by using past individual rates is a reduction of 1% in mean squared forecast error for the market rate.

In Table 4 and 5 we present the corresponding results for the 22 lightly traded stocks in our sample. It appears from Table 4 that the evidence for market lead is even stronger here than in the case of heavily traded stocks. Moreover, we notice from Table 5 that the relationships, though still of modest strength, are rather

Table 2.　Tests for Market Leads and Lags:
Heavily Traded Stocks; *F*-Statistics

Stocks	Maximum Lag 5 Days, Dependent Variable		Maximum Lag 10 Days, Dependent Variable	
	R_{jt}	R_{mt}	R_{jt}	R_{mt}
1	6.458***	3.620***	3.994***	2.034**
2	2.768**	0.838	1.673*	0.671
3	2.666**	0.432	2.730***	0.463
4	8.239***	1.255	4.525**	1.475
5	1.491	2.369**	3.257***	1.740*
6	2.194*	0.584	1.735*	1.077
7	2.322**	2.493**	3.053***	1.436
8	1.591	0.828	1.739*	1.483
9	3.411***	2.847**	2.652***	1.973
10	1.975*	1.358	1.816*	0.670
11	1.413	1.492	0.993	0.977
12	2.845**	0.668	2.368***	0.876
13	6.822***	1.848	4.428***	1.690
14	2.709**	0.714	1.784*	0.981
15	3.645***	0.189	2.693***	0.315
16	2.136	1.165	2.805	1.016
17	1.365	1.509	1.643*	1.000
18	3.889***	1.365	4.395***	0.954
19	7.989***	1.399	4.880***	1.057
20	2.262**	2.110*	3.717***	1.578
21	1.216	2.000*	1.865**	1.212
22	1.194	2.706**	1.554	2.441***
23	3.061***	1.138	2.769***	0.883
24	2.998**	1.509	2.788***	1.725**
25	0.952	0.551	1.084	0.663
26	1.619	0.744	1.742*	0.864
27	3.018**	1.355	1.968**	0.822

Notes:　*Significant at 10% level.
　　　** Significant at 5% level.
　　　***Significant at 1% level.

weak for the lightly traded stocks. Mean squared error ratios are less than 0.97 for 7 stocks when the maximum permitted lag is 5 days, and for 6 stocks when the maximum permitted lag is 10 days. Nevertheless, the smallest value found for this ration is still as much as 0.942 in the former case and 0.931 in the latter. It seems pretty clear that, while strong statistical evidence of lags can be found, only modest gains can be expected in trying to exploit these lags in the prediction of future individual rates of return on a daily basis, even for lightly traded stocks. As is to

Table 3. Tests for Market Leads and Lags:
Heavily Traded Stocks; Mean Squared Error Ratios

	Maximum Lag 5 Days, Dependent Variable		Maximum Lag 10 Days, Dependent Variable	
	R_{jt}	R_{mt}	R_{jt}	R_{mt}
Smallest	0.9077	0.991	0.957	0.990
0.97-0.99	2	0	4	0
0.98-0.99	2	0	10	0
0.99-1.00	21	17	12	12
More than 1.00	2	10	1	15

Table 4. Tests for Market Leads and Lags:
Lightly Traded Stocks; *F*-Statistics

	Maximum Lag 5 Days, Dependent Variable		Maximum Lag 10 Days, Dependent Variable	
Stocks	R_{jt}	R_{mt}	R_{jt}	R_{mt}
1	4.915***	0.897	3.612***	0.928
2	7.352***	0.566	3.460***	0.853
3	2.571**	0.508	1.794*	0.945
4	13.405***	2.097*	8.288***	2.604***
5	4.930***	1.775	3.336***	1.686*
6	2.615	1.250	1.759*	1.059
7	7.463***	0.525	5.327***	0.568
8	8.598***	1.393	5.093***	0.783
9	2.734**	0.708	2.121**	1.026
10	8.195***	0.279	4.854***	0.628
11	6.378***	1.373	3.958***	1.763*
12	0.923	0.118	1.022	0.524
13	4.474***	0.276	3.312**	0.629
14	2.699**	1.240	1.758*	2.160**
15	8.328***	1.461	5.050***	1.162
16	3.750***	1.352	2.573***	1.023
17	2.988**	0.880	2.125**	1.009
18	1.337	0.954	1.611*	0.856
19	2.636**	2.046*	1.628*	1.122
20	3.184***	1.728	1.794*	1.935**
21	11.333***	1.461	7.211***	2.051**
22	2.372**	3.035***	1.682*	2.299**

Notes: *Significant at 10% level.
** Significant at 5% level.
***Significant at 1% level.

Table 5. Tests for Market Leads and Lags:
Heavily Traded Stocks; Mean Squared Error Ratios

	Maximum Lag 5 Days, Dependent Variable		Maximum Lag 10 Days, Dependent Variable	
	R_{jt}	R_{mt}	R_{jt}	R_{mt}
Smallest	0.942	0.990	0.931	0.984
0.93-0.94	0	0	1	0
0.94-0.95	1	0	1	0
0.95-0.96	1	0	1	0
0.96-0.97	5	0	3	0
0.97-0.98	1	0	4	0
0.98-0.99	5	0	4	3
0.99-1.00	8	10	7	7
More than 1.00	1	12	1	12

be expected, we see from the tables that little is to be gained in attempting to use the individual rates for lightly traded stocks to predict the market rate.

We were concerned that our findings could be influenced by the omission of a relevant variable related to both individual rates and market rate. Accordingly, we repeated our analysis subtracting the risk-free interest rate from individual and market rates; that is, we tested for leads and lags between R_{jt}^* and R_{mt}^*, where

$$R_{jt}^* = R_{jt} - R_{ft}; \qquad R_{mt}^* = R_{mt} - R_{ft},$$

and R_{ft} is the risk-free rate, for which we employed the daily Federal Funds rate, obtained from the *Wall Street Journal*. Qualitatively our findings are unchanged. The null hypotheses of no leads or lags are very often rejected at the usual significance levels. However, in terms of mean squared error ratios, the relationships found are not terribly strong. Once again, the strongest relations appear to involve the market rate leading the rate of return on lightly traded stocks. Since the overall findings are similar to those in Tables 2 to 5, these results are not reported here.[3]

INTERTEMPORAL CASUAL RELATIONSHIPS BETWEEN MARKET AND INDIVIDUAL STOCK RETURNS

The analysis above provides results for a given period. It would be interesting to see whether the lead-lag relationship between market and individual stock returns may change over time. Also, we have restricted the order of autoregression to a fixed number K. This imposition may become troublesome when analyzing the intertemporal variations of the returns relationships because the order of autoregrssion may change over time as well as as across different securities. To explore the intertemporal stationarity of the dynamic market model, we apply to a more extensive dataset covering 1962-1986 a general dynamic structure, vector ARMA model (VARMA), proposed by Zellner and Palm (1974) and Sims (1980). This dynamic structure is capable of incorporating all competing hypotheses for returns relationships.

A General Dynamic Structure

A dynamic structure of any two economic variables, x and y, is composed of two elements: a within-variable relationship and a between-variable relation. Pierce (1979) suggests using "innovation variance" to separate these two elements. From a vector Gaussian process, $x_1, ..., x_t$, and $y_1, ..., y_t$, three innovation variance, $\tilde{\sigma}_x^2$, σ_x^2 and $\bar{\sigma}_x^2$, are defined as follows:

$$\tilde{\sigma}_x^2 = Var\left(x_t \mid x_{t-1}, ..., x_1\right), \tag{5}$$

$$\sigma_x^2 = Var\left(x_t \mid x_{t-1}, ..., x_1, y_{t-1}, ..., y_1\right), \tag{6}$$

$$\bar{\sigma}_x^2 = Var\left(x_t \mid x_{t-1}, ..., x_1, y_t, y_{t-1}, ..., y_1\right). \tag{7}$$

Likewise, $\tilde{\sigma}_y^2$, σ_y^2, and $\bar{\sigma}_y^2$ can be similarly defined. In general, these innovation variances are functions of time t. However, when x_t and y_t follow a general VARMA model, they are asymptotically independent of time t. These three variances are free from the "contamination" of a within-variable effect, and the difference among these three variances reveal the nature of between-variable effect, and the differences among these three variances reveal the nature of between-variable relations. Hence, the between-variable relations can be measured by the following modified coefficients of determination:

$$R_{x \cdot y}^2 = 1 - \frac{\sigma_x^2}{\tilde{\sigma}_x^2}, \qquad \bar{R}_{x \cdot y}^2 = 1 - \frac{\bar{\sigma}_x^2}{\sigma_x^2}$$

where $R_{x \cdot y}^2$ measures the marginal effect of past y on x and $\bar{R}_{x \cdot y}^2$ measures that of current y on x. The marginal effects of x on y, $R_{y \cdot x}^2$ and $\bar{R}_{y \cdot x}^2$, can be similarly defined.

Using these measurements of marginal effect, we can define five dynamic relations between x and y as follows:

A. x and y are *independent*, $x \wedge y$, if and only if

$$R_{x \cdot y}^2 = R_{y \cdot x}^2 = \bar{R}_{x \cdot y}^2 = \bar{R}_{y \cdot x}^2 = 0 \tag{8}$$

B. x and y are *contemporaneously related*, x$\leftrightarrow$ y, if and only if

$$R^2_{x \cdot y} = R^2_{y \cdot x} = 0 \quad \text{and} \quad \bar{R}^2_{x \cdot y} > 0 \quad \text{or} \quad \bar{R}^2_{y \cdot x} > 0. \tag{9}$$

C.   There is a *unidirectional relation* from y to x, $x \Rightarrow y$, if and only if

$$R^2_{x \cdot y} = 0 \quad \text{and} \quad R^2_{y \cdot x} > 0. \tag{10}$$

D.   There is a *unidirectional relation* from y to x, $x \Leftarrow y$, if and only if

$$R^2_{y \cdot x} = 0 \quad \text{and} \quad R^2_{x \cdot y} > 0. \tag{11}$$

E.   There is a *feedback relation* between x and y, $x \Leftrightarrow y$, if and only if

$$R^2_{x \cdot y} > 0 \quad \text{and} \quad R^2_{y \cdot x} > 0. \tag{12}$$

These definitions may be easily generalized to cases where x and y are two sets of variables. Pierce and Haugh (1977) and Pierce (1979) show that the above definitons of dynamic relations are equivalent to the Granger-Wiener causality described in Granger (1969).

A Vector ARMA Test

The vector ARMA model allows us to check all possible relations in a more systematic way. Testing the competing theories is regarded as a nonnested multiple decision problem, where all hypotheses are examined in a systematic way. Following Zellner and Palm (1974) and Sims (1980), we use a vector ARMA (VARMA) structure to represent the reduced form of the underlying econometric system. The order of the VARMA model can be determined by a procedure developed in Tiao and Tsay (1983). The association between the parameter constraints and the dynamic relationships in the VARMA formulation can be found in Kang (1981). Corresponding to each hypothesis, the parameters of the model are estimated by the maximum likelihood method developed in Hillmer and Tiao (1979), and the likelihood ratio statistic is calculated.

To examine the hypotheses in a systematic way, we take a position that a hypothesis should not be rejected in favor of a more restrictive one unless sufficient evidence indicates otherwise. Consequently, the proposed procedure starts from the most general hypothesis and then examines the relative validity of competing hypotheses in an increasing order of parametric restrictiveness. Details for this procedure can be seen in Chen and Lee (1990).

We report Table 6 the order of the VARMA model for each stock. Again, except for a few cases, the time series fit to the AR process very well and the order of the process does not exceed 5. Note that some stocks are dropped because of missing observations in our extended sample period. The whole period includes 6,151 observations (the first daily return is missing in the CRSP tape). It is then divided

Table 6.   Model Specification: Market Returns and Stock Returns

Stocks	Whole Period (2-6125)	Period 1 (2-1231)	Period 2 (1232-2461)	Period 3 (2462-3691)	Period 4 (3692-4921)	Period 5 (4922-6152)
			Heavily Traded Stocks			
2	AR(1)	MA(1)	AR(3)	AR(2)	AR(1)	AR(1)
3	AR(2)	MA(1)	AR(3)	AR(2)	AR(1)	AR(2)
4	AR(1)	AR(1)	AR(3)	AR(2)	AR(1)	AR(1)
5	MA(3)	ARMA(1,1)	AR(1)	AR(1)	AR(1)	AR(1)
6	AR(1)	AR(1)	AR(3)	AR(2)	AR(1)	AR(1)
7	AR(2)	AR(1)	AR(3)	AR(2)	AR(2)	AR(1)
8	AR(3)	AR(1)	AR(2)	AR(1)	AR(1)	AR(1)
9	AR(3)	MA(1)	AR(3)	AR(3)	AR(1)	AR(1)
10	AR(3)	AR(1)	AR(3)	AR(2)	AR(1)	AR(1)
12	AR(3)	MA(1)	AR(3)	AR(3)	AR(1)	AR(1)
13	AR(1)	AR(1)	AR(3)	AR(1)	AR(1)	AR(1)
14	AR(1)	AR(1)	AR(3)	AR(2)	AR(1)	AR(1)
15	AR(3)	AR(1)	AR(3)	AR(2)	AR(1)	AR(1)
16	AR(3)	AR(1)	AR(3)	AR(2)	AR(1)	AR(1)
17	AR(3)	AR(1)	AR(3)	AR(1)	AR(1)	AR(1)
19	MA(1)	AR(1)	AR(3)	AR(2)	AR(1)	AR(1)
20	AR(3)	AR(1)	AR(1)	AR(2)	AR(1)	AR(1)
21	AR(3)	AR(1)	AR(3)	AR(2)	AR(1)	AR(1)
23	AR(3)	AR(1)	AR(3)	AR(1)	AR(1)	AR(1)
25	AR(3)	AR(2)	AR(3)	AR(2)	AR(1)	AR(2)
24	AR(3)	AR(2)	AR(3)	AR(2)	AR(1)	AR(1)
26	AR(3)	AR(1)	AR(3)	AR(3)	AR(1)	AR(1)
27	AR(1)	AR(1)	AR(3)	AR(3)	AR(1)	AR(1)
			Lightly Traded Stocks			
11	ARMA(1,1)	AR(1)	AR(3)	AR(3)	AR(1)	AR(1)
12	AR(2)	AR(2)	AR(3)	AR(3)	AR(1)	AR(1)
13	AR(3)	AR(1)	AR(3)	AR(3)	AR(1)	AR(1)
17	AR(1)	AR(1)	AR(3)	AR(3)	AR(1)	AR(1)
20	AR(3)	AR(1)	AR(3)	AR(3)	AR(1)	AR(1)
22	AR(1)	AR(1)	AR(3)	AR(3)	AR(1)	AR(1)

into five subperiods. We report the results only for those stocks that have complete daily records in the whole period.

Table 7 reports the results based on the VARMA test. A 1% critical value is selected for the likelihood ratio test. It is found that the relations between market

Table 7.   The Dynamic Relations between Market Returns and
Stock Returns: Backward Procedure, 1% Critical Values[a]

Stocks	Whole Period (2-6125)	Period 1 (2-1231)	Period 2 (1232-2461)	Period 3 (2462-3691)	Period 4 (3692-4921)	Period 5 (4922-6152)
			Heavily Traded Stocks			
2	$R_{mt} \Rightarrow R_t$	$R_{mt} \Rightarrow R_t$	$R_{mt} \Rightarrow R_t$	$R_{mt} \Rightarrow R_t$	$R_{mt} \leftrightarrow R_t$	$R_{mt} \leftrightarrow R_t$
3	$R_{mt} \Rightarrow R_t$	$R_{mt} \leftrightarrow R_t$	$R_{mt} \Rightarrow R_t$	$R_{mt} \Rightarrow R_t$	$R_{mt} \leftrightarrow R_t$	$R_{mt} \leftrightarrow R_t$
4	$R_{mt} \Rightarrow R_t$	$R_{mt} \Rightarrow R_t$	$R_{mt} \Rightarrow R_t$	$R_{mt} \Rightarrow R_t$	$R_{mt} \Rightarrow R_t$	$R_{mt} \Rightarrow R_t$
5	$R_{mt} \Leftarrow R_t$	$R_{mt} \Rightarrow R_t$	$R_{mt} \Rightarrow R_t$	$R_{mt} \Rightarrow R_t$	$R_{mt} \leftrightarrow R_t$	$R_{mt} \Rightarrow R_t$
6	$R_{mt} \leftrightarrow R_t$	$R_{mt} \leftrightarrow R_t$	$R_{mt} \leftrightarrow R_t$	$R_{mt} \Rightarrow R_t$	$R_{mt} \leftrightarrow R_t$	$R_{mt} \leftrightarrow R_t$
7	$R_{mt} \leftrightarrow R_t$	$R_{mt} \leftrightarrow R_t$	$R_{mt} \Rightarrow R_t$	$R_{mt} \Rightarrow R_t$	$R_{mt} \Rightarrow R_t$	$R_{mt} \leftrightarrow R_t$
8	$R_{mt} \leftrightarrow R_t$	$R_{mt} \leftrightarrow R_t$	$R_{mt} \Rightarrow R_t$	$R_{mt} \leftrightarrow R_t$	$R_{mt} \Rightarrow R_t$	$R_{mt} \Rightarrow R_t$
9	$R_{mt} \Leftrightarrow R_t$	$R_{mt} \leftrightarrow R_t$	$R_{mt} \Rightarrow R_t$	$R_{mt} \Rightarrow R_t$	$R_{mt} \leftrightarrow R_t$	$R_{mt} \Leftarrow R_t$
10	$R_{mt} \Rightarrow R_t$	$R_{mt} \leftrightarrow R_t$	$R_{mt} \Leftrightarrow R_t$	$R_{mt} \Rightarrow R_t$	$R_{mt} \leftrightarrow R_t$	$R_{mt} \leftrightarrow R_t$
12	$R_{mt} \leftrightarrow R_t$	$R_{mt} \leftrightarrow R_t$	$R_{mt} \Leftrightarrow R_t$	$R_{mt} \leftrightarrow R_t$	$R_{mt} \Rightarrow R_t$	$R_{mt} \Rightarrow R_t$
13	$R_{mt} \Rightarrow R_t$	$R_{mt} \leftrightarrow R_t$	$R_{mt} \Rightarrow R_t$	$R_{mt} \Rightarrow R_t$	$R_{mt} \Rightarrow R_t$	$R_{mt} \Rightarrow R_t$
14	$R_{mt} \Rightarrow R_t$	$R_{mt} \leftrightarrow R_t$	$R_{mt} \Rightarrow R_t$	$R_{mt} \Rightarrow R_t$	$R_{mt} \leftrightarrow R_t$	$R_{mt} \leftrightarrow R_t$
15	$R_{mt} \Rightarrow R_t$	$R_{mt} \leftrightarrow R_t$	$R_{mt} \Rightarrow R_t$	$R_{mt} \Rightarrow R_t$	$R_{mt} \leftrightarrow R_t$	$R_{mt} \leftrightarrow R_t$
16	$R_{mt} \Rightarrow R_t$	$R_{mt} \leftrightarrow R_t$	$R_{mt} \Rightarrow R_t$	$R_{mt} \Rightarrow R_t$	$R_{mt} \Rightarrow R_t$	$R_{mt} \leftrightarrow R_t$
17	$R_{mt} \Rightarrow R_t$	$R_{mt} \Rightarrow R_t$	$R_{mt} \Rightarrow R_t$	$R_{mt} \Leftarrow R_t$	$R_{mt} \leftrightarrow R_t$	$R_{mt} \leftrightarrow R_t$
19	$R_{mt} \Rightarrow R_t$	$R_{mt} \Rightarrow R_t$	$R_{mt} \Rightarrow R_t$	$R_{mt} \Rightarrow R_t$	$R_{mt} \leftrightarrow R_t$	$R_{mt} \Rightarrow R_t$
20	$R_{mt} \Rightarrow R_t$	$R_{mt} \Rightarrow R_t$	$R_{mt} \Rightarrow R_t$	$R_{mt} \Rightarrow R_t$	$R_{mt} \Leftarrow R_t$	$R_{mt} \leftrightarrow R_t$
21	$R_{mt} \Leftrightarrow R_t$	$R_{mt} \Leftarrow R_t$	$R_{mt} \Rightarrow R_t$	$R_{mt} \Rightarrow R_t$	$R_{mt} \leftrightarrow R_t$	$R_{mt} \leftrightarrow R_t$
23	$R_{mt} \Rightarrow R_t$	$R_{mt} \Rightarrow R_t$	$R_{mt} \Rightarrow R_t$	$R_{mt} \Leftrightarrow R_t$	$R_{mt} \leftrightarrow R_t$	$R_{mt} \leftrightarrow R_t$
25	$R_{mt} \Rightarrow R_t$	$R_{mt} \Leftarrow R_t$	$R_{mt} \Rightarrow R_t$	$R_{mt} \Rightarrow R_t$	$R_{mt} \leftrightarrow R_t$	$R_{mt} \leftrightarrow R_t$
24	$R_{mt} \Rightarrow R_t$	$R_{mt} \Rightarrow R_t$	$R_{mt} \Rightarrow R_t$	$R_{mt} \Rightarrow R_t$	$R_{mt} \leftrightarrow R_t$	$R_{mt} \leftrightarrow R_t$
26	$R_{mt} \Rightarrow R_t$	$R_{mt} \leftrightarrow R_t$	$R_{mt} \Rightarrow R_t$	$R_{mt} \Rightarrow R_t$	$R_{mt} \leftrightarrow R_t$	$R_{mt} \leftrightarrow R_t$
27	$R_{mt} \Rightarrow R_t$	$R_{mt} \Rightarrow R_t$	$R_{mt} \Rightarrow R_t$	$R_{mt} \Rightarrow R_t$	$R_{mt} \leftrightarrow R_t$	$R_{mt} \leftrightarrow R_t$
			Lightly Traded Stocks			
11	$R_{mt} \Rightarrow R_t$	$R_{mt} \leftrightarrow R_t$	$R_{mt} \Rightarrow R_t$	$R_{mt} \Rightarrow R_t$	$R_{mt} \Rightarrow R_t$	$R_{mt} \Rightarrow R_t$
12	$R_{mt} \Rightarrow R_t$	$R_{mt} \leftrightarrow R_t$	$R_{mt} \Rightarrow R_t$	$R_{mt} \leftrightarrow R_t$	$R_{mt} \leftrightarrow R_t$	$R_{mt} \Rightarrow R_t$
13	$R_{mt} \Rightarrow R_t$	$R_{mt} \Rightarrow R_t$	$R_{mt} \Rightarrow R_t$	$R_{mt} \wedge R_t$	$R_{mt} \Rightarrow R_t$	$R_{mt} \leftrightarrow R_t$
17	$R_{mt} \Rightarrow R_t$	$R_{mt} \Rightarrow R_t$	$R_{mt} \leftrightarrow R_t$	$R_{mt} \Rightarrow R_t$	$R_{mt} \leftrightarrow R_t$	$R_{mt} \leftrightarrow R_t$
20	$R_{mt} \Rightarrow R_t$	$R_{mt} \Rightarrow R_t$	$R_{mt} \Rightarrow R_t$	$R_{mt} \Rightarrow R_t$	$R_{mt} \Rightarrow R_t$	$R_{mt} \Rightarrow R_t$
22	$R_{mt} \Rightarrow R_t$	$R_{mt} \Rightarrow R_t$	$R_{mt} \Rightarrow R_t$	$R_{mt} \Rightarrow R_t$	$R_{mt} \leftrightarrow R_t$	$R_{mt} \Rightarrow R_t$

and individual stocks are not quite stable over time—only 2 stocks (stocks 4 and 20) show consistent relationship over the 5 subperiods. Examining the case of the whole period among the 23 heavily traded firms, we observe the relationship that the market rate leads the rate of return on individual stock $(R_m \Leftrightarrow R_t)$ for 16 firms. Such relationship is found in all 6 lightly traded stocks. The results are quite consistent with those obtained by the traditional Granger test in Section II. However, when we examine the results over time, the situations are not that clear. During periods 2 and 3, the relationship $(R_{mt} \Rightarrow R_t)$ is still supported by the empirical results (20 out of 23 heavily traded stocks and 5 out of 6 lightly traded stocks reveal such relationship for period 2, 19 out of 23 and 4 out of 6 for period 3.) On the other hand, a contemporaneous relation $(R_{mt} \leftrightarrow R_t)$ that is consistent with the traditional static market model of (1), is found adequate for 12, 16, and 16 out of 23 heavily traded stocks during periods 1, 4, and 5, respectively. There are a few cases exhibiting feedback and independent relations between market and individual stock returns. Since the frequencies of such events are relatively low, we may regard them as a consequence of market variations.

In summary, we find mixed results on the intertemporal relationship between market and individual stock returns. For periods 2 and 3, we obtain the relationship $R_{mt} \Rightarrow R_t$. During periods 1, 4, and 5, a contemporaneous relation $(R_{mt} \leftrightarrow R_t)$ is better supported by the data.

IMPLICATIONS OF THE EMPIRICAL RESULTS

The empirical results of the previous sections provide some evidence supporting the existence of a dynamic market model, confirming the findings of Reinganum (1982). However, while Reinganum's major concern is with the precision of ordinary least squares estimates of beta, we have focused attention on assessing the strength of the dynamic aspects of the relationship and distinguishing between practical significance and statistical significance.[4] Using the criterion of prediction mean squared error, we have found that the practical importance of the dynamic specification is not terribly great, though market leads over lightly traded stocks returns do not appear to be somewhat stronger than those over heavily traded stock returns. Certainly we have found strong evidence for the existence of leads and lags, but it appears that, for many practical purposes, these will be only of minor importance. Hence, while we find strong statistical evidence of market inefficiency, the extent of that inefficiency appears not to be very severe. This finding is generally consistent with Hillmer and Yu's (1980) concerns about markets' adjustment speed with respect to information release. Moreover, two additional factors suggest that any underlying relationships may be even weaker than we have reported. Newbold (1978) has shown that, if one or other of a pair of time series variables is measured with errors, spurious causal relationships can arise between the measured variables, and any true relationship can be magnified.

Since the market rate of return index used in practice is a proxy for the unobserved "true" rate, measurement errors could constitute a partial explanation of some of our findings of dynamic relationships. In addition, Tiao and Wei (1976) have shown that, through time aggregation, inherently unidirectional relationships can take on the spurious appearance of feedback. This could account for our rather surprising finding that rates of return for some lightly traded stocks appear to lead as well as lag behind the market rate. Although it is impossible to quantify the effects of these two factors, they must be kept in mind when attempting to interpret empirical findings on dynamic specification.

The empirical results also provide evidence of structural changes in the dynamic relationship between the market and individual stock returns. We find both the order of lags and the nature of the relationship (lead or lag) may change over time. To the extent that the lead and lag terms are important for an unbiased estimation of the systematic risk, researchers should carefully examine the intertemporal relations between returns series before they apply Dimson's aggregate coefficient method to estimate betas from the dynamic market model.

MODEL

In this paper, we have considered the possibility of departure from the simple static market model for individual rates of return, contemplating the existence of leads and lags in the system. Using long series of daily data, for both heavily traded and lightly traded stocks, we have found statistical evidence indicating that the simple market model is often misspecified against alternatives involving a market lead. This evidence is particularly strong for the lightly traded stocks. A multiple hypotheses testing procedure and the VARMA test are employed to investigate the intertemporal relationship between market and individual stock returns. We find that the structure of the dynamic relations changes over time. Consequently, applying any fixed-order lead-lag structure to a dynamic market model over different time periods might result in improper estimation of security betas. To obtain more accurate estimates of the systematic risk, researchers should carefully scrutinize return series and examine the stability of the fitted model.

NOTES

1. Any instantaneous relationship between the two series is absorbed in the off-diagonal elements of the covariant matrix.

2. These are the most and least heavily traded stocks on which we are able to obtain complete daily records in the sampling period. Trading volume is used to provide this measure.

3. These results are available from the authors.

4. In principle, our results support both the Dimson (1979) and Reinganum (1982) methods of estimating beta coefficients. However, our results indicate that the market lag variables in their specifications are likely to be less important than the market lead variables.

REFERENCES

Ansley, C.F., & Newbold, P. (1979). Multivariate parial autocorrelations. Proceedings of Business and Economic Statistics Section, American Statistical Association, 349-353.

Chen, C., & Lee, C.J. (1990). A vector of ARMA test on the the Gibson paradox. *Review of Economics and Statistics, 72,* 96-107.

Dimson, E. (1979). Risk measurement when shares are subject to infrequent trading. *Journal of Financial Economics, 7,* 197-226.

Granger, C.W.J. (1969). Investing causal relations by econometric models and cross-spectral methods. *Econometrica, 37,* 424-438.

Hannan, E.J. (1980). the estimatino of the order of an ARMA process. *Annals of Statistics, 8,* 1071-1081.

Hillmer, S.C., & Tiao, G.C. (1979). Likelihood function of stationary multiple autoregressive moving average models. *Jounral of American Statistical Association, 74,* 652-660.

Hillmer, S.C., & Yu, P.L. (1980). Markets' adjustment speed with respect to information release. *Jounral of Financial Economics, 7,* 321-345.

Kang, H. (1981). Necessary and sufficient conditions for causality testing in multivariate ARMA models. *Jounral of Time Series, 2,* 95-101.

Nelson, C.R., & Schwert, G.B (1982). Tests for predictive relationship between time series variables: A Monte Carlo investigation. *Jounral of American Statistical Association, 71,* 11-18.

Newbold, P. (1978). Feedback induced by measurement errors. *International Economic Review, 19,* 787-791.

Pierce, D.A. (1979). R^2 measures for time series. *Journal of the American Statistical Association, 74,* 901-910.

Pierce, D.A., & Haugh, L.D. (1977). Causality in temporal systems: Characterizations and survey. *Jounral of Econometrica, 5,* 265-293.

Reinganum, M.R. (1982). A direct test of Roll's conjecture on the firm size effect. *Jounal of Finance, 37,* 27-35.

Sims, C.A. (1972). Money, income and causality. *American Economic Review, 62,* 540-552.

Sims, C.A. (1980). Macro-economic and reality. *Econometrica, 48,* 1-48.

Tiao, G.C., & Tsay, R.S. (1983). Multiple time series modeling and extended sample cross-correlations. *Journal of Business and Economic Statistics, 1,* 43-56.

Tiao, G.C., & Wei, W.S. (1976). Effect of temporal aggregation on the dynamci relationship of two time series variables. *Biometrika, 63,* 513-523.

Zellner, A., & Palm, F. (1974). Time series analysis and simultaneous equation econometric models. *Journal of Econometics, 2,* 17-54.

VOLUME AND INTERVENTION EFFECTS ON YEN/DOLLAR EXCHANGE RATE VOLATILITY, 1977-1979

Robert A. Connolly and William M. Taylor

ABSTRACT

Current research shows exchange rate volatility is time varying. This paper presents empirical estimates of the effects of central bank intervention and turnover volume on daily spot exchange rate volatility. The observed conditional volatility is the net result of market forces and intervention activity. We find that unexpectedly large turnover volume and intervention volume are both associated with relatively high conditional volatility. Our data indicate that the Bank of Japan often intervenes on days that would otherwise have relatively high conditional volatility. These interventions appear to have only limited success in resisting market forces so that conditional volatility net of intervention activity is still larger on intervention days. Intervention effects also depend on the underlying policy environment.

Advances in Financial Planning and Forecasting,
Volume 5, pages 181-200.
Copyright © 1994 by JAI Press Inc.
All rights of reproduction in any form reserved.
ISBN:1-55938-421-2

INTRODUCTION

Since the adoption of the flexible foreign exchange (FX) rate system in the early 1970s, FX rates have displayed higher, unstable volatility. This instability in FX rate changes and their volatilities is well documented. It has been reported by Mussa (1979), Cumby and Obstfeld (1981), Hodrick and Srivastava (1984), Bollerslev (1987), Jorion (1988), Giovannini and Jorion (1989), Hsieh (1989), and Hodrick (1989), among others.

It is important to explain this time variation in FX rate volatility for several reasons. First, volatility is a central feature of modern asset-pricing theory. Econometric evaluations of these theories must properly account for the causes and form of conditional volatility. Second, FX rate volatility is important in pricing derivative assets such as currency options. Sensible pricing and trading strategies clearly depend on understanding the determinants of FX rate volatility. Third, there is some international trade analysis [see, e.g. Cushman (1986)] suggesting that volatile FX rates may raise the risk and lower the volume of trade.

Financial economic research accords a prominent role to information release as the proximate source of price volatility. For example, Admati and Pfleiderer (1988) develop a model of trading patterns relating volume and volatility in markets with liquidity and informed traders. Ross (1989) provides a no-arbitrage model in which the variance of price changes and the rate of information flow are directly related. On the empirical side, Patell and Wolfson (1984) find in the equity market that large increases in the variance of intraday returns follow earnings announcements. The empirical literature on mixtures of distributions is generally based on using the rate of information flow as the mixing variable that controls the sampling from distributions with different variances.[1]

This paper focuses on central bank intervention volume and turnover volume as proxies for the rate of information arrival in the spot FX market. Specifically, we investigate the relationships of intervention volume with the conditional mean and variance of daily changes in spot FX rates. Our empirical work examines these relationships in the Tokyo spot FX market in the late 1970s. Further, our analysis addresses these relationships in the context of major changes in underlying economic policy.[2]

Government releases of economic data and announcements of policy changes are examples of information releases with possible volatility effects. A number of studies, including Dornbusch (1980), Frenkel (1981), Edwards (1982), Hakkio and Pearce (1985), Ito and Roley (1987), and Hardevoulis (1988) examine the effects of "news" (represented as unexpected changes in economic variables) on FX rates. The economic variables include the spread between short-and long-term interest rates, money supply, inflation, and industrial production.

Recently, some researchers have developed models in which central bank actions are signaling devices.[3] In these models, sterilized interventions can affect FX rates because they communicate inside information to exchange market participants. In the context of these models, the volume and direction of intervention may reveal information about government economic policy that may be unavailable or unbelievable from other sources.

For example, Stein (1989) considers a signaling model of monetary policy announcements in which the Fed can credibly signal information to the market by limiting itself to declaring preferences over ranges of interest rate or FX rate outcomes. On the empirical side, Marston (1988) finds some support for the signaling view in the market response to the G-5 meeting in September 1985, which ended with an announcement that the central banks would cooperate to insure further depreciation of the dollar. Even though there was virtually no change in interest differentials, significant FX rate volatility followed the announcement. Dominguez (1989) studies the effects of coordinated and unilateral central bank interventions over the 1985-1987 period using a model in which central bank interventions affect FX rates by conveying inside information and/or changing market expectations. She concludes that some episodes of unilateral intervention significantly influence market expectations. Coordinated interventions had longer-lived and significantly different expectations effects.

A critical factor in these models of intervention signaling is the credibility of central bank policy. Intervention activities that are consistent with trader perceptions of monetary policy are more likely to be credible. Inconsistent intervention and monetary policy may raise volatility because traders have greater difficulty separating signal from noise in the central bank's behavior. Thus, the effect of intervention on spot FX rate volatility depends on the information environment. The credibility of government policy, past policy choices (which may reveal the central bank's reaction function), and recent market history are all important aspects of that information environment.

In our view, central bank interventions may have several, potentially different effects on FX rate volatility. To the extent that central bank interventions communicate new information to market participants, interventions may increase short-term FX rate volatility. As an empirical matter, we would not expect such interventions to be routine since they are most likely to accompany major shifts in government policy and such shifts are infrequent. Much intervention activity appears to be directed at smoothing movements in FX rates, a "leaning against the wind" policy. If the bank's intervention policy is to reduce FX rate change volatility by leaning against the wind, the intervention activity may reduce volatility (relative to freely floating FX rates), particularly if the policy is credible.[4] Models of central bank resistance to FX rate changes, such as Corrado and Taylor (1986), conclude that specific intervention rules can reduce the variance of FX rate changes relative to the variance of freely floating FX rate changes. In their model, the central bank consistently and predictably follows a specific intervention rule.

Thus, depending on the underlying policy, we might expect different volatility effects to accompany central bank interventions. Our aim is to provide empirical evidence on this question. We explore this issue by focusing on the specific case of the Bank of Japan's intervention in the Tokyo spot FX market for the October 1977-December 1979 period.

The next section describes the dataset we use, Japanese macroeconomic and financial policies, and changes in those policies during the sample period. Section 3 develops the econometric models of daily FX rate changes and conditional volatility that we estimate. In section 4, we discuss our empirical results. A summary and conclusions are offered in Section 5.

DATA AND POLICY:
JAPAN IN THE LATE 1970s

Our examination of the intervention-volume-volatility relationship uses data for the Tokyo spot FX market. Taya (1983) reports daily data on the ¥/$ FX rate, Bank of Japan (BOJ) intervention volume, and U.S. dollar turnover volume in the Tokyo market.[5] Our sample contains 559 daily observations from October 3, 1977, through December 31, 1979. This period is interesting at least in part because of the major policy changes in Japan, independent BOJ actions in financial markets, and the apparent lack of integration of the Tokyo capital markets with those in Europe and the United States. These features will be discussed in more detail in this section.

Figures 1-4 graph the daily ¥/S FX rate, changes in log (FX rates), intervention volume, and turnover volume, respectively. Figure 1 shows the FX rate generally falling until October 1978 and rising (through not monotonically) through the end of the sample period. BOJ intervention involved dollar support through October 1978 and yen support from November 1978 through the end of the sample. Figure 2 indicates no particular pattern in FX rate changes other than some relatively large changes. As Figure 3 shows, intervention volume exhibits considerable bunching with very large spikes. During the sample period, the BOJ frequently intervened on a sequence of days rather than on isolated days. Figure 4 graphs daily turnover volume.

Table 1 provides the descriptive statistics for the changes in log (FX rates) and turnover volume for the entire sample, BOJ dollar buy days, BOJ dollar days, and nonintervention days.[4] The mean log (FX rate) change is negative on dollar buy days and is positive on sell days. The table also shows the statistics for the first and second subperiods, which correspond to the dollar support and yen support periods, respectively. Average turnover volume (in hundreds of millions of dollars) is larger on dollar sale days than on dollar buy days. This may only reflect the fact that all dollar sales were in the second subsample, where volume is on average higher than during the first subsample. Volume appears to be smaller on nonintervention days than intervention days, though the difference is small for dollar purchase days. The other sample moments for both variables vary across subsamples.

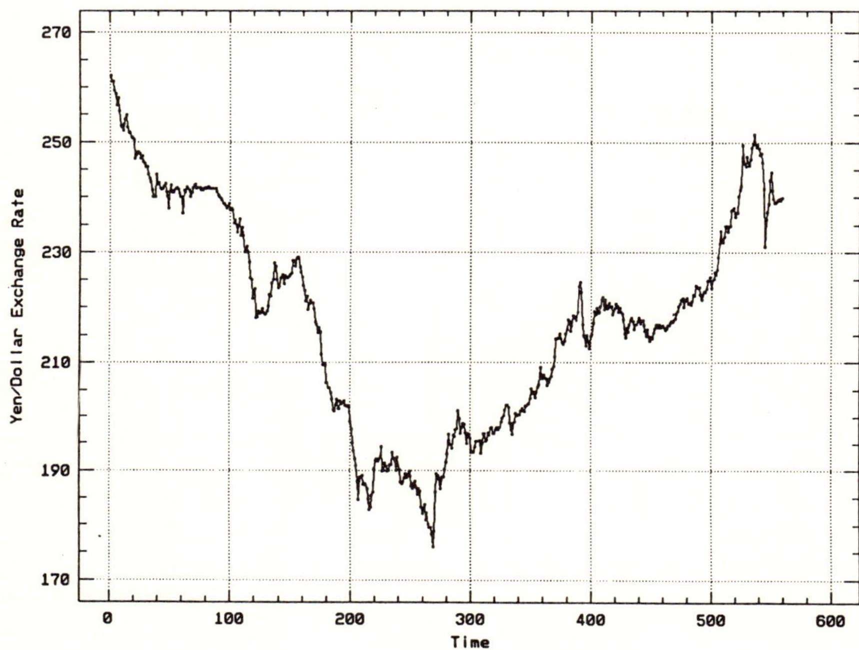

Figure 1.   Daily ¥/$ exchange rate, Oct. 1977-Dec. 1979

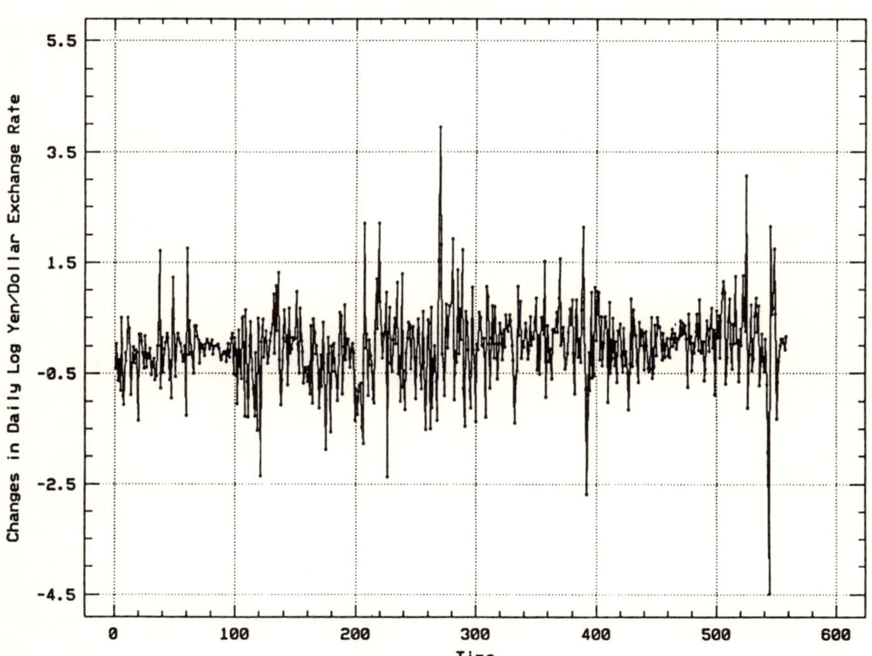

Figure 2.   Changes in daily log (¥/$ rate), Oct. 1977-Dec. 1979

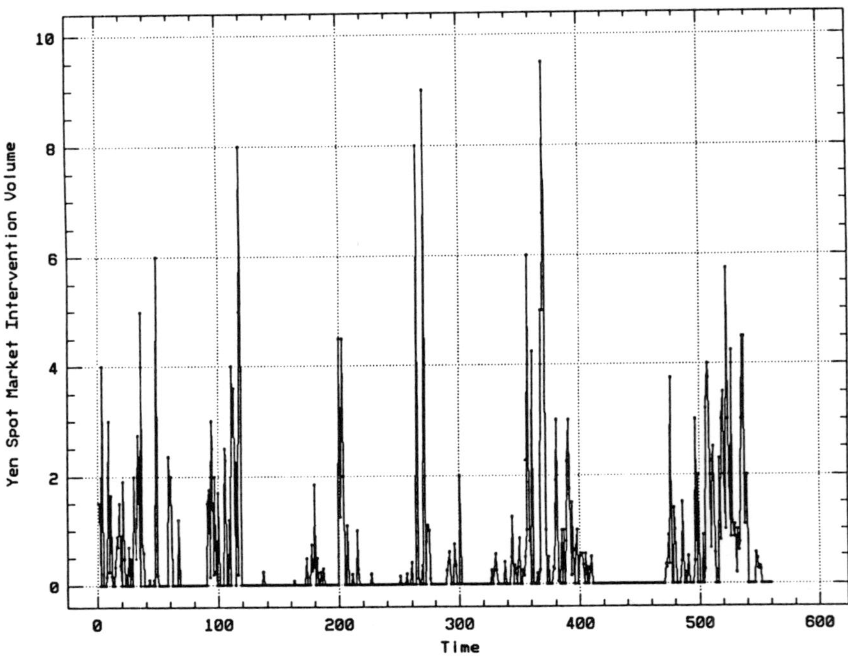

Figure 3.　　BOJ intervention volume, Oct. 1977-Dec. 1979

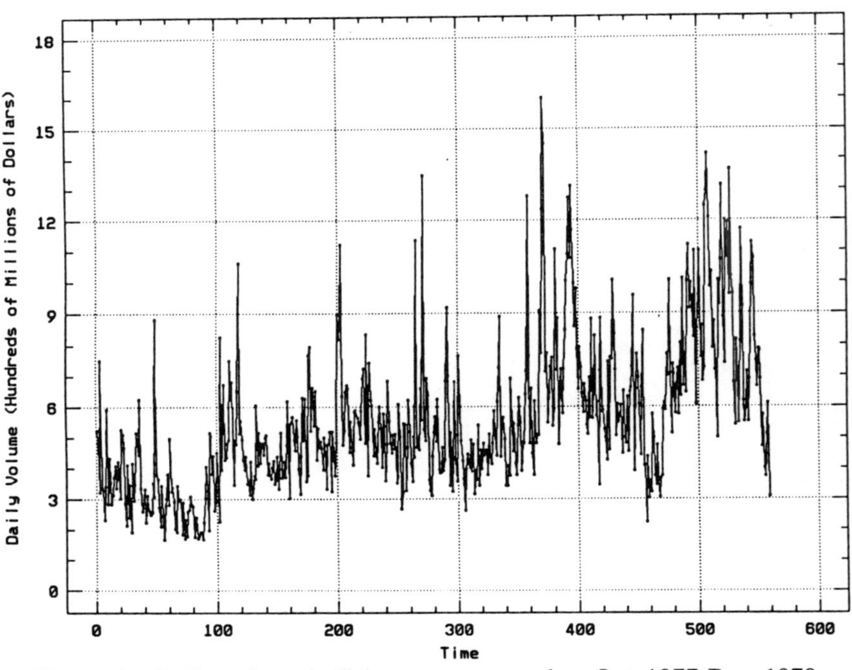

Figure 4.　　Daily volume in Tokyo spot yen market, Oct. 1977-Dec. 1979

Table 1.   Descriptive Statistics on the Daily Changes in ¥/$
Spot Log (FX) Changes and Turnover Volume[a]

Period	Number of observations	Mean	Variance	Skewness	Kurtosis
Δln (FX)					
All days	556	−0.0161	0.5075	−0.0516	5.533*
Buy days	87	−0.4784*	0.5911	2.211*	12.26*
Sell days	108	0.2814*	0.5269	−0.0750	3.685*
No intervention days	360	0.0005	0.3943	−0.9372*	8.482*
$ support period	268	−0.1485*	0.4235	−0.0251	1.845*
¥ support period	288	0.1072	0.5559	−0.1901	8.070*
Volume					
All days	556	5.566*	5.944	1.173*	1.556*
Buy days	87	5.414*	4.446	1.269*	2.357*
Sell days	108	8.205*	7.143	0.6523*	−0.1757
No intervention days	360	4.797*	3.225	0.9329*	1.208*
$ support period	268	4.408*	2.699	1.051*	2.246*
¥ support period	288	6.645*	6.561	0.9681*	0.6497*

Notes: [a] An asterisk on the mean indicates the estimate is significantly different from zero at the .01 level. For skewness (kurtosis), the asterisk indicates the estimate is significantly different from 0 (3), the value consistent with the data being drawn from a normal distribution. One observation in the second subsample had both buy and sell activity but the volumes were offsetting. We have deleted this observation to calculate the above statistics for the buy and sell subsamples.

A number of changes in Japanese financial, regulatory, and macroeconomic policy occurred over this period. The 1970s were a period of gradual liberalization of Japanese financial markets culminating in virtually total financial decontrol in 1980. Before deregulation, foreign exchange transactions were restricted as part of a general program of capital controls.[7] Japanese authorities promoted capital exports from 1976 until late 1978. Beginning in mid-1977, Japanese security firms and others were permitted to acquire foreign securities and Japanese foreign exchange banks had expanded overseas lending authority. Capital imports were discouraged. A 50% reserve requirement was placed on yen accounts owned by foreigners in 1977 and it was raised to 100% the following year.

In late 1978, the expansionary macroeconomic and financial policy of the previous few years was reversed as the Japanese current account sank into deficit, the yen begin depreciating, and OPEC announced a second round of sizable oil price increases. The Japanese government liberalized capital import restrictions in February 1979 by eliminating reserve requirements on yen accounts. Nonresidents were permitted access to the Gensaki (short-term bond repurchase) market and negotiable-rate yen-denominated CDs were introduced in May 1979[8] Overseas lending by banks was discouraged. These policies were intended to stem the depreciation of the yen.

In view of the major policy changes during the sample period, our empirical analyses use dummy variables to split the sample at the end of October 1978 to permit changes in coefficients. Our approach is consistent with the finding of Loopeski (1984) that the intervention-FX rate relationship differs before and after November 1, 1978.

The data do not include contemporaneous intervention data for other countries, but there are several reasons why it is reasonable to assume that the BOJ intervention volume captures the effects that are most important in the Tokyo market during this period[9] First, during the yen appreciation period, unilateral capital controls were in place (see Ito, 1986). Argy describes BOJ policy during this period as directed at FX rate management through capital controls and direct interventions[10] He accords capital controls a significant role in reversing the appreciation of the yen. Also, tests by Ito (1988) reject interest rate parity during this period and he attributes this to the effectiveness of capital controls.[11]

Second, accounts of central bank behavior during this period indicate independent action by the BOJ. The BOJ rarely intervened outside the Tokyo market, and other central banks just as infrequently conducted operations in the Tokyo market. Loopesko's attempts to evaluate the effectiveness of coordinated intervention were compromised by the very few examples of coordinated intervention, (see p. 270). Further, Taya reports no clear evidence that BOJ intervention spilled over into the European exchange markets.

Finally, the evidence indicates the Tokyo capital markets were not integrated with other major capital markets in the sample period. Gültekin, Gültekin, and Penati (1989) tested for integration of the Tokyo capital markets before and after 1980. They did not find evidence of integration for the period including our sample period. This result is consistent with the lack of interest rate parity found by Ito during this period.

A MODEL OF INTERVENTION, TURNOVER VOLUME, AND EXCHANGE RATE VOLATILITY

We now develop an econometric model relating the expected value and the conditional volatility of daily FX rate changes to intervention volume and turnover volume. The descriptive statistics in Table 1 and our description of policy in Section 2 indicate that the mean equation should accommodate the possibility of changing coefficients across the subperiods.[12] Following Frenkel(1981), "news" about economic fundamentals may lead to FX rate changes.[13] With these considerations in mind, we specify the basic mean equation as:

$$\Delta \ln (FX_t) = \alpha_1 UP_t + \alpha_2 DOWN_t + \sum_{j=1}^{8} \beta_j TPSPRU_{t-j} + e_t, \tag{1}$$

where $\Delta\ln(FX_t)$ is the daily change in log (FX rates) from time t-1 to t, UP_t ($DOWN_t$)is a dummy variable equal to 1 in the dollar (yen) support subperiod and 0 otherwise, and e_t is the error term. The $TPSPRU_{t-j}$ are the lagged unexpected term premium differentials between the two countries.[14]

We use the unexpected term premium as our news measure. The U.S. term premium is defined as the 90-day Treasury bill rate less the 30-day Treasury bill rate. For Japan, the term premium is the bill rate less the call loan rate. The term premium spread is the U.S. term premium (at t - 1) minus the Japanese term premium (at t). The difference in timing is required by the significant offset in trading hours between the U.S. and Japanese capital markets.[15] Our news measure is defined as the observed minus the expected term premium differential. We measure the expected values as the predicted values from an autoregressive model for the term premium differentials. The details of these estimates are not reported here but are available from the authors on request.

The term premium (long rate-short rate) in each country gives information about expected future movements in interest rates. In an informationally efficient market system, differences in the term premium between two countries should reflect expectations about relative interest rate movements.[16] In turn, these expectations ought to affect FX rate movements.[17]

The general treatment of FX rate follows recent studies in financial economics (see, e.g., Schwert 1990; Schwert & Seguin, 1990). These studies apply suggestions from Davidian and Carroll (1987) for estimating conditional variance functions of form:

$$V[\Delta\ln(FX_t) \mid \Omega_{t-1}] = f(\mathbf{X}_t'\beta)\,\sigma^2, \tag{2}$$

where Ω_{t-1} represents the information set at time $_{t-1}$, $f(\cdot)$ is a function that shifts the variance σ^2, depending on the linear combination β of explanatory variables $\mathbf{X}_t$.[18] Davidian and Carroll find that estimates of conditional standard deviations that are based on the residuals from the estimated mean regression are more robust to departures from conditional normality than models using residuals or squared residuals (as in ARCH and GARCH models).[19]

The model of the conditional standard deviation of $\Delta\ln(FX_t)$ that we estimate is:

$$|\hat{u}|_t = \sigma_1 UP_t + \sigma_2 DOWN_t + \sigma_3 M_t + \sigma_4 NVOLU_t + \sigma_5 IBVOLU_t$$

$$+\sigma_6 ISVOLU_t + \sum_{i=1}^{4} \rho_i |\hat{u}|_{t-i} + \rho_5 M_{t-1} |\hat{u}|_{t-1} + v_t, \tag{3}$$

where $|\hat{u}|_t$ is the product of the absolute residual from Equation (1) and $(\pi/2)^{1/2}$(see, e.g, Schwert, 1990) and v_t is the error term. The explanatory variables in equation (3) are UP_t ($DOWN_t$), a dummy variable that is 1 for the dollar (yen) support and 0 otherwise; M_t is the unexpected net turnover dollar volume; $IBVOLU_t$, the unexpected intervention dollar buy volume; and $ISVOLU_t$ the unexpected intervention dollar sell volume.

Our focus on unexpected volume presumes information is conveyed by turnover volume that differs from "normal".[20] To measure unexpected net turnover volume, we estimate separate models for intervention volume and total market volume. We compute unexpected net turnover volume as unexpected (or residual) total market volume less unexpected (or residual) intervention volume.[21] This seems more appropriate than calculating net volume directly and taking the residuals from a model of net volume because in real FX markets, traders must estimate both total volume *and* central bank volume. Computations that begin by calculating net volume directly assume that at least one of the component series in known.[22]

We also use the central bank intervention volume model to compute unexpected intervention volume. To measure $IBVOLU_t$ and $ISVOLU_t$, we separate the unexpected intervention volume series into two data series covering buy days (when the central bank bought dollars) and sell days (when the central bank sold dollars). Our formulation allows asymmetries in the volatility response to purchases and sales by the central bank. Given the patterns of actual intervention behavior, this specification captures differences in intervention volatility effects related to policy changes.[23]

The UP and DOWN variables permit conditional volatility to vary between the yen appreciation and dollar appreciation periods. The data in Table 1 show the unconditional variance of FX rate changes is 31% higher in the yen support than the dollar support segment of the time series. In our specification, conditional volatility can also be different on Monday relative to other days of the week. This is consistent with results from equity market studies and FX market volatility models.[24]

Finally, our specification also permits volatility persistence as captured by the lagged dependent variables in equation (3).[25] There is ample evidence of such persistence in the volatility of FX rate changes.[26] The final term, an interaction between the lagged Monday dummy variable and lagged volatility, eliminates any spillover effects of the lagged absolute residual if the previous day is a Monday.

Based on the preceding discussion, we expect $\sigma_4 > 0$ because positive, unexpected turnover volume should indicate new information which in turn raises volatility. To the extent that positive, unexpected central bank intervention volume conveys information to the market, we expect σ_5 and σ_6 will also be positive. There is, however, another potential explanation for these signs. The observed, unexpected FX rate change impounds both intervention effects and market forces. If the BOJ's effect is primarily due to a consistent leaning against the wind policy, unexpected intervention volume may still be positively correlated with daily, observed volatility. This result follows from two characteristics of bank interventions. First, if the bank follows a leaning against the wind policy, the bank will be more likely to intervene on days when the unexpected FX rate changes is large and in the undesired direction. Second, Loopesko and others have found central bank interventions are not particularly influential in affecting FX rates. Thus, while the BOJ is more likely to intervene on days with high volatility, it is unlikely that the intervention will completely offset market forces. Consequently, observed volatility may be larger on intervention days than on days when the central bank does not intervene. Interpreting estimates of equation (3) may hinge, in part, on understanding other details of the intervention process.

We expect $\rho_i > 0$, indicating the autoregressive nature of conditional volatility that has been reported in other studies (see note 24). We also expect $\sigma_3 > 0$ (Monday volatility is higher) and $\sigma_1 \neq \sigma_2$ since the unconditional variances appear quite different for the two subsamples.

We estimate Equations (1) and (3) by an iterative weighted least squares process also used in Schwert (1990) and Schwert and Seguin (1990). As suggested by Davidian and Carroll, initial estimates of Equations (1) and (3) are by least squares. Then, using standard deviation estimates from Equation (3), we reestimate Equation (1) using weighted least squares. Residuals from the weighted least squares estimates are unweighted and used to reestimate Equation (3). Davidian and Carroll recommend three iterations between the two equations but we stopped at two iterations because estimates were unaffected by further iteration.

EMPIRICAL RESULTS

We report the results of our empirical work in Tables 2-4. We turn first to the estimates of the mean Equation (1), which are reported in Table 2. The data appear

Table 2. Iterated Estimates of Mean Equation (1) [a]

Variable	Coefficient	Standard error
Up_t	0.1158*	0.0212
DOWN_t	-0.0331	0.0377
TPSPRU_{t-1}	0.0574	0.0717
TPSPRU_{t-2}	0.0843	0.0700
TPSPRU_{t-3}	-0.0512	0.0480
TPSPRU_{t-4}	0.0306	0.0570
TPSPRU_{t-5}	0.0349	0.0619
TPSPRU_{t-6}	0.0080	0.0715
TPSPRU_{t-7}	-0.0268	0.0658
TPSPRU_{t-8}	0.0200	0.1925

Notes: [a] An asterisk indicates a coefficient estimate is statistically significant at the .01 level. To calculate the standard errors, we have used the same heteroscedastic - and autocorrelation-resistant covariance matrix estimator employed by Schwert and Seguin (1990).

Table 3.   Iterated Estimates of Volatility Equation $(3)^a$

Variable	Coefficient	Standard error
M_t	0.3963*	0.1005
UP_t	0.2934*	0.0500
$DOWN_t$	0.2444*	0.0570
$IBVOLU_t$	0.1996*	0.0716
$ISVOLU_t$	0.0844*	0.0269
$NVOLU_t$	0.1658*	0.0211
$\|\hat{u}\|_{t-1}$	0.1837*	0.0708
$\|\hat{u}\|_{t-2}$	0.0225	0.0387
$\|\hat{u}\|_{t-3}$	0.1238*	0.0460
$\|\hat{u}\|_{t-4}$	0.0745*	0.0336
$M_t\|\hat{u}\|_{t-1}$	0.0309	0.0430

Notes: [a] An asterisk indicates a coefficient estimate is statistically significant at the .01 level. To calculate the standard errors, we have used the same heteroscedastic-and autocorrelation-resistant covariance matrix estimator employed by Schwert and seguin(1990).

Table 4.   Average Mean Equation (1) Residuals
by Period and Intervention Activity^a

Intervention action	Number of observations	Mean	Variance	Skewness	Kurtosis
Dollar support period					
Buy dollars	59	−.5342*	4063	.2946	1.572*
Sell dollars	0				
No intervention	179	.0291	.3891	−.0371	2.784*
Yen support period					
Buy dollars	10	−.0494	3.096	1.490	1.874
Sell dollars	109	.1872*	.5536	.0555	3.442
No intervention	170	−.1201*	.4140	−1.531*	10.58*

Notes: [a] An asterisk on the mean indicates the estimate is significantly from 0 at the .01 level. For skewness and kurtosis, the asterisk indicates the estimate is significantly from 0 and 3, the values consistent with the data being drawn from a normal distribution.

to have a strong trend element for the dollar support period (UP). For the yen support period (DOWN), the trend has the opposite sign but is statistically insignificant. None of our unexpected term premium differential variables are statistically significant. We found this result held even with a smaller number of lag values. The Box-Pierce Q-statistic for the model has an insignificant p-value of only .35.

Table 3 contains estimates of our volatility model [Equation(3)]. We find our expectations about the relationship between volatility, turnover volume, and intervention volume are borne out by the data. Positive, unexpected turnover volume is associated with higher conditional volatility. This result echoes findings from other speculative markets and supports financial models that connect information flow, turnover volume, and volatility. Positive, unexpected central bank intervention volume, whether purchasing or selling dollars, is also correlated with higher volatility.

As noted above, one interpretation of this result is that unexpected central bank intervention volume conveys information to FX markets that leads to higher volatility. Alternatively, there may be unexpectedly large intervention volume because the central bank is responding to unusually high volatility. Causality tests cannot discriminate between these explanations because the issue turns on contemporaneous correlation. As an alternative, we investigated the patterns of mean equation residuals and central bank intervention volume. Table 4 reports the results of this analysis. We find that when the mean residual is negative (positive), the central bank is consistently buying (selling) dollars. This accords closely with a central bank intervention policy oriented toward smoothing large changes in FX rates. Even with this intervention, unexpected FX rate changes are still unusually large on average relative to nonintervention days. This is because on average BOJ interventions do not offset market movements completely. Thus positive, unexpected intervention is on average positively related to daily volatility.

Interestingly, the volatility effects of unexpected dollar purchases are nearly two and one-half times as large as in the case of dollar sales. One plausible explanation for this result may be different underlying economic policies and conditions in the two subperiods.

Estimates reported in Table 3 also show that the autoregressive character of conditional volatility noted in earlier studies persists, even after accounting for turnover volume-and central bank-related volatility influences. The sum of the coefficients on these lagged volatility terms is .4045 with a standard error of .0649 (significant at the .01 level). This may indicate the possible existence of other factors, including policy variables, which could further explain the persistence of conditional volatility. There was no evidence that a longer lag structure added explanatory power to the conditional volatility model.

Finally, conditional volatility is higher on Monday, the same finding reported in other studies. Also, based on the coefficient estimates for UP and DOWN, the differences between baseline conditional volatility in the two subsamples are about 20%. This difference in conditional volatility may be related to the major changes in policy between the two subperiods.[27]

SUMMARY AND CONCLUSIONS

In this paper, we have studied the effects of central bank spot intervention volume and turnover on the volatility of daily FX rates. The empirical results for Japan in the period from October 1977 through December 1979 suggest these are important determinants of conditional volatility. Turnover volume, net of identified BOJ volume, is positively related to conditional daily volatility.

Unambiguous interpretation of the positive correlation between conditional FX rate volatility and unexpected central bank intervention volume is difficult.

Dominguez's results show that central bank interventions in the 1985-1987 period changed market expectations, presumably by changing the information set. However, we lean to the interpretation that this correlation in our data is the net result of a BOJ volatility-reducing intervention policy. The data appear to indicate that BOJ intervention involved trading in a direction that would be expected to mitigate that volatility. However, the observed conditional volatility is still larger on intervention days than on nonintervention days. This appears to be consistent with results reported by Loopesko and others indicating the difficulties central banks encounter in resisting undesired FX rate movements.

Our discussion of FX rate volatility suggested that the policy environment might play a role in understanding the effects of intervention and turnover volumes. Our empirical models permit coefficients to vary across the major policy change in the sample period. We find that the effects per dollar of intervention volume do change across the sample's two subperiods. We do not wish to overstate the strength of the evidence on this issue for several reasons. First, it is difficult to date policy shifts exactly and existing econometric models do not permit the data to select the shift in the *variance* function. Further, since there is no consensus FX rate model, it is virtually impossible to develop a close correspondence between policy shifts and FX rate behavior. The empirical results do, however, suggest strongly the importance of checking model stability over long periods in which business conditions and economic policy may change.

The methods used in this study can, in principle, be applied to other currencies and time periods. The econometric model can also be extended to include other determinants of FX rate changes and volatility. A major impediment to research in this area remains the difficulty of obtaining reliable data on central bank activities and policy changes, and daily data on macroeconomic factors related to FX rates.

APPENDIX

This appendix reports estimates of the models we used to generate expected values of total trading volume and central bank intervention volume. Our trading volume model is based on the synthesis suggested by Karpoff(1987) supplemented by autoregressive terms and day of the week dummy variables. In particular, our specification is

$$\text{TVOL}_t = b_0 + \sum_{i=1}^{4} b_i \text{TVOL}_{t-i} + b_5 \Delta\ln(\text{FX}_{t-1})\text{DOWN}_{t-1}$$

$$+ b_6 \Delta\ln(\text{FX}_{t-1})\text{UP}_{t-1} + b_7 \text{TIME}_t$$

$$\sum_{j=1}^{4} b_{j+7} \text{IVOL}_{t-j} + \sum_{m=1}^{4} d_m \text{DOW}_m + \varepsilon_t, \tag{A1}$$

where TVOL is total market volume, TIME is a time trend variable, IVOL is intervention volume, and DOW are day-of-the-week variables. Karpoff argues that there may be asymmetric volume responses to positive and negative price changes. The asymmetry occurs because there are different costs of taking short and long positions in the asset. The Tokyo spot FX market corresponds to this description fairly closely for this time period; short positions in the yen were very difficult to achieve. The TIME trend variable is included to capture market growth. Its inclusion is based on the theoretical development in Tauchen and Pitts (1983). If the central bank attempts to moderate FX rate changes and its reaction function is known by traders (even with error), then central bank interventions may increase volume. Traders may try to trade against the central bank because the bank's intervention activities will consist of buying at above market prices or selling at below market prices if the intent is to moderate FX rate changes. The DOW variables are included in view of results reported in Jain and Joh (1987) and in other volume-price chane studies. OLS estimates of the model are reported in Table A1. We did some experiments with other time series models and alternative lag lengths, but we were unable to improve on the model (A1).

Our basic intervention volume model includes an autoregressive lag structure in intervention volume along with several potential determinants of the central bank's intervention intensity:

$$\text{IVOL}_t = c_o + \sum_{i=1}^{4} c_i \text{IVOL}_{t-i} + \sum_{j=1}^{3} c_{j+4} \Delta \ln(\text{FX}_{t-j}) + c_8 [\Delta \ln(\text{FX}\cdot\text{DOWN})]_{t-1}$$

$$+ c_9 \text{CUMRET}_{t-1} + c_{10}(\text{CUMRET}\cdot\text{DOWN})_{t-1} + \varepsilon_t \qquad (A2)$$

where CUMRET is the cumulative percentage change in the ¥/$ FX rate over the previous 5 trading days. The leaning-against-the-wind intervention model implies a correspondence between intervention volume and the size of exchange rate changes. Our specification includes several lag values of FX rate changes because the timing of the central bank's response is not known a priori. It also seems possible the central bank may respond to cumulative movements in FX rates so we have included this variable as well. We have included interactions of these FX rate changes with a dummy variable (DOWN) to account for any shifts in the central bank's reaction function between the yen appreciation and depreciation episodes.

Because IVOL is bounded below at zero, a Tobit procedure is quite appropriate for estimating (A2). The difficulty with applying Tobit is the significant residual serial correlation. Standard asymptotic distribution theory for Tobit regressions does not incorporate a serial correlation correction or the presence of lagged dependent variables among the regressors.[28] Since our interest is generating forecasts of intervention volume, not inference, we relied on OLS estimates. These estimates are reported on the right-hand of Table A1.

Table A1.   Estimated Total Volume and
Central Bank Intervention Volume Models[a]

Total Market Volume			Intervention Volume	
Variable	*Estimate*	*Std. Error*	*Variable*	*Estimate*
$\Delta\ln(FX_{t-1})UP_{t-1}$	0.3940*	.1821	$IVOL_{t-1}$	0.2690
$\Delta\ln(FX_{t-1})DOWN_{t-1}$	−0.2519	.1847	$IVOL_{t-2}$	0.1063
$TVOL_{t-1}$	0.3173*	.0582	$IVOL_{t-3}$	0.0769
$TVOL_{t-2}$	0.1757*	.0574	$IVOL_{t-4}$	0.0074
$IVOL_{t-3}$	0.0485	.0578	$\Delta\ln(FX_{t-1})$	−0.0290
$TVOL_{t-4}$	0.0657	.0525	$\Delta\ln(FX_{t-2})$	−0.1858
$IVOL_{t-1}$	0.2016*	.0753	$\Delta\ln(FX_{t-3})$	0.0024
$IVOL_{t-2}$	−0.0400	.0771	$\Delta\ln(FX_{t-1})DOWN_{t-1}$	0.4090
$IVOL_{t-3}$	0.0432	.0773	$CUMRET_{t-1}$	3.585
$IVOL_{t-4}$	−0.0923	.0741	$CUMRET_{t-1}DOWN_{t-1}$	8.961
$TIME_t$	0.0033*	.0007	CONSTANT	0.2475
$MONDAY_t$	−0.2404	.2237		
$TUESDAY_t$	0.2751	.2218	R^2=.185 DW=2.00	
$TUESDAY_t$	0.0379	.2196		
$FRIDAY_t$	−0.3504	.2206		
CONSTANT	1.094*	.2559		
R^2=.574 DW=1.99				

Notes: [a] An asterisk indicates an estimate is statistically significant at the .05 level. Up is 1 for the yen appreciation period and 0 otherwise. DOWN is 1 for the yen depreciation period and 0 otherwise. TVOL is total market volume in hundreds of millions of dollars. IVOL is central bank intervention volume in hundreds of millions of dollars. TIME is a time trend. MONDAY, TUESDAY, THURSDAY, and FRIDAY are dummy variables, which are 1 for those days of the week and 0 otherwise. CUMRET is the cumulative change in log exchange rates over the past 5 trading days.

ACKNOWLEDGMENT

We gratefully acknowledge the helpful comments of Amir Barnear, Klaus Fischer, Fumiko Nagata, and seminar participants at the Financial Management Association, the Second Texas Finance Symposium, the University of California-Irvine, the University of Minnesota, and the Western Finance Association. Kwang Lee provided research assistance. The first author had financial support from research grants at the University of California-Irvine. The second author had support from a Halliburton Foundation Grant. The usual caveat applies.

NOTES

1.   Tauchen and Pitts (1983) present a joint model of trading volume and price changes that is closely tied to the mixture of distributions hypothesis.

2.   Lastrapes(1989) demonstrates that shifts in monetary policy regimes materially affect empirical estimates of GARCH conditional

3.   Obstfeld (1988) reviews some of this work. Other empirical analyses of central bank intervention activities are Wonnacott (1982), Rogoff (1984), Loopesko (1984), and Dominguez (1989).

4.   It may argued, of course, that since the central bank will almost always abandon its defense of a particular FX rate, the real effect of leaning against the wind is to spread underlying volatility over a longer time period. We will not address this issue directly here.

5.   Dominguez (1989) obtained intervention data from the Bundesbank for her study. Loopesko's analysis was based on confidential central bank intervention for the Group of Seven finance ministers. Rogoff (1984) and Davutyan and Pippenger (1989) used previously available data on Canadian intervention activities during the 1950s.

6.   Computations in the paper were made using RATS, Verson 3.10

7.   Argy (1982) concludes these capital controls affected the ¥/$ FX rate.

8.   We found no evidence that any of our empirical estimates were affected by the May 1979 liberalizations, so this issue is not explicitly addressed in the reported analyses.

9.   In her study of coordinated interventions, Dominguez had to estimate U.S. intervention volume data but she could only construct a dummy intervention variable for BOJ.

10.   If capital controls are the primary tool of FX rate management, the information content of spot market interventions may be reduced. This enhances the importance of checking for stability across policy subperiods in our empirical models.

11.   We confirmed Ito's results using our data.

12.   We do not include direct intervention effects in our mean FX rate change equation for two reasons. First, the existing literature finds only very small intervention effects on mean FX rate changes. In regressions not reported here, we found the same was true for our sample. Second, none of our volatility model results depend on including (or excluding) intervention measures from the mean equation.

13.   In addition to Frenkel's article, see Ch. 7 of Baillie and McMahon (1989) for a survey of models relating FX rate changes and news including references to other papers. Hakkio and Pearce (1985) use a similar model in their investigation of how FX rates react to economic news.

14.   We tried several different lag lengths on TPSPRU but none of our results depended on the particular lag length.

15.   The daily interest rate data are from the Citibank Foreign Exchange database.

16.   Frenkel (1981), p. 686, fnote. 23) suggests this formulation of the news model. Other studies of domestic asset pricing have also used term premium measures (see, e.g., Chen, Roll, & Ross, 1986).

17.   Implicit in our formulation is a forward-looking expectations model of the FX rate in which today's FX rate depends on a weighted average of future, expected FX rates. See Dominguez (1989) for more details.

18.   Among the functional forms of $f(\cdot)$ investigated in the literature are the ARCH, GARCH, and exponential GARCH models. Schwert (1990) uses a particularly tractable and easily estimated linear form. Davidian and Carroll (1987) also contains several suggested models.

19.   In contrast, Kandel and Stambaugh (1990) use GMM to estimate their mean and volatility equations.

20.   In equity market trading volume models [see Karpoff (1987) for a survey], return volatility is related to the level of trading volume. Unlike equity instruments, FX has value as a medium of exchange. Accordingly, there is some positive, base level of trading in the spot FX markets that is directly related to underlying trade flows, capital movements, and commercial transactions.

21.   The total turnover volume and central bank intervention models we estimated are not reported here but details are available from the authors.

22.   Dominguez (1989) reports that for her 1985-1987 sample period, market participants could usually observe the source and magnitude of central bank intervention activities at the time those operations were underway.

23.   In our sample, all sales of dollars by the BOJ occurred in the second subsample. The great majority of the dollar purchases happened during the first subsample. Thus, the two unexpected intervention volume measures probably capture volatility effects of unexpected purchases and sales of dollars along with any shifts in policy from the dollar support to yen support period.

24.   For evidence from the equity markets, see, e.g., French and Roll (1986). The spot FX volatility model estimates reported in Baillie and McMahon (1987) and Hsieh (1989), among others, all show Monday volatility is different from other days of the week.

25.   We experimented with other lag lengths in equation (3) without any change in our inferences about the effects of unexpected trading and intervention volume on conditional volatility.

26.   See, e.g., Engle and Bollerslev (1986), Bollerslev (1987), Baillie and McMahon (1989), and Hsieh (1989).

27.   In Connolly and Taylor (1990), we found very similar results using a GARCH model of conditional volatility.

28.   Poirier and Rudd (1988) have developed some analysis of PROBIT models with dependent observations. There are significant difficulties to overcome in making their analysis applicable to the problem considered here but these issues are beyond the scope of this paper.

REFERENCES

Admati, Anat R., & Pfleiderer, Paul, (1988), A theory of intraday patterns: Volume and price variability, *Review of Financial Studies, 1*, 3-40.

Argy, V. (1982), Exchange-rate management in theory and practice, *Princeton Studies in International Finance, 50.*

Baillie, Richard, & McMahon, Patrick, (1989), *The foreign exchange market: Theory and econometric evidence,* New York: Cambridge University Press.

Bollerslev, Tim (1987). A conditionally heteroscedastic time series model for speculative prices and rates of return. *Review of Economics and Statistics, 69*, 542-547.

Chen, Nai-fu, Roll, Richard & Ross, Stephen A. (1986), Economic forces and the stock market. *Journal of Business, 59*, 388-403.

Connolly, Robert A., & Taylor, William M. (1990). The impact of central bank intervention on exchange rate volatility. Working paper.

Corrado, Charles J. & Taylor, Dean (1986). The cost of a central bank leaning against a random walk. *Journal of International Money and Finance, 5*, 303-314.

Cumby, R.E., & Obstfeld, M. (1981). A note on exchange-rate expectations and nominal interest differentials: A test of the Fisher hypothesis. *Journal of Finance, 36*, 697-704.

Cushman, David O. (1986). Has exchange risk depressed international trade? The impact of third country exchange risk. *Journal of International Money and Finance,5*, 361-380.

Davidian, Marie, & Carroll, R.J. (1987). Variance function estimation. *Journal of the American Statistical Association, 82*, 1079-1091.

Davutyan, Nurhan & Pippenger, John (1989). Excess returns and official intervention: Canada 1952-1960. *Economic Inquiry, 27*, 489-500.

Dominguez, Kathryn Mary (1989). Market response to coordinated central bank intervention. Working paper 3192, National Bureau of Economic Research, Cambridge, MA.

Dornbusch, Rudiger (1980). Exchange rate economics: Where do we stand? *Brookings Paper on Economic Activity,* 143-185.

Edwards, Sebastian (1982). Exchange rates and news: A multi-currency approach, *Journal of International Money and Finance, 1*, 211-224.

Engle, Robert F. & Bollerslev, Tim (1986). Modelling the persistence of conditional variances. Econometric Reviews, 5, 1-150.

French, Kenneth R. & Roll (1986). Stock return variances: The arrival of information and the reaction of traders, *Journal of Financial Economics, 17*, 5-26.

Frenkel, Jacob A. (1981). Flexible exchange rates, prices, and the role of news: Lessons from the 1970s. *Journal of Political Economy, 89*. 665-705.

Giovannini, A., & Jorian, P. (1989). The time variation of risk and return in the foreign exchange and stock markets. *Journal of Finance, 44*, 307-325.

Gültekin, Mustafa N., Bulent, N. Gültekin, & Penati, Alessandro (1989). Capital controls and international capital markets segmentation: The evidence from the Japanese and American stock markets. *Journal of Finance, 44*, 849-870.

Hakkio, Craig, & Pearce, Douglas K. (1985). The reaction of exchange rates to economic news. *Economic Inquiry, 23*, 621-636.

Hardevoulis, Gikas, (1986). Economic news, exchange rates and interest rates. *Journal of International Money and Finance, 7*, 23-36.

Hodrick, Robert. (1989). Risk, uncertainty, and exchange rates. *Journal of Monetary Economics, 23*, 433-459.

Hodrick, R.J., & Srivastava, S. (1984). An investigation of risk and return in forward foreign exchange. *Journal of International Money and Finance, 3*, 5-29.

Hsieh, David (1989). Modelling heteroscedasticity in daily foreign exchange rates. *Journal of Business and Economics Statistics, 7*, 307-317.

Ito, Takatoshi (1986). Capital controls and covered interest parity between the yen and the dollar. *Economic Studies Quarterly, 37*, 223-241.

Ito, Takatoshi (1988). Use of (time-domain) vector autoregressions to test uncovered interest parity. *Review of Economics and Statistics 70*, 296-305.

Ito, Takatoshi, & Roley, Vance V. (1987). News from the U.S. and Japan: Which moves the yen/dollar exchange rate? *Journal of Monetary Economics, 19*, 255-277.

Jain, Prem C., & Joh, Gun-Ho (1987) The dependence between hourly prices and trading volume. *Journal of Financial and Quantitative Analysis, 23*, 269-283.

Jorion, P. (1988). On jump processes in the foreign exchange and stock markets. *Review of Financial Studies, 1*, 427-445.

Kandel, Shmuel, & Stambaugh, Robert F. (1990). Expectations and volatility of consumption and asset returns. *Review of Financial Studies, 3*, 207-232.

Karpoff, Jonathan M. (1987). The reaction between price changes and trading volume: A survey. *Journal of Financial and Quantitative Analysis, 22*, 109-126.

Lastrapes, William D. (1989). Exchange rate volatility and U.S. monetary policy: An ARCH application. *Journal of Money, Credit, and Banking, 21*, 66-77.

Loopesko, B.E. (1984). Relationships among exchange rates, intervention, and interest rates: An empirical investigation. *Journal of International Money and Finance, 3*, 257-277.

Marston, R.C. (1988). Exchange rate policy reconsidered. In M. Feldstein (Ed.), *International Economic Cooperation*. (Chicago: University of Chicago Press.)

Mussa, Michael L. (1979). Empirical regularities in the behavior of exchange rates and theories of the foreign exchange market. *Carnegie-Rochester Conference Series on Public Policy, 11*, 9-57.

Obstfeld, Maurice. (1988). The effectiveness of foreign-exchange intervention: Recent experience. Working paper 2796, National Bureau of Economic Research, Cambridge, MA.

Patell, James M. & Wolfson, Mark A. (1984). The intraday speed of adjustment of stock prices to earnings and dividend announcement. *Journal of Financial Economics, 13*, 223-252.

Poirier, Dale, & Rudd, Paul (1988). Probit with dependent observations. *Review of Economic Studies, 55*, 593-614.

Rogoff, Kenneth (1984). On the effects of sterilized intervention: An analysis of weekly data. *Journal of Monetary Economics, 14*, 133-150.

Ross, Stephen. (1989). Information and volatility: The no-arbitrage martingale approach to timing and resolution irrelevancy. *Journal of Finance, 44*, 1-18.

Schwert, G. William (1990). Stock volatility and the crash of '87. *Review of Financial Studies, 3*, 77-102.

Schwert, G. William, & Seguin, Paul J. (1990). Heteroscedasticity in stock returns. *Journal of Finance, 45*, 1129-1155.

Stein, Jeremy C. (1989). Cheap talk and the Fed: A theory of imprecise policy announcements. *American Economic Review, 79*, 32-42.

Tauchen, George, & Pitts, Mark (1983). The price variability-volume relationship on speculative markets. *Econometrica, 51*, 485-505.

Taya, T. (1983). Effectiveness of exchange market intervention in moderating the speed of exchange rate movements: An empirical study of the case of Japan. In D. Bigman and T. Taya, (Eds.), *Exchange rate and trade instability: Causes, consequences, and remedies* (pp. 217-255) Cambridge: Ballinger.

Wonnacott, Paul (1982). U.S. intervention in the exchange market for DM, 1977-1980. *Princeton Studies in International Finance, 51*.

DIVIDEND POLICY, ASYMMETRIC INFORMATION, AND SIGNALING:
AN EMPIRICAL TEST

Said M. Elfakhani and Larry J. Merville

ABSTRACT

In a world of asymmetric firm information, managers can use dividend changes in signaling private information. This research proposes a multiple signals-attributes model, from which two testable implications are formed, and tests for the existence of a dividend information effect around dividend announcement dates. The model and empirical tests suggest that a dividend signal can have three dimensions: (1) clarity (neutral, positive, or unclear), (2) direction (favorable or unfavorable), and (3) significance (high or low). The results show that changes in financial statements and dividends may resolve all or some uncertainly about the firm's future cash flows. In particular, we find: (1) firms that use more signals to signal the same number of attributes are more valuable and (2) signals that reduce information ambiguity are more valuable than those which do not.

Conventional finance theory posits that the value of a firm is the expected cash flows discounted at the risk-adjusted rate of return. The market increases the value

Advances in Financial Planning and Forecasting,
Volume 5, pages 201-225.
Copyright © 1994 by JAI Press Inc.
All rights of reproduction in any form reserved.
ISBN:1-55938-421-2

of the firm only if the expected rate of return, rather than dividend yield, exceeds the market required rate. Following this reasoning, dividend payments should not theoretically change the total risk of the firm nor increase its perceived value.

In practice, firms are reluctant to change their dividend policies. The discrepancy between theory and practice raises several questions. For example, what are the factors that dictate the firm's decision to pay or not to pay dividends? How do investors perceive changes in dividend levels?

This research examines the role of dividend policy as a superior signaling device to deliver inside information to the market. It relates the dividend signal to balance sheet signals, which are other forms of management signaling instruments. The argument is that the dividend announcement is a complicated piece of information about capital investment and capital structure decisions as well as internal liquidity strength and, perhaps, agency costs of the firm.

Miller and Modigliani (1961) pioneered the literature on dividend irrelevancy and the valuation of the firm. The irrelevancy argument considers dividends only as cash recycling between now and the future. However, when the assumption of a perfect market is relaxed, the argument loses most of its credibility. In addition, this theory cannot explain the apparent conflict with practice. This has triggered an extensive debate on what Black (1976) calls the dividend policy puzzle.

Studies by Lintner (1956), Fama and Babiak (1968), and Black (1976) show that firms in the United States behave as if they have target dividend policies from which they are reluctant to deviate. These studies suggest that U.S. corporations raise their dividend payments only when they are confident they can maintain them over the long term. One implication of these findings is that dividend announcements may contain new information related to the firm's power to generate future profits. This information, not known to the public, is signaled to the market. Support for this information content hypothesis can be found in several past studies such as those of Pettit (1976), Charest (1978), Asquith and Mullins (1983), Healy and Palepu (1988), Wansley and Lane (1987), and more recently Wansley, Sirmans, Shilling, and Lee (1991).

The signaling of new information via dividends assumes that information asymmetry exists between management and market participants including existing shareholders. The market believes that management knows more about current and future profitability. Therefore, the market expects a truthful signal in that direction. A formal dividend signaling theory is developed by Ross (1977), Bhattacharya (1979, 1980), Hakansson (1982), and Makhija and Thompson (1986). More recently, John and Williams (1985) and Miller and Rock (1985) provide one signal (dividends or earnings)-one-attribute (cash flows from capital budgeting) signaling models. John and Kalay (1982), Asquith and Mullins (1986), Ambarish, John, and Williams (AJW; 1987), and Ofer and Thakor (1987) advance models with a maximum of one attribute (cash flows from capital investment) and two signals (for example, dividend and net new issues). In this context, Ofer and Siegel (1987) report that earnings forecasts that adjust for unexpected dividend changes improve the predictability of firm future performance. This presents supportive empirical evidence for a signaling theory of dividends.

Current signaling theory, however, is restrictive. It postulates that asymmetric cash flow information reflects only one attribute (capital investment). Other pertinent factors such as the financing decision and liquidity problems can influence forecasts of future cash flows that are not accounted for in current models. Furthermore, current theory restricts the number of signals used by management. For example, Ofer and Thakor (1987) assume that debt is zero. This implicitly denies the use of the financing decision as a signaling device. Other studies challenge the superiority of dividend signals over other types of signals, such as Miller and Rock (1985) who argue that the role of the dividend signal is to help predict current earnings, which in turn signal future earnings.

To summarize, the precise way in which the market uses the dividend policy of the firm is still an open theoretical question. The usefulness of dividends as a signal versus other sources of signals is still a testable query. Empirically, dividend announcements appear to produce new information for the market.

This paper argues that the signaling effect of dividend change must be evaluated in light of balance sheet variables changes. Thus, dividend change can convey some information on the firm's value in some cases, and none in others. We develop a model that extends current signaling models in two important ways: (1) by allowing for two attributes (focusing on two information sources, capital investment and capital structure) both of which affect the present value of future cash flows of the firm and (2) by developing a signaling mechanism in which the dividend signal is integrated with other firm (balance sheet) signals. We also propose a testing methodology to examine the information content of dividends around their announcement dates.

The first section proposes a signaling model in which dividend announcements signal future cash flows from one or two attributes. In the next section, hypotheses are formed to test the theory and data are described. The results and interpretations of the tests are then given, and the final section concludes the paper.

THE SIGNALING MODEL AND TESTS

Before proposing the signaling model, we define four terms used frequently in the paper:

Attribute: *Private information* about the *effect* of the firm's state variable on the cash flows generated by a managerial decision.

Signal: A device (proxy) that delivers private information (attribute) to outsiders. A signal must be credible and *efficient* in the sense that it can communicate all private information at lower cost than other dissipative signals.

Clarity: A measure of the *clearness* of the signal. Effects of clarity on stock price reaction can be positive, negative, or neutral, depending on the direction (favorable or unfavorable) of the signal. *Unclear* signals may draw opposing reactions.

Direction: Private attributes can reflect *favorable* or *unfavorable* news. Favorable news signals invite positive stock price adjustment.

Extant signaling models usually define the firm's attribute as private information about asset investment (in place or opportunity to invest). The value of this attribute is related to a state variable that affects the firm's cash flows. AJW propose a nonmimicry model that uses changes in dividends and investments to signal one attribute about total cash flow from capital investment. Sometimes it takes two signals to signal one attribute so that another firm of lower value cannot mimic the signal. In all cases, their model perceives that only investment news affects firm value. Normally, the market uses total cash flows to compute the firm's present value. Source of cash flows, however, can arise from assets (already in place or future opportunities) as well as liabilities.

In this paper, we allow for two firm attributes (capital investment and financing) and multiple signals (balance sheet and dividend changes) in the process of providing new information about the firm's total cash flows.[1] We let net cash flows depend on the value of a state variable that affects the firm's present value. The number of binding nonmimicry constraints in our model is a function of the number of attributes to signal.

Insiders (managers and board of directors) prefer to report their corporate attributes truthfully to outsiders (external stockholders), who correctly price the firm in the market. This wish, however, is sometimes plagued by lack of credibility. Thus, other means of signaling are required.

This paper suggests a two-stage signaling model. Balance sheet changes act as a phase 1 signal followed almost immediately by a dividend change (phase 2 signal). The effect of the interaction between earnings and dividend announcements on abnormal returns is documented by Kane, Lee, and Marcus (1984). Also, Wansley and Lane (1987) use financial ratios to relate changes in the financial characteristics of the firm to its initiation of a dividend payment. We propose that in most cases this prescribed sequence can lead to a complete or almost complete assessment of firm value. This approach takes the path described next.

Day-to-day change in the firm's operations is not observable by outside shareholders. Thus, marginal investors wait for interim balance sheet releases, among other events, to assess the firm's approximate standing. The argument presented here is that these releases may present information on both assets and liabilities in place of future directions. Although financial statements are susceptible to possible manipulation, the market is not fooled by such actions and is likely to infer useful private information. Investors discover the firm's operational decisions as expressed by balance sheet changes from one period to another. These changes are made at the discretion of management and therefore can be used as phase 1 information signals.[2]

However, the flow of information and the level of common knowledge are not complete. Therefore, balance sheet changes alone cannot clear up all confusion or uncertainty about the firm's expected future. For instance, an increase in fixed assets account translates as a signal of expected incremental cash inflows. However, under more complex changes, the exact meaning of this signal by itself may not be clear to the market.

Under those circumstances, dividends offer some useful information not present in announcements of earnings and audited financial statements. Investors use this information in revising their valuation of the firm by reassessing its future returns. This provides the second phase of the signaling process, thus completing a set of information on firm value.

The interpretation of the information content of dividend announcements is conditioned on earnings and financial statement information released earlier. In this context, changes in the balance sheet and dividend policy help reveal firm attributes and their directions.

In our model, we allow for two firm attributes at a time. Let two such attributes be signaled by the *proxies*: changes in investment (I) and debt financing (B). In addition, changes in near cash (C) also provide signals about a third firm attribute, its internal liquidity.[3] It requires at least two signals to communicate simultaneously insider information about two of the attributes of the firm to the market. Thus, the model requires additional balance sheet variables to satisfy both the nonmimicry constraints and the sources and uses of funds equation for a given firm. The proxy variables for the attributes can be viewed as (more) direct signals, while the additional balance sheet and dividend change variables can be thought of as supporting signals, but all are part of the total signaling process of the firm.

The following general assumption are made in order to develop and test the signaling model:

1. Insiders know more than the market about attributes affecting future cash flows of the firm.

2. Each financial attribute is directly related to a change in the balance sheet (for example, the investment attribute relates to $I \gtrless 0$). Insiders use these changes as signals of the asymmetric information to the common shareholders.

3. Outsiders inspect the changes in financial statements but often cannot fully infer the inside information.

4. Firms are of two types, lower value and higher value.[4] Managers of both types prefer to communicate their corporate attributes truthfully to outsiders. Higher-value firms select expensive-to-mimic signals induce lower-value firms not to replicate them (nonmimicry conditions).

5. The firm is owned by a homogeneous clientele of investors. This clientele represents a consensus group with homogeneous expectations about the firm

value. A consensus investor holds a personal portfolio and meets the demand for liquidity by buying or selling the stock at the equilibrium price.

6. The market is efficient in the semi-strong form. In a world of uncertainty, however, it can take the market time to assimilate complex or conflicting (favorable and unfavorable) information. In this case, balance sheet and dividend signals by themselves may not serve to clarify the ambiguity.

7. All changes in the firm's balance sheet between a balance sheet release and a dividend announcement are zero.[5]

8. Stock returns are independent and stationary over time with finite variance. Therefore, portfolio returns of a large sample have a log-normal distribution.

The Model

We define near cash (CA) as current assets minus inventory. We set investment (FA) as all fixed assets plus inventory. Debt (DP) represents short- or long-term liabilities including preferred stocks. Common stock account (CS) includes common stocks (par) and paid-in capital, while retained earnings account (RE) is handled separately.

Knowing that sources of funds are equal to uses, then changes in these balance sheet accounts satisfy

$$D + I = C + B + S \tag{1}$$

where

D = dividends paid,
I = value of new investment in real assets,
C = value of reduction in near crash,
B = market value of new debt, and
S = market value of new stock.

During each quarter q of firm operation, the following scenario takes place:

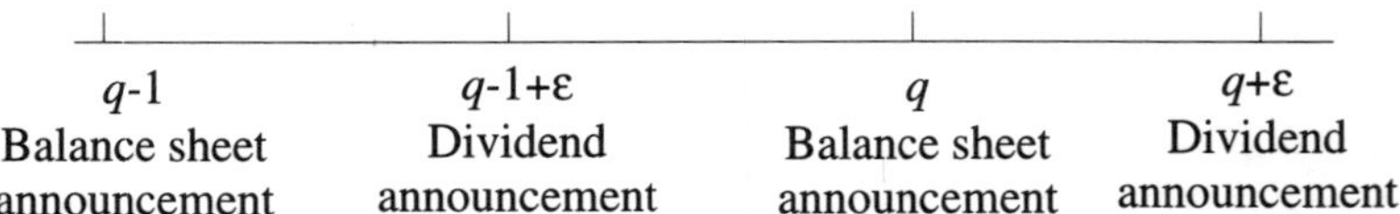

where $q = 1,\ldots, T$; ε = few days into quarter q during which management first publishes its financial statements and then decides the dividend amount, announced later at date $q+\varepsilon$.[6]

In this design, any changes (positive or negative) in near cash, investment, debt and preferred stock, common stock, or retained earnings are known upon the release of the new balance sheet of quarter q. Notice that changes in retained earnings reflect dividends paid at $(q-1+\varepsilon)$ and earnings accumulated over the same quarter, that is:

$$\Delta RE_q = E_q - D_{q-1+e} \tag{2}$$

where E_q = earnings realized at time q.

In the model we extend the fourth assumption above to let there be two j values (1, 2) for each attribute. We assume that values of different attributes are all consistent with only one firm type (higher *or* lower value). The type 1 firms relate to the value of a state variable that has a lower present value of cash flows, everything else the same. More valuable firms (type 2) have higher present values.

Insiders create a dividend policy to increase the wealth of the consensus shareholder, who has both liquidated and retained ownership. Consistent with AJW, our one-period maximand is:[7]

$$\text{Max}\left\{ (1 - t_p) D + P_e R + \frac{Q - R}{Q + N} \sum_{T+1}^{T+K} F(S_k^j) \right\} \tag{3}$$

where[8]

t_p =   marginal personal tax rate,
D =   total dividends,
P_e =   *ex dividend* price per share j,
Q =   number of outstanding shares,
R =   number of shares sold on personal account by the consensus investor in order to meet his demand for liquidity,
N =   number of new shares bought or sold at price P_e,
T =   number of nonmimicry constraints,
K =   total number of firm attributes,
$F(S_k^j)$ =   total present value of after-tax cash flows of the firm conditioned on attribute k, and
S_k^j =   balance sheet change signal for attribute k of firm j.

In this problem, insiders choose the optimal balance sheet and dividend changes that maximize the wealth of their shareholders. Outsiders (external stockholders) solve their personal portfolio problems, subject to the firm's sources and uses of funds (1), so to determine their demand for the firm's stock. This in turn determines their targeted demand for liquidity $L(D,P)$, which is the liquidity of the consensus stockholder, who meets his demand for liquidity L by buying or selling shares R in the common stock at *ex* dividend price such that

$$L(D, P) = (1-t_p)D + P_e R \tag{4}$$

where

P = total *cum* dividend market value of common stock j.

It must be noted that in order to thwart any arbitrage around the *ex* dividend date, the total *cum* dividend market value, P, of common stock J, must satisfy

$$P = P_e + (1\text{-}t_p)D/Q \tag{5}$$

Let us insert (1), (4), and (5) into the maximand (3). This presents an equivalent problem to equation (3) and is particularized for two attributes as:

$$V^j(D, I, B, C, S) = L(D, P) + \frac{P - L(D, P)}{P + t_p D + I - C - B} \sum_{k=1}^{2} F(S_k^j) \tag{6}$$

where

J = firm type (j=1, 2),
K = attribute (k=1, 2),

One implication of the model is that insiders work on solving the problem in Equation (3) to increase to increase shareholders' wealth, V^j, in (6). They foresee that investors notice the true value of the firm in response to the dividend change. Outsiders buy or sell stock j to optimize their utility from liquidity $L(D,P)$ and the market value of outstanding shares held in stock after the *ex* dividend day.

Another feature of the model is that multiple corporate signals (balance sheet and dividend signals) can reveal information about one or two attributes (investment and financing). These signals are generated by different combinations of the five sources and uses of funds variables described in (1). Each combination can satisfy the maximand.

The balance sheet change variables include three sets: (a) firm attributes, (b) nonmimicry constraints, and (c) sources and uses of funds (1). The assumption in the model is that the more valuable firms use binding nonmimicry constraints to separate their signals about their firms' attributes from those of less valuable firms. Corollary 1 in Appendix A shows that, for informationally efficient signaling to exist, the relationship among the minimum number of balance sheet change variables (BS), the total number of attributes (K), the type of the firm (j), the maximum number of binding nonmimicry constraints (T_M), and the minimum number of variables needed to guarantee the equality of sources and uses of funds is

$$B\,S \geq K + T_M + 1 \quad \text{and} \quad T_M = j^k - 1$$

where the 1 represents a variable required to guarantee the sources and uses of funds condition in Equation (1) with a minimum BS of 5. T_M depends on the number of attributes (K) and firm type (j) per attribute. For lesser-value firms, however, it is possible that BS is smaller than $K + T_M$. In Equations (3) and (6), the number of balance sheet change variables (BS) and the maximum number of binding nonmimicry constraints (T_M) restrict the number of attributes (K) that can be efficiently signaled. It follows from the above relation that the condition for K reduces to $K \leq BS - (J^K-1) - 1 = BS - J^K$.

So, if $J=2$ and $K=2$ then BS=6, which supersedes conditions imposed by Equation (1). Thus, the higher-value firm cannot efficiently signal two attributes simultaneously. In our model, BS=5 and for $J=2$, that implies $K \leq 5 - 2^K$. This condition only holds if $K=1$. For the more valuable firms ($J=2$), we require two balance sheet change variables to send a clear signal on one attribute and one change variable to reflect the liquidity level. This is necessary to satisfy the binding nonmimicry constraint and the sources and uses of funds condition. With BS=5, signaling more than one attribute ($K>1$) leads to a signal that may not be clear as to intended stock price effect.

The Components of Dividend Signals

The dividend signal is conditioned on the prior earnings announcement and the balance sheet signals. If the balance sheet signals are perfectly clear about the net effect of inside information, then the role of the dividend signal diminishes. For instance, if the firm undertakes a positive NPV project, then the market interpretation of this signal is straightforward, other things being equal. Similar is the case of a change in capital structure that is implemented ti improve the firm's future after-tax cash flows. Under such conditions, the size of the dividend change signal confirms the information about the direction (favorable or unfavorable) and significance (high or low) of the inside information being signaled. This will be reflected in the stock price reaction after the dividend announcement. We identify these cases of the signaling mechanism as *"neutral."* That is, a dividend signal is neutral when there is only one possible value inference about the attribute(s) signaled before *and* after the dividend announcement.

There are occasions when many balance sheet changes imply two (or more) attributes with conflicting (or opposing) types of information. Balance sheet signals may not always be clear about the net effect of the inside information signaled when more than one attribute is involved. Therefore, ambiguity about the firm's net attribute is not clear before the dividend announcement. Afterward, the dividend announcement *may* help resolve some or all ambiguity about the firm's present value. Thus, the dividend signal can have a clarifying role as well as directional and significance roles.

If the dividend announcement signal provides clarification of the ambiguity, then a significant move in stock price (up or down) can develop, everything else the same. We consider this signal clarity A *"positive."* A dividend signal is positive if the effect of the direction of the attributes on firm valuation becomes clear after the dividend announcement.

Sometimes, the conflict in inside information about the attributes signaled by the balance sheet remains unresolved after the dividend signal. We call this signal "unclear." In this case a divided signal is not enough to make clear the firm's true state. However, this is not to say that an unclear signal has zero value, as it should not have the same value as a positive signal.

Thus, we propose that the dividend signal has at least three components: (1) clarity (neutral, positive, or unclear), (2) direction [favorable (+) or unfavorable (−)], and (3) significance (high or low) as shown in Figure 1. We empirically verify that actual stock price changes depend on these three dimensions of the dividend signal.

Creation of Signal Categories

The firm's balance sheet change variables are first divided into three sets:

$$\delta_1: \quad I, B, C, \qquad \delta_2: \quad C, S, \qquad \delta_3: \quad D$$

States are classified according to attribute changes (δ_1), nonmimicry constraints and sources and uses of funds condition(δ_2), and dividend signals (δ_3).[9]

The states are partitioned into four Q_j^i categories. The i indexes the number of balance sheet change variables ($i=1$, fewer; $i=2$, more). Also, i relates to the dividend change ($i=1$, $\Delta D=0$; $i=2$, $\Delta D\neq 0$). The j marks signal clarity ($j=1$, neutral; $j=2$, positive). The conditions for being in each Q_j^i category are as follows:[10]

	Q_1^1	Q_1^2	Q_2^1	Q_2^2
#$\delta_1 \neq 0$	=1	=1	=2	=2
#$\delta_2 \neq 0$	≤2	≤2	≤2	≤2
#δ_3	0	≠0	0	≠0
$\sum_1^3 \neq 0$	2	3	3	4

where $\sum_1^3 \# \neq 0$ means the total number of balance sheet change variables is not equal to zero in sets δ_1, δ_2, and δ_3.

Testable Implications

In Appendix B, we show that the necessary condition for a discrete stock price change for one attribute in a three attribute case is

$$\Delta P_j \gtreqless 0 \qquad \text{if} \qquad \frac{\partial P/\partial D}{\partial P/\partial k} \gtreqless 1 \tag{7}$$

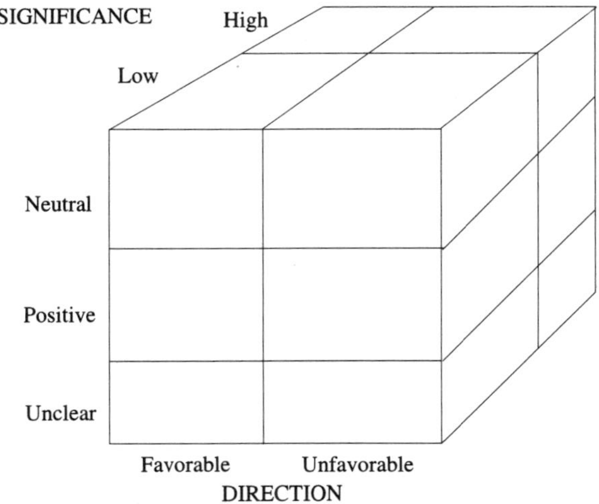

Figure 1.　Dividend Signal Components

where

P_j　　　= price of firm j common stock,

$\partial P/\partial D$ = partial derivative of P_j with respect to D, and

$\partial P/\partial k$ = partial derivative of P_j with respect to $k = I, B,$ or C.

The dividend signal is in the marketplace a few days after the release of a balance sheet investment (S_1^j; $\Delta I \neq 0$), financing (S_2^j; $\Delta B \neq 0$), or internal liquidity (S_3^j; $\Delta C \neq 0$) signal. However, it is the combination of the two signals that determines the net effect on the stock price.

While the specific value of $\partial P/\partial D$ or $\partial P/\partial k$ depends on the assumed functional form of $F(S_k^j)$ in Equation (6), their ratio, which depends on the general properties of $F(S_k^j)$, determines the effect of one attribute signal k. The ratio $[(\partial P/\partial D) \div (\partial P/\partial k)]$ for the capital investment, financing, and internal liquidity signals are derived in Appendix B for the more valuable firms $j=2$ as

$$-\frac{(\partial P/\partial D)}{\partial P/\partial I} = \frac{t_p}{F'(I)-1} < 1,$$

$$-\frac{(\partial P/\partial D)}{\partial P/\partial B} = \frac{t_p}{I-F'(-B)1} < 1, \qquad (8)$$

$$-\frac{(\partial P/\partial D)}{\partial P/\partial C} = \frac{t_p}{I-F'(-C)1} < 1,$$

Thus, the more valuable firms in the one-attribute signaling case require at least three variables to signal their information about the attribute. Less valuable firms, however, require no more than two variables. Also, we assume that $F'(S_k^j) > 1$ for the more valuable $j=2$ firm and <1 for the less valuable $j=1$ firm, if $s_k^j > 0$ and vice versa.

There are several testable implications of the theory described by expressions (6), (7), and (8). For the same level of signal clarity and number of attributes, firms that use fewer balance sheet change variables should be less valuable than those that use more. This stems from the nonmimicry condition advocated by more valuable firms. Another set of possible testable implications is that signals that improve signal clarity should be more valuable than those which do not, everything else the same. Both sets of implications are tested next.

TEST DESIGN AND DATA SOURCES

Sampling Criteria and Data Sources

Firms on the Compustat quarterly tape and Center for Research in Security Prices at the University of Chicago (CRSP) Master File Returns were filtered to the following restrictive criteria:

1. Firms use the same quarterly fiscal system (December).
2. Public utilities and banks are discarded because they have regulated constraints on earnings and dividend payment.
3. Firms reporting negative earnings for two consecutive quarters are obliterated for those two quarters.[11] Firms with negative earnings in one quarter and positive earnings in the quarters around it are sampled.
4. Nonquarterly dividends are removed from our sample. Also, we dismiss nonregular (extra, special, and year-end) dividends because they are predictable and short-lived.
5. Stock splits declared on or near the dividend announcement day suspend the dividend event.
6. Cash dividends announced on the same day as stock dividends are in the sample since they are nontaxable distributions and therefore should not disqualify the dividend event.
7. A firm that undertakes a merger or an acquisition during any period is excluded for the year in which it occurs. This is to avoid any possible noise from unusual changes in earnings' level or dividend policy.
8. Noisy events around the estimation period are discarded. Examples include major management changes, significant lawsuits, and labor disputes. This filter allows for close examination of the dividend information effect.
9. Firms that announce earnings and financial statements shortly (within 45 days) after dividend announcements are deleted in this study.[12]
10. As in Ahrony and Swary (1960), firms must have their earnings and financial statements made at least 5 days before dividend announcements but

    not earlier than 20 days. *Exdividend* days should occur within 5 days after dividend announcement days.

11. Less actively traded stocks must trade at least on the announcement day to qualify in the sample.

The sampling period is from January 1, 1976, through December 31, 1985. Book values of quarterly cash balances, investment, leverage, common stocks (including paid-in capital), retained earnings, earnings per share, and earnings' announcement dates are available on the Standard and Poor's Quarterly Compustat Tape. Dividends per share, dividend announcement dates, *ex* dividend days, and daily stock prices and returns are available on the CRSP tape. Dates of earnings and dividend announcements are from CRSP or from *Annual Wall Street Journal Index*. Omitted dividend announcement and *ex* dividend dates are available from the *Wall Street Journal* or *Annual Wall Street Journal Index*.

Design Description

The sampled data are arranged so they describe all possible combination of balance sheet changes in one period (quarter) before the dividend announcement.

Changes from one quarter to another quarter in near cash, capital investment, debt (and preferred), and common stocks are indexed as positive, negative, or zero changes. The change in the four major items of the balance sheet, as described earlier, allows for 3^4 or 81 different states (θ). Each state represents a unique combination of these changes. For each state, several substates (θ_s) can arise depending on the direction of the dividend signal.

The direction of the signal reflects the dividend change from one quarter to another quarter. Initially, these changes are classified as increases, decreases, stable, omissions, or remissions. Increases (decreases) occur when dividends paid in the current quarter, q, are larger (smaller) than those paid in last quarter, q-1. Stability refers to the case where no change in dividends has occurred from the prior period. Firms that have paid dividends for some time and omit paying them for one period fall in the omission group. Omitted dividends cases are treated as decreases in dividends.[13] For sampling purposes, sudden remissions (initiations) of dividend policy are regarded as increases in dividends. Therefore, changes in dividend classes are three: positive, negative, or zero.

Thus, theoretically there is a maximum of 243 distinct substates. The final number of states and substates increases by three conditions:

1. The states are confined to three attribute signals (I, B, C). Other signals are allowed if they act to satisfy the nonmimicry and funds flow conditions.
2. Many states are infeasible.[14] They cannot exist anytime there are unequal or opposite changes in assets and liabilities. This suggests that sourced and

uses of funds are unequal. Therefore, we discard unfeasible cases from consideration.

3.   There are sampling constraints related to the number of events that fall within a substate. If there are few or no sample points in one substate, then we drop it since it provides little or no empirical testing opportunity. Similarly we remove the case where there are many sample points but only a few firms (less than 5) in one substate (θ_s), Of course, there is no sense in testing information content of dividends when firms use the same policy over time.

Test Procedures

The now classical procedure for testing event studies is to investigate whether there are abnormal stock returns around or on the announcement date. One accepted methodology for using daily data relies on the use of mean-adjusted returns. This method is shown by Brown and Warner (1985) to be as good as the market model in detecting abnormal daily returns. It only requires the assumption that the returns generating process is stationary. This method does not require a determination of risk type (systematic or unsystematic). Also, it does not entail a specification of the market portfolio as in the market model. However, this approach requires dividend announcements not be clustered in few calendar days. Otherwise, it will lose its advantage over using the market model. Because our research design includes many substates distributed over various periods, clustering turns out to be not a serious problem.

The mean-adjusted returns model assumes that the return-generating process for stock i is stochastic of the form

$$\tilde{R}_{i,t} = \hat{\mu}_i + \tilde{\varepsilon}_{i,t} \tag{9}$$

where $E(\tilde{\varepsilon}_{i,t}) = 0$ and $\text{Cov}(\tilde{\varepsilon}_{i,t}, \tilde{\varepsilon}_{i,t-1}) = 0$ for all i, t; $\tilde{R}_{i,t}$ = return on (firm) stock i at day t; and $\hat{\mu}_i$ = unbiased estimate of the mean return of stock i before the event period.

In our problem, each substate has several firms sampled at different times and is an event to study. In this context, we test the clarity (neutral, positive, or unclear) and direction (favorable or unfavorable) of the dividend announcement by analyzing normal returns around the date of the announcement. Therefore, the following event methodology steps are taken:

1. Let us define around each dividend announcement date a period of 10 trading days: 4 days before the announcement day, the announcement day, the day

after, and 4 days after the announcement day. A nonevent period is set at 15 trading days in length ending at least 10 days before the earnings announcement date. This period must be as free as possible of any other related announcement effects.[15]

2. Compute the abnormal returns for event sample k $[e_{jk}(i,q)]$ in substate (j) at time t in quarter q:

$$\text{AR}_{jk}(i,t) = (R_{i,t} - \mu_i), \qquad t = 4,\dots,0,\dots,+5, \quad j=1,\dots,\theta_s, \quad k=1,\dots,N_s(j) \tag{10}$$

where

$\text{AR}_{jk}(i,t) =$ abnormal return for event sample k at day t in substate j,
$R_{i,t} \qquad =$ return on stock i *at day* t,
$\hat{\mu}_i \qquad = (1/15) \sum_{t=-15}^{-1} R_{i,\tau}$
$\theta_s \qquad\;\; =$ number of substates, and
$N_s(J) \quad\; =$ number of sample points in substate j.

3. Compute the average abnormal returns by forming an equally weighted portfolio of all individual abnormal returns for each event day t;

$$\overline{\text{AR}}_{s,t} = (1/N_s) \sum_{k=1}^{N_s} \text{AR}_{jk}(i,t) \tag{11}$$

4. Compute the average abnormal returns for the nonevent period by forming an equally weighted portfolio of all individual abnormal returns for each nonevent day t:

$$\overline{\text{AR}}_{s,t} = (1/N_s) \sum_{k=1}^{N_s} \text{AR}_{jk,t} \tag{12}$$

5. Compute the time average abnormal return for each event over the nonevent period:

$$\overline{\overline{\text{AR}}}_{s,\tau} = (1/15) \sum_{k=-15}^{-1} \text{AR}_{s,t} \tag{13}$$

6. Compute an estimated standard deviation of the average abnormal returns over the nonevent period for substate j:

$$\hat{\sigma}_s = (1/\sqrt{14}) \sqrt{\sum_{\tau=-15}^{-1} (\overline{\text{AR}}_{s,\tau} - \overline{\overline{\text{AR}}}_{s,\tau})^2} \tag{14}$$

7. Standardize the portfolio abnormal returns for each event day t:[16]

$$\widehat{\overline{\text{AR}}}_{s,t} = \overline{\text{AR}}_{s,t} / \hat{\sigma}_s \tag{15}$$

8. Define the testable hypothesis for every day t of substate j (event) period. The null hypothesis H_o is $\overline{AR}_{s,t} = 0$, with alternative hypothesis H_A:

$$\widehat{\overline{AR}}_{s,t} \neq 0.$$

To test the hypothesis in step 8, use the following Student t-statistic:

$$t^* = \widehat{\overline{AR}}_{s,t}/\hat{\bar{\sigma}}_s \tag{16}$$

where $\hat{\sigma}_s = 1$.

For each substate, event days are grouped into three subperiods (n). The first period includes preannouncement days $-4,\ldots,-1$. The second period includes both the announcement days 0 and 1. Announcement day 1 accounts for effect of dividend announcement made late afternoon in day 0, which may not be captured by the market until the next day. The third subgroup includes postannouncement days $2,\ldots,5$. It is now possible to form the cumulative average abnormal returns (CAR) for each substate j. To do so, define $t = -4,\ldots-1$, for $n=1$; $t=0,1$, for $n=2$; $t=2,\ldots,5$, for $n=3$. We repeat steps 2 through 7 above and add step 9:

$$9.\ \overline{CAR}_{s,n} = \sum_{t=1}^{J_n} \overline{AR}_{sn,t}$$

$$t^* = \overline{CAR}_{s,n}/\sqrt{J_n}\,\hat{\sigma}_s \tag{17}$$

where J_n is the number of days in subperiod n and $\hat{\bar{\sigma}}$ equals 1.

The purpose of dividing the substate period into three subperiods is to detect any differences in the stock market reaction to dividend signals before, on, or after the announcement.

To test for abnormal stock returns over the entire substate period, we modify (17) to read

$$\overline{CAR}_s = \sum_{t=-4}^{+5} \overline{AR}_{s,t}$$

$$t^* = \overline{CAR}_s/\bar{\sigma}_s\sqrt{10} \tag{18}$$

HYPOTHESES

We propose two hypotheses pertinent to the testable implications stated in above. The first hypothesis focuses on firm value and the number of balance sheet change variables used in signaling. The second hypothesis addresses the clarity of the signal.

Hypothesis 1: For the same clarity of signal, firms that use fewer balance sheet change variables to signal the same number of attributes are less valuable than firms that use more.

Hypothesis 2: For the same level of firm value, a positive signal is more valuable than a neutral signal.

Hyphothesis 1 establishes the relationship between the value of the firm and the number of signals used. Hypothesis 2 confirms the association of a change in signal clarity and stock price reaction.

Hypothesis 1 is tested by comparing the abnormal returns between sample points with fewer balance sheet changes ($i=1$) *and* those of more balance sheet changes ($i=2$). This is performed for the neutral signal ($j=1$) set (Q_1^1, Q_1^2) *and* positive signal ($j=2$) set (Q_2^1, Q_2^2). Alternatively, for hypothesis 2, the sample points with fewer balance sheet changes and more balance sheet changes are examined across neutral *and* positive signal sets (Q_1^1, Q_2^1) and (Q_1^2, Q_2^2), respectively.[17]

RESULTS AND INTERPRETATIONS

Table 1 displays a listing of substates for the Q_j^i categories by clarity and dividend sign change. One can see that the total number of substates is about equal for firms using more balance sheet change variables or less. The table also shows that twice as many substates send positive signals as neutral signals.

Table 2 is a companion table to Table 1, and shows the number of sample points for the substates of each class of Table 1. The table shows that more firms use dividend policy to dispatch positive signals. Nineteen percent of balance sheet change combinations (i.e., substates) include dividend increases, while only 5 percent of dividend decreases exist. This observation confirms earlier evidence that most firms prefer to maintain stable dividend policy. Also, there is a preference for dividend increases over decreases when possible.

Table 3 reports the cumulative abnormal returns for the Q_j^i categories shown for the before, on, and after event periods as well as for the overall 10-day period. Obviously the overall cumulative abnormal returns are much higher for firms using more balance sheet change variables than for those using fewer $(Q_1^2$ vs. Q_1^1 *or* Q_2^2 vs. $Q_2^1)$. This supports the hypothesis that for the same level of signal clarity (neutral *or* positive), firms that use more changes in balance sheet are more valuable. Also, positive signals have higher absolute value abnormal returns than neutral signals $(Q_2^1$ vs. Q_1^1 *or* Q_2^2 vs. $Q_1^2)$. This sustains the conclusion that for the same firm valuableness, clarity of the signal matters.

In Table 3, the figures in parentheses are the percentages of the substates that are significant at the .05 level. They are to be compared to the significance of

Table 1. Substates Classified by Signal Clarity and Dividend Change for the Sample Period 1976-85 with all Substates having 5 or More Sample Points (Fewer Balance Sheet Changes, $i=1$; More Changes, $i=2$)

Dividend sign/clarity	Dividend increases (+) ($i=2$)	Dividend decreases (-) ($i=2$)	Stable dividends (0) ($i=1$)	Total
Neutral signals ($j=1$)	7	1	5	13
Positive signals ($j=2$)	7	3	17	27
Total	14	4	22	40

Table 2. Sample Points Classified by Signal Clarity and Dividend Change for the Sample Period 1976-85 Based on 15 Nonevent Sample Days (Fewer Balance Sheet Changes, $i=1$; More Changes, $i=2$)

Dividend sign/clarity	Dividend increases (+) ($i=2$)	Dividend decreases (-) ($i=2$)	Stable dividends (0) ($i=1$)	Total
Neutral signals ($j=1$)	173	26	473	672
Positive signals ($j=2$)	162	55	893	1110
Total	335	81	1366	1782

Table 3. CAR for the Q_j^i Categories (Numbers in Parentheses Are Percentage of Substates that Are Significant at the .05 Level)

Category	Cumulative abnormal returns			
	Before (-4 to -1)	*On* ($0,1$)	*After* ($+2$, to $+5$)	*Overall* (-4, to $+5$)
Q_1^1	-1.080 (0)	-0.022 (0)	0.943 (0)	-0.159 (0)
Q_1^2	0.071 (12)	2.768* (12)	1.484 (12)	4.323* (25)
Q_2^1	-0.931 (0)	0.262 (0)	-0.342 (12)	-1.011 (35)
Q_2^2	1.984 (10)	2.479 (40)	-0.070 (10)	4.393* (70)

Notes: Testing dividend signals using the conventional mean-adjusted returns methodology. CARs are cumulative of standardized portfolio average abnormal returns for the sub-event periods and the total event. T-statistics are marked by asterisks. The sampling period is 1975-1985.

*Significant at .10 level.

[a]Portfolio Q_i^j are

Q_1^1; fewer signals, neutral signals;

Q_1^2; more signals, neutral signals;

Q_2^1; fewer signals, positive signals;

Q_2^2; more signals, positive signals.

CAR all statistically significant, then the corresponding percentage of the sub-states should show a high percentage of significance at the .05 level. The table demonstrates that the more valuable firms $(Q_1^2$ and $Q_2^2)$ dominate the less valuable firms $(Q_1^1$ and $Q_2^1)$ in every column except one (the after column for (Q_2^1). Similarly, the positive signals $(Q_2^1$ and $Q_2^2)$ dominate the neutral signals $(Q_1^1$ and $Q_1^2)$ in overall cumulative abnormal returns.

Inferences from Table 3 are investigated in Table 4. Tests are pertinent to examining hypotheses 1 and 2. The table exhibits results of a pairwise *t*-test for the groups in Table 3. The difference in overall cumulative abnormal returns is significantly different from zero for (Q_1^1, Q_1^2), (Q_2^1, Q_2^2) and (Q_1^1, Q_2^1) . This supports the conclusion that neither hypothesis 1 nor 2 should be rejected. Thus, irrespective of signal clarity, firms that use more balance sheet signals are more valuable. Also, for signals of less valuable firms the level of clarity (positive or neutral) is essential for inducing significant adjustments of stock prices.

Inspection of group pair (Q_1^2, Q_2^2) inTable 4 shows that the return differences are significant before and after the event but not overall event period. This is due to a sign reversal. One possible explanation is that the value of the firm surfaces as more important than the clarity of the signal to the market (hypothesis 1 versus hypothesis 2 overall returns). Thus, the difference in signal clarity for the more valuable firms emerges as not as crucial as it is for the less valuable firms.

Finally, in Table 5 we show the *F*-test results for volatility differences in all tests of Table 4. It is seen that the differences in mean CAR not ascribe to differences in risk (variance).

Table 4.   Paired *t*-Test of Hypotheses 1 and 2
(*t*-Statistics Marked by Asterisks).[a,b]
Sampling Period 1975-1985

	Hypothesis[c]	Before (-4 to -1)	On (0,1)	After (+2 to +5)	Overall (-4 to +5)
1	(Q_1^1, Q_1^2)	-2.019**	-4.894**	-0.950	-7.863**
	(Q_2^1, Q_2^2)	-4.223**	-3.212**	-0.395	-7.830**
2	(Q_1^1, Q_1^2)	-0.292	-0.558	2.526**	1.676*
	(Q_2^1, Q_2^2)	-2.851**	0.431	2.316**	-0.104

Notes: [a]**Significant at .05 level; *; significant at .10 level.
[b]The *t*-values are calculated as follows

$$ t = \frac{\overline{CAR}_1}{J_{n1}\sqrt{\dfrac{1}{J_{n1}} + \dfrac{1}{J_{n2}}}} - \frac{\overline{CAR}_2}{J_{n2}\sqrt{\dfrac{1}{J_{n1}} + \dfrac{1}{J_{n2}}}} $$

[c]Hypothesis 1:   Valuable vs. less valuable firms given same clarity of signal and number of attributes.
Hypothesis 2:   Neutral vs. positive signals given same firm value

Table 5.   *F*-Test for Volatility Differences in Paired Tests of Table 4[a]

Hypothesis[c]	Before (-4 to -1)	On (0,1)	After (+2 to +5)	Overall (-4 to +5)
1 (Q_1^1, Q_1^2)	0.654	0.586	0.500	0.433
(Q_2^1, Q_2^2)	0.840	0.685	1.012	0.822
2 (Q_1^1, Q_2^1)	0.841	0.572	0.650	0.595
(Q_1^2, Q_2^2)	1.079	0.669	1.314	1.129

Notes: [a]**, Significant at .05 level; *,significant at .10 level.
[b]Hypothesis categories defined in Table 3.

CONCLUSION

Early literature on dividend signaling by John and Williams (1985) and Miller and Rock (1985) suggests one signal (earnings or dividend) and one attribute (cash flows from capital investment). More recently, Asquith and Mullins (1986), Ambarish, John and Williams (1987), and Ofer and Thakor (1987) propose models with two signals (e.g., dividend and net new issues, *or* dividend and stock repurchase) and one attribute (cash flows from capital investment) for all equity firms. In this paper we advance and test a version of a signaling model that integrates balance sheet and dividend signals and allows for two firm attributes (focusing on capital investment and financing). In our model, the dividend signal has three possible dimensions: (1) clarity (neutral, positive, or unclear), (2) direction (favorable or unfavorable), and (3) significance (high or low). Clarity marks the extent of comprehension of corporate signals. A favorable direction induces positive stock price adjustments during the announcement period and vice versa. Significance is measured by the strength of market response to the signals.

The clarity of the signal (neutral or positive) is tested along with the number of balance sheet and dividend signals. In particular, we find (1) that firms that use more signals to signal the same number of attributes are more valuable, and (2) that signals that increase information clarity are more valuable than those which do not.

The results of our study confirm the notion that dividend announcements are but part of a complex signaling process. Depending on the prior condition of the firm, the signal is either favorable or unfavorable to the stock price. The reason for this is explained by the type and clarity of the dividend signal itself.

The positive clarity signal evokes more response from the capital markets. This is because this type of signal provides new and valuable information that is not present in a neutral group signal. The market response to a neutral signal depends solely on the directions and size of the changes.

Future research will focus on extending signaling models for another attribute, agency costs. Also, since a dividend signal can sometimes be unclear, it is compelling to know when such a signal is valuable and when it becomes cost prohibitive.

APPENDIX A: DERIVATION OF BINDING NONMIMICRY CONSTRAINTS AND MINIMUM NUMBER OF BALANCE SHEET CHANGE VARIABLES

Corollary 1: If the number of firm attributes is k, the number of firm types per attribute is j, and the number of balance sheet changes is BS, then (a) the maximum number of binding nonmimicry constraints T_M is $T_M = j^K - 1$, and (b) the minimum number of balance sheet change variables BS necessary for an efficient signal is $BS_{min} = K + T_M + 1$ where $+ 1$ represents the sources and uses of funds condition.

Proof: A firm of type j can mimic any single attribute of another firm. For K attributes, the maximum number of mimicking firms in $j \times j^x \ldots {}^x j^k = j_k$. Since the case of a firm that has the lowest value for each attribute may be included in j but is never mimicked, then the maximum number of binding nonmimicry constraints TM, is $TM = j^k = 1$.

For signaling efficiency to hold for all firms, the minimum number of balance sheet change variables (BS_{min}), must equal the number of attributes (K), the maximum number of binding nonmimicry constraints (T_M), plus the sources and uses of funds condition. Thus, $BSmin = K + T_M + 1$.

APPENDIX B: DERIVATION OF PRICE CHANGES FOR THREE ATTRIBUTES

Let Vj in (3) for the signal pair (D,X) be given as

$$V^j(D, X, S) = L(D, P) + \frac{P - L(D, P)}{P + t_p D + X} F(X) \tag{A1}$$

where $X = I, -B, -C$. The minus signs on B and C reflect the fact that they appear on the right-hand side of the sources and uses of funds condition (1).

The first-order conditions for the price change effects are

$$\partial P / \partial D = t_p \frac{(P - L)}{t_p D + X + L} \tag{A2}$$

$$\partial P / \partial X = \delta (1 - F'(X)) \frac{(P - L)}{t_p D + X + L} \tag{A3}$$

where $\delta = \pm 1$ as $X \gtrless 0$.

Consider the following attribute functions:

$$F(I) = a + b\,G(I): \quad G' > 0,\ G' < 0,\ G''(\infty) > 0,\ a,b > 0 \tag{A4}$$

$$F(B) = (1-t_c)(-B) - W(-B): \quad W' < 0,\ W'' < 0,\ t_c > 0,\ W(B) = W(-B),\ W'(B)$$
$$= -W'(-B) \tag{A5}$$

$$F(-C) = -d + A(-C): \quad A'(C, A'' < 0,\ d > 0,\ A(C) = A(-C),$$
$$A'(C) = -A'(-C) \tag{A6}$$

where a,b,d are constraints; t_c is the corporate tax rate; $G(\ )$ is an investment function; $W(\ )$ is the bankruptcy cost function; and $A(\ )$ is the internal liquidity cost function.

Applying (A3) to (A4)-(4-6) yields:

$$\partial P/\partial I = (1 - bG'(I))\frac{P-L}{t_p D - I + L} \tag{A7}$$

$$\partial P/\partial B = -(t_c + W'(-B))\frac{P-L}{t_p D - B + L} \tag{A8}$$

$$\partial P/\partial C = -(1 - A'(-C))\frac{P-L}{t_p D - C + L} \tag{A9}$$

Therefore, the price effect ratios are:

$$-\frac{\partial P/\partial D}{\partial P/\partial I} = \frac{t_p}{bG'(I) - 1} \tag{A10}$$

$$-\frac{\partial P/\partial D}{\partial P/\partial B} = \frac{t_p}{t_c + W'(-B)} \tag{A11}$$

$$-\frac{\partial P/\partial D}{\partial P/\partial C} = \frac{t_p}{1 - A'(-C)} \tag{A12}$$

For the more valuable firms, we assume that $bG'(I) \gg 1$, which implies $-(\partial P/\partial D \div \partial P/\partial I) < 1$, where t_p is around .30 for many investors. Also, $t_c > W'(B)$ for the more valuable firms and since $W'(B) = W'(-B)$, then $tc + W'(-B)$ is positive and presumably greater than t_p. Finally, internal liquidity cost for the more valuable firms are assumed to be small, that is, $1 - A'(-C) > t_p$. Any of these conditions leads to a positive stock price response $\Delta P > 0$ if ΔD and $\pm\Delta X$ are both positive. Less valuable firms may or may not satisfy the $-(\partial P/\partial D \div \partial P/\partial X) < 1$ condition for a positive price response.

ACKNOWLEDGMENTS

We thank Mohammed Chaudhury; Jim Overdahl; members of the Finance Workshop, UT-Dallas; participants of the Northern Finance Meetings, Ottawa; and anonymous referees of this journal. All errors are the authors'.

NOTES

1. According to Rozeff (1982), agency costs can relate to dividend policy. We argue that changes in the balance sheet can also signal the agency attribute. However, the agency attribute is dropped from our model because agency can be manifested in more than one balance sheet measure.

2. This idea is implicitly embodied in the analyses of Kane, Lee, and Marcus (1984) and Miller and Rock (1985).

3. Since we know that the C variable can play other roles in firm signaling, such as completing the sources and uses of funds equation or helping to satisfy the nonmimicry constraints, we do not focus on it as one of our two attributes in the model development section. However, we do not include C as a proxy for one of the two possible attributes in the empirical tests after analyzing a three-attribute model presented in Appendix B.

4. This assumption is consistent with other signaling models (e.g.; AJW). Although other types of firms may exist in between, the analysis here is restricted to the two types to avoid unnecessary complications and for ease of empirical testing.

5. Earnings and financial statements announcements are assumed to be made before dividend announcements (see note 12).

6. See note 12.

7. Equation (3) differs from Equation (5) in AJW in two important aspects: First, the firm value is a function of all five sources and uses of funds variables described in-equation (1); this adds the financing decision attribute. Second, function $F(\ )$ represents the present value of all after-tax future cash flows for *multiple attributes* including the investment attribute. Moreover, the model meets the engers (1987) conditions for an informationally consistent equilibrium and conforms with the revelation principle of Harris and Townsend (1985).

8. In this formulation, all depreciation tax shield effects are captured in the $F(S_k^j)$ functions. Management and the board of directors decide on D and N while external stockholders represented by a consensus investor make decisions on R.

9. See note 3 for the rationale of including C in both δ_1 and δ_2.

10. Consistent with Corollary 1 in Appendix A, to be a neutral signal $T_M \leq \delta_2^M + \delta_3^M$ *and* BS $\geq K+T_M+1$, where M = maximum number. For positive signals $T_M > \delta_2^M + \delta_3^M$ *or* BS $< K+T_M+1$. For an unclear signal $T_M > \delta_M^2 + \delta_3^M$ *and* BS $< K+T_M+1$.

11. Although this can be a selection bias, we do not expect managers or investors to rely as much on dividends as an important signaling device when they have concern about the firm's survival. This criterion, however, resulted in only a 3% reduction in the number of observations.

12. Approximately 40% of the firms on the Compustat tape used in the study announced their earnings and financial statements after announcing their dividends. Since it is not obvious that earnings second signals are perfect substitutes for dividends second signals, they were separated. Future analysis in this area is planned by the authors.

13. This is consistent with Kalay and Lowenstein (1985). They maintain that boards of directors normally announce omission of dividend payments for several quarters in advance. These predictions are, therefore, known to the market. This would limit any negative effect to a dividend omission.

14. In the case of changes in C, I, or B, a band of $\pm\%$ is placed around the zero (stable) change state to account for classification error. This has the effect of converting 13 infeasible states into feasible states.

15.   In 70% of the sample points, the announcements period is no more than seven days. In 15% of the sample, the nonevent period was less than 15 days in length and they were dropped from the sample. The short non event period is set to filer out other related announcement effects; however, we did allow the nonevent period to be 20 days with no discernible effects on the results.

16.   The portfolio is standardized each day t to account for the possibility that N_s could change each day.

17.   By focusing on these categories only 25 states and 40 substates are examined. The remaining states will be examined in future research.

REFERENCES

Aharony, J. & Swary, I. (1980). Quarterly dividend and earnings announcements and stockholders returns: An empirical analysis. *Journal of Finance, 35,* 1-12.

Ambarish, R., John, K., Williams, J. (1987). Efficient signaling with dividends and investments. *Journal of Finance, 42,* 321-342.

Asquith, P. & Mullins D. Jr. (1983). The impact of initiating dividend payments on shareholders' wealth. *Journal of Business, 56,* 77-96.

_______ (1986). Signaling with dividends, stock repurchases, and equity issues. *Financial Management,* 15, 27-44.

Bhattacharya, S. (1979). Imperfect information, dividend policy and the bird in hand fallacy. *Bell Journal of Economics, 10,* 259-270.

Bhattacharya, S. (1980). Non-dissipative signaling structure and dividend policy. *Quarterly Journal of Economics, 95,* 1-24.

Black, F. (1976). The dividend puzzle. *Journal of Portfolio Management,* 5-8.

Brown, S.J. & Warner, J.B. (1985). Using daily stock returns: The case of event studies. *Journal of Financial Economics, 4,* 3-31.

Charest, G. (1979). Dividend information, stock return and market efficiency II. *Journal of Financial Economics, 6,* 297-330.

Engers, M. (1987). Signaling with many signals. *Econometrica, 3,* 663-674.

Fama, E. & Babiak, H. (1968). Dividend policy: An empirical analysis. *Journal of American Statistical Association, 63,* 32-61.

Hakansson, N. (1982). Dividend policy and valuation: Theory and tests. *Journal of Finance, 37,* 415-442.

Harris, M. & Townsend R. (1985). Resources allocation under asymmetric information. *Econometrica, 49,* 33-64.

Healy, P.M. and Palepu, K.G. 1988. Market rationality and dividend announcements. *Journal of Financial Economics,* 149-176.

John, K. & Kalay, A. (1982). Costly contracting and optimal payout constraints. *Journal of Finance, 37,* 457-70.

_______ John, K. & Williams J. (1985), Dividends, dilution, and taxes: A signaling equilibrium. *Journal of Finance, 40,* 1053-1070.

Kalay, A. & Lowenstein, V. (1985). Predictable events and excess returns: The case of dividend announcements. *Journal of Financial Economics, 4,* 423-449.

Kane, A., Lee, & Y. & Marcus A. (1984). Earnings and dividend announcements: Is there a corroboration effect? *Journal of Finance, 39,* 1091-1099.

Lintner, J. (1956). Distribution of income among dividends, retained earnings, and taxes. *American Economics Review, 46,* 97-113.

Makhija, A. Thompson, H. (1986). Some aspects of equilibrium for a cross-section of firms and signaling profitability with dividends: A note. *Journal of Finance, 41,* 249-254.

Miller, M. & Modigliani, F. (1961). Dividend policy, growth and valuation of shares. *Journal of Business, 34*, 411-433.

Miller, M. & Rock, K. (1985). Dividend policy under asymmetric information. *Journal of Finance, 40*, 1031-1052.

Ofer, A.R. & Siegel, D.R. (1987). Corporate financial policy, information, and market expectations: An empirical investigation of dividends. *Journal of Finance, 42*, 889-912.

Ofer, A.R. & Thakor, A.V. (1987). A theory of stock price responses to alternative corporate cash disbursement methods: Stock Repurchases and dividends. *Journal of Finance, 42*, 365-394.

Pettit, R. (1976) The impact of dividend and earnings announcements: A reconciliation. *Journal of Business, 49*, 86-96.

Ross, S. (1977). The determination of financial structure: The incentive signaling approach. *Bell Journal of Economics, 8*, 23-40.

Rozeff, M. (1982). Growth, beta and agency costs as determinants of dividend payout ratios. *Journal of Financial Research, 5*, 249-259.

Wansley, J.W. & Lane, W.R. (1987). A financial profile of the dividend initiating firm. *Journal of Business Finance and Accounting, 14*, 425-436.

Wansley, J.W., Sirmans, C.F., Shilling, J.D., and Lee, Y.J. (1991). Dividend change announcement effects and earnings volatility and timing. *Journal of Financial Research, 14*, 37-50.

HETEROGENEOUS DISCOUNT RATES AND MODELS OF EXHAUSTIBLE RESOURCES

A.G. Malliaris and Silvana Stefani

INTRODUCTION

According to the now famous *Hotelling rule* established in Hotelling (1931), the price of an exhaustible resource must grow at a rate equal to the rate of interest, both along an efficient extraction path and in a competitive resource industry equilibrium. If we denote by $p(0)$ the initial period price and by $p(t)$ the price at period t, we can write

$$p(t) = p(0)e^{rt} \tag{1.1}$$

where r is the rate of interest. If we assume that this interest rate r is equal to society's optimal discount rate between future and present, Hotelling showed that the competitive resource owner would deplete at the social optimal rate.

The intuition behind the Hotelling rule is simple. The present value of a unit of resource extracted must be the same in all periods if there is to be no gain from

Advances in Financial Planning and Forecasting,
Volume 5, pages 227-247.
Copyright © 1994 by JAI Press Inc.
All rights of reproduction in any form reserved.
ISBN:1-55938-421-2

shifting extraction among periods. For the present value of price, or price net of extraction cost, to be the same in all periods, the undiscounted value must be growing at precisely the rate of interest. Put differently, suppose that price net of extraction cost is expected by producers to be rising too slowly, say below the interest rate r. Then resource deposit is not a good way to hold wealth. Producers will try to liquidate their resource deposits by increasing current production and by investing their revenues at the higher $r\%$. But as production increases, the current price must decrease along the demand curve. Thus, initial pessimistic price expectations lead to current price decreases. Similar reasoning suggests that if prices are expected to grow faster than the interest rate r, then the value of resource deposits would grow faster than any other form of wealth, which may cause speculative withholding of production and higher current prices.

It is reasonable to conclude that the role that society's optimal discount rate plays is very important. Solow (1974, p. 10) emphasizes that "the pure theory of exhaustible resources is trying to tell us that, if exhaustible resources really matter, then the balance between present and future is more delicate than we are accustomed to think; and pretty important and one ought not to be casual about it."

The purpose of this paper is to analyze the role of the firm's and the market's discount rate in several representative partial equilibrium models of exhaustible resources. More specifically, we use the elementary theory of finance to write the expected discount rate of the firm δ as the sum of the expected risk-free rate of interest r and the term $\beta\,(r_M\text{-}r)$, where r_M denotes the expected return on a diversified portfolio of assets, usually called market return, and β is a measure of the covariance between the market rate and the return on the particular asset in question. Symbolically we write

$$\delta = r + \beta\,(r_M\text{-}r) \tag{1.2}$$

The current literature on exhaustible resources simply assumes that $\delta = r$ because $r_M = r$ or $\beta = 0$. In other words it is assumed that firms in the extraction of exhaustible resources receive no premium over the risk-free rate of return or that such firms are viewed as assuming no financial risk, that is, $\beta = 0$. Of course, this is an oversimplification and in order to be more realistic we plan to remove this assumption. In this paper, we no longer assume that $\beta\,(r_M - r) = 0$. Instead we consider firms in the business of extracting exhaustible resources each facing a specific discount rate δ_i, which can be written as

$$\delta_i = r + \rho_i \tag{1.3}$$

where r is as before the risk-free interest rate, say the short-term return on a 3-month Treasury bill and $\rho_i = \beta_i\,(r_M - r)$ is the excess return required to compensate for the particular risks that the specific ith firm, $i = 1, \dots, k$, assumes. There is no reason a priori why ρ_i should be the same for each firm, particularly if one considers the experience of oil-producing firms, which operate under dissimilar production, financial, and political risks across the international economy. Adelman (1986) lists several factors that determine ρ_i and therefore the firm's discount rate δ_i. Brealey and Meyers (1981) estimate that the real risk-free rate is approximately 2%, $\beta = 1.07$ for the oil industry and $r_M - r = 8.8\%$. Therefore, the average δ for the oil industry is about 11%.

THE HOTELLING MODEL

Consider the ith firm that solves the following problem:

$$\max_{v^{(i)}} \int_0^\infty p(t) v^{(i)}(t) e^{-\delta_i t} dt \qquad (2.1)$$

subject to the constraints on the total stock of the resource $X_0^{(i)}$, that is,

$$\dot{X}(t) = -v^{(i)}(t) \quad with \ X^{(i)}(0) = X_0^{(i)} \qquad (2.2)$$

where $p(t)$ denotes price and $v^{(i)}(t)$ denotes output of the ith firm, i=1,$\ldots k$, both during period t. The discount rate δ_i is as in (1.3). In this simplified model we assume that extraction costs are zero. Forming the current-value Hamiltonian, we write

$$H^{(i)}(t) = p(t) v^{(i)}(t) - q^{(i)}(t) v^{(i)}(t) \qquad (2.3)$$

where $q^{(i)}(t)$ is the current costate variable. Note that $H^{(i)}(t) = e^{\delta_i t} \tilde{H}^{(i)}(t)$ is the discounted Hamiltonian and $q^{(i)}(t) = e^{\delta_i t} \lambda^{(i)}(t)$, where $\lambda^{(i)}(t)$ is the discounted costate variable. It is more convenient to use the current-value Hamiltonian and costate rather than discounted variables. Time t is not an explicit argument of $p(t)$ and $v^{(i)}(t)$. Thus the equations describing the optimal path will be autonomous (Kamien and Schwartz, 1981). We compute the first-order condition for optimality:

$$\partial H^{(i)}/\partial v^{(i)} = p(t) - q^{(i)}(t) = 0 \qquad (2.4)$$

From (2.4) we obtain

$$\dot{p}(t)/p(t) = \dot{q}^{(i)}(t)/q^{(i)}(t) \qquad (2.5)$$

Combining (2.5) with the expression for $q^{(i)}(t)$ from

$$\partial H^{(i)}/\partial X = \dot{q}^{(i)} - \delta_i q^{(i)}(t) = 0 \qquad (2.6)$$

we obtain

$$\dot{p}(t)/p(t) = \delta_i \qquad (2.7)$$

which is the Hotelling rule result. Suppose that the market price of the exhaustible resource follows

$$\dot{p}(t)/p(t) = \alpha \qquad (2.8)$$

and assume that firm i which just solved (2.1) subject to (2.2), is a perfectly competitive firm that faces (2.8) parametrically. How can (2.7) and (2.8) be compared? It seems reasonable that the firms whose discount rate $\delta_i \geq \alpha$ will produce and supply the resource, while those with $\delta_i < \alpha$ could not be sufficiently compensated and therefore will not produce. Put it in different words, in a partial equilibrium analysis, the ith producer takes as given the price evolution of the resource given by (2.8). If this producer's discount rate $\delta_i \geq \alpha$, the future market price discounted to present by the firm's discount rate δ_i will yield a lower present value of the resources and thus induce the firm to sell such resources at the higher market price. Conversely, if $\delta_i < \alpha$, the present value of the reserves discounted by δ_i will be worth more the current market price and thus cause this ith firm to withhold the resource.

This elementary analysis suggests a modification of the Hotelling rule to take into account heterogeneous discount rates. Assuming no extraction costs and a large number of competitive producers with a distribution of discount rates $\{\delta_i\}$ i = i, ..., k, market supply and demand conditions require that price grows exponentially at a rate α so that the quantity supplied by all firms with $\delta_i \geq \alpha$ meets the market demand. If the market price increases at a rate faster than and if the distribution of $\{\delta_i\}$ does not change, then fewer firms will continue their production and if market price grows at a rate lower than certain marginal firms will enter the production process.

This paper attempts to generalize the Hotelling result by allowing heterogeneous discount rates among the producing firms. Using partial equilibrium analysis and deterministic optimal control techniques we show how the optimal policies of the representative firm are affected by financial risk. More specifically we study the following.

First, we analyze the constant-cost case and then the case where costs depend on the resource stocks. For this purpose, two representative forms are considered, each characterized by a different discount, attributed to different financial risk, and their optimal policies are compared.

With constant costs, the firm with discounts greater than the rate of the growth of the market price will all produce at maximum capacity.

When the costs depend on the resource in the ground, the amount of available resource turns out to be essential in order to assess whether a higher financial risk would imply a faster output policy. More specifically, we show that the riskier firm will be faster in depleting its available stock when it has more resource than the less risky firm. However, more resource scarcity may result in a more conservative policy even though the producing firm has a higher financial risk. This last result depends also on the shape of the cost function, as shown in a theorem and an example.

Moreover, we also study the role of shifts in the market discount rate, that is, we analyze the impact of a change in the market discount on the optimal policy of a producer. The problem studied in this: as a result of a change in demand, the growth rate of the market price Q changes, what is the impact of such a change in Q on the optimal policy of firm i with discount rate δ_i?

We consider first the case when costs are independent of the market price growth rate; in this case we give a necessary and sufficient condition for faster initial depletion when the market discount increases. When costs are dependent on the market discount rate a sufficient condition for the shadow price to decline as the market discount rate increases is given.

Finally, an example shows that slower depletion may occur at a rising market discount. This happens when the costs are too high to be sustained, due to the scarcity of the resource, or because of the financing costs for the capital required for extraction.

It may be worth mentioning that statements may be found in the literature concerning faster depletion when the discount rate is rising. Some authors, such as Adelman (1986 (1986), refer to a discount rate specific for each producer and claim that a higher discount may lead to faster depletion. Others refer to the market discount rate, that is, when there is a shift in the economy, production should be faster; see, for instance, Solow (1974) and Pindyck (1978a).

The results presented in this paper clarify and give mathematical support to several conjectures found on this issue in the literature. For example, in the next section, we clarify the importance of the amount of the available resource for producers with heterogeneous discounts, and show the results depend critically on this condition. In contrast, Devarajan and Fisher (1981) review several major contributions on exhaustible resources and do not specify the role of resource stocks. Similarly our results in the subsequent section 4, which refer to shifts in the valid under some particular hypotheses, show that different situations may occur. In fact, an increase of the market rate does not necessarily imply faster depletion. This last result is consistent with Farzin (1984).

NON NEGLIGIBLE COSTS

In this section, we first give our general methodological framework and then study the two major cases: when costs are constant and when extraction costs depend on the reserves of the exhaustible resource. In order to analyze more closely the effect of a different discounting on the optimal policies, we consider two firms in a competitive environment, each characterized by a different discount rate.

The General Setting

Suppose the discount rates δ_1 and δ_2 are such that $\delta_1 > \delta_2$, that is $\rho_1 > \rho_2$, according to (1.3). Therefore, we assume that firm 1 faces a higher financial risk than firm 2.

We also assume that the two firms have the same cost function and decide their strategy according to the same pattern, except possibly the initial level of resource. The general optimization problem is

$$\underset{v^{(i)}}{Max} \int_0^\infty [p(t) - C(X)] v^{(i)}(t) \exp[-(r + \rho_i)t] \, dt \tag{3.1}$$

subject to

$$X(t) = -v^{(i)}(t) \quad X^{(i)}(0) = X_0^i, \quad i = 1, 2$$

with cost function $C(X)$ such that $C_x \leq 0$; $v^{(i)}$ denotes the extraction rate, with $0 \leq v^{(i)} \leq \bar{v}$ (where $\bar{v}$ denotes the maximum production capacity for both firms).

Form the current-value Hamiltonian

$$H^{(i)}(t) = [p(t) - C(X)] v^{(i)}(t) - q^{(i)}(t) v^{(i)}$$

and obtain

$$-(r + \rho_i) q^{(i)} + q^{(i)} = C_x^{(i)}, \quad i = 1, 2 \tag{3.2}$$

where $q^{(i)}$ is the current costate variable for the ith firm. For the current-value Hamiltonian and costate, recall the remarks given regarding Equation (2.3). The necessary condition for optimality is

$$\partial H^{(i)}/\partial v^{(i)} = p(t) - C(X) - q^{(i)}(t) = 0 \tag{3.3}$$

and according to Arrow and Kurz (1970) and Benveniste and Scheinkman (1982), the transversality condition requires

$$\lim_{t\to\infty} X(t)\, q^{(i)}(t)\, \exp\left[-(r+\rho_i)t\right] = 0$$

Since the objective function is linear in the control variable, we may possibly get "bang-bang" solutions. However, we are interested in the singular paths, that is, those solutions that hold when (3.3) is satisfied; otherwise (3.3) should be ≤ 0 for $v^{(i)} = 0$ or ≥ 0 for $v^{(i)} = \bar{v}$.

Differentiating (3.3) with respect to time we get

$$\dot{q}^{(i)}(t) = \dot{p}(t) - C_X \dot{X}, \quad i = 1, 2 \tag{3.4}$$

Equation (3.2) and (3.4), from the state equation, it follows that

$$(r+\rho_i)\, q^{(i)} + C_X v^{(i)} = \dot{p} - C_X \dot{X} = \dot{p} + C_X v^{(i)}, \quad i = 1, 2 \tag{3.5}$$

Therefore, we conclude that

$$q^{(i)}(t) = \dot{p}(t) / (r+\rho_i), \quad i = 1, 2 \tag{3.6}$$

which gives the optimal singular path for the costate variable (shadow price) for each firm. Note that the difference between the two optimal strategies is given only by ρ_i, because both producers are price-takers. Then, one could conclude that a simple comparison between the two shadow prices (which give the value of the resource underground for each producer) at time 0 may indicate which one of the two would produce more. That is, the one with lower shadow price, or equivalently with higher financial risk, would begin to produce faster. We show that this is in general true only when costs are constant, that is, when extraction costs are independent of the available resource. This corresponds to the Hotelling case with nonnegligible costs.

Constant Costs

In this case we have $C_X = 0$. This is well-known Hotelling rule, which states (as already mentioned above) that the resource price net of the extraction costs must rise at the market discount rate, assuming free competition. Extraction costs are assumed constant and in fact the rule holds only when costs are constant; this is rather obvious from the methodology of control theory, but in 1931 it was not so! See also Gordon (1967). When cost are negligible we get (2.4) and (2.5). Note that (3.2) and (3.3) combined, for $C_X = 0$, give the Hotelling rule.

The effect of an increase in the discount rate cannot be directly seen in the optimal output, given the singularity of the problem. The optimal output is not unique and any policy that satisfies the initial and final binding conditions of the resource path is optimal. In fact, the value of the stock is independent of the actual extraction policy, since its price rises at the market discount rate. See Gordon (1967) or Dasgupta and Heal (1979). The analysis will then be carried out through the shadow prices for the two firms. It is easy to see that even with constant costs, $C(X) = m$, and assuming for simplicity that they are the same for all firms in the market, condition (3.6) together with (3.3) still need to be satisfied by the two shadow prices, on the singular path. However, under the Hotelling hypothesis it is known that (3.3) must hold in the market according to (2.8), that is,

$$p(t) - m = \dot{p}(t)/\alpha \tag{3.7}$$

This equation is obtained from (3.3) and (3.6) when $C_X = 0$ by assuming that the discount rate is equal to α. It follows then that for both firms the singular path condition cannot be sustained because

$$p(t) - m = \dot{p}(t)/\alpha > \dot{\rho}(t)/(r + \rho_2) > \dot{\rho}(t)/(r + \rho_1) \tag{3.8}$$

since $\alpha < r + \rho_2 < r + \rho_1$ from the suceeding section. This is true particular when $t = 0$, in which case from (3.6) we conclude

$$q^{(i)}(0) < p(0) - m, \quad i = 1, 2$$

This is the condition for production at maximum capacity for Hotelling firms. The following theorem summarizes the result.

Theorem 1.   At constant extraction costs, firms with discount rates δ_i higher than the market price growth rate will all produce at maximum capacity.

Note that this holds irrespective of the resource available for each firm. Theorem 1 holds of course also when one of the two firms has α as discount rate and the other is characterized by a higher financial risk. Therefore, while the market firm will be following an arbitrarily optimal policy, provided (3.3) is satisfied, the riskier firm will produce at maximum capacity up to the data of exhaustion of its resource. See also Malliaris and Stefani (1991).

Costs Depending on Reserves

Let us consider next a more general setting, in which costs depend on the resource available. Theorem 2 shows that, if in addition to $\delta_1 > \delta_2$ we also postulate that $X^{(1)}(0) \geq X^{(2)}(0)$, then faster depletion is reinforced by the availability of greater initial resource stocks.

However, if $\delta_1 > \delta_2$ and $X^{(1)}(0) < X^{(2)}(0)$, no conclusion can be drawn. In this last case we will see that the shape of the cost function is also important, as Theorem 3 and *Example* 1 will show.

These results establish previous claims that higher discounts in an heterogeneous environment may lead to faster depletion, such as in Adelman (1986).

Theorem 2. If two producers of an exhaustible resource are prices takers, have different discount rates $r + \rho_1$, $r + \rho_2$ with $\rho_1 > \rho_2$, and the same cost function $C(X)$ then

(i) if $X^{(1)}(0) \geq X^{(2)}(0)$

$$v^{(1)}(0) = \bar{v}, \quad v^{(2)}(0) = v^*(0) \ (singular \ path)$$

or

$$v^{(1)}(0) = v^*(0) \quad (singular \ path), \quad v^{(2)}(0) = 0$$

(ii) if $X^{(1)}(0) < X^{(2)}(0)$ no conclusion can a priori be drawn as Theorem 3 and Example 1 will show.

Proof: We will separate the two cases $X^{(1)}(0) = X^{(2)}(0)$ and $X^{(1)}(0) > X^{(2)}(0)$. For the first case $X^{(1)}(0) = X^{(2)}(0)$, it is clear that both producers cannot follow simultaneously the singular path at $t=0$. In fact, (3.3) and 3.6) combined give

$$p(0) - C(0) = \dot{p}(0)/(r + \rho_i), \quad i = 1 \ or \ 2 \tag{3.9}$$

Assume that firm 2 is following the singular path, then (3.9) holds for $i=2$. Therefore,

$$p(0) - C(0) > \dot{p}(0)/(r + \rho_1)$$

since $\rho_1 > \rho_2$. This is the condition for production at maximum capacity of firm 1. If on the contrary, (3.9) holds for $i=1$, then

$$p(0) - C(0) < \dot{p}(0)(r + \rho_2)$$

since $\rho_1 > \rho_2$, which is the condition for firm 2 to produce nothing.

In the second case $X^{(1)}(0) > X^{(2)}(0)$ also one of the two firms cannot follow the singular path at $t = 0$. If this were true, we would have

$$p(0) - C^{(1)}(0) = \dot{p}(0)/(r + \rho_1) \qquad (3.10a)$$

$$p(0) - C^{(2)}(0) = \dot{p}(0)/(r + \rho_2) \qquad (3.10b)$$

where $C^{(1)}(0) = C^{(2)}(0)$. Solving for $\dot{p}(0)$ and p(0) we get $p(0) < 0$, which is absurd, otherwise production would never take place in the market. Thus only one of the two (3.10) may hold. Assume (3.10b) holds. Then, solving for $p(0)$ from the left-hand side of (3.10a) we get

$$\dot{p}(0)/(r + \rho_2) + C^{(2)}(0) - C^{(1)}(0) > \dot{p}(0)/(r + \rho_1)$$

which is the condition for firm 1 to produce at maximum capacity. If on the contrary we assume that (3.10a) holds, a similar argument gives the condition for firm 2 to produce nothing. See Figures 1 and 2 for possible optimal paths. This completes the proof.

When $X^{(1)}(0) < X^{(2)}(0)$, nothing, can be said a priori. A simple result and an example will show different behaviors for the two firms. Specifically, in this case the shape of the cost function is also important. Theorem 3 shows that if the riskier firm has less initial resource, it will be producing faster than the less risky, provided that the cost is a concave function, it will be producing faster than the

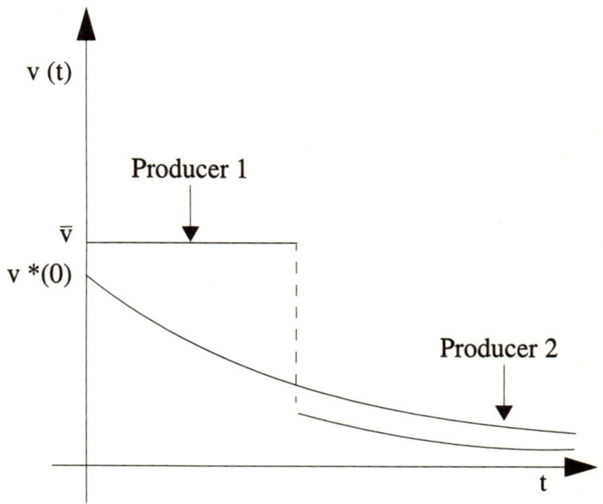

Figure 1. $X^{(1)}(0) \geq X^{(2)}(0)$, Producer 2 Singular

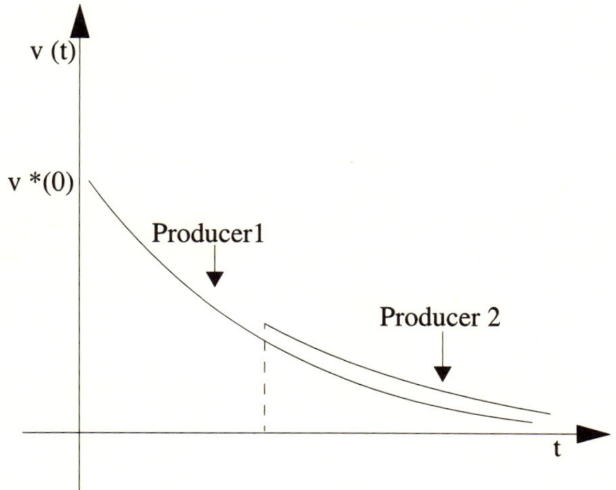

Figure 2. $X^{(1)}(0) \geq X^{(2)}(0)$ Producer 1 Singular

less risky, provided that the cost is a concave function of the resource stock and the marginal price is increasing at $t=0$. Note that this last condition is always satisfied when the price has an exponential path. On the other hand, Example 1 shows that slower depletion occurs for the riskier firm when cost is a convex function of the resource stock.

Theorem 3. Consider two exhaustible resource producers with different discount rates $r + \rho_1$ and $r + \rho_2$, $\rho_1 > \rho_2$, such that

$$X^{(1)}(0) < X^{(2)}(0)$$

If $C_{XX} \leq 0$ and $\ddot{p}(0) > 0$ then $v^{(1)}(0) = v^{(2)}(0)$.
Proof: From (3.2) and (3.6) we obtain

$$v^{(i)}(0) = [\dot{p}(0) - \ddot{p}(0)/(r + \rho_i)] / [-C^{(i)}x(0)], \quad i = 1, 2$$

If $C_{XX} \leq 0$, then $C_X^{(2)}(0) \leq C_X^{(1)}(0) < 0$. Therefore,

$$v^{(1)}(0) > v^{(2)}(0)$$

if

$$\dot{p}(0) - \ddot{p}(0)/(r + \rho_1) > \dot{p}(0) - \ddot{p}(0)/(r + \rho_2)$$

which is true because $\rho_1 > \rho_2$. This completes the proof.

The following example shows that the riskier firm may be slower in production, when the extraction costs are a convex instead of a concave function of reserves.
Example 1:   Assume, as throughout this section, $\rho_1 > \rho_2$, and consider as in Bohi and Toman (1984), price and cost functions of the form.

$$p(t) = p(0)\ \exp(\gamma t),\quad C(X) = m/X,\quad m \in R^{+}$$

Note that, since in this case costs depend on the reserves, the market price cannot follow (2.6) but, if exponential, it should rise at a rate strictly less than Q. This can be seen from the market condition (3.7), where we have $C=C(X(t))$ instead of the constant m. From

$$p(t) - C(X(t)) = \dot{p}(t)/\alpha$$

it follows that

$$\dot{p}(t)/p(t) < \alpha$$

We assume here an exponential path at a rate $\gamma < \alpha$; see Pindyck (1978b), Dasgupta and Heal (1979), Miller and Upton (1985). As it has been stressed in the previous section, when costs are constant, the condition for both producers to extract now must still hold in this case and in fact it is obviously satisfied because

$$r + \rho_1 > r + \rho_2 > \alpha > \gamma$$

Then from (3.6)

$$q^{(i)}(t) = \gamma p(0)\ \exp(\gamma t)/(r + \rho_i),\quad i = 1, 2 \tag{3.11}$$

From the market condition (3.3) and 3.11) we get

$$C^{(i)}(X) = p(t) - q^{(i)}(t) = p(0)\exp(\gamma t) - \gamma p(0)\exp(\gamma t)/(r+\rho_i)$$

$$= p(0)\exp(\gamma t)(r+\rho_i-\gamma)/(r+\rho_i), \quad i = 1, 2 \qquad (3.12)$$

Knowing that $C(X) = m/X$, from this last equation we get the expression for the optimal resource stock along the optimal path,

$$X^{(i)}(t) = m(r+\rho_i)(\exp(-\gamma t)/[p(0)(r+\rho_i-\gamma)], \quad i) = 1, 2$$

From the state equation we write

$$v^{(i)}(t) = -\dot{X}^{(i)}(t)$$
$$= \gamma m(r+\rho_i)\exp(-\gamma t)/[p(0)(r+\rho_i-\gamma)], \quad i = 1, 2 \qquad (3.14)$$

For $t=0$, we immediately see from this last equation that

$$v^{(1)}(0) < v^{(2)}(0) \qquad (3.15)$$

Since $\rho_1 > \rho_2$, and computing the derivative of $v^{(i)}(t)$ from (3.14) with respect to time we also get

$$\dot{v}^{(1)}(0) > \dot{v}^{(2)}(0) \qquad (3.16)$$

From (3.15) we see that the riskier firm starts producing less than the less risky firm and from (3.16) we conclude that the rate of the riskier firm is slower. Again from (3.14) note that producer 1 will produce less than the producer 2 during *all* the lifetime of the resource.

As we pointed out already, costs are crucial. It is easy to see that, from (3.6) and (3.3),

$$C^{(i)}(X(t)) = m/X^{(i)}(t) = p(t) - \dot{p}(t)/(r+\rho_i), \quad i = 1, 2 \qquad (3.17)$$

Clearly, even though we assumed the same cost function for the two firms, the different outputs cause different paths for the resource stocks and therefore for costs.

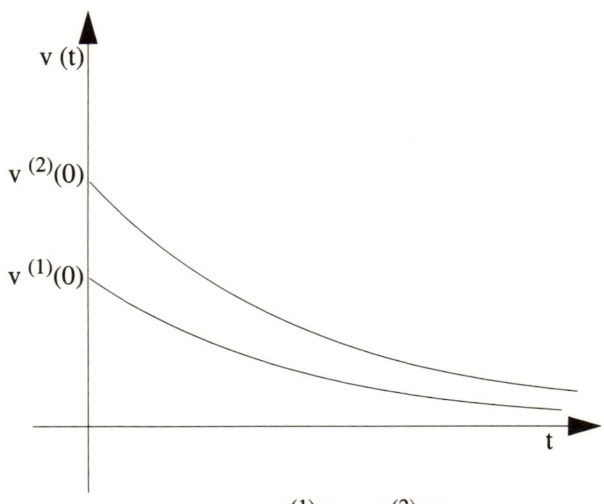

Figure 3. $X^{(1)}(0) < X^{(2)}(0)$

From (3.17) we see that $C^{(i)}(X(t))$ depend on the discount rate, thereby reversing a faster depletion effect, which an increase in the discount could imply.

Furthermore, since both firms are price-takers, as the price follows an exogenous path, then $v^{(1)}(t)$ must be lower than $v^{(2)}(t)$ in order to offset the corresponding higher costs $C^{(i)}(t)$. Note also that $C(X)$ is a convex function of X.

SHIFTS IN THE MARKET

The analysis carried out in the former sections considered two firms with different discount rates operating during the same time period.

In an analogous way, we may study a firm facing shifts in the market conditions, that is, we can study the comparative dynamics of a firm at two different time periods due to certain changes. (See figure 3)

The General Setting

Formula (1.2) depends on the value of r. It obviously follows that, as market conditions change, the firm will also change its discount. Furthermore, since α depends on the distribution of $(r + \rho_i)$, a change in r will cause a corresponding change in α. A possible change in the resource price path, in particular at $t = 0$, may also occur in this case. Assume for simplicity that $\delta = \alpha$, that is, consider a representative firm whose discount rate equals the equilibrium market discount rate.

We study two cases: when costs are independent and when they are dependent on the market discount rate α.

We will give first a necessary and sufficient condition for faster depletion at a rising discount rate, when costs are constant and independent of α. It turns out that when these conditions are not satisfied we may possibly have slower depletion and correspondingly rising market prices, when the market condition rate α is rising.

Note, however, that costs dependent on are more likely to occur because, unless they are constant, $C(X)$ should always depend on α, through $X(t)$ and the optimal $v(t)$. When costs are dependent on α theorem 5 will give a sufficient condition for the shadow price of the resource t to decline as α increases. This will allow us to draw further conclusions about a possible decline of the market price of the resource when the market discount rate increases. Furthermore, Example 2 will show how a conservative policy, that, is slower depletion, emerges in a particular case in which the cost function is rising fast with respect to α, under some hypotheses on the marginal price.

Finally, an insight is given about the common belief found in the literature that higher discounts imply faster depletion [Pindyck (1978a), or see Farzin (1984) for a review]. It is not actually clear what is the rationale behind such a claim. We will suggest here a possible explanation through a simple criterion.

Costs Independent of Market Discount

Here we give a necessary and sufficient condition for faster initial depletion when the market discount rate increases. While a shift in α would obviously change the future price path, we are interested in analyzing possible changes in the initial price $p(0)$. Note that costs independent of α must be constant, as we remarked before.

Theorem 4.   When costs are independent of α

$$p_\alpha(0) < \quad if \quad q(0) > \dot{p}_\alpha(0)$$

Proof: Condition (3.7) must still hold on the singular path. Taking its partial derivative with respect to α, we get

$$q_\alpha(t) \;=\; [\dot{p}_\alpha(t)/\alpha] - [\dot{p}(t)/\alpha^2] \;=\; [\dot{p}_\alpha(t)/\alpha] - [q(t)/\alpha] \tag{4.1}$$

which is in particular true for $t = 0$.

From (4.1), since $p_\alpha(0) = q_\alpha(0)$, the market condition (3.3)

$$p_\alpha(0) \;=\; [\dot{p}_\alpha(0)/\alpha] - [q(0)/\alpha] \tag{4.2}$$

Then $p_\alpha(0) < 0$ if and only if

$$q(0) > \dot{p}_\alpha(0).$$ (4.3)

This completes the proof.

From Theorem 5 it follows that if condition (4.3) does not hold, depletion may be slower, that is, $p_\alpha(0) > 0$.

Costs Dependent on the Market Discount

Farzin (1984) already has studied the Hotelling case with constant costs dependent on the market discount, showing that rising discount rates do not necessarily imply faster initial depletion of the resource source. Therefore, we analyze here the case in which costs depend on the resource stock. As we pointed out in Example 1, the price path will be constantly under the exponential path at rate α, when costs depend on the reserves. Therefore, in this case the effect of a change in α on the future price is not so apparent as when costs are independent of market discount.

The following theorem holds in the particular case $\dot{p}_\alpha(t) \leq 0$, that is, when the time derivative of price is a decreasing function of α.

Theorem 5.   When $\dot{p}_\alpha(t) \leq 0$ then $q_\alpha(t) < 0$.

Proof: Observe that (3.7) must hold on the singular path. Then for each t,

$$q_\alpha(t) = \dot{p}_\alpha(t)/\alpha - \dot{p}(t)/\alpha^2$$ (4.4)

which is negative when $p_\alpha(t) \leq 0$. This completes the proof.

Theorem 5 implies that, under the given hypothesis, it is the shadow price of the resource, that is, the price of the resource net of the extraction costs, that is declining as α increases. From (3.3), the market condition, we obtain also

$$q_\alpha(t) = p_\alpha(t) - C_\alpha(X) < 0$$ (4.5)

when in particular $t = 0$ (4.5) does not necessarily imply $p_\alpha(0) < 0$ as it may also be

$$0 < p_\alpha(0) < C_\alpha(X(0))$$ (4.6)

this, of course, says that depletion can be slower as market rates are rising.

As further consideration, we give an example that shows that slower depletion occurs when the cost is rising as fast as α is increasing.

Example 2: Consider the same price and cost functions as in Example 1, that is,

$$p(t) = p(0)\exp(\gamma t), \quad C(X) = m/X, \quad m \in R^{+} \tag{4.7}$$

In order to ensure production, the condition $\gamma < \alpha$ must hold, as already discussed in Example 1.

We assume here that a shift in a may change the initial price $p(0)$ but has no effect on the future path. In other words, $p(0)$ depends on α while γ does not.

The optimal policy is therefore as in (3.14), with

$$r + \rho_i = \alpha, \quad v(t) = \gamma m \alpha \exp(-\gamma t) / [p(0)(\alpha - \gamma)] \tag{4.8}$$

and

$$C(X(t)) = p(0)\exp(\gamma t)[(\alpha - \gamma)/\alpha] \tag{4.9}$$

as in (3.12). From (4.9) we get, for $t = 0$, by putting $C(X(0)) = C(0)$,

$$p(0) = C(0)[\alpha/(\alpha - \gamma)] \tag{4.10}$$

By taking the derivative with respect to α in this equation we get

$$p_\alpha(0) = [C_\alpha(0)\alpha(\alpha - \gamma) - \gamma C(0)]/(\alpha - \gamma)^2 \tag{4.11}$$

If the condition

$$C_a(0) > \gamma C(0)/[\alpha(\alpha - \gamma)] \tag{4.12}$$

holds, immediately conclude from (4.11) that

$$p_\alpha(0) > 0 \tag{4.13}$$

which means that an increasing a may imply initial market price or an equivalently slower depletion of the resource for the representative firm. Furthermore, as $X(t) = m/C(X(t))$, it follows that

$$X_\alpha(t) = -mC_\alpha(X(t))/C^2(X(t))$$

Then, at $t = 0$,

$$C_\alpha(0) = -C^2(0)X_\alpha(0)/m$$

By substituting this into (4.12) we get

$$X_\alpha(0) < -\gamma X(0)/[\alpha(\alpha - \gamma)] \qquad (4.14)$$

The explanation is the following: α is increasing and costs are increasing too much [see (4.12)], it is as if the resource is becoming too scarce [see (4.14)]. Then the market price must rise enough to satisfy the singular condition $p(0) - C(0) = q(0)$; otherwise, no one would produce anything [$q(0) > p(0) - C(0)$].

We conclude by giving some explanation about the widespread belief that higher discount implies faster depletion. Consider a producer maximizing his discounted profit according to

$$W(0) = \underset{v(t)}{Max}\int_0^\infty [p(t) - C(X)]v(t) \exp(-\alpha t)\ dt$$

$$= \int_0^\infty [p(t) - C(X)]v^*(t) \exp(-\alpha t)\ dt \qquad (4.15)$$

subject to

$$\dot{X}(t) = -v(t)$$

where $v^*(t)$ is the optimal policy. The statement that "higher rates cause a more rapid depletion" could be possibly based on the idea that "in order to maintain the optimum, the policy should be...." Then in order to sustain an increase in the market discount, $W(0)$ should satisfy

$$W_\alpha(0) \geq 0 \qquad (4.16)$$

or , accordingly, for a decrease $W_\alpha(0) \leq 0$.

It can immediately be seen from (4.16) and (3.3) that

$$W(0) = \int_0^\infty q(t) v^*(t) \, (\exp(-\alpha t)) \, dt$$

and

$$W_\alpha(0) = \int_0^\infty q_\alpha(t) v^*(t) + q(t) v_\alpha^*(t)$$

$$-t q(t) v^*(t) \exp(-\alpha t) \, dt \tag{4.17}$$

or using the discounted shadow price $\lambda(t) = q(t) \exp(-\alpha t)$,

$$W_\alpha(0) = \int_0^\infty [\lambda_\alpha(t) v^*(t) + \lambda(t) v^*(t)] \, dt \tag{4.18}$$

We consider the simpler case when costs are independent of α. Assuming (4.16) as a reasonable criterion, when costs are independent of α, from (4.17) we get

$$W_\alpha(0) = \int_0^\infty [q_\alpha(0) v^*(t) + q(0) v_\alpha^*(t)] \, dt$$

$$= \int_0^\infty [p_\alpha(0) v^*(t) + q(0) v_\alpha^*(t)] \, dt \tag{4.19}$$

This equation is obtained from (3.2) and (3.3) when $C_x = 0$ because

$$q(t) = q(0) \exp(\alpha t) \quad \text{and} \quad p(t) = m + q(0) \exp(\alpha t)$$

which implies

$$W_\alpha(0) = \int_0^\infty [q_\alpha(0) v^*(t) + q(0) v_\alpha^*(t)] \, dt$$

Note that the same result would be obtained if we allowed a finite horizon $[0,T]$ provided $v^*(T)=0$.

If we want (4.19) to be nonnegative, we might require $v_\alpha^*(t) > 0$; if we further assume some monotonicity on $v^*(t)$, we may have in particular $v_\alpha^*(t) > 0$ in $[0, \tau]$ and consequently $p_\alpha(0) < 0$. But this is of course just one of the two possibilities, as we could also require

$$p_\alpha(0) > 0 \quad \text{and} \quad v_\alpha^*(t) < 0$$

which are also possible.

Note that all this happens along the singular path, that is, when the market condition is satisfied. Note also that the exponential in (4.15), which one would think could make "things go fast to zero," has disappeared. This is also reasonable, as the necessary condition for optimality (market condition) gives indifference between extraction now or later.

SUMMARY

In this paper we attempt to introduce the notion of the firm's discount rate as used in the context of modern financial theory. This leads us to considering heterogeneous firms with respect to discount rates due to dissimilar risks.

Our analysis follows the partial equilibrium approach and our techniques used are those of deterministic optimal control. The problem addressed is as follows: Given a market of an exhaustible resource that has attained an equilibrium with the market price growing at a rate α, what is the optimal policy of a given competitive firm with a discount rate δ_i? We offer answers to this problem in two cases: when extraction costs are fixed and when they depend on the reserve stock. In three theorems and an example we show conditions that induce the riskier firm to deplete faster and when such result does not hold. This analysis clarifies conditions that justify the previously claimed conjectures.

We also study the comparative statistics of the individual firm as it responds to changes in the market discount rate α. In two theorems and an example we analyze the impact of a change in on the firm's behavior and again clarify certain conjectures previously advanced in the exhaustibles resources literature.

Much more remains to be done on this important subject of introducing financial considerations in the theory of exhaustible resources. One approach that might be fruitful would be using the methods of stochastic calculus and control, as presented in Malliaris and Brock (1982), to generalize our results. Another possibility is to analyze the role of risks in oligopolistic markets of exhaustible resources.

ACKNOWLEDGMENTS

We are thankful to Piera Mazzoleni, Stanley Pliska, and Linda Salchenberger for encouragement and numerous critical comments that have helped us improve our work. This work was partially supported by the grant M.P.I. 1986/87, which made it possible for S. Stefani to be a visiting scholar at Loyola University of Chicago during 1988. The useful comments of an anonymous referee and the expositional suggestions of C.F. Lee are gratefully acknowledged.

REFERENCES

Adelman, M.A. (1986). Oil producing countries discount rates. *Resources and Energy, 8* 309-329.
Arrow, K.J. & Kurz, M. (1970). *Public investment, the rate of return and optimal fiscal policy.* London: Johns Hopkins Press.

Brealey, R & Myers, S. (1981). *Principles of corporate finance.* New York: McGraw Hill.

Benveniste, L.M. & Scheinkman, J.A. (1982). Duality theory for dynamic optimization models of economics: The continuous time case. *Journal of economic theory,* 27, 1-19.

Bohi, O.R. & Toman, M.A. (1984). *Analyzing nonrenewable resources supply.* Washington, DC: Resources for the future.

Dasgupta, P.S. & Heal, G.M. (1979). *Economic theory and exhaustible resources.* Oxford: Cambridge University Press.

Devarajan, S. & Fisher, A.C. (1981). Hotelling's economics of exhaustible resources: Fifty years later. *Journal of Economic Literature, 19,* 65-73.

Farzin, Y.H. (1984). The effect of the discount rate on depletion of exhaustible resources. *Journal of Political Economy, 92,* 841-851.

Gordon, R. L. (1967). A reinterpretation of the pure theory of exhaustion. *Journal of Political Economy, 75,* 274-286.

Hotelling, H. (1931). The economics of exhaustible resources. *Journal of Political Economy, 39,* 137-175.

Kamien, M.I. & Schwartz, N.L. (1981). *Dynamics optimization: The calculus of variations and optimal control in economics and management.* New York: North-Holland.

Malliaris, A.G. & Brock, W.A. (1982). *Stochastic methods in economics and finance.* New York: North-Holland.

Malliaris, A.G. & Stefani, S. (1991). Heterogeneous discount rates: A generalization of Hotelling's rule. In Hamalainen R. and H. Ehtamo (eds), *Dynamic Games in Economic Analysis.* New York: Springer-Verlag.

Mazzoleni, P. (1983). *Sullo sfruttamento ottimo di risorse naturali esauribili.* Padua: Ciclografica.

Miller M.H. & Upton C.W. (1985). A test of the Hotelling valuation principle. *Journal of Political Economy, 93,* 1-25.

Pindyck, R.S. (1978a). Gains to producers from the cartelization of exhaustible resources. *Review of Economics and Statistics, 60,* 238-251.

Pindyck, R.S. (1978b). The optimal exploration and production of non-renewable resources. *Journal of Political Economy, 86,* 841-861.

Solow, R.M. (1974). The economics of resources or the resources of economics. *American Economic Review: Papers and Proceedings, 64,* 1-14.

Stiglitz, J.E. (1976). Monopoly and the rate of extraction of exhaustible resources. *American Economic Review, 66,* 655-661.

THE EMPIRICAL RELATIONSHIP BETWEEN INVESTMENT AND FINANCING DECISION:
A SWITCHING SIMULTANEOUS-EQUATION APPROACH

Cheng-few Lee and Chau-Chen Yang

ABSTRACT

Switching simultaneous equations model proposed by Lee, Maddala, and Trost (1979) was used to examine the relationship between investment and financing decisions simultaneously for firms that issue new shares and those that do not. The results show that dividend decisions do not have negative impact on the investment decisions of firms. In order words, we found no evidence that dividend policies may hamper the investment activity of firms.

Advances in Financial Planning and Forecasting,
Volume 5, pages 249-264.
Copyright © 1994 by JAI Press Inc.
All rights of reproduction in any form reserved.
ISBN:1-55938-421-2

INTRODUCTION

Modigliani and Miller (mm; 1958, 1963) have established that in perfect capital markets the value of a firm is independent of how the firm finances its investments. An implication of this theorem is that investment decisions should be independent of dividend decisions. However, capital markets are not perfect. The empirical validity of this result is subject to further examination.

Dhrymes and Kurz (1967), Fama (1974), McDonald, Jacquillant, and Nussenbarum (1975), McCabe (1979), and Peterson and Benesh (1983) intended to verify the empirical relationships between the investment and financing decisions. These studies essentially focused on determining whether market imperfections have been of sufficient magnitude to lead to joint determination of investment, dividend, and external financing decisions. Most of the studies showed that external financing does have a positive impact on investments. Nevertheless, there are no conclusive results concerning whether dividends compete with investments for internal sources of funds.

The primary purpose of this paper is to provide further evidence pertaining to the empirical relationship between investment and financing decisions using a different econometric model. The econometric model used in this paper is the one proposed by Lee, Maddala, and Trost (1979): the switching simultaneous-equations model. The interaction between the investment and financing decisions is examined simultaneously for both the firms that issue new shares and those which do not. The rationale for using the new issue as a switch is to indirectly involve new equity financing in the investment/financing simultaneous equations. New equity financing has become an important issue in recent finance signaling literature, because it might be regarded as a negative signal to investors. Myer's (1984) and Donaldson's (1961) financing pecking order proposition treat it as a last resort for financing investments. Hence we treat new equity, and not any other financing investments, as a switch point in this paper. However, new equity financing had been excluded in the simultaneous-equations system in previous studies either because it was thought to be unimportant or for lack of sufficient data. The inclusion of the new issue in the simultaneous equation as a switch will provide more valuable information than previous tests.

The next briefly surveys the results of previous relevant studies. The subsequent section discusses the model and data along with the empirical methodology. After that, empirical results are presented. The final section has concluding comments.

A BRIEF LITERATURE SURVEY

A series of previous empirical studies on the MM propositions were done through the estimation of a system of simultaneous equations. Generally, these studies incorporate several equations with endogenous and exogenous variables. Endogenous variables in each equation are used to examine their impact on another

Table 1. Econometric Models of the Firm

	Dhrymes and Kurz (1967)	*Fama* (1974)	*McDonald, Jacquillat, Nussenbaum* (1975)
Decisions	Investment Dividend New Debt	Investment Dividend	Investment Dividend New Debt
Types of analysis	Cross-sectional	Time-series	Cross-sectional
Years analyzed	1951-1960	1946-1968	1962-1968
Estimation techniques	OLS, 2SLS, 3SLS	OLS, 2SLS	OLS, 2SLS
Number of firms	181	298	75[a]
Support for MM theorem that investment and financing decisions are independent	Reject	Support	Support

	McCabe (1979)	*Peterson and Benesh* (1983)	*Proposed*
	Investment Dividend New Debt	Investment Dividend New Debt	Conditional-investment Dividend Debt
	Cross-sectional	Cross-sectional	Cross-sectional and pooled cross-sectional, and time-series
	1966-1973	1975-1979	1978-1987
	OLS, 2SLS	OLS, 3SLS, SUR	Switching regression model with simulta- neous equations in the second stage
	112	534-538	
	Reject	Reject	

Notes: [a]Include 2 French firms only.

endogenous variable, the dependent variable. They usually represent the uses and sources of funds. Exogenous variables in each equation represent financial characteristics of the firm that determine the level of various uses and sources.

External equity financing was often precluded as an endogenous variable in the system of simultaneous equations in previous studies, because it was believed to be unimportant or it was difficult to acquire data. The Compustat tape provides external equity financing data after 1971, while most of the studies that this paper follows use data primarily prior to 1971. Thanks to the availability of the data on external equity financing and other related data after 1971, this paper will explicitly incorporate external equity financing in the system of equations.

The MM theorems do not completely preclude interdependence between a firm's investment and financing decisions. The only interdependence not proposed by MM is that the financing decisions impact directly on investment decisions. Relationships between investment and financing variables do not violate

MM's theorems if the causation is from the former to the latter.[1] Previous studies on the interdependence hypothesis, except Peterson and Benesh (1983), focus on the justification of using simultaneous-equations estimating techniques, in contrast to ordinary least squares (OLS), and interpreting the sign and statistical significance of the coefficients of endogenous variables. Two-stage least-square (2SLS) and three-stage least-squares (3SLS) methods have often been employed in these studies. In addition to 2SLS and 3SLS methods, Peterson and Benesh (PB., 1983) employed the seemingly unrelated regression (SUR) method to test the interdependence hypothesis. PB set up two simultaneous-equations system. One of them assumes that dividends and debt-financing decisions have no impact on the investment decision of a firm; the other assumes that investment, dividends and debt-financing decisions interact with each other. PB's approach is to compare these two structural models by testing the implied restrictions upon reduced-form coefficients. If the restrictions are rejected, the conclusion is that they fail to support MM's propositions. Table 1 briefly describes the major studies in this area and their conclusions with respect to MM theorems.

From Table 1, we see that Fama (1974) employed time-series analysis, while others employed cross-sectional analysis. Fama's time-series analysis supported MM's theorem. For the cross-sectional analyses, McDonald, Jacquillant, and Nussenbaum (MJN; 1975) used French firms' data, and others used American firms' data. Yet all but MJN rejected MM's theorem. Also, the periods and the number of firms for these studies are quite different across studies. The rejection of the significance of the coefficients of the endogenous variables in the investment structural equation, that is, the coefficients of dividends and new debt financing.

In imperfect capital markets, investment and dividend outlays should be considered as competing with each other for the use of funds. The dividend coefficient should be negative. An increase in debt provides more funds for investments. Thus, the coefficients of new debt should be positive. Dhrymes and Kurz (DK., 1967) find that the coefficient for dividends in the investment equation is both negative and significant in 8 of the 10 years examined, McCabe (1979) and PB (find the same to be true in 5 of the 8 years and 4 of the 5 years, respectively. PB's SUR approach also confirms their findings from the 3SLS analysis that MM's theorem should be rejected. The coefficient of new debt variable is positive and significant in the investment equation for 6 out of the 8 years in McCabe's study, and for 3 out of 10 and 3 out of 5 in DK's and PB's studies, respectively. On the other hand, Fama's 2SLS time-series study shows that the coefficient for the dividend variable in the investment equation has an opposite sign (positive) about 60 percent of the time, and the corresponding t values show little relationship between the investment and the dividend variables. MJN's study shows that the dividend variable has a positive sign in all of the years and is significant for 5 of the 7 years examined. MJN suggest that the positive sign of dividend coefficient is not inconsistent with MM's theorem. They interpret the positive dividend as a proxy for a lagged capital stock variable or a proxy for "economic earnings" under French accounting practices.

SIMULTANEOUS-EQUATIONS SYSTEM AND METHODOLOGY

The Model

This simultaneous-equations system is composed of three structural equations: investment, dividend, and new debt. The three endogenous variables are new investment in plant and equipment, change in dividend payments, and new long-term debt. The first two endogenous variables are used in Fama (1974). The new-debt variable is used in other related studies. Basically, these variables are associated with the uses and sources of funds. The other factor, new external equity financing, which is also related to the uses and sources of funds is directly incorporated into this structural system. In other words, a conditional structural system is developed. The simultaneous equations are analyzed given the condition of whether a firm issues new shares or not.

The three-equation model employed in this paper is similar to those of earlier studies except for the condition of whether firms issue new shares or not.

Let $I=1$ denote the condition when a firm issues new shares, and $I=0$ denote the condition when a firm does not issue new shares. The simple simultaneous equations are:

when $I=1$,

$$\delta\text{INV}_t = a_{11} + a_{12}\delta D_t + a_{13}\text{ND}_t + a_{14}Q_t + a_{15}\text{INV}_{t-1}$$
$$+ a_{16}\delta\text{SAL}_t + e_{12t}$$
$$\delta D_t = b_{11} + b_{12}\delta\text{INV}_t + b_{13}\text{ND}_t + b_{14}P^*_t + b_{15}D_{t-1}$$
$$+ b_{16}D_{t-2} + e_{11t}$$
$$\text{ND}_t = C_{11} + C_{12}\delta\text{INV}_t + C_{13}\delta D_t + C_{14}P_{t-1} + C_{15}\text{IRT}_{t-1}$$
$$+ C_{16}\text{COFVR}_t + e_{13t} \tag{1}$$

When $I=0$

$$\delta\text{INV}_t = a_{21} + a_{22}\delta D_t + a_{23}\text{ND}_t + a_{24}Q_t + a_{25}\text{INV}_{t-1}$$
$$+ a_{26}\delta\text{SAL}_t + e_{22t}$$
$$\delta D_t = b_{21} + b_{22}\delta\text{INV}_t + b_{23}\text{ND}_t + b_{24}P^*_t + b_{25}D_{t-1}$$
$$+ b_{26}D_{t-2} + e_{21t}$$
$$\text{ND}_t = C_{21} + C_{22}\delta\text{INV}_t + C_{23}\delta D_t + C_{24}P_{t-1} + C_{25}\text{IRT}_{t-1}$$
$$+ C_{26}\text{COFVR}_t + e_{23t}$$

where δINV_t, is new plant and equipment at period t; Q_t is sales plus change in inventories; Pt is net income before extraordinary items plus depreciation; P^*_t is P_t minus preferred dividends; Dt is common dividends; $SALt$ is sales; $IRTt$ is interest over long-term debt; D_t, P_t, INV, δ INV, ND, RD, and Q are normalized by lagged net sales; COFVR is coefficient of variation of net operating income plus depreciation.

Each structural equation contains two endogenous variables and several exogenous variables. Most of the explanatory variables used in the investment and dividend structural equations have been used by Fama (1974), and those in the new-debt structural equation were used by other studies, which have not been subject to critiques. Industry dummy variables are not employed in the thesis, because PB have found no significance of these variables.

To transform a conditional simultaneous-equations system into a simple simultaneous-equations system, a variable, which is related to the probabilities of issuing or not issuing new shares by the firm, must be added to each structural equation. This variable can be estimated by the probit model, which will be further discussed in the following section. Here we discuss the explanatory variables used in the probit model, which estimates the probabilities referred to above. The following equation is used for the probit model:

$$\delta CS_t^* = b_0 + b_1 NI_{t-1} + b_2 RET_{t-1}$$
$$+ b_3 TDMKT_{t-1} + b_4 COFVR_t + b_5 SALG_t - u_t \tag{2}$$

where δCS_t^* is a dummy variable, 1 or 0, to denote whether a firm issues new shares or not; NI is net income plus depreciation over sales; RET is stock return; TDMKT is long-term debt over market value of common equity; COFVR is the coefficient of variation of EBIT over a period of 10 years; SALG is sales growth rate; t denotes the period.

NI is used because the internal funds generated in a previous period will affect the need for financing in current period. RET is also a explanatory variable because it is believed that firms tend to time the flotation of new shares. When the stock price is overestimated or fairly reflected, firms have more motivation to issue new shares than when the price is underestimated. TDMKT reflects the condition of debt capacity of the firm. If a firm has a high TDMKT ratio, it implies that the firm may have to issue new shares for financing. COFVR denotes the business risk of the firm. High-risk firms may have difficulty obtaining new debt, and thus may have to resort to external equity financing. SALG is used because higher sales growth rate is supposed to be accompanied by more investments.

Data

Annual data were collected for empirical studies in this paper. These data were obtained from the Compustat files.

The Compustat Industrial file, ANNALLII, which includes 20 years of annual data, will be used to acquire the information for cross-sectional study. ANNALLII file is composed of three files: ANNPSTII, ANNFUII, and ANNRESII. ANNP-STII covers financial data for primary industries. ANNFUII covers financial data for firms listed in OTC. ANNRESII contains financial data for firms that are excluded from ANNPSTII and ANNFUII due to bankruptcy, merger, acquisition, liquidation, or becoming private. Annual data in the period 1978-1987 will be used for analysis.

In order to examine whether expectation of sales growth will affect a firm's investment and financing decisions, total sample firms are also divided evenly into three groups: high-growth, medium-growth, and nongrowth firms. The projected sales growth rate by Value Line will be used as a proxy for the expectation of sales growth by the firm. Ranked according to the ascending projected sales growth rate, the first one,-third of total sample firms are classified as nongrowth firms, and the last one-third are classified as high-growth firms. The results for these two groups will be compared. Quarterly data are not used for this purpose.

Any firm that violates any of the following criteria will be excluded from the sample:

1. The firm must not belong to the firms in the industry with industry number (DNUM) between 4000 and 5000 or between 6000 and 7000. Therefore, financial institutions, utility industry, and transportation industry are excluded.
2. The firm must have complete observations for all the variables in study in the year for cross-sectional analysis.
3. For grouped firms, the projected sales growth rates must be available from Value Line.

Cross-sectional data were used to analyze the impact of firm's decision to issue new shares on the interactions among their investment, dividend, and debt-financing decisions. In each year, any firm that meets the selection criteria was included in the sample. Therefore, the number of sample firms varied in each year. The largest sample size for annual data was 517, while the smallest was 367. Average sample size was 438.

Methodology

A simultaneous-equation switching regression model by Lee, Maddala, and Trost (1979) was used for the empirical tests. There are two stages in the model. In the first stage, a criterion function is set up to decide whether a firm issues new shares or not. Two regimes are classified accordingly. The probabilities of issuing new shares or not can be estimated by the probit model in this stage. In the second stage, a system of simultaneous equations is constructed, which incorporates the probabilities estimated in the first stage.

The switching regression models was first proposed by Goldfeld and Quandt (1973). There are two stages in the model, which can be expressed as
First stage:

$$I_i = \tau' z_i - e_i$$

Second stage:

$$\text{Regime 1:} \quad y_i = \beta_1' X_{1i} + e_{1i}, \quad \text{iff } I_i > 0$$

$$\text{Regime 2:} \quad y_i = \beta_2' X_{2i} + e_{2i}, \quad \text{iff } I_i \leq 0 \tag{3}$$

where I is an index of 1 or 0; z is a vector of explanatory variables; τ is a vector of regression coefficients.

In their model, Goldfeld and Quandt assume that e_i is independent of $e1_i$ and e_{2i}. Maddala and Nelson's (1975) "Switching regression model with endogenous switching" assumes the existence of correlation between e_{i1}, e_{i2}, and e_i. The covariance matrix of e_{i1}, e_{i2}, and e_i is expressed as

$$\Sigma = \begin{bmatrix} \sigma_1^2 & \sigma_{12} & \sigma_{1e} \\ & \sigma_2^2 & \sigma_{2e} \\ & & \sigma_2 \end{bmatrix} \tag{4}$$

Since τ is estimable up to a scale factor the covariance matrix can be redefined as

$$\Sigma = \begin{bmatrix} \sigma_1^2 & \sigma_{12} & \sigma_{1e} \\ & \sigma_2^2 & \sigma_{2e} \\ & & 1 \end{bmatrix} \tag{5}$$

As assumed, ei and $e1i$ or $e2i$ have bivariate normal distribution. Hence, according to Johnson and Kotz (1972),

$$E(e_{1i} \mid I_i = 1) = E(e_{1i} \mid e_i \leq \tau' z_i) = -\sigma_{1e}(\phi/\Phi)$$

$$= -\sigma_{1e} * (W_{1i}) \tag{6}$$

$$E(e_{2i} \mid I_i = 0) = E(e_{2i} \mid e_i > \tau' z_i) = \sigma_{2e}(\phi/1-\Phi))$$

$$= \sigma_{2e} * (W_{2i}) \tag{7}$$

where ϕ is a density function and Φ is a cumulative density function.

Equations in the second stage can be rewritten as

$$y_i = \beta_1'X_{1i} - \sigma_{1e}W_{1i} + u_{1i}, \quad \text{for } I_i = 1 \tag{8}$$

$$y_i = \beta_2'X_{2i} + \sigma_{2e}W_{2i} + u_{2i}, \quad \text{for } I_i = 0 \tag{9}$$

where $u1i$ and $u2i$ are the new residuals, with zero means:

$$u_{1i} = e_{1i} + \sigma_{1e}W_{1i} \tag{10}$$

$$u_{2i} = e_{2i} + \sigma_{2e}W_{2i} \tag{11}$$

where

$$W_{1i} = \phi(\tau'Z_i)/\Phi(\tau'Z_i), \quad \text{for } I_i = 1$$

$$W_{2i} = \phi(\tau'Z_i)/\Phi(\tau'Z_i)/[1 - \Phi(\tau'Z_i)], \quad \text{for } I_i = 0$$

and τ_i are obtained in the first-stage estimation, $i=1,2,\dots,$ n. Thus, in the simultaneous system, that is, Equation (1), if the residuals in each structural equation are replaced according to (10) or (11), then this system will become an unconditional simultaneous-equations system. Maddala (1983) has shown the way to estimate the coefficients in each structural equation and their unbiased and consistent estimates of standard errors. Maddala's method of estimation in the second stage is similar to the instrumental variable approach as used in the 2SLS and 3SLS methods, except that several procedures are taken to correct the bias incurred by incorporating the probability variable in the second stage.

EMPIRICAL RESULTS

Prediction of New External Equity Financing

Prior to the analysis of those simultaneous decisions referred to above, it is necessary to analyze how a new equity financing decision can be determined by certain exogenous variables. This is the first stage of the two-stage switching regression model applied in this thesis. The function in the first stage is called a criterion function which decides whether a firm issues new shares or not. The probabilities of issuing new shares are thus estimated.

The explanatory variables used are NI_{t-1}, RET_{t-1}, $SALG_t$, and $COFVR_t$, which are the net income in a previous period, the debt-equity ratio, the return on stock at a previous period, the sales growth rate, and the coefficient of variation of income before interest and taxes, respectively. Based on the results from annual

Table 2. First-Stage Results—Probit Model (Annual Data)[a]

Year	Constant	NI_{t-1}	$TDMKT_{t-1}$	RET_{t-1}	$SALG_t$	$COFVR_t$
78	−1.729*	−0.957	0.2617*	−0.025	1.275*	1.341*
	(−8.533)	(−.837)	(3.022)	(−.607)	(3.146)	(4.065)
79	−1.85*	−0.222	0.404*	−0.03	0.725*	0.766*
	(−8.982)	(−.234)	(4.266)	(−.669)	(2.041)	(2.728)
80	−2.108*	0.231	0.226**	0.025	1.366*	1.196*
	(−10.157)	(.339)	(1.978)	(1.016)	(4.002)	(3.802)
81	−1.361*	−1.291	0.205*	0.0012	1.517*	0.082
	(7.541)	(−1.227)	(2.307)	(.069)	(4.544)	(.362)
82	−1.164*	−2.216	0.263*	−0.0015	1.663*	0.151
	(−5.888)	(1.558)	(1.895)	(−.042)	(3.221)	(1.119)
83	−1.11*	−1.674*	0.726*	−0.084**	1.204*	0.415
	(−6.367)	(−2.029)	(5.68)	(−1.908)	(2.864)	(1.546)
84	−1.232*	−3.77*	0.465*	−0.047	1.714*	0.301
	(−5.955)	(−2.747)	(3.164)	(−1.083)	(3.872)	(1.034)
85	−1.088*	−3.164*	0.563*	−0.0067	1.274*	0.2775
	−5.841)	(−2.446)	(4.296)	(−.187)	(2.769)	(1.096)
86	−1.74*	−1.924	0.569*	0.03	0.9*	0.985*
	(−7.607)	(−1.460)	(3.627)	(1.287)	(2.272)	(2.452)
87	−1.291*	−1.392	0.655*	0.0096	0.536**	0.0012
	(−7.668)	(−1.294)	(4.481)	(.444)	(1.661)	(.014)

Notes: [a]Chi-squared statistics are always significant at the .002 level.
   *Significant at the 5% level.
   **Significant at the 10% level.

data in Table 2, it is found that the coefficient of NI_{t-1} has the correct sign (negative) for 9 of the 10 years in the study and is significant for 3 years. The coefficient of $TDMKT_{t-1}$ has the correct sign (positive) and is significant in each of the years examined. On the other hand, RET_{t-1} has the wrong sign (negative) for 6 out of 10 years, but is significant only in 1 year, 1983. $SALG_t$ is always significant in each year and has the correct sign (positive). $COFVR_t$ is significant and positive for 4 of the ten years examined.

In all, the debt-equity ratio ($TDMKT_{t-1}$) and the sales growth rate ($SALG_t$) are always significantly associated with the issuance of new shares and their regression coefficients have the correct signs. NI_{t-1} is significant and negative in the first 3 years of the period 1983-1987, while $COFVR_t$ is significant and positive in the first 3 years of 1978-1982. This finding indicates that in the beginning of a recession period, 1978-1982, business risk ($COFVR_t$) dominates net income (NI_{t-1}) in playing an important role in deciding whether to issue new shares. But in an economic recovery period, 1983-1985, net income dominates business risk.

This implies that during a recession period, the more fluctuation in a firm's profitability, the more likely it is to issue new shares, holding other conditions unchanged. Firms are uncertain about their cash inflow during a recession period, and may have difficulties in acquiring sufficient funds through debt. Thus, they

Table 3. Empirical Results For the Investment Model in the Two-Stage Switching Regression Model (Annual Data); Dependent Variable: δINV_t

| | Explanatory endogenous variables | | | | | |
| | δD_t | | ND_t | | Adjusted R^2 | |
Year	I=1	I=0	I=0	I=0	I=1	I=0
78	8.065*	5.37*	1.145*	0.584*	0.8861	0.2535
	(2.778)	(2.94)	(9.07)	(2.87)		
79	11.34*	0.485	1.08*	1.162*	0.6330	0.5729
	(2.42)	(.321)	(4.6)	(9.387)		
80	1.96*	7.77*	−0.325**	2.022*	0.6026	0.6557
	(2.07)	(3.886)	(−1.676)	(9.29)		
81	9.485	28.79*	0.893*	0.6525	0.7043	0.082
	(1.259)	(5.079)	(5.19)			(.362)
82	14.09**	5.12*	1.116*	0.7621	0.4054	0.151
	(1.97)	(3.683)	(4.006)			(1.119)
83	2.7	−1.64	0.431	0.354*	0.2140	0.1822
	(.736)	(−1.438)	(1.181)	(3.347)		
84	4.218	21.62*	0.513	1.237*	0.1902	0.2620
	(3.372)	(4.62)	(1.44)	(4.76)		
85	−2.25	24.09*	0.237**	−0.501	0.6800	0.2435
	(−.331)	(5.23)	(1.651)	(−1.34)		
86	11.57**	12.47*	0.241*	0.359*	0.2733	0.3531
	(1.68)	(5.01)	(2.714)	(2.18)		
87	0.741	17.18*	0.239*	−0.735	0.7378	0.5244
	(.495)	(6.99)	(3.01)	(−4.77)		

Notes: *Significant at the 5% level.
**Significant at the 10% level.

Table 4. Empirical Results For the Investment Model in the
Two-Stage Switching Regression Model
(Growth Group Data); Dependent Variable: δINV_t

| | Explanatory endogenous variables | | | | | |
| | δD_t | | ND_t | | Adjusted R^2 | |
Subgroup (period)	I=1	I=0	I=0	I=0	I=1	I=0
Growth	−3.837	9.25*	0.088	1.09*	0.6305	0.5676
(78-82)	(−0.694)	(4.223)	(.362)	(7.868)		
Nongrowth	−0.031	5.667*	1.06*	0.576*	0.5788	0.4702
(78-82)	(−.039)	(6.827)	(3.746)	(3.199)		
Growth	−0.335	4.082*	0.13	0.027	0.4519	0.2193
(83-87)	(−.108)	(2.199)	(1.118)	(.099)		
Nongrowth	0.594	10.86*	0.391	−0.582*	0.6746	0.2703
(83-87(	(.135)	(5.117)	(1.233)	(−3.02)		

Notes: *Significant at the 5% level.
**Significant at the 10% level.

tend to resort to external equity financing to finance current investment or to preserve funds for future need.

During a recovery period, firms tend to be optimistic. Thus, they do not regard the historical fluctuation in their earnings as a crucial factor when making their external equity financing decisions. Firms' net income, not business fisk, plays an important role in making their external equity financing decision. The more profitable a firm's business in a previous period, the less likely it is to issue new shares in current period.

The chi-squared statistics are always significant at a level less than .002, which demonstrates that at least one variable is significantly different from zero. Furthermore, the accuracy of predicting firms' issuing or not issuing new shares ranges from 78.8 to 87.8 percent, which is very high. These prove the appropriateness of employing those explanatory variables in the first stage.

MM's Independence Theorem

The sign and significance of the coefficient of financing variables, that is, dividend and new debt, in the investment equation are used to examine the influence of these two variables on the investment decision of the firm. Two cases, that is, when a firm issues new shares and when it does not, will be discussed separately. Again, for convenience, $I=1$ denotes the former case and $I=0$ denotes the latter. Tables 3 and 4 present the results for the annual and grouped data, respectively. The results for $I=0$ and $I=1$ will be discussed separately.

$I=0$ (Firms Do Not Issue New Shares)

When $I=0$, the results from both the annual and grouped data show that the coefficients of the dividend variable are positive most of the time. For annual data, the coefficient is positive and significant in 8 out of 10 years; for grouped data, regardless of the group of time period, each coefficient is positive and significant.

This result is not consistent with the results in Dhrymes and Kurz (1967), McCabe (1979), and PB where the dividend coefficients are mostly significant and negative. The dividend coefficient is significant and positive most of the time. As indicated in a previous section the positive coefficient of dividend should not be interpreted as a positive impact of dividend on investment. The dividend variable should be interpreted alternatively. It may be interpreted as a proxy for the earnings prospect of a firm. As the earnings prospect becomes favorable, a firm will increase dividend payments and also increase investment in plant and equipment. This interpretation is consistent with Miller and Modigliani's (1961) dividend information content hypothesis and does not violate MM's original independence proposition. Thus, when firms do not want to issue new shares, though capital markets are imperfect, the degree of imperfection is not large enough to violate MM's independence proposition.

Table 5. Empirical Results For the Investment Model in Two-Stage Switching Regression Model (Pooled Time-Series and Cross-Sectional Data); Dependent Variable = δINV_t

I	dD_t	ND_t	Constant	Q_t	INV_{t-1}	$NSAL_t$	Adjusted R^2
	13.142*	.017	.543*	−.592*	.182*	.699*	.4602
$I=1$	(7.079)	(.207)	(2.807)	(−2.99)	(11.79)	(3.59)	
	16.368*	.929*	−.798*	.748*	.027*	−.749*	.3112
$I=0$	(16.025)	(9.810)	(−6.94)	(6.580)	(3.052)	(−6.24)	

Notes: *Significant at the % level.

$I=1$ (Firms Issue New Shares)

When $I=1$, the results from the annual data show that only 5 out of 10 years have significant and positive dividend coefficient. The results from the grouped data show no significant dividend coefficient at all. As in the case when $I=0$, we conclude that MM's proposition is not rejected.

But it is interesting to note that the effect of the dividend variable is different for the recession and the prosperity periods. There are 4 years in the recession period 1978-1982 when we have a significant and positive dividend coefficient. The positive effect of the dividend variable on the investment variable exist only 1 year during the prosperity period 1983-1987. In the first period, the magnitude of the change in dividend increases as the investment increases. Yet in the next period, this relationship almost vanishes.

Based on the information content hypothesis of dividends, the implication of this finding may be that when firms want to issue new shares in a bear market, they use larger dividend payments along with investment projects to signal favorable growth opportunities. Larger increases in dividend payments signal a firm's favorable earnings potential and help to boost its stock price, which in turn increases the proceeds from the floating of new shares. Without the dividend serving as a signal, a firm's stock price may be underestimated during a bear market, and the firm may have difficulty in issuing new shares, while in the postrecession period, the stock price may have reflected the true value of a firm, or it may have been overestimated. A firm that wants to issue new shares to finance investment does not need to distribute more dividends to boost stock price. Thus, the association between the change in dividends and investment variables becomes insignificant in the investment equation during a postrecession or bull market period.

The other interesting question is why the dividend coefficients are mostly positive and significant in the period 1978-1987, when firms do not issue new shares. An explanation is that when firms do not issue new shares, they usually have sufficient internal funds or debt capacity; larger dividends reflect larger current or expected future earnings, which induce larger investments. An increase in dividends is not meant to boost stock price, but to demonstrate confidence in long-term earnings prospects. Thus, in this case, dividends do convey information on firms' earnings, but do not serve as a signal to boost stock price.

SUMMARY AND CONCLUSIONS

Investment, dividend, and external financing decisions are long-run decisions of the firm. External financing can be further divided into decisions related to common equity, debt, and other hybrid instruments. These financing decisions represent a major inflow or outflow of funds. The investment decision is closely related to the long-run value of the firm. The dividend decision is indirectly related to the long-run value of the firm too. External financing is necessary if the internally generated funds of a firm are not enough to support its investment and dividend decisions. In the perfect capital markets, as proposed by MM (1958, 1961), a firm's long run value should be solely determined by its investment decision, not affected by either its dividend or its external financing decision. However, in imperfect capital markets, the investment decisions may interact with the dividend or external financing decisions of a firm. Therefore, the interactions between the investment and financing decisions have been the focus of such articles as Dhrymes and Kurz (1967), Fama (1974), McDonald, Jacquillat, and Nussenbaum (1975), McCabe (1979), and PB.

The key argument of these articles is whether the dividend is competing with investment for the use of funds in a firm. MM's (1958) proposition indicates that the cutoff point of the investment of a firm should be independent of its financing decisions. Thus, the implication is that the investment decision of a firm is independent of its external financing or dividend decision. However, Dhrymes and Kurz (1967) propose that dividends compete with investments in the allocation decision process.

These articles primarily use the 2SLS, 3SLS, or SUR estimators to test the interactions between the investment and dividend decisions and give inconclusive results concerning the impact of the dividend decision on the investment decision. The data used by these articles do not include new external equity financing in the analyses, which happens to be very important in the development of signaling theory. Myers and Majluf (1984) and Asquith and Mullins (1986) demonstrate the adverse information effect of new external equity financing, even though John and Williams (1985) do not regard new equity financing as an unfavorable signal under certain conditions.

This thesis not only incorporates the new equity financing data and other updated data into the analysis, but also employs a new approach to estimating a simultaneous-equations system. A simultaneous two-stage switching regression model by Lee, Maddala, and Trost (1979) is employed for the analysis, which has not been used in the estimation of a simultaneous system in finance.

The empirical results of the thesis are used to test the interaction between the investment and the dividend decisions. The sample is rearranged according to (1) the decision of issuing or not issuing new shares and (2) the projected sales growth rates. The dividend policy behavior across firms is investigated in a simultaneous-decisions framework. Lee, Wu, and Djarraya's (1987) generalized dividend adjustment model is used as the dividend structural equation in the simultaneous-equations system. It is applied here to incorporate a partial adjustment model and the information content of dividends into the analysis of the dividend behavior of firms.

The empirical results of this thesis do not provide any evidence that the dividend decision has a negative impact on the investment decision. This does not reject MM's (1958) original proposition that the cutoff point of a firm's investment decision is not affected by its dividend or external financing decision.

The expectation of sales growth rates does not seem to affect the firm's simultaneous determination of its investment, dividend, and external financing decisions. The results from the grouped data do not distinguish one group from the other.

The results apparently indicate that American stock markets are progressing toward less imperfect capital markets. The results suggest that favorable investments may frequently be adopted regardless of what financing a firm may use or how much dividend payments a firm maintains. The degree of imperfection in the capital markets does not seem to be large enough to affect a firm's investment decision. Thus, as MM's proposition states, a firm's long-term value should be independent of its dividend and external financing decisions.

NOTE

1. Miller (1987) has carefully explored this type of concept.

REFERENCES

Asquity, P. & Mullins D.W. Jr. (1986) Equity issues and offering dilution. *Journal of Financial Economics* 15. (1/2), 61-89.

Donaldson, G. (1961). *Corporate debt capacity: A study of corporate debt policy and the determination of corporate debt capacity.* Boston: Division of Research, Harvard Graduate School of Business Administration.

Dhrymes, P.J. & Kurz, Mordecai (1967). Investment, dividend and external finance behavior of firms. In R. Ferber (ed.), New York: *Determinants of investment behavior.* Columbia University Press.

Fama, E.F. The empirical relationships between the dividend and investment decisions of firms. *American Economic Review 64*, 304-318.

Goldfeld, S.M. & Quandt, R.E. (1973). The estimation of structural shifts by switching regressions. *Annals of Economic and Social Measurement 2*, 475-485.

John, K. & Williams, J. (1985). Dividends, dilution and taxes: A signaling equilibrium. *Journal of Finance*, 1053-1070.

Johnson, N.L. & Kotz, S. (1972). *Distributions in statistics: Continuous multivariate distribution.* New York: Wiley.

Lee, C.F., Wu, & Djarraya, (1987). *Journal of Econometrics 35*, 267-285.

Lee, L.F., Maddala, G. & Trost, R.P. (1979). Testing for structural change by D-methods in switching simultaneous equation models. *Proceedings of the American Statistical Association (Business and Economics Section)*, 423-426.

Maddala, G.S. (1983) *Limited-dependent and qualitative variables in econometrics.* Cambridge: Cambridge University Press.

Maddala, G.S. & Nelson, F.D. (1975) Switching regression models with exogenous and endogenous switching. *Proceedings of the American Statistical Association (Business and Economics Section*, 423-426.

McCabe, G.M. (1979). The empirical relationship between investment and financing: A new Look. *Journal of Financial and Quantitative Analysis*, 14, 119-135.

McDonald, J.G. Jacquillant B., and Nussenbaum, M. (1975). Dividend, investment and financing decisions: Empirical evidence on French firms. *Journal of Financial and Quantitative Analysis*, 10, 741-755.

Miller, M.H. & Modigliani, F. (1961). Dividend policy, growth, and the valuation of shares. *Journal of Business* 34(4), 411-433.

Modigliani, F. & M. Miller H. (1958) The cost of capital, corporation finance and the theory of investment. *American Economic Review, 48*(3), 261-297.

Modigliani, F. & M. Miller, H. (1963). Taxes and cost of capital: A correction. *American Economic Review*, 433-443.

Myers, S. (1984). The capital structure puzzle. *Journal of Finance* 39(3), 575-592.

Myers & Majluf, N. (1984). Corporate financing and investment decisions when firms have information that investors do not have. *Journal of Financial Economics 13*,(2) 187-222.

Peterson, P.P. & Benesh, G.A. (1983). A reexamination of the empirical relationship between investment and financing decisions. *Journal of Financial and Quantitative Analysis,* 18(4), 439-453.

A TIMELINE APPROACH TO DAILY CASH FLOW FORECASTING

Tom W. Miller and Bernell K. Stone

ABSTRACT

A timeline approach to daily cash flow forecasting focuses on significant events and delays associated with the cash flow process. The cash flow timeline provides a framework for designing an information-based daily cash flow forecasting system. This forecasting system uses known information for timeline events, patterns representing the delays in the cash flow process, and probabilistic scheduling for generating future daily cash flows. A range of cash flow timeline information can be used concurrently so that the accuracy of the forecasts improves as time passes and additional information becomes available and the forecasting horizon is extended. Essential information (about the amount and timing of future cash flows) used to manage the short-term portfolio is provided by this daily cash flow forecasting system.

Advances in Financial Planning and Forecasting,
Volume 5, pages 265-281.

INTRODUCTION

When corporations designed and developed paper-based decision support systems to be used to manage their cash flows, they divided the cash flow timeline into limited, isolated segments. For example, separate, independent systems and databases were provided for sales order processing, credit granting, invoicing, receivables management, cash collection, cash concentration, purchase order processing, payment scheduling, payables management, cash disbursement, disbursements funding, short-term borrowing and lending, and accounting purposes. These paper-based systems and databases seldom interfaced or exchanged information with each other.

As corporations converted their decision support systems from paper to electronics, they built electronic versions of their paper-based systems without redesigning them to exploit the additional potential provided by computer technology. Existing technology makes it possible to design and develop a unified, integrated decision support system for the entire cash flow timeline. Such a design will eliminate significant duplication of effort and suboptimization. Currently, the same basic information is entered many different times by different people at different points along the cash flow timeline. This multiple entry of the same basic information is inefficient and increases the likelihood of an error occurring somewhere in the corporation's information system. In addition, different management groups have been given responsibility for different segments of the cash flow timeline. This has resulted in conflicting objectives and management groups working against each other. Many corporations are beginning to recognize these problems and are becoming increasingly interested in integrating their fragmented decision support systems for managing their cash flows.

THE CASH FLOW TIMELINE

A firm's cash flows are composed of inflows, outflows, and intrafirm flows. Inflows come from external sources. Outflows go to external uses. Intrafirm cash flows move from collection accounts to central accounts (concentration accounts and investment accounts) to disbursement accounts. The cash flow timeline portrays the essential features of the cash flow process. For inflows, it schedules significant events and delays from the initiation of the selling process through the receipt of available balances and updating or records. For outflows, significant events and delays from the initiation of the buying process through the loss of available balances and updating of records are scheduled. Reaping the benefits of rapidly evolving electronic technology requires an integrative, systems approach to cash management.

Hill and Ferguson (1985) have presented a conceptual model that divides the cash flow timeline into two portions: an inflow portion and an outflow portion.

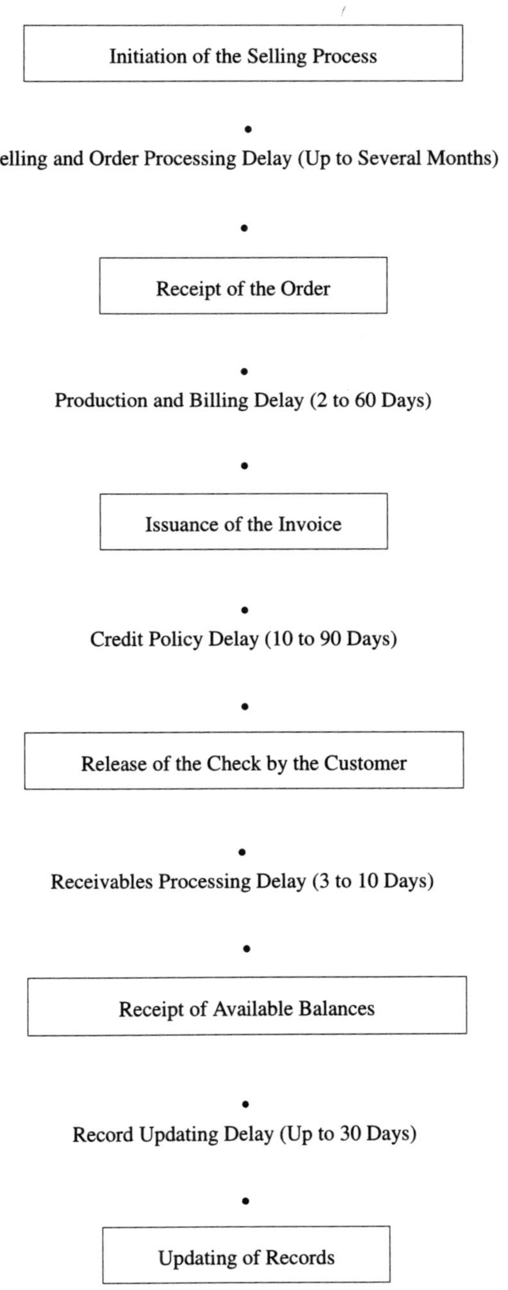

Figure 1.   The New Collection Timeline Definition

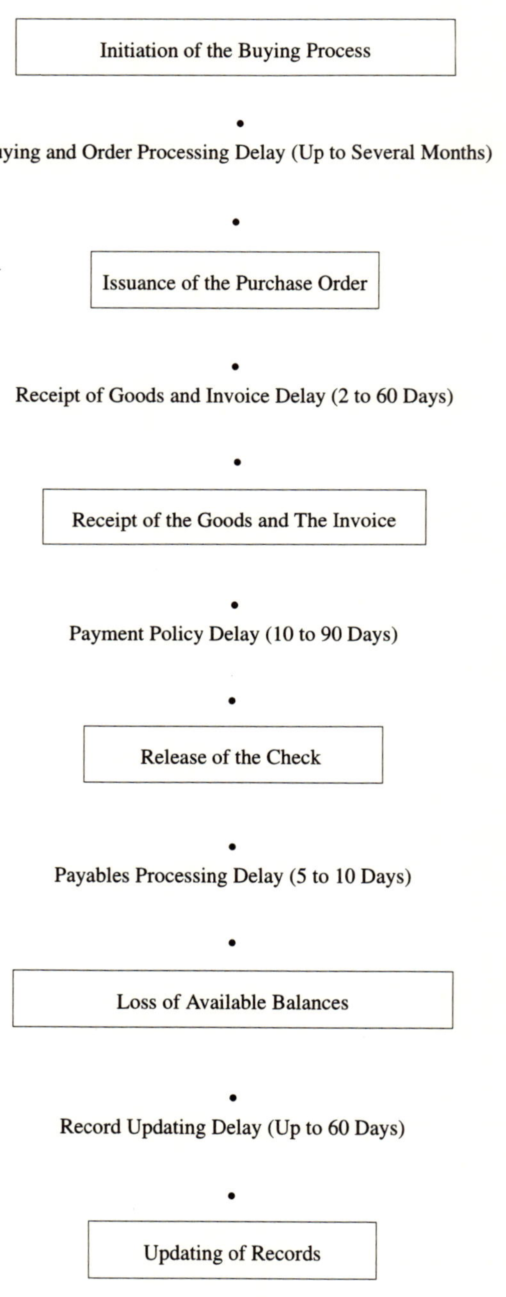

Figure 2.   The New Disbursement Timeline Definition

Figure 1 shows the segments for collections, the inflow portion, and figure 2 shows the segments for disbursements, the outflow portion, for the typical firm.

For most corporations, six significant events are separated by five different delays for both the inflow and outflow portions of the cash flow timeline. These events for the inflow portion of the cash flow timeline are:

1. initiation of the selling process,
2. receipt of the order,
3. issuance of the invoice,
4. release of the check by the customer,
5. receipt of available balances, and
6. updating of records.

For the outflow portion of the cash flow timeline, the events are

1. initiation of the buying process,
2. issuance of the purchase order,
3. receipt of the goods and the invoice,
4. release of the check,
5. loss of available balances, and
6. updating of records.

The delays are associated with five common segments for the inflow portion of the cash flow timeline:

1. The *selling and order processing* segment is the interval of time from when the selling process begins until the order is received. This period may last up to several months.
2. The *production and billing* segment is the time interval from when the order is received until the invoice is issued. This period typically lasts from a few days to 2 months.
3. The *credit policy* segment is the interval of time from when the invoice is issued until the check is mailed by the customer. The length of this segment depends upon the firm's credit policy and collection effort. This period typically lasts from 10 days to 3 months.
4. The *receivables processing* segment is the time interval from when the customer mails the check until available balances are received. This interval includes mail, processing, and availability delays. This period typically lasts from 3 to 10 days.
5. The *record updating* segment for receivables is the interval of time from when available balances are received until accounting records are updated. This period typically lasts from a few days to a month.

The delays for the outflow portion of the cash flow timeline are also associated with five common segments:

1. The *buying and order processing* segment is the time interval from when the buying process begins until a purchase order is issued. This period may last up to several months.
2. The *receipt of goods and invoice* segment is the interval of time from when the purchase order is issued until the goods and the invoice are received. This period typically lasts from a few days to 2 months.
3. The *payment policy* segment is the time interval from when the invoice is received until the check is mailed. The length of this segment depends upon the firm's payment policy with respect to taking discounts and stretching. This period typically lasts from 10 days to 3 months.
4. The *payables processing* segment is the interval of time from when the check is mailed until available balances are lost. This period typically lasts from 5 to 10 days.
5. The *record updating* segment for disbursements is the time interval from when available balances are lost until accounting records are updated. This period may last up to two months.

Traditional cash management has focused on the receivables-processing segment of the cash flow timeline for collections and on the payables-processing segment of the timeline for disbursements. Figures 3 and 4 show the portions of the cash flow timeline that are the domain of traditional cash management. Electronic order entry, electronic invoicing, optical scanning, image processing, and electronic settlement will reduce the lengths of the delays associated with the segments along the cash flow timeline. Focus needs to be shifted from the individual segments of the cash flow timeline to an integrated view of all of the segments (Beehler, 1984; Hill & Ferguson, 1985; Napoli, 1984). Today, capturing the data for the entire timeline is impossible or inconvenient for most companies. Companies need to build the information and decision support systems and organizational structures that will facilitate an integrated approach to the management of the significant events and delays along the cash flow timeline (Hill & Ferguson, 1985)

The short-term investment portfolio, which includes cash balances and financial instruments used for both borrowing and lending, serves as both a source and a sink for the cash flow timeline (Miller, 1988). Funds flow from the end of the receivables-processing segment of the inflow portion of the cash flow timeline to the short-term investment portfolio. Funds flow from the short-term investment portfolio to the end of the payables-processing segment of the outflow portion of the cash flow timeline.

Management of the cash flow timeline should consider the net yield on the short-term investment portfolio as well as the costs associated with the segments along the timeline (Miller, 1988). As a company integrates the management of its cash flow timeline, it should incorporate daily cash flow forecasting in its information and decision support system. Information associated with events along the

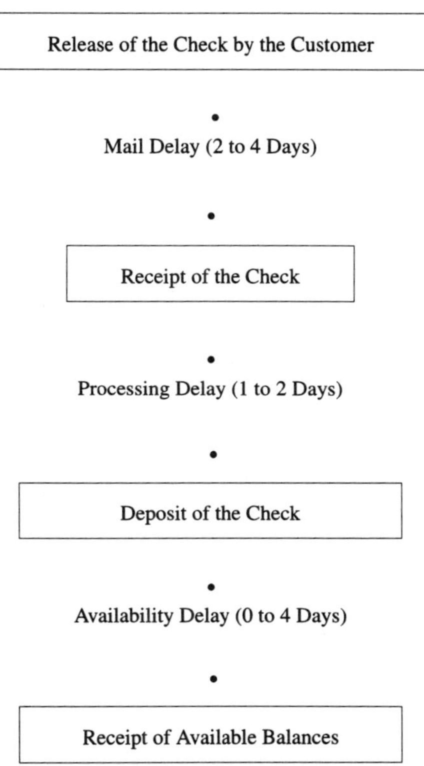

Figure 3.   Traditional Definition of the Collection Timeline

cash flow timeline can be used to generate daily cash flow forecasts. These cash flow forecasts can be used along with information from the cash flow timeline to integrate the management of the significant events and delays along the timeline and the management of the short-term portfolio (Austin, Maier, & Vander Weide, 1980; Maier & Vander Weide, 1978, 1982; Stone, 1986).

FORECASTING DAILY CASH FLOWS

Distribution and scheduling are generic approaches to cash flow forecasting.

Distribution

Distribution is an approach that uses a probability distribution to map a total cash flow for a given time period into the associated daily cash flows. When this

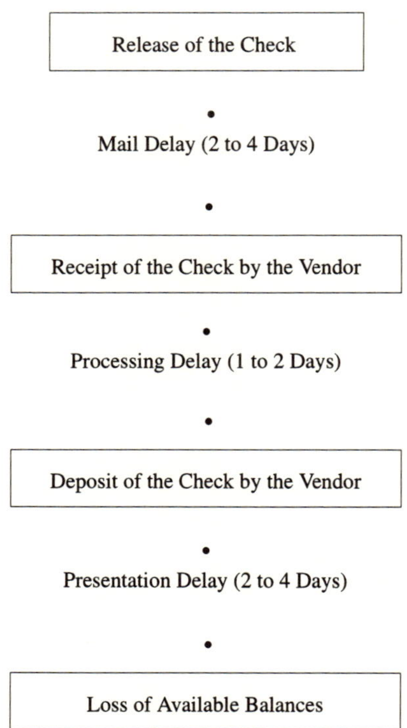

Figure 4.   Traditional Definition of the Disbursement Timeline

approach is utilized, the cash flow forecasting task is separated into three steps. The total cash flow for the time period is estimated, the intraperiod cash flow patterns are estimated, and the estimated total cash flow and the cash flow patterns are used to generate the daily cash flow to the days within the period. The distribution approach has been used for collections to map a total cash flow for a month into the daily cash flows for the days within the month (Stone & Miller, 1987; Stone & Wood, 1977).

Scheduling

Scheduling is an information-based approach to cash flow forecasting. It uses information that precedes a cash flow to determine the timing and amount of the resulting future cash flow. Scheduling may be either deterministic or probabilistic. When the total cash flow associated with the information occurring on a given day is assigned to *one* specific future day, deterministic scheduling should be employed. When the total cash flow associated with information occurring on a given day is spread over a *range* of future days, probabilistic scheduling should be used. In such situations, a probability distribution is used to assign the total cash flow associated with the information occurring on the given day to the range of future days. Deterministic scheduling is a degenerate form of probabilistic scheduling.

The deterministic scheduling approach has been used for cash flows resulting from electronic dividend payments, tax payments, lease payments, insurance premium payments, retirement benefits, and debt service payments. The probabilistic scheduling approach has been applied to disbursements to map the total dollar amount of checks released on a given day into the daily cash outflows associated with these checks (Maier, 1982; Maier, Robinson, & Vander Weide, 1981; Stone & Miller, 1983) It has been used for collections to map the total dollar amount of credit sales for a given month into the monthly cash inflows associated with these sales (Stone, 1972). It can also be used for collections or disbursements to map the total dollar amount of the cash flows associated with credit sales or credit purchases occurring on a given day into the future daily cash resulting from these sales or purchases.

Using Cash Flow Timeline Information

Information taken from the selling and order-processing, production and billing, credit policy, and receivables-processing segments of the inflow portion of the cash flow timeline can be used to generate forecasts of future cash inflows. Similarly, information from the buying and order-processing, receipt of goods and invoice, payables policy, and payables-processing segments of the outflow portion of the cash flow timeline can be utilized to generate forecasts of future cash outflows. Using information that occurs later on the cash flow timeline generally provides more accurate forecasts of future cash flows. However, use of information that occurs earlier on the timeline extends the forecast horizon. Figures 5 and 6 show how the use of information for different events on the cash flow timeline extends the horizon for the daily cash flow forecasts.

Information from the receivables-processing and payables/processing (Maier, 1982; Maier, Robinson, & Vander Weide, 1981; Stone & Miller, 1983) segments of the cash flow timeline can be used to generate relatively accurate short-term forecast for horizons up to about 10 days, information from the credit policy and payment policy segments of the cash flow timeline can be used to extend the forecasting horizon up to about 100 days with some loss of accuracy, information from the production and billing and receipt of goods and invoice segments of the cash flow timeline can be used to extend the forecasting horizon up to about 160 days with a little more loss of accuracy, and information from the selling and order-processing segments of the cash flow timeline can be used to extend the forecasting horizon up to several months with some more loss of accuracy. All of these forms of cash flow timeline information can be utilized concurrently so that

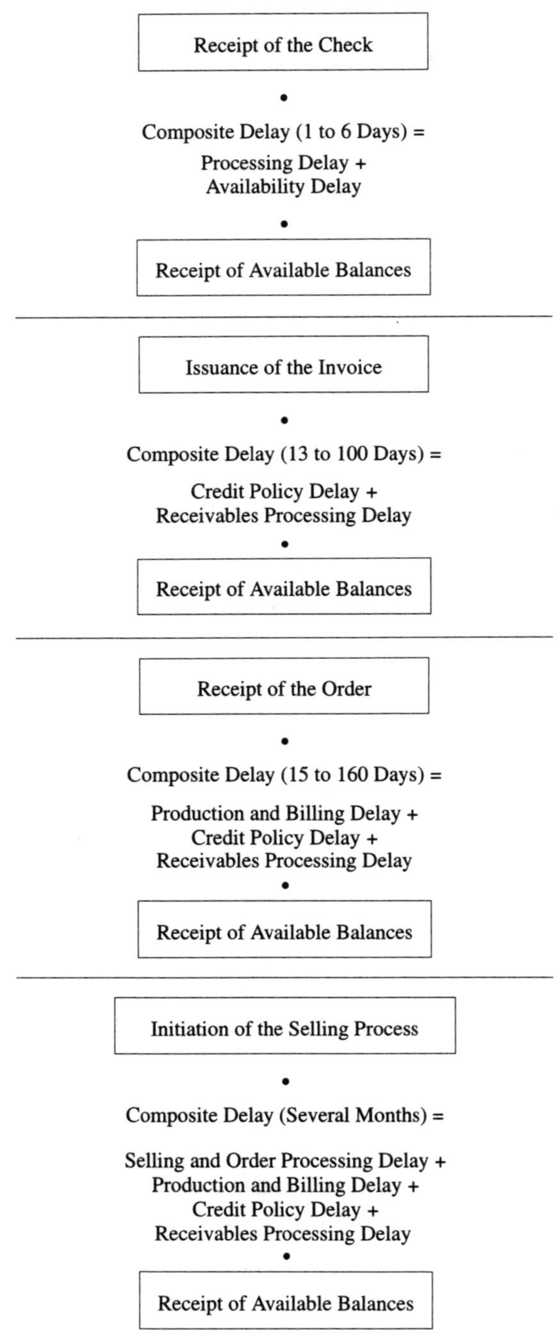

Figure 5.   Extending the Forecasting Horizon for Collections

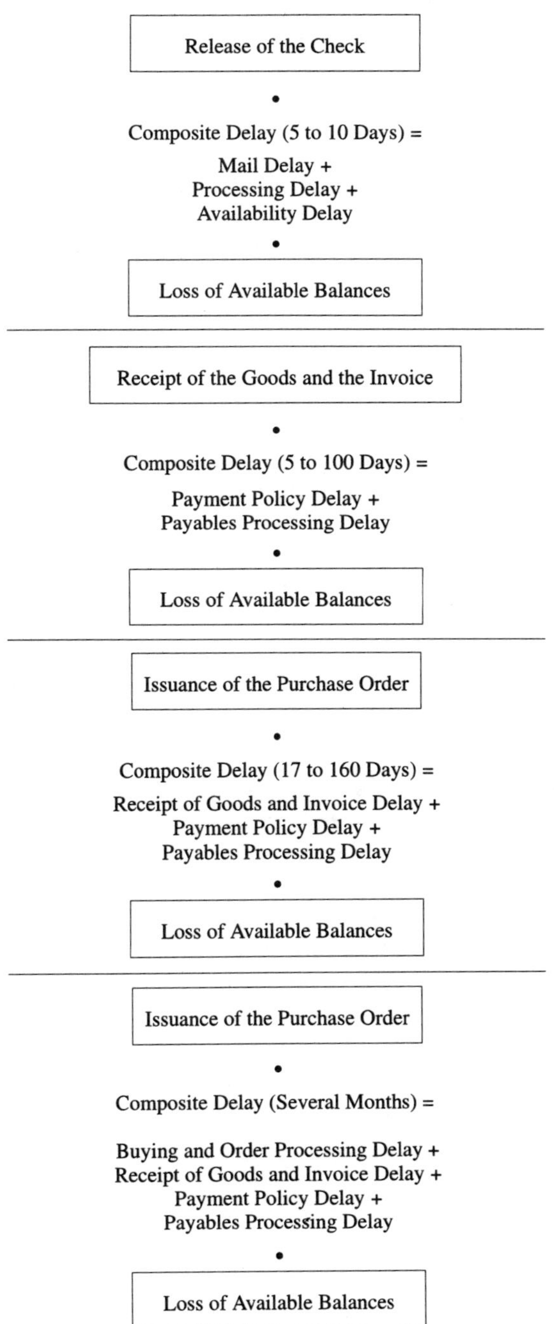

Figure 6.   Extending the Forecasting Horizon for Disbursements

the forecasts can be improved as time passes and additional timeline information becomes available.

Separating Cash Flows into Components

To obtain statistically stable patterns, cash flows need to be separated into components that can logically be expected to have similar behavior (Stone & Miller, 1981, 1985). Division of cash flows into components for product lines, operating groups, or subsidiaries is one logical approach. Cash flow patterns will usually differ for products with different credit terms. Sales may need to be separated into credit classes or credit quality groups.

FORECASTING DAILY CASH FLOWS ASSOCIATED WITH CASH FLOW TIMELINE EVENTS

The probabilistic scheduling approach can be used to forecast daily cash flows associated with cash flow timeline events. When payment behavior is reasonably stable over time, forecasts can be based on the time distribution of daily cash flows associated with a cash flow timeline event. The time distribution of cash flows is referred to as the cash flow pattern. The proportions of the total cash flow associated with information for a cash flow timeline event occurring on a specified day that become cash flows on subsequent days characterize the daily cash flow pattern. The cash flow pattern and the schedule of past (known) timeline events can be used to generate a schedule of future daily cash flows. In this way, each day's cash flow timeline information can be transformed into a schedule of future cash flows. Then, the total cash flow for a given future day can be obtained by combining the appropriate daily cash flows.

The cash flow horizon can be defined as the number of days required for all of the cash flows associated with the information for the cash flow timeline event to affect available balances. The cash flow pattern measures the fractions of the total cash flow associated with cash flow timeline events that affect balances after specific delays. These proportions are calculated by dividing the daily cash flows associated with a given day's cash flow timeline event that occur after a specific delay by the total cash flow associated with the timeline event. The cash flow proportions are defined as

$$\text{PROPOTION}_i = \text{FLOW}_{ti}/\text{DOLLAR}_t \tag{1}$$

for $i = 1, \ldots, I$, where I denotes the cash flow horizon; FLOW_{ti} is the dollar amount of the cash flow occurring on day $t+i$ associated with the cash flow timeline event occurring on day t; and DOLLAR_t is the dollar amount of the total cash flow associated with the cash flow timeline event occurring on day t. The total dollar amount of the cash flow occurring on day T can be calculated by summing all of the cash flows resulting from past cash flow timeline events. The total cash flow on day T is given by

$$\text{TOTAL}_T = \text{FLOW}_{T-1,1} + \text{FLOW}_{T-2,2} + \ldots + \text{FLOWS}_{T-I,I}$$

$$= \sum_{i=1}^{I} \text{FLOW}_{T-i,i} \tag{2}$$

Alternatively, the total cash flow on day T can be calculated by summing all of the products of the cash flow proportions and the dollar amounts of the total cash flows associated with past cash flow timeline events over the cash flow horizon:

$$\text{TOTAL}_T = \text{PROPORTION}_1 \text{DOLLAR}_{T-1} + \text{PROPORTION}_2 \text{DOLLAR}_{T-2}$$

$$+ \ldots + \text{PROPORTION}_I \text{DOLLAR}_{T-I}$$

$$= \sum_{i=1}^{I} \text{PROPORTION}_i \text{DOLLAR}_{T-i} \tag{3}$$

Time-Varying Behavior

Certain types of time-varying payment behavior can be modeled by using a constant set of cash flow proportions that are associated with an assumed stable cash flow pattern. Weekends, holidays, seasons, interest rates, and economic conditions may cause shifts in the underlying stable cash flow pattern (Miller & Stone, 1985).

Weekend Effects

Weekends disturb the normal cash flow patterns. Customers do not make payments on weekends. The company's available balances are not increased or decreased on weekends. Mail is delayed on weekends. The company's and the banks' processing operations are interrupted and workloads are shifted by weekends. The cash flows that would normally occur on an immediately after weekends are shifted to later business days. Such cash flows are usually shifted 1 or 2 days. Therefore, these weekend shifts can be treated as disturbances to the normal cash flow pattern.

Holiday Effects

The normal cash flow patterns are disturbed by holidays in much the same way as by weekends. Customers do not make payments and banks do not clear checks on holidays. Mail is delayed and workloads are shifted by holidays. The cash flows that would normally occur on holidays are shifted to later business days. The actual shifts depend on the length of the holiday (1 or 2 business days) and the position of the holiday within the week (beginning of the week, middle of the week, or end of the week). The effects of holidays can also be treated as disturbances to the normal cash flow pattern.

Seasonal Effects

Seasonality of cash flows refers to systematic variation over time. Such seasonality can be decomposed into two components: systematic variation in the amount of cash associated with the timeline event and systematic variation in cash flow patterns. The dollar amounts of cash associated with various timeline events are often highly seasonal. This type of seasonality is completely incorporated in the daily cash flow forecast because information for the actual dollar amounts associated with the cash flow timeline event is used to generate the forecast. The cash flow patterns may not be very seasonal. If the cash flow patterns vary systematically with the seasons, seasonality can be treated as a disturbance to the normal pattern.

Interest Rate Effects

Interest rates may also disturb normal cash flow patterns. Payments may be delayed more and discounts may for forgone when interest rates are high. When interest rates are low, payments may be made more promptly and discounts may be taken. Consequently, cash flow patterns may be shifted by abnormal levels of interest rates.

Economic Activity

When general economic conditions are good, payments may be made in a timely fashion. When general economic conditions are bad, payments may be delayed. The level of economic activity disturbs the normal cash flow patterns so that cash flows are speeded up in good times and slowed down in bad times. The cash flow patterns may be modified to incorporate such disturbances.

Synthesis

Schedules of the dollar amounts of cash flows associated with the timeline events and cash flow patterns can be used to forecast future daily cash flows. Estimates of cash flow patterns should reflect the effects of weekends, holidays, seasons, interest rates, and economic activity. Cash flow pattern parameters need to incorporate the time-varying behavior. Cash flow patterns can be modeled to incorporate the effects of weekends, holidays, seasonality, interest rates, and general economic conditions (Miller & Stone, 1985)

Using Cash Flow Patterns to Forecast Daily Cash Flows

Estimates of the cash flow pattern parameters and schedules of past cash flow timeline event dollar amounts can be used to generate forecasts of resulting future cash flows. The daily cash flow associated with a specific type of cash flow timeline event can be forecasted by using

$$FORECAST_t = \sum_{I=1}^{I} ESTIMATE_i DOLLAR_{t-i} \tag{4}$$

where $FORECAST_t$ is the dollar amount of the cash flow forecasted for business day t, $ESTIMATE_i$ is the estimate of $PROPORTION_i$, and $DOLLAR_{t-i}$ is the dollar amount of the total cash flow associated with the cash flow timeline event occurring on day t-i.

Information Required

Actual cash flow data can be used to parameterize and measure the accuracy of the forecasting models. Historical information indicating, the amounts and the timing of the cash flows associated with the various cash flow timeline events is required to estimate the cash flow patterns. A company can simply record the required information for the cash flow timeline events. Information can be obtained from the sales entry, order entry, invoicing, payment scheduling, check release, and balance reporting systems. Bank accounts can be designed to provide information on when available balances change. Zero-balance accounts can be used to facilitate the data collection process. In addition, measures can be developed for interest rate and economic activity disturbances and historical databases can be maintained. This type of information can typically be obtained from public sources.

SUMMARY

As the scope of cash management is broadened and the company designs and develops the information system required to support an integrative, systems approach to cash flow timeline management, it should also design and develop an information-based daily cash flow forecasting system. The probabilistic scheduling approach can be used to produce such a forecasting system. This approach uses information about cash flow timeline events and cash flow patterns associated with cash flow timeline delays to forecast future daily cash flows. Cash flow patterns can be modeled to incorporate the effects of weekends, holidays, seasons, interest rates, and general economic conditions. Cash flow timeline information ranging from the receivables-processing segment to the selling and order-processing segment for the inflow portion of the timeline and from the payables-processing segment to the buying and order-processing segment of the outflow portion of the timeline can be used concurrently so that the forecasting horizon is extended and the accuracy of the forecasts improves as time passes and additional timeline information becomes available. This type of forecasting system can accommodate changes in the lengths of the delays in the inflow and outflow portions of the timeline brought about by future technological developments as the treasury function moves away from paper toward electronics. These daily cash flow forecasts provide essential information used to integrate the management of the short-term portfolio (Maier & Vander Weide, 1978) with the management of the events and delays along the inflow and outflow portions of the cash flow timeline (Hill & Ferguson, 1985). The effects of cash flow timeline changes can be analyzed. Maturity structures can be chosen and financial instruments can be selected for both borrowing and lending. Timeline management and short-term portfolio management decisions can be coordinated.

REFERENCES

Austin, J., Maier, S.F., & Vander Weide, J.H. (1980) General Telephone's experience with a short run financial planning model. *Cash Management Forum* (June), 3-6.

Beehler P. J. (1984) Treasury management evolution. *Journal of Cash Management, 4,*(January/February), 10-19.

Hill, N.C & Ferguson D.M, (1985). Cash flow timeline management: The next frontier of cash management. *Journal of Cash Management, 5*(May/June), 12-22.

Maier, S.F., Insulated controlled disbursing: A technique for coping with noon presentment and other possible check system changes. *Journal of Cash Management,* 1(November), 32-37.

Maier, S.F., Robinson, D.W., & Vander Weide, J.H. (1981). A short-term disbursement forecasting model. *Financial Management, 10*(Spring), 9-20.

Maier, S.F. & Vander Weide, J.H. (1978). A practical approach to short-run financial planning. *Financial Management,* 8(Winter), 10-16.

Maier, S.F. & Vander Weide, J.H. (1982). A decision-support system for Managing a short-term financial instrument portfolio. *Journal of Cash Management,* 2(March), 20-25.

Miller T.W., (1988) A systems view of short-term investment management. *Advances in Working Capital Management,* 1.

Miller, T.W. & Stone B.K. (1985). Daily cash flow forecasting and seasonal resolution: Alternative models and techniques for using the distribution approach. *Journal of Financial and Quantitative Analysis, 20*(September), 335-352.

Napoli, M.J. Jr. (1984). Float reduction along the cash flow timeline. *Journal of Cash Management,* 4(July/August), 44-47.

Stone, B.K. (1972). The payment-pattern approach to the forecasting and control of accounts receivable. *Financial Management,* 1(Spring), 72-84.

Stone, B.K. (1986) The use of forecasts and smoothing in control-limit models for cash management. *Financial Management,5*(Autumn), 65-82.

Stone, B.K. & Miller, T.W. (1983). Forecasting disbursement funding requirements: The clearing pattern approach. *Journal of Cash Management*, *3*(October/November), 67-78.

Stone, B.K. & Miller, T.W. (1981). Daily cash forecasting: A structuring framework. *Journal of Cash Management*, *1*(October), 35-50.

Stone, B.K. & Miller, T.W. (1985). Daily cash forecasting. In Frank J. Fabozzi and Leslie N. Masonson (eds.), *Corporate cash management: Techniques and Analysis,* 120-141. Homewood, IL: Dow Jones-Irwin.

Stone, B.K. & Miller T.W. (1988). Daily cash forecasting with multiplicative models of cash flow patterns. *Financial Management*, *16* (Winter), 45-54.

Stone, B.K. & Wood R.A. (1977). Daily cash forecasting: A simple method for implementing the distribution approach. *Financial Management*, 6(Fall), 40-50.

A MARKOV PROCESS SOLUTION TO THE DEMAND-FOR-CASH PROBLEM

Kevin J. Leonard

ABSTRACT

In this paper, we consider a Markov process model for optimizing the operating cash
of a firm. We use a stochastic inventory model in which we assume that the input
process (receipt of cash) is Poisson and the cash disbursement time is exponentially
distributed. We derive steady-state probabilities of reaching various cash levels and
illustrate some important characteristics of such systems. As well, an application of
this model is provided that allows for the justification of assumptions and the
evaluation of the model's effectiveness.

INTRODUCTION

In this paper, we concentrate on one area of cash management: the demand for
cash by a firm in the short term. We consider a company that pools all of its cash
in one account, called the concentration account. This account is funded by the net
cash flow of the firm each day (cash received minus cash disbursed). When the

Advances in Financial Planning and Forecasting,
Volume 5, pages 283-301.
Copyright © 1994 by JAI Press Inc.
All rights of reproduction in any form reserved.
ISBN:1-55938-421-2

cash in the account becomes too excessive, a transfer of some amount is made to an interest-earning short-term investment portfolio at a cost. A second cost, an opportunity or holding cost, is incurred on the cash not being utilized—sitting idle in the concentration account. On the other hand, if the cash becomes low, then some of the funds in the portfolio are liquidated and transferred to the cash account at a cost—which is not necessarily the same as the transfer cost in the opposite direction. If the transfer is not made, then the cash account could become depleted, thereby incurring a shortage cost.

The objective of previous models that have been presented in the literature to solve the "demand-for-cash" problem is primarily to find the optimal level of cash to have in the concentration account (often within a specified interval) so as to minimize the total cost of management of such an account with regard to the costs stipulated above.

Many such models have been proposed (e.g.) Girgis, 1968; Neave, 1970; Miller & Orr, 1966. The variations in the models are due to the assumptions the authors made with respect to the distribution to the net cash flow, type of costs involved, and time of transfers. Unfortunately, very little application of these models has occurred in business. The reasons are mainly due to the complexity of the models, the need for the user to have a significant level of mathematical sophistication, and, most often, the unrealistic nature of the models themselves. One recent additional argument is that transaction costs have become insignificant compared to opportunity or holding costs, to the point where the cash management problem is trivial: minimize cash balances subject to any compensating balance constraint. However, these compensating balances are often dictated by the fluctuations in cash balances. If cash balances can be brought down further through effective cash management, the need for cash reserves or compensating balances will be reduced further, creating additional cost saving.

We propose a new model in an attempt to solve the "optimal cash balance" dilemma. Its development emphasizes the application of this model to a real business setting involving an existing Canadian small business. The assumptions and validity of the model are addressed.

LITERATURE REVIEW

Early work in the field of cash management was performed by Baumol (1952) and Tobin (1956). These models considered cash to be an inventory item with deterministic demand. Models that followed treated the demand for cash as being stochastic in nature and these included Girgis (1968) and Neave (1970). Research by Constantinides (1976) considered a continuous-time model with stochastic demand and allowed for positive and negative balances, where the optimal policy took the simple form (d, D, U, u).

A well known cash management model was proposed by Miller and Orr (1966). They stated that for many firms, the typical pattern of cash flows is not a simple one, but rather a complex, irregular one. The cash balance (receipts minus disbursements) fluctuates irregularly (and to some extent, unpredictably) over time in both directions. The cash balance builds up when receipts exceed payments and it declines when the opposite is true. Should the build-up become excessive, then a transfer should occur - taking money from a ready cash account and transferring it to interest bearing alternatives. On the other hand, should there be a significant decline in the cash balance, a transfer should again occur - transferring money from interest paying items to cash in order to restore the cash balance to an adequate working level. The presentation of the Miller-Orr model concentrated on the special yet realistic scenario of the symmetric, zero- or no-drift case where cash inflows and outflows are equal over a short time frame.

A subsequent cash management model was proposed by Milbourne, Buckholtz, and Wasau (1982). This model considered cash as a simple random walk, which rises or falls at points in time. They assumed a Markov process model in discrete time and discrete state space, where in each time period the cash balance either increases, decreases, or remains constant.

This model contained two boundaries and two return points of the form (d,D,U,u) as opposed to one return point (Miller-Orr). When the cash balance falls below d, it is returned to a level of $D;$ similarly, when it rises above u, it is returned to U. Otherwise, no transfers are made. One of the major findings of this research was the optimality of this particular money-holding rule when the cash balances at each point in time are serially independent.

A STOCHASTIC MODEL FOR CASH MANAGEMENT

The model proposed here pertains solely to cash management in the short term. Basically, two separate short-term assets—ready cash in a concentration account *and* an interest-bearing account—are considered. Transfers between these two accounts can occur almost instantly (and always within the same day) but will incur a cost (transfer cost). There are no shortage costs, since it is assumed there will be no shortages or overdrafts.

The objective of the model is to find an optimal level of cash to have on hand by minimizing the transfer and opportunity (holding) costs.

The main feature of this model pertains to the fluctuations of the cash balance [denoted by $C(t)$], which is assumed to follow a Markov process in continuous time and a finite number of states (discrete state space). The model, similar to the Miller-Orr model, has two boundary points $(R,S+1)$, but will contain two return points (M, M') similar to the Neave (1970) model and later Milbourne, Buckholtz and Wasan (1982). The cash balance will be allowed to wander freely while remaining within the boundary limits. However, once the cash balance reaches

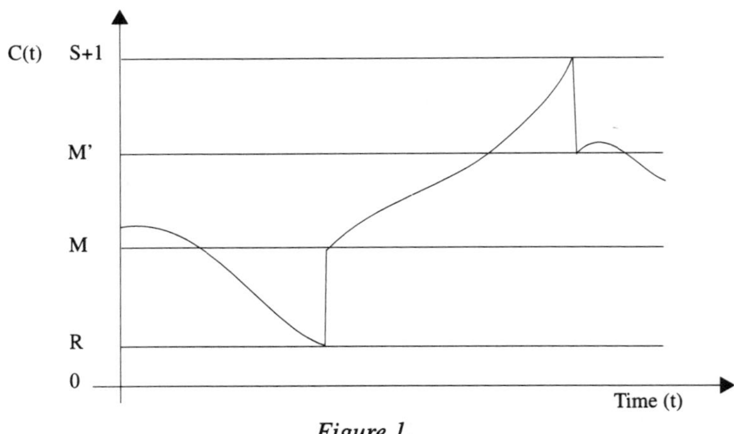

Figure 1.

S+1, the upper limit, a transfer is made from the cash account to the interest-bearing account in the amount of $(S$+1$) - M'$. The balance then returns to a value of M'. If the cash balance reaches a level of R (the lower boundary), then a transfer is made from the interest-bearing account to the ready cash state in the amount of $M - R$. The cash balance then returns to a value of M. A realization of the stochastic behavior of the model is given in Figure 1.

The cash balance changes continuously and is basically the net difference between cash receipts and cash disbursements. We consider the stochastic inventory model, where we assume the input process (receipt of cash) is Poisson with mean rate δ and the disbursement of cash is exponentially distributed with parameter μ. The ratio of cash receipt to cash payment rates is denoted by τ (where $\tau = \delta/\mu$).

JUSTIFICATION OF THE MODEL

First, the application of Markov chains (and by extension, queuing theory) to inventory theory and problems is not new. (For one reference, See Karlin & Taylor, 1975). What is novel about this application is that a continuous-time Markov process is applied to the cash management inventory problem, where cash is considered as an inventory item that can increase as well as decrease within the time period.

Second, some elaboration of the distributional assumptions concerning cash receipts and disbursements is required. In other applications of queuing theory to the classic inventory problem (see Gaver & Thompson, 1973, for example), the arrival of the demand for the inventory item is assumed to follow a stationary Poisson process with mean rate δ. When stock of the item reaches a reorder point, a replenishment order is placed. This order must await its turn at the production facility. The waiting time from the moment the reorder is placed until the item is received is a random variable independent from one reorder to the next and is assumed to follow an exponential distribution.

In the application employed in this model, the arrival of cash is assumed to be independent of the time period and follows a stationary Poisson process. The disbursement of cash is a random variable that is independent of time from one payment to the next and is assumed to follow an exponential distribution.

THE COST FUNCTION

There are three costs associated with this model: (1) the transfer cost per transfer associated with transferring money from interest-bearing accounts to the cash accounts called C_1, (2) the cost of transferring money from cash to the portfolio called C_2, and (3) the cost of holding cash in the ready state (forfeiting the opportunity of earning a higher return in the portfolio called C_3.

The total cost of having too little cash is the cost C_1 per transfer multiplied by the probability of running out of cash (reaching level R). The only way of reaching state R is by being in state $R+1$ and having a cash disbursement of one unit, which occurs with rate μ. A Shortage event occurs then in time interval $(t, t+\Delta t)$ with probability

$$P\{C(t) = R+1\}\mu\, dt \tag{1}$$

The expected number of such events over time t is obtained by integrating

$$\int_0^T P\{C(t) = R+1\}\mu\, dt = \mu\int_0^T P\{C(t) = R+1\}\, dt \tag{2}$$

The expected number of shortages during a unit time interval then results when Equation (2) is divided by T and the long-run expected number of shortages per unit time is approached as T becomes large. But for any state i, it can be shown that

$$\lim_{T\to\infty} \frac{1}{T}\int_0^T P\{C(t) = i\}\, dt = \pi_i \tag{3}$$

where π_i are the steady-state probabilities. Hence, the long-run shortage of cash rate is shown to be $\mu\pi_{R+1}$. Consequently, the expected cost of being short of cash is

$$C_1\mu\pi_{R+1} \tag{4}$$

where C_1 is the cost per transfer from the portfolio to the cash account.

Similarly, the cost of having too much cash on hand (excess) is the cost of a transfer multiplied by the probability of having excess cash (reaching level $S+1$).

The only way to reach state $S+1$ is by having the process in state S and having a cash receipt that occurs with rate δ. Thus, a transfer is initiated in the time interval $(t, t+\triangle t)$ with probability

$$P\{C(t) = S\}\delta\ dt \tag{5}$$

and the long-run excess cash rate is calculated as $\delta\pi_s$. Consequently, the expected cost of having too much cash is

$$C_2\delta\pi_s \tag{6}$$

where C_2 is the cost per transfer from the cash account to the portfolio.

The carrying cost associated with the holding of cash is a function of the cash in the concentration account during the time period is denoted by

$$\sum_{i=R}^{S} \pi_i i \tag{7}$$

If we let C_3 represent the difference in rate of return between the earning power of the portfolio and of the cash account over the duration of the time period, then the holding cost of cash is

$$C_3 \sum_{i=R}^{S} \pi_i i \tag{8}$$

The total cost function then is given by

$$C(S, M', M, R) = C_1\mu\pi_{R+1} + C_2\delta\pi_s + C_3\sum_{i=R}^{S} \pi_i \cdot i \tag{9}$$

MODIFICATIONS

In an attempt to apply this model to a business environment, the general inventory model was modified somewhat by assuming that the lower boundary (R) was equal to zero. The logic behind this assumption is that with instantaneous transfers, there is no need to have a buffer stock of cash (in the amount of

R-0). Instantaneous transfers at any time during the day are rapidly becoming a reality in business. Thus once the cash balance hits the lower bound [$C(t) = R$], the transfer is made (at least within the same day) and the balance returns to M. The cash balance will never fall below R, implying that the lower bound should be at a minimum (in order to reduce opportunity costs), which is achieved at $R=0$.

As a result, the total cost function is

$$C(S, M', M, R = 0) = C_1 \mu \pi_1 + C_2 \delta \pi_s + C_3 \sum_{i=1}^{S} \pi_i i \qquad (10)$$

Let us now turn to the problem of finding an expression for the values of π_i from π_1 to π_s. Consider $C(t)$ as a Markov process, continuous in time, and a finite discrete state space $(1, 2, \dots M, M+1, t\dots, M', M'+1, \dots, S-1, S)$. The transition diagram illustrating the behavior of cash in the states is shown in Figure 2.

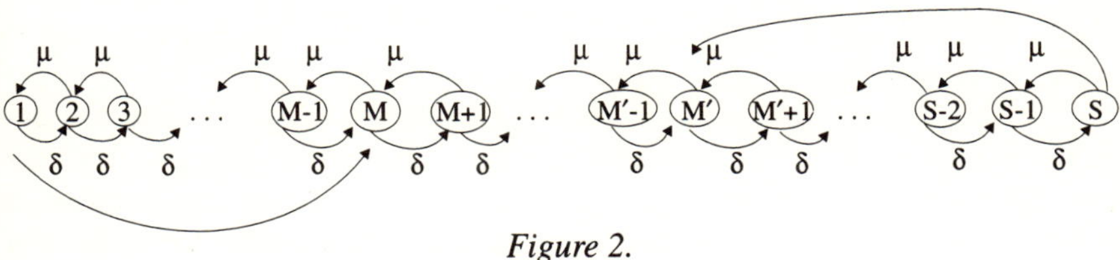

Figure 2.

With this Markov assumption, the balance equations can be calculated straight-forwardly (see Appendix 1 for calculations).

MINIMIZATION OF THE COST FUNCTION

Expressing the cost equation in full, we have

$$C(S, M', M, R) = \frac{C_1 \mu (1-\tau)^2 (1-\tau)^{S-M'+1} + C_2 \delta (1-\tau)^2 (1-\tau^M) \tau^{S-M}}{(M-\tau^M)(1-\tau^{S-M'+1}) - (S-M'+1)\tau^{S-M'+1}(1-\tau)(1-\tau^M)} + C_3 \sum_{i=1}^{S} \pi_i i \qquad (11)$$

in the asymmetric case, where cash inflows and cash outflows are not forced to be equal, that is, $\tau \gtrless 1$. In the symmetric case ($\tau = \delta/\mu = 1$), the cost equation can be represented by

$$C(S, M', M, R) =$$

$$+ C_3 \sum_{i=1}^{S} \pi_i i$$

$$(M)(S + M' + 1)(S - M' + 1)\, 2C_1\mu\,(S - M' + 1) + 2C_2\delta\,(M) \qquad (12)$$

If we wish to find the minimum of this cost function with respect to the three variables M, M', and S, we can follow standard minimization techniques. This involves taking the partial derivatives of this function with respect to each variable, setting the derivatives equal to zero, and solving simultaneously. (The partials derivative equations for the general asymmetric case are presented in Appendix 2.)

As can be seen, due to the complexity of these simultaneous equations, solving for a unique solution using standard procedures would not yield satisfactory results. The variables are transcendentally interrelated and a closed-form solution cannot be obtained.

In the short term, however, a reasonable solution can be found under the no-drift, symmetric case. If we consider a very short time horizon, then the assumption of equal cash inflows and outflows is quite realistic. The solution procedure described above applied to the cost equation for t =1 (the symmetric, no-drift case) yields the following results from the partial-derivative equations:

$$M' = \frac{\delta C_2}{C_3}$$

$$M' = \frac{(2S\delta C_2) + (2\delta C_2) + (S^2 C_3) - C_3}{C_3}$$

$$M = \frac{(S - M' + 1)^2 C_1 \mu}{C_3(2S + 2) - C_2\delta(S + 2) - C_3(S + M' + 1)(S - M' + 1)}$$

To employ this model, the values of $C1$, $C2$, and $C3$ have to be ascertained for the specific application and then substituted into the above equations to determine the optimal values for M, M', and S.

APPLICATION OF THE MODEL

In this paper, novel ideas were raised with respect to the construction of a new cash management model. Of these, the most interesting and perhaps most questionable relates to the assumptions of the distributions of the cash receipts and cash disbursements. Rather than attempting to defend these assumptions theoretically, we selected a real business firm and we analyzed its pattern of receipts and payments to justify these assumption.

The firm (referred to as ABC Company) that was selected was a medium-sized company with five branch offices distributed across Canada. This firm is a wholesaler of industrial and electrical products and deals mainly with the Canadian industry, although it does possess some clients and suppliers in the American and European markets. ABC Company deals solely with one bank in Canada and presently uses many features offered for cash centralization (see, for example, Anvari, 1983).

After the firm was selected, the nature of the data required had to be determined. It was decided that analysis of daily cash flow for a period of 2 months would be sufficient. Hence data were collected from May 1 to June 30, which accounted for 43 working days. There is no definitive rule concerning the amount of data to collect. It was this author's opinion that anything less than 2 months would jeopardize the validity of the nonparametric tests that were performed to verify the distributional assumptions. Unfortunately, due to restrictions placed by the firm, it was not possible to obtain a larger sample. The limitations of this application as a result of the small sample size are so noted.

The usual practice of cash management research is to analyze the history of the net cash flow of a firm (for example, Homonoff & Mullins, 1975). The net cash flow per day is basically just the cash receipts minus the cash disbursements. The distribution of the net cash is then followed for a specified period of time, indicating whether it was positive or negative, at which point analysis is performed on the data relating to the goals of the particular researchers.

Here, a different approach was taken. Following the suggestions of Stone and Miller (1981), the daily net cash was separated into the cash inflows and the cash outflows. Therefore, the cash receipts and the cash disbursements per day were examined independently. The justification is that the rate of cash inflow is assumed to be independent of the cash outflow—in the short term. They are both related to the success of the business, but there is very little relation between these two variables in the short run. Hence, when they are considered together, the fluctuations of one negate the fluctuations of the other and some degree of statistical smoothing occurs. This then makes forecasting and estimation extremely difficult. Some of this difficulty can be eliminated when the receipts and payments are analyzed alone. It was this procedure that was followed to find the population distribution from which the cash inflows and outflows originate.

Another feature of this research was that the stochastic portion of the cash flow was emphasized. There is often a portion of the receipts or payments that is deterministic. For example, in the cash disbursements, payments for payroll, for leased equipment, for rental of automobiles, and for long-term debt are all examples of disbursements that are constant and known in advance with certainty. It is these items that should be removed from the statistical analysis. There is no need to try to predict the occurrence of these items when they are already known. Thus the analyses of the cash receipts and cash payments distributions deal solely with the stochastic element of the cash flows that remains once the deterministic portion has been identified and removed.

To this end, for the cash receipts, every check received must be identified as either being a predictable occurrence (deterministic in nature) or being a random occurrence (stochastic). Then all of the stochastic items are pooled together and studied as to their distribution and behavior. The same analysis is then performed for the cash payments. Although it could be argued that any company's cash payments should be comprised of only deterministic elements, a large part of the cash outflow remains stochastic in nature. This is due to the mail or delivery service, the efficiency of the processing of the check by the payee, and the efficiency of the check-clearing systems. Thus, even though the date of check issuing is known, the actual timing of the disbursements of funds from the cash account remains unknown.

Therefore, in order to analyze the stochastic component for one firm over a 43-day period, every check and direct withdrawal and deposit made must be examined and recorded. (See Appendix 4 for a complete discussion on the goodness-of-fit tests employed to test for the distributional assumptions relating to cash receipts and disbursements.)

The Application

To test this Markov model in a real business setting, the results were compared to that of the Miller-Orr model. For proper comparison purposes, all cost components were equalized (i.e., transfer and opportunity costs were the same). Further, the no-drift case was used in both cases. For short-term cash management, the symmetric case is most realistic (Miller & Orr, 1966). Additionally, in the data captured, the ratio of cash receipts to cash disbursements was very close to 1 (δ/μ = 1.1091; see Appendix 4), further supporting the zero -drift case.

One assumption of this application is that the time period relating to the cost equations is 1 day. Thus, the objective is to minimize the cost of cash management per day. This fits in well with the cash manager's role because very often the only time the manager has confirmed information on the cash account is from the end-of-day balances. Hence, at the end of the day, the manager can review the cash activity and calculate the cost of management with respect to holding and transfer costs.

One feature of the Markov model is that it considers cash in continuous-time-discrete-state-space process. Cash is divided into unit increments, but there is no restriction on how the unit is defined. The only restriction made is the assumption that all disbursements and all receipts are defined by the same unit. Thus, in the time from one transaction to the next (within the day) cash has either increased by

Table 1A.   Comparison of Application Results.[a] Case 1: No-Drift Case

Miller-Orr Model	
Miller-Orr model	
Holding cost	0.001
Transfer cost	10
Variance of daily change in cash balance	40,754,223
Optimal values	
Lower bound	0
Return point (z)	10,700
Upper bound (h)	32,100
Markov model	
Holding cost	0.001
Transfer cost	10
Ratio of receipts/disbursements	1
optimal values	
Lower bound (R)	0
Lower return point (M)	3600
Upper return point (M')	37,000
Upper bound ($S+1$)	75,700

	Miller-Orr	*Markov*
Number of transfers	8	11
Transfer cost	80	110
Total cash balances	2,757,567	1,531,718
Holding cost	2,757.57	1,531.72
Total cost	2,837	1,641

Reduction using Markov model: 42.16%

Notes: [a]Each model, with parameters as calculated above, was employed to manage the cash balances over a 43-day, 2-month period. Below are the individual cost components and the overall cost for both models.

one unit or decreased by one unit. This argument is similar in the time period that cash would either increase by m dollars or decrease by m dollars. The principle is the same except we have defined m dollars to be equal to a more general definition of one unit. In the application highlighted in this paper, the unit is defined as one Canadian dollar.

A final consideration of this application is that there are only two accounts: cash and an interest-earning portfolio. This is, in fact, quite realistic. The interest-bearing account in reality consists of all the short-term investments of the firm, which is not in a liquid cash position. This can take the form of money invested in commercial paper, Treasury bills, and bankers' acceptances (or similar-short-term investments). The actual rate of interest accrued in this account is the weighted average of the rate of return from all the investments in the portfolio. The specific

Table 1B.   Comparison of Application Results.[a]

Miller-Orr model	
Holding cost	0.1
Transfer cost	100
Variance of daily change in cash balance	40,754,223
Optimal values	
Lower bound	0
Return point (z)	4,960
Upper bound (h)	14,900
Markov model	
Holding cost	0.1
Transfer cost	100
Ratio of receipts/disbursements	1
optimal values	
Lower bound (R)	0
Lower return point (M)	650
Upper return point (M')	3700
Upper bound $(S+1)$	4,030

	Miller-Orr	*Markov*
Number of transfers	35	42
Transfer cost	3,500	4,200
Total cash balances	246,361	114,195
Holding cost	24,636.10	11,419.50
Total cost	28,136	15,619

Reduction using Markov model: 44.49%

Notes: [a]Each model, with parameters as calculated above, was employed to manage the cash balances over a 43-day, 2-month period. Below are the individual cost components and the overall cost for both models.

ingredients of the portfolio are not important in this calculation—all that must be known is the interest rate earned therein.

The Results

Basically information relating to the cost parameters C_1, C_2, and C_3 is needed. For presentation purposes, two different cost structures are utilized. As can be seen from Table 1, both models were compared and evaluated under the *same two* completely different cost scenarios. The Markov model performs better than the Miller-Orr model in both cases. In fact, the Markov model performs substantially better. In both cases the cost savings is greater than 40 percent.

In the first case, transfer costs are very small compared to opportunity costs per day (10/0.001 = 10,000). This is often the case with contemporary cash management situations. As a result, few transfers and cash balances tend to become large. Even though the Markov model has more transfers, it has substantially reduced cash holdings (compared to Miller-Orr). Cost reduction is approximately 42 percent.

In the second case, transfer costs are more significant, but are still small in comparison to holding costs per day (100/0.1 = 1000). Here there are many more transfers (again the Markov model produces more transactions). However, the Markov model once again produces a much lower overall cost, with a reduction of about 44.5 percent compared to the Miller-Orr result.

Apart from the cost savings benefit, the primary structural advantage of this model over other cash management models in the literature is that this model allows for a completely random cash flow. With the continuous-time Markov process, there is no restriction on the timing of the cash disbursements or cash receipts: they can take place any time during the day (which is possible with an on-line cash management computer system).

Another advantage of the model pertains to the transfer cost coefficients. The actual values are *not* assumed to be equal, which is a limitation in some models, and this allows the model to be applicable to many categories of firms in a wide variety of environments. Both C_1 and C_2 can also be further segmented into a fixed and variable component. This will allow for a partially fixed transfer cost as well as possible variable component driven by the actual size of the amount of cash transferred.

CONCLUSION

In this paper, a new and completely stochastic model for cash management was developed. Its application was discussed and its advantages were elaborated upon.

This model does have its limitations. The assumptions of the probability distributions have only been tested against one firm. This does not ensure universal application. This assumption should be tested more thoroughly.

A second shortcoming is that the state space is discrete and not continuous. This requires the executive of the firm to set a unit level depending on the firm. Ideally, one would like to consider the cash flow as being continuous in nature and then the definition of a unit would not be required. It would then permit any volume of cash to be received at any time.

Finally, an assumption inherent in this model is a common assumption occurring in most models: there are only two accounts available for short-term funds (as noted above). This assumption further requires a pooling of the company's cash in a cash account prior to performing the management function of the cash.

However, with modern advanced capabilities in place in banking systems across the world, this pooling requisite should be quite easily accomplished.

APPENDIX 1:   CALCULATION OF
THE BALANCE EQUATIONS

$$- (\mu + \delta)\, \pi_1 + \mu\pi_2 = 0 \tag{A1}$$

$$\delta\pi_{i-2} - (\mu + \delta)\, \pi_i + \mu\pi_{i+1} = 0$$

$$= 0, \quad \text{for} \quad 2 \leq i \leq M - 1, \quad M + 1 \leq i \leq M' - 1, \quad M' + 1 \leq i \leq S - 1 \tag{A2}$$

$$\mu\pi_1 + \delta\pi_{M-1} - (\mu + \delta)\, \pi_M + \mu\pi_{M+1} = 0 \tag{A3}$$

$$\delta\pi_{M'-1} - (\mu + \delta)\, \pi_{M'} + \mu\pi_{M'+1} + \delta\pi_s = 0 \tag{A4}$$

$$\delta\pi_{s-1} - (\mu + \delta)\, \pi_s = 0 \tag{A5}$$

In order to derive the steady-state probabilities, we require the normalizing equation:

$$\sum_{i=1}^{S} \pi_i = 1 \tag{A6}$$

Solving equations (10) and (1A)-(4A) in terms of π_1, we get

$$\frac{1 - \tau^K}{1 - \tau}\pi_1, \quad \text{for } 1 \leq K \leq M \tag{A7}$$

$$\pi_k = \frac{\tau^{K-M}(1 - \tau^M)}{1 - \tau}\pi_1, \quad \text{for } M + 1 \leq K \leq M' \tag{A8}$$

$$\frac{\tau^{K-M}(1 - \tau^M)(1 - \tau^{S-K+1})}{(1 - \tau)(1 - \tau^{S-M'+1})}\pi_1, \quad \text{for } M' + 1 \leq K \leq S \tag{A9}$$

$$\pi_s = \frac{\tau^{S-M}(1 - \tau^M)}{1 - \tau^{S-M'+1}}\pi_1, \quad \text{for } \tau = \delta/\mu < > 1. \text{ Also} \tag{A10}$$

$$K\pi_1, \quad \text{for } 1 \leq K \leq M \tag{A11}$$

$$\pi_K = M\pi_1, \quad \text{for } M + 1 \leq K \leq M' \tag{A12}$$

$$\frac{M(S - K + 1)}{S - M' + 1}\pi_1, \quad \text{for } M' + 1 \leq K \leq S \tag{A13}$$

$$\pi_s = \frac{M}{S - M' + 1} \cdot \pi_1, \quad \text{for } \tau = \delta/\mu = 1 \tag{A14}$$

Now by equation (6A) we have

$$\sum_{i=1}^{S} \pi_i = \sum_{i=1}^{M} \pi_i + \sum_{i=M+1}^{M'} \pi_i + \sum_{i=M'+1}^{S} \pi_i = 1 \tag{A15}$$

Substituting for π_i from Equations (7A)-(10A) into (A15) and solving for π_1 yields

$$\tag{A16}$$

$$\pi_1 = \frac{(1-\tau)^2 (1-\tau^{S-M'+1})}{(M-\tau^M)(1-\tau^{S-M'+1}) - (S-M'+1)\tau^{S-M+1}(1-\tau)(1-\tau)(1-\tau^M)}$$

and hence

$$\tag{A17}$$

$$\pi_s = \frac{(1-\tau)^2 (1-\tau^M)\tau^{S-M}}{(M-\tau^M)(1-\tau^{S-M'+1}) - (S-M'+1)(1-\tau)(1-\tau^M)}$$

Likewise, substituting for π_1 yields

$$\pi_1 = \frac{2}{M(S+M'+1)} \tag{A18}$$

and hence,

$$\pi_s = \frac{2}{(S-M'+1)(S+M'1)} \tag{A19}$$

for $\pi = 1$.

These values van then be substituted in the cost function [Equation (10) in order to obtain the optimal values of M, M', and S in either the symmetric or asymmetric case.

APPENDIX 2: PRESENTATION OF PARTIAL-DERIVATIVE EQUATIONS—THE ASYMMETRIC CASE

For M: $\dfrac{1-\tau^M}{1-\tau} - M(1-\tau)(\ln \tau)\tau^M C_3[(M-\tau^M)(\tau^{M'+1})$

$$(S-M'+1)\tau(1-\tau)] - [(C_1)\tau^{M'} - C_2) - C_3 M(1-\tau)(\tau M^{M'})]$$

$$X[\tau(\ln \tau)(\tau^M)] = 0 \tag{A20}$$

For M': $[C_1 (\ln\ \tau) (\tau^{-M'}) - C_3/1 - \tau/] [(M - \tau^M) (1 - \tau^{S-M'+1})$

$$(S - M' + 1) (\tau^{S-M+1}) (1 - \tau) (1 - \tau^M)]$$

$$X [(M - \tau^M)] (-\ln\ \tau) (\tau^{-M'}) + (1 - \tau)] = 0 \qquad \text{(A21)}$$

For S: $[(\ln\ \tau) S + 1] (-C_3) + C_{1\tau}^{-M'+21} + C_2 \tau - 1)$

$$X \{ [(1 - \tau) (\tau^{S+1}) \{ (S - M' + 1) (\ln\ \tau - 1) + 1 \}]$$

$$+ (\ln\ \text{t-1}) (M - \tau^M) (\ln\ \tau) \tau^{S-M'+1} \}$$

$$[(- C_1 \tau^{-M'+1} + C_2 \tau (\ln\ \tau) (\ln\ \tau)] = 0 \qquad \text{(A22)}$$

APPENDIX 3:   JUSTIFICATION OF THE USE OF THE COST FUNCTION

Before any further calculations, we investigate the form of this cost function. We proceed to calculate the second-order partial derivatives (which were continuous), which form the Hessian matrix. The Hessian matrix that results is a diagonal matrix and its represented by $\delta \cdot I_{3\text{x}3}$, where

$$\delta = \{ C\theta^2 \tau^M (S - M') + (\ln\ \tau) \tau^M \frac{(C_3 - B)}{\tau - 1}, C_3, C_3 \frac{(\tau^2 - 1)}{\tau} \}$$

$$\theta = \ln\ \tau$$

This Hessian matrix is diagonal w ith entries all positive. Thus it is a positive-definite matrix. Referring to a lemma proposed by Zangwill (1969), we see that this p roves convexity of the cost function.

Lemma: Let h have continuous second partial derivatives. Then h is concave (convex) if and only if the Hessian matrix is negative (positive) semidefinite.

In summary, by the convexity of the cost equation, we are justified in equating first-order partial derivatives to zero, solving and obtaining the global minimum point. [By its convexity, as well, we are also justified in using the two-boundary-two-return-point model of Neave (1970).]

APPENDIX 4:   TESTS FOR VALIDITY OF DISTRIBUTIONAL ASSUMPTIONS

The Cash Receipts

The first assumption of this model is that the cash receipts follow a Poisson distribution. This assumption was justified by performing a chi-square goodness-of-fit test on the data. Recall that all the deterministic factors were eliminated and the test was performed solely on the random portion. The Poisson distribution is a discrete distribution and so the data were placed into classes ranging from zero to 7.5 and over (the data are given in units of tens of thousands of dollars). The midpoint of the classes was used as the discrete value. The frequency of the data occurring within these classes was then noted. The determination of the estimate for the true parameter δ is basically just the value of the arithmetic mean of the sample data. This is the best estimate of the population mean and must be implemented so that the test can be executed.

Once the test was performed, one violation occurred in the expected frequency column (f_e). The theory states that each class should have an expected frequency off 5 or more when the sample size is small. Since there are only 9 classes and the sample size is only 43, some of the classes were grouped and the probabilities and the expected frequencies were recalculated.

The test statistic resulting from this chi-square test was 9.2438, and the table value (at $\alpha = .05$) is 9.49. The actual critical value (p-value) obtained through interpolation is estimated to be $p = 0.059$. Hence at the .05 level of significance, there is insufficient evidence to indicate that the true population distribution is some distribution other than the Poisson distribution.

The significance of this fact should not be undermined. Although the test was only performed on data from one company, this does indeed illustrate that the assumption of Poisson-distributed cash receipts is not unreasonable.

The Cash Disbursements

As was the case with the cash receipts, the assumption of the cash disbursements must also be tested. Once again, the deterministic element was removed from the cash outflow before proceeding. The exponential distribution differs from the Poisson distribution in that it is a continuous distribution and, as such, is better applied to a Kolmogorov-Smirnov-type test: the Lilliefors test for the exponential distribution (the data is in thousands of dollars). In this instance, this appears to be the most powerful test.

As can be seen, the test statistic, which is the largest absolute deviation, is 0.111538. The calculation of the estimate of the true parameter μ is merely the arithmetic mean of the daily cash and so the decision is not to reject the null hypothesis. The actual critical value (p-value) is estimate to be near 0.45.

Test for the Distribution of Cash Reciepts

H_o: The population distribution from which the cash receipts are drawn is Poisson

H_A: The population distribution of the cash receipts cannot be assumed to be Poisson

In this application:

$$\delta = 37{,}228, \quad \text{Observed } \chi^2 = 9.2438, \quad \text{degrees of freedom} = 4, \quad p\text{-value} = 0.59$$

Test for the Distribution of Cash Disbursements

H: The random sample follows the exponential distribution

H_a: The random sample does not follow the exponential distribution

The test statistic is the largest absolute deviation that equaled

$$|\,F^*(X) - S(X)\,| = 0.111538 \qquad p\text{-value} = 0.45$$

In this application:

$$\delta = 37{,}228, \quad \mu = 33{,}566, \qquad \tau = \delta/\mu = 1.1091 = 1.00$$

To reiterate what was stated in Appendix 3, this test demonstrates that the assumption that the cash disbursements are exponentially distributed is not unfounded. This is not to proclaim that one firm is representative of the entire population of business firms. However, it does clearly illustrate that the assumptions are reasonable ones. Many researchers in the past have attempted to verify assumptions of the cash flow without the same degree of success (Emery, 1981). Therefore, the usage of Poisson arrival and exponential disbursements is not only mathematically tractable but also not unrealistic.

REFERENCES

Akerloff, G.A. (1929). Irving Fisher on his head: The consequences of constant thresholds—Target monitoring of money holdings. *Quarterly Journal of Economics* (May).

Anvari, M (1981). An application of inventory theoretical models to cash collection. *Decision Sciences*.

Anvari, M (1983). Cash concentration systems in Canada: An example of national banking. *Journal of Cash Management* (June/July).

Archer, S.H. (1966). A model for the determination of firm cash balances. *Journal of Financial and Quantitative Analysis* (March).

Baumol, W (1952). The transaction demand for cash: An inventory theoretic approach. *Quarterly Journal of Economics* (November).

Beehler, P.J. (1983). *Contemporary cash management.* New York: 1093.

Conover, W.J. (1980). *Practical nonparametric statistics.* New York: J. Wiley.

Consantinides, G.M. (1976). Stochastic cash management with fixed and proportional costs. *Management Science*, 22(August).

Emery, G.W. (1981). Some empirical evidence on the properties of daily cash flow. *Financial Management* (Spring).

Eppen, G.D., & Fama E.G. (1969). Cash balance and simple dynamic portfolio problems with Economic Review, 10.

Gaver, D.P., & Thompson G.L. *Programming and probability models in operations research.* (1968). Brooks/Cole.

Girgis, N.M. (1968). Optimal cash balance levels. *Management Science* (November).

Homonoff, R., & Mullins D.W. (1975). *Cash management.* Washington, DC: Heath.

Karlin, S., & Taylor, H.M. (1975). *A first course in stochastic processes.* New York: *Academic Press.*

Leonard, K.J. & Khalil, Z.S. (1984). A Markov process model for cash management. *Mathematical modelling in science and technology.* New York: Pergamon.

Leonard, K.J. (1979). A short term cash management model. Unpublished M.B.A. thesis, Concordia University, Montreal.

Leonard, K.J. (1985). Demand for cash: A cash management problem. Unpublished Ph.D. research paper, Concordia University, Montreal.

Milbourne, R.D., Buckholtz, R.D., & Wasan, M.T. (1982). Cash balances as a random walk. Second Canadian Conference on Applied Statistics, Concordia University.

Milbourne, R.D. (1983) Cash management with fixed and variable transfer costs. Discussion Paper #434, 1983.

Miller, M.H., & Orr, D. (1966). A model of the demand for money by firms. *Quarterly Journal of Economics, 80.*

Neave, E.H. (1970). The stochastic cash balance problem with fixed costs for increases and decreases. *Management Science.* (March).

Sethi, S.P., & Thompson, G.L. (1970). Application of mathematical control theory to finance: Modelling simple dynamic cash balance problems. *Journal of Financial and Quantitative Analysis, 5.*

Stone, B.K., & Miller, T.W. (1981). Daily cash forecasting: A strategic framework. *Journal of Cash Management.* (October).

Tobin, J. (1956). The interest elasticity of transaction demand for money. *Review of Economics and Statistics.* (August).

Zangwill, W.I. (1969). *Nonlinear programming: A unified approach.* New York: Prentice-Hall.

AGENCY COSTS, ASYMMETRIC INFORMATION, AND ALTERNATIVE CAPITAL STRUCTURE:

THEORY AND EVIDENCE

Gili Yen, Eva C. Yen, and Cheng-few Lee

ABSTRACT

Ever since the publication of Modigliani and Miller's path-breaking paper, what determines capital structure has attracted scholars' wide attention. This study will attack the issue from the perspective of asymmetric information. We show that a decrease in informational asymmetry between owner-managers and investors will reduce the fraction of inside equity, the nonpecuniary benefits, and the debt-equity ratio.

Advances in Financial Planning and Forecasting,
Volume 5, pages 303-317.
Copyright © 1994 by JAI Press Inc.
All rights of reproduction in any form reserved.
ISBN:1-55938-421-2

INTRODUCTION

Based on the mechanism of arbitrage, Modigliani and Miller (1958) have shown that the capital structure under a restrictive set of assumptions has no bearing on the market value of the firm. In other words, there exists no optimal capital structure. Ever since the publication of their path-breaking paper, what determines capital structure has attracted scholars' wide attention. Nonetheless, a consensus has still to be reached.

Scholars in favor of the hypothesis of value maximization tend to argue that a trade-off exists between the tax benefits and financial distress (including bankruptcy) costs of debt. This trade-off produces an optimal debt-equity ratio. Among others, Myers (1984) and Bradley, Jarrell, and Kim (1984) are the most eminent examples. In contrast, built on the hypothesis of managerial utility maximization, Jensen and Meckling (1976) developed a theory of the ownership structure of the firm. In our opinion, Jensen and Meckling (1978) have correctly put emphasis on the notion of agency costs. Unfortunately, the notion has exerted a much smaller influence in their joint paper than it deserves since Jensen and Meckling argued in the same paper that an outside owner, as a partial holder of residual claims, is only willing to pay his fractional ownership times the expected value he had in mind given the induced wealth reduction brought about by the opportunistic behavior of the owner-manager. In other words, on their assumption that the owner-manager's opportunistic behavior is perfectly perceived by the investors, the agency costs will be fully borne by the agents themselves. Besides, it is extremely difficult to measure empirically the magnitude of agency costs, let alone estimate their influences.

The research objective of the present study is twofold: On the theoretical front, to widen the applicability of Jensen and Meckling's model, the assumption that outside shareholders or, for that matter, potential investors are able to make unbiased estimates of wealth changes associated with agents' opportunistic behavior is relaxed. On the empirical front, the testable implications drawn from the proposed model, especially the impact of information asymmetry on the capital structure, will be examined. Special emphasis is put on the variable *information asymmetry* simply because it is a variable so often mentioned yet so scarcely tested.

At this point, we have briefly described the issue involved and the research objective of the present study. The remaining portion of the paper is organized in the following way. The first section develops an expanded theoretical model that shows that the degree of information asymmetry, given the presence of agency costs, between the owner-manager and the investor is crucial as far as the capital structure is concerned. With the aid of simulation, testable implications are drawn from the proposed model in the subsequent section. The next section examines empirically the impact of degree of information asymmetry on alternative capital structures. The last section presents conclusions.

MODEL DEVELOPMENT AND ITS TESTABLE IMPLICATIONS

In this section we develop a single-period model that captures the essence of the tax advantage and bankruptcy costs trade-off models of Bradley, Jarrell, and Kim (BJK; 1984), the agency costs of equity arguments of Jensen and Meckling (JM; 1976), and the asymmetric information existing between the owner-manager and outsiders.[1] The following assumptions are used to derive the new model:

1. There exists a single manager (the peak coordinator) with an ownership interest in the firm.

2. The entrepreneur-manager's money wages are held constant throughout the period analyzed.

3. All outside equity shares are nonvoting.

4. No complex financial claims such as convertible bonds or preferred stocks or warrants can be issued.

5. The size of the firm is fixed.

6. No monitoring or bonding activities are possible.

7. The firm faces a constant statutory marginal tax rate.

Notations used to derive the new model are as follows:

$\tilde{X}$:   the firm's end-of-period value before taxes and debt payments

N: market value of the stream of the manager's expenditures on nonpecuniary benefits, that is, managerial perquisites consumption

$\hat{Y}$:   the total end-of-period promised payment to bondholders

t_c: the constant statutory marginal tax rate faced by the firm

r_0:   1 plus the rate of return on default-free, tax-exempt bonds

S_0:   the beginning-of-period value of the firm's outside stocks

S_i: the beginning-of-period value of the firm's inside stocks

B: the beginning-of-period value of the firm's bonds

δ: the ratio of nonpecuniary benefits consumed by the owner-manager as perceived by outsiders

k: costs of financial distress per dollar of the end-of-period value of the firm

α: the fraction of inside equity

$\tilde{Y}_{s0}$:   the gross end-of-period returns to outside stockholders

$\tilde{Y}_{si}$:   the gross end-of-period returns to inside stockholders

$\tilde{Y}_b$:   the gross end-of-period returns to bondholders

V: the beginning-of-period market value of the firm

Under the above assumptions and definitions of the model, the uncertain end-of-period pretax returns to the firm's owner-manager, outsiders, and bondholders can be written as follows:

$$\tilde{Y}_{si} = \begin{cases} \alpha\,(\tilde{x} - N - \hat{Y})\,(1 - t_c), & \tilde{x} \geq N + \hat{Y} \\ 0, & \tilde{x} < N + \hat{Y} \end{cases} \tag{1}$$

$$\tilde{Y}_{s0} = \begin{cases} (1 - \alpha)\,(\tilde{x} - \delta N - \hat{Y})\,(1 - t_c), & \tilde{x} \geq \delta N + \hat{Y},\, 0 \leq \delta \leq 1 \\ 0, & \tilde{x} < \delta N + \hat{Y} \end{cases} \tag{2}$$

$$\tilde{Y}_{b} = \begin{cases} \hat{Y}, & \tilde{x} \geq N + \hat{Y} \\ (\tilde{x} - N)\,(1 - k,) & 0 \leq \tilde{x} < N + \hat{Y} \\ 0, & \tilde{x} < 0 \end{cases} \tag{3}$$

The owner-manager utility function for wealth and perquisites is represented as follows:

$$\underset{\alpha,\, N,\, \hat{Y}\,|\,\delta,\, k}{\text{Max}} U\,[\alpha V, N]$$

subject to

$$V = \frac{E(\tilde{Y}_{si}) + E(\tilde{Y}_{s0}) + E(\tilde{Y}_{b})}{r_0} = S_i + S_0 + B \tag{4}$$

where

$$E(\tilde{Y}_{si}) = \int_{N + \hat{Y}}^{\infty} \alpha\,(\tilde{x} - N - \hat{Y})\,(1 - t_c)f(\tilde{x})\ d\tilde{x} \tag{5}$$

$$E(\tilde{Y}_{s0}) = \int_{\delta N + \hat{Y}}^{\infty} (1 - \alpha)\,(\tilde{x} - \delta N - \hat{Y})\,(1 - t_c)f(\tilde{x})\ d\tilde{x} \tag{6}$$

$$E(\tilde{Y}_{b}) = \int_{0}^{N + \hat{Y}} (\tilde{x} - N)\,(1 - k)f(\tilde{x})\ d\tilde{x} + \int_{N + \hat{Y}}^{\infty} \hat{Y}f(\tilde{x})\ d\tilde{x} \tag{7}$$

$$V = \frac{1}{r_0}\left[\int_{N + \hat{Y}}^{\infty} \alpha\,(\tilde{x} - N - \hat{Y})\,(1 - t_c)f(\tilde{x})\ d\tilde{x} \right.$$

$$\left. + \int_{\delta N + \hat{Y}}^{\infty} (1 - \alpha)\,(\tilde{x} - \delta N - \hat{Y})\,(1 - t_c)f(\tilde{x})\ d\tilde{x} \right.$$

$$+ \int_{0}^{N+Y} (\tilde{x} - N)(1-k)f(\tilde{x})\ d\tilde{x}$$

$$\left. + \int_{N+\hat{Y}}^{\infty} \hat{Y}f(\tilde{x})\ d\tilde{x} \right) \tag{8}$$

Equation (8) shows that the value of the firm is equal to the present value of the sum of three expected values. The owner-manager's decision involves setting optimal values for the following three variables: α, the fraction of inside equity; N, the level of nonpecuniary benefits consumed by the owner-manager; and $\hat{Y}$, the end-of-period payment promised to bondholders. Differentiating V with respect to α, N, and Y yields the first-order condition of Equations (9), (10), and (11), where U_α, $U_{\hat{Y}}$, and U_N are the partial derivatives $\frac{\partial U}{\partial \alpha}$ $\partial U / \partial \hat{Y}$, and $\partial U / \partial N$, respectively:

$$U_\alpha - \lambda V_\alpha = 0 \tag{9}$$

$$U_{\hat{Y}} - \lambda V_{\hat{Y}} = 0 \tag{10}$$

$$U_N - \lambda V_N = 0 \tag{11}$$

where

$$V_\alpha = \frac{(1-t_c)}{r_0} \left(\left. G(\tilde{x}) \right|_{N+\hat{Y}}^{\infty} - \left. NF(\tilde{x}) \right|_{N+\hat{Y}}^{\infty} - \left. \hat{Y}F(\tilde{x}) \right|_{N+\hat{Y}}^{\infty} \right.$$

$$\left. - \left. G(\tilde{x}) \right|_{\delta N+\hat{Y}}^{\infty} + \left. \delta NF(\tilde{x}) \right|_{\delta N+\hat{Y}}^{\infty} + \left. \hat{Y}F(\tilde{x}) \right|_{\delta N+\hat{Y}}^{\infty} \right)$$

$$\partial G(\tilde{x}) / \partial \tilde{x} = \tilde{x}f(\tilde{x})$$

$$V_{\hat{Y}} = \frac{(1-t_c)}{r_o} [\alpha F(N+\hat{Y}) + (1+\alpha)F(\delta N+\hat{Y}) - 1]$$

$$- k\hat{Y}f(N+\hat{Y}) - F(N+\hat{Y}) + 1$$

$$V_N = \frac{-(1-\alpha)(1-t_c)}{r_0} \delta[1 - F(\delta N+\hat{Y})] - \frac{\alpha(1-t_c)}{r_0}[1 - F(N+\hat{Y})]$$

$$- k\hat{Y}f(N+\hat{Y}) - (1-k)f(N+\hat{Y})$$

In Equations (12), (13), and (14), $F(\cdot)$ is the cumulative probability density function of x. It might be of interest at this juncture to compare our model with the Modigliani-Miller model or the Bradley-Jarrell-Kim trade-off model. In Modigliani and Miller's model, $V_{\hat{Y}}$ is set at zero. Even so, a firm's leverage decision is still relevant to its optimal capital structure through Equations (12) and (14). As for Bradley-Jarrell-Kim, the trade-off involved exists not only between the expected tax advantage of debt and expected leverage-related costs, but also between other agency costs.

Let us now move on to examine the comparative statics of the proposed model. This can be done by differentiating the optimality conditions (9)-(11) with respect to each of the relevant exogenous variables. Specifically, differentiating Equations (9)-(11) with respect to δ and k yields the following cross-partial derivatives:

$$\begin{bmatrix} U_{\alpha\alpha}-\lambda V_{\alpha\alpha} & U_{\alpha\hat{Y}}-\lambda V_{\alpha\hat{Y}} & U_{\alpha N}-\lambda V_{\alpha N} & -V_{\alpha} \\ U_{\hat{Y}\alpha}-\lambda V_{\hat{Y}\alpha} & U_{\hat{Y}\hat{Y}}-\lambda V_{\hat{Y}\hat{Y}} & U_{\hat{Y}N}-\lambda V_{\hat{Y}N} & -V_{\hat{Y}} \\ U_{N\alpha}-\lambda V_{N\alpha} & U_{N\hat{Y}}-\lambda V_{N\hat{Y}} & U_{NN}-\lambda V_{NN} & -V_{N} \\ -V_{\alpha} & -V_{\hat{Y}} & -V_{N} & 0 \end{bmatrix} \begin{bmatrix} \partial\alpha/\partial\delta \\ \partial\hat{Y}/\partial\delta \\ \partial N/\partial\delta \\ \partial\lambda/\partial\delta \end{bmatrix} = \begin{bmatrix} \lambda V_{\alpha\delta} \\ \lambda V_{\hat{Y}\delta} \\ \lambda V_{N\delta} \\ V_{\delta} \end{bmatrix}$$

(15)

$$\begin{bmatrix} U_{\alpha\alpha}-\lambda V_{\alpha\alpha} & U_{\alpha\hat{Y}}-\lambda V_{\alpha\hat{Y}} & U_{\alpha N}-\lambda V_{\alpha N} & -V_{\alpha} \\ U_{\hat{Y}\alpha}-\lambda V_{\hat{Y}\alpha} & U_{\hat{Y}\hat{Y}}-\lambda V_{\hat{Y}\hat{Y}} & U_{\hat{Y}N}-\lambda V_{\hat{Y}N} & -V_{\hat{Y}} \\ U_{N\alpha}-\lambda V_{N\alpha} & U_{N\hat{Y}}-\lambda V_{N\hat{Y}} & U_{NN}-\lambda V_{NN} & -V_{N} \\ -V_{\alpha} & -V_{\hat{Y}} & -V_{N} & 0 \end{bmatrix} \begin{bmatrix} \partial\alpha/\partial k \\ \partial\hat{Y}/\partial k \\ \partial N/\partial k \\ \partial\lambda/\partial k \end{bmatrix} = \begin{bmatrix} \lambda V_{\alpha k} \\ \lambda V_{\hat{Y}k} \\ \lambda V_{Nk} \\ V_{k} \end{bmatrix}$$

(16)

where

$$\begin{bmatrix} U_{\alpha\alpha}-\lambda V_{\alpha\alpha} & U_{\alpha\hat{Y}}-\lambda V_{\alpha\hat{Y}} & U_{\alpha N}-\lambda V_{\alpha N} & -V_{\alpha} \\ U_{\hat{Y}\alpha}-\lambda V_{\hat{Y}\alpha} & U_{\hat{Y}\hat{Y}}-\lambda V_{\hat{Y}\hat{Y}} & U_{\hat{Y}N}-\lambda V_{\hat{Y}N} & -V_{\hat{Y}} \\ U_{N\alpha}-\lambda V_{N\alpha} & U_{N\hat{Y}}-\lambda V_{N\hat{Y}} & U_{NN}-\lambda V_{NN} & -V_{N} \\ -V_{\alpha} & -V_{\hat{Y}} & -V_{N} & 0 \end{bmatrix} > 0$$

(17)

$$V_{\alpha\alpha} = 0$$

(18)

$$V_{\alpha\hat{Y}} = \frac{(1-t_c)}{r_0} [F(N+\hat{Y})-F(\delta N+\hat{Y})]$$

(19)

$$V_{\alpha N} = \frac{(1-t_c)}{r_0} [F(N+\hat{Y})-\delta F(\delta N+\hat{Y})]$$

(20)

$$V_{N\alpha} = \frac{(1-t_c)}{r_0} \{\delta[1-F(\delta N+Y)]-[1-F(N+\hat{Y})]\}$$

(21)

$$V_{N\hat{Y}} = f(N + \hat{Y})\left[\frac{\alpha(1 - t_c)}{r_0} - 1\right] + \frac{\delta(1 - \alpha)(1 - t_c)}{r_0} f(\delta N + \hat{Y}) - k\hat{Y}f'(N + \hat{Y}) \tag{22}$$

$$V_{NN} = f(N + \hat{Y})\left[\frac{\alpha(1 - t_c)}{r_0} - (1 - k)\right]$$

$$+ \frac{(1 - \alpha)(1 - t_c)}{r_0}\delta^2 f(\delta N + \hat{Y}) - k\hat{Y}f(N + \hat{Y}) \tag{23}$$

$$V_{\hat{Y}\alpha} = \frac{(1 - t_c)}{r_0}[F(N + \hat{Y}) - F(\delta N + \hat{Y})] \tag{24}$$

$$V_{\hat{Y}\hat{Y}} = f(N + \hat{Y})\left[\frac{\alpha(1 - t_c)}{r_0} - k - 1\right]$$

$$+ \frac{(1 - \alpha)(1 - t_c)}{r_0}f(\delta N + \hat{Y}) - k\hat{Y}f'(N + \hat{Y}) \tag{25}$$

$$V_{\hat{Y}N} = f(N + \hat{Y})\left[\frac{(1 - t_c)}{r_0} - 1\right]$$

$$+ \frac{\delta(1 - \alpha)(1 - t_c)}{r_0}f(\delta N + \hat{Y}) - k\hat{Y}f'(N + \hat{Y}) \tag{26}$$

$$V_{\alpha\delta} = \frac{(1 - t_c)}{r_0}[1 - F(\delta N + \hat{Y})] \tag{27}$$

$$V_{\hat{Y}\delta} = \frac{(1 - t_c)(1 - \alpha)}{r_0}f(\delta N + \hat{Y})N \tag{28}$$

$$V_{N\delta} = \frac{-(1 - \alpha)(1 - t_c)}{r_0}\{[1 - F(\delta N + \hat{Y})] - \delta f(\delta N + \hat{Y})N\} \tag{29}$$

$$V_{\alpha k} = 0 \tag{30}$$

$$V_{\hat{Y}k} = -\hat{Y}f(N + \hat{Y}) \tag{31}$$

$$V_{Nk} = -\hat{Y}f(N + \hat{Y}) + F(N + \hat{Y}) \tag{32}$$

TESTABLE IMPLICATIONS

After formally setting up the model, the testable implications can be then drawn with the aid of simulation. To make simulations manageable, however, we assume that the representative owner-manager's utility function belongs to the Cobb-Douglas type. Moreover, the probability density of the firm's end-of-period value before taxes and debt payments is assumed to be uniformly distributed between 0 and B. Under these two conditions, the first-order conditions can be rewritten as follows:

$$\frac{t_c B - (k + t_c)\hat{Y} - [1 - (1 - t_c)(\alpha + \delta - \alpha\delta)]N}{B} = 0 \tag{33}$$

$$\frac{\beta_1(1 - t_c)(\alpha + \delta - \alpha\delta)B - \beta_1\left[1 - k - (1 - t_c)(\alpha + \delta^2 - \alpha\delta^2)\right]N - \beta_1[1 - t_c(\alpha + \delta - \alpha\delta)]\hat{Y}}{B}$$

$$\frac{+ \alpha\beta_2(1 - t_c)(1 - \delta)[2B - 2\hat{Y} - (1 + \delta)N]}{2B} = 0 \tag{34}$$

$$\frac{1}{2B}\left\{(-2k + 1 - t_c)\hat{Y}^2 + \left[-2 + 2k + (1 - t_c)(\alpha + \delta^2 - \alpha\delta^2)\right]N^2\right.$$

$$+ Z[(1 - t_c)(\alpha + \delta - \alpha\delta) - 1]\hat{Y}N$$

$$\left. + 2Bt_c\hat{Y} - 2B(1 - t_c)(\alpha + \delta - \alpha\delta)N + (1 - t_c)B^2\right\} = r^0\bar{V} \tag{35}$$

We assume the numerical values for β_1, β_2, B, and t_c are 0.7, 0.3, 50,000, 0.3, and 0.4, respectively. We further assume that the set of α comes as follows: $S_a = \{0.0000001, 0.1, 0.2, 0.3, 0.4, 0.5, 0.6, 0.7, 0.8, 0.9, 1.0\}$. The results are reported in Table 1.

In summary, the simulation of the model provides the following testable implications: When the ratio of nonpecuniary benefits consumed by the owner-manager as perceived by outsiders increases, the following three items all decrease: (1) the fraction of inside equity, (2) promised payment to bondholders, and (3) managerial perquisites consumption. Based on the testable implications stated above, our major proposition concerning corporate financing decision can be established as follows: As the degree of information asymmetry existing between

Table 1.   Owner-Manager's Optimal Decisions under
Different Degrees of Information Asymmetry

Endogenous variables	Ownership structure	Capital structure	Managerial utility
Degree of information asymmetry	α	Y	N
$\delta = 0.8$	0.4	15,043	7,351
$\delta = 0.6$	0.7	0.7	17,136

Table 2.　Comparison of Debt to Equity Ratio between Companies
Listed on Stock Exchange and Companies Unlisted on Stock Exchange

Industry	1984		1985		1986	
	Listed	Unlisted	Listed	Unlisted	Listed	Unlisted
Canned food	1528.77	166.93	145.10	138.42	110.72	147.65
Frozen food	4376.96	221.24	–	–	–	–
Flour mill	126.33	268.66	128.20	219.96	97.32	666.06
Vegetable oil & feed	748.89	294.70	164.04	258.88	143.79	307.70
Seasoning	101.64	354.90	128.60	413.39	88.13	249.73
Other foods	146.01	292.35	164.48	347.74	128.44	342.86
Cotton textile	235.03	283.54	236.76	230.82	221.83	231.94
Wool textile	133.64	397.62	154.42	342.22	314.11	417.27
Man -made fibers	220.97	221.93	179.76	191.77	157.57	209.49
Man-made fiber textiles	248.16	187.76	192.83	208.90	225.97	188.19
Apparel	228.55	283.61	165.36	232.63	170.57	246.38
Dyeing & finishing	239.26	209.35	187.62	176.59	124.35	418.81
Paper & pulp	125.93	215.92	117.89	169.44	127.16	184.08
Plastics	191.01	217.16	98.20	144.52	82.28	156.21
Plastics processing	201.72	340.91	155.33	327.05	107.75	224.96
Rubber	156.16	172.55	156.25	121.37	141.01	123.56
Sporting goods	–	–	–	–	–	–
Pharmaceuticals & pesticides	87.31	121.61	96.15	143.76	114.82	149.47
Chemicals	148.26	191.70	146.44	170.88	139.41	186.00
Coatings, paints, & resins	138.44	210.78	–	–	–	–
Detergent	106.82	86.53	102.46	123.00	63.85	89.99
Electrical & electronics	173.59	251.99	150.87	220.86	126.53	273.67
Wire & cable	186.25	289.71	150.07	201.12	109.25	176.29
Machinery	123.28	436.46	318.31	312.81	349.06	313.47
Iron & steel	334.82	577.99	328.42	388.92	–	–
Steel products	–	–	–	–	51.04	404.33
Other metal products	160.07	250.89	158.04	263.41	130.95	385.46
Motor vehicles & equipment	154.11	260.70	144.91	262.60	138.83	313.11
Cement	102.10	92.14	93.61	104.25	87.34	94.07
Plywood, wooden, bamboo products	468.09	269.76	355.93	291.83	1476.49	233.41
Tannery & leather goods	–	–	–	–	–	–
Miscellaneous	973.24	205.90	137.18	195.12	125.84	287.17

Notes:　*a*—indicates that there exist no listed companies in this industry.

the owner-manager and the outside shareholder (or potential investor) decreases,
in other words, as the fraction of information perceived by the latter group
increases, the debt-equity ratio becomes lower than it would otherwise be.

EMPIRICAL RESULTS

The data representing the top 500 private enterprises during the period from 1984 to 1986 are used to examine the relation between δ and capital structure. They are compiled from *The Largest Industrial Corporations in the Republic of China*. Because an explicit managerial statement (including statement of earnings, statement of financial position, statement of changes in financial position, and other related information), signatures by certified accountants, and a formal auditing report are required for listed companies, we would expect companies listed on the stock exchange to have a higher value of δ when compared with their unlisted counterparts. Based on simulation, the reduction in $\hat{Y}$ as a result of a higher δ would lead us to expect that listed companies will carry a lower debt-equity ratio.

After classifying the sample firms into two groups, namely, companies listed on the stock exchange market versus companies not listed on the stock exchange market, we calculate debt-equity ratios associated with listed versus unlisted companies in 32 industries. Table 2 shows the results. For the year 1984, there are 20 cases out of 29 in which debt-equity ratios for the listed group are lower than those for unlisted group. For 1985, there were 21 cases out of 27 in which listed companies have lower debt-equity ratios. Similarly, for 1986, there are 23 cases out of 27 in which listed companies have lower debt-equity ratios. Based on these results, the null hypothesis that no difference exists between the average debt-equity ratios of these two groups can be rejected at a .01 level of significance.

A direct comparison between the listed companies versus the unlisted companies reveals that the listed companies in relative terms carry lower debt-equity ratios as predicted by our model. In other words, our proposition that —although the agency costs are present for both listed and unlisted firms—the opportunistic behavior of the owner-manager is more constrained because the degree of information asymmetry is less severe in the case of listed companies is borne out by the intergroup comparison.

To provide some further evidence, in what follows we set up a regression model that enables us to examine the impact of the degree of asymmetric information on financing decisions in the presence of other explanatory variables. By consulting previous studies such as Kim and Sorenson (1986) and checking the availability of data, in addition to the pivotal crucial dummy variable characterizing "listing" or "nonlisting," included in the model are earnings before taxes (GROW), the variation in earnings before taxes (STDINC) operationally defined as the positive square root of the variation in earnings, and the balance sheet value of the assets (ASSETS).

The rationale for GROW is provided by Myers's hypothesis (1977) that firms with large growth opportunities will use less debt in optimality. An alternative explanation may result from the use of historical growth data to proxy future growth. GROW may also be related to the availability of internal funds. Tradi-

Table 3. Regression Results for the Debt-Equity Ratio

Independent variable: Industry	Const.	Assets	STDINC	GROW	DL	R^2	F	n
	3.33	.002**	−.14**	−.007	5.20**			
Canned food	(3.16)	(3.48)	(-3.55)	(−.31)	(2.40)	.16	3.45	77
	2.71	−.001	.08	.07	−2.57			
Flour mill	(1.70)	(−1.39)	(1.64)	(.88)	(−1.30)	.11	1.52	56
	3.56	−.0001	−.004	.02	−1.58**			
Seasoning	(9.42)	(−.31)	(−.31)	(.70)	(−2.58)	.42	5.57	36
	3.11	.0002	−.02**	.008	−1.24**			
Other foods	(9.52)	(1.51)	(−.2.66)	(.36)	(−2.40)	.11	3.51	114
	1.77	.002**	−.003	−.008	−1.98*			
Wool textile	(1.60)	(2.87)	(−.25)	(−.49)	(−1.78)	.21	3.46	56
	3.32	−.001**	.05**	.03	−2.03*			
Vegetable oil & feed	(5.27)	(−1.97)	(4.00)	(.50)	(−1.81)	.08	4.43	199
	2.29	.0001	−.002	.003	−.17			
Cotton textile	(14.67)	(.99)	(−1.20)	(.78)	(−.42)	.01	0.53	245
	1.57	.00001	.0007	−.04	−.71			
Man-made fibers	(2.72)	(.19)	(.37)	(−.68)	(−1.07)	.02	0.62	105
	−2.52	−.002	.04	−.009	5.71			
Man-made fiber textiles	(−.61)	(−.84)	(.86)	(−.10)	(.56)	.004	0.26	263
	2.91	.00003	.004	−.0008	−1.55*			
Apparel	(8.32)	(−.43)	(1.10)	(−.03)	(−1.78)	.02	0.96	194
	2.57	−.0001	.004	−.004	−.88			
Dyeing & finishing	(5.16)	(−1.12)	(1.17)	(−.56)	(−1.00)	.05	0.71	54
	2.11	.00002	−.003*	.02	−.40*			
Paper & pulp	(15.28)	(.30)	(1.82)	(1.63)	(−1.75)	.23	7.44	106
	2.10	.0001**	−.003**	−.008	−.64			
Plastics	(9.05	(2.51)	(−2.92)	(−1.39)	(−1.59)	.13	2.88	83
	2.76	.00009	−.003	−.12	−1.08			
Plastics processing	(11.41)	(1.03)	(−1.32)	(−1.36)	(−1.26)	.003	1.53	205

(continued)

Table 3. (continued)

Rubber	1.45 (9.13)	.0004** (4.17)	−.02** (−4.04)	−.02 (−1.37)	−.03 (−.12)	.28	5.90	67
Pharmaceuticals & pesticides	1.25 (6.90)	.0008** (3.01)	−.022** (−2.15)	.01 (.80)	−.27 (−1.28)	.42	5.41	35
Electrical & electronic, computer & peripheral, electric machinery	2.67 (7.31)	.00002 (.22)	−.004 (−.72)	−.18** (−18.63)	−.02 (−.02)	.48	87.98	381
Wire & cable	2.01 (9.15)	.0006** (3.48)	−.02** (−3.78)	−.02 (−1.02)	−.22 (−.45)	.27	5.29	62
Machinery	4.17 (6.44)	−.0003 (−1.19)	.004 (.42)	.002 (.06)	1.72 (.79)	.03	0.60	81
Iron & steel	2.98 (2.40)	−.0003 (−.21)	.08** (2.86)	-.05 (−1.57)	−18.44** (−3.69)	.17	4.45	94
Steel products	4.43 (5.19)	.0006 (.81)	−.02 (−1.14)	.01 (.36)	−5.16 (−.71)	.01	0.46	206
Other metal products	2.07 (3.69)	−.0002 (−.36)	.05 (1.56)	−.03 (−.70)	−3.79* (−1.78)	.05	1.21	105
Motor vehicle & equipment	2.75 (9.56)	.0004** (2.28)	−.008** (−2.89)	−.003 (−.12)	−2.16** (−1.97)	.08	2.78	129
Cement	.94 (7.10)	.0001** (3.28)	−.004** (−3.59)	−.004 (−.42)	.06 (.34)	.16	3.42	75
Plywood, wooden, bamboo, products	5.72 (2.91)	−.001 (−.54)	−.03 (−.65)	−.003 (−.02)	3.97 (.70)	.02	0.34	92
Tannery & leather goods	6.96 (3.15)	.002 (.42)	−.45 (−1.34)	−.23 (−.46)	−.000 (n.a)	.13	1.62	37
Miscellaneous	2.24 (4.11)	−.0005* (−1.86)	.03** (3.52)	.04 (.87)	−2.55 (−1.56)	.08	3.36	151

Notes: **Statistically significant at the 5% level.
*Statistically significant at the 10% level.

314

tional finance textbooks argue that firms with high degrees of business risk have less capacity to sustain high financial risk, and thus will use less debt. However, Myers arrives at the opposite conclusion. Firms with large business risk may have a lower agency cost of debt, and thus optimally borrow more. STDINC is a proxy for business risk in our model. Many earlier empirical studies allude to the argument that large diversified firms have more debt capacity than do small firms [See Ferri and Jones (1979), Flath and Knoeber (1980), Schneller (1980), Scott (1972), Scott and Martin (1975).] However, Myers presents an analysis of the interaction between diversification and optimal debt. He concludes that there should be no consistent relationship between them. We use ASSETS as a proxy for firm size.

The regression results are shown in Table 3 which reveals a number of issues for consideration. It is important to note that a huge variation in debt ratios is left unexplained. The conclusion, as argued by Kim and Sorensen (1986), is that debt decision is to a large extent determined nonsystematically by managers across firms. Nevertheless, several of the variable coefficients give insights to the determinants of the debt decision.

ASSETS is significant in ten industries. Among them, eight are significantly positive. STDINC is significant in twelve industries. Among them, nine are significantly negative. The results of the ASSETS variable being significantly positive tends to be in agreement with the traditional notion that large diversified firms have more debt capacity. STDINC, which measures operating risk, has significantly negative coefficients. This result also tends to confirm the traditional notion that firms with high business risk have lower debt capacity.

The dummy variable (DL) is significant in ten industries. Among them, nine are significantly negative as expected. The findings indicate that firms listed on the stock exchange have lower debt/equity ratios. The result by itself is interesting. Kim and Sorensen found that firms heavily owned by insiders tend to finance projects with greater amounts of debt. They provided three possible explanations of these findings. One interpretation addresses the issue of corporate control. Insider firms may have incentives to issue debt to finance growth. Second, firms with heavy insider ownership would issue debt to avoid the costs of external equity. A third interpretation is that insider firms have lower agency costs of debt. If we provide the fourth reason that firms with heavy insider ownership would have less asymmetric information, then our findings are consistent with the findings of Kim and Sorensen.

CONCLUDING REMARKS

In this paper, we develope a model of optimal capital structure in which agency costs and information asymmetry are explicitly taken into account. On the basis of comparative statics, simulation shows that a decrease in informational asymmetry reduces the debt-equity ratio.

We classify the sample firms into two groups, namely, firms listed on the stock exchange market versus firms not listed on the stock exchange market. We expect the former has less informational asymmetry when compared with the latter. The results show that listed firms have lower debt-equity ratios, as expected. An additional regression model is applied to control for the possible influences exerted by other explanatory variables. The results, although somewhat weaker, show again that listed firms have lower debt-equity ratios. Based on the reinforcing empirical results, we therefore conclude that the implications of the model are borne out by the empirical analysis.

APPENDIX

The structural relationships between the Jensen-Meckling (JM), Bradley-Jarrell-Kim (BJK), and Yen-Yen-Lee (YYL) model can be summarized in Table A1.

Table A1   Structural Relationships between BJK, JM, and YYL Models

JM	*BJK*	*YYL*
Max. managerial utility	Max. firm's value	Max. managerial utility
$N > 0$ (agency costs)	$N = 0$ (no agency costs)	$N > 0$
$\delta = 1$ (perfect information)	$\delta = 1$	$0 < \delta < 1$ (asymmetric information
$0 < \alpha' < 1$	$\alpha = 1$	$0 < \alpha < 1$
$(B + S_0 + S_i)$ fixed	max. $(B + S)$	$(B + S_0 + S_i)$ fixed

NOTE

1.   See Appendix for the explicit comparison between the BJK model and the JM model.

REFERENCES

Black, F., "Valuation of corporate claims," *The Journal of Finance*, July 1984, pp. 539-607.

Bradley, M., Jarrell, G.A., & Kim, E.H. (1984). On the existence of an optimal capital structure: Theory and evidence. *Journal of Finance* (July), 557-880.

Demsetz, H. & Lehn, K. "The structure of corporate ownership: causes and consequences," *Journal of Political Economy,* Dec. 1985, pp. 1155-1177.

Fama, E.F., "Agency problems and the theory of the firm," *Journal of Political Economy*, April 1980, pp. 288-307.

Fama, E.F. & M.C. Jensen, "Agency problems and residual claims," working paper series no. MERC 82-16, Graduate School of Management, University of Rochester, 1982.

———— , "Separation of ownership and control," working paper series no MERC 82-14, Graduate School of Management, University of Rochester, 1982.

Ferri, M.G. and M.H. Jones, "Determinants of financial structure: A new methodological approach," *Journal of Finance*, 34, June 1979, pp. 631-644.

Flath, D. and C.R. Knoeber, "Taxes, failure costs, and optimal industry capital structure: An empirical test," *Journal of Finance*, March 1980, pp. 99-117.

Furubotn, E.G. and S. Pejovich, "Property rights and economic theory: A survey of recent literature," *Journal of Economic Literature*, Dec. 1972, pp. 1137-1162.

Jensen, M.C. & Meckling, W.H. (1976). Theory of the firm: Managerial behavior, agency costs and ownership structure. *Journal of Financial Economics*, *3*, 305-360.

Jones, E. P., S. P. Mason, and E. Rosenfeld, "Contingent claims analysis of corporate capital structures: An empirical investigation," *The Journal of Finance*, July 1984, pp. 611-625.

Kim, W.S. & Sorensen, E.H. (1986). Evidence on the impact of the agency costs of debt on corporate debt policy. *Journal of Financial and Quantitative Analysis*, *21* (June), 131-144.

Kraus, A. and R.H. Litzenberger, "A state preference model of optimal capital structure," *Journal of Finance*, Sep. 1973, pp. 911-922.

Lee, C.F., C.C. Wu and D. Han and M. Hoque, "On the capital asset pricing model with dividend signaling," *Journal of Financial and Quantitative Analysis*, forthcoming, 1991.

Litzenberger, R., "Some observations on capital structure and the impact of recent recapitalizations on share prices," *Journal of Financial and Quantitative Analysis*, 21, March 1986, pp. 59-71.

Mayers, D. and C. W. Smith, Jr., "Ownership structure and control- The mutualization of stock life insurance companies," *Journal of Financial Economics*, 16, 1985, pp. 73-98.

Modigliani, F. & Miller, M. (1958). "The cost of capital, corporation finance and the theory of investment. *American Economic Review*, *53*,(June), 261-176.

——— , (1984). The capital structure puzzle. *Journal of Finance* (July), 575-592.

Norton, E., "Determinants of capital structure: A survey," *Advances in Financial Planning and Forecasting*, Vol. 3, 1989, pp. 323-350.

Ross, S.A., "The determination of financial structure: The incentive-signaling approach," *Bell Journal of Economics*, 8, Spring 1977, pp. 23-40.

Schall, L.D., "Taxes, inflation and corporate financial policy," *The Journal of Finance*, March 1984, pp. 105-126.

Schneller, M.I., "Taxes and optimal capital structure of the firm," *Journal of Finance*, 35, March 1980, pp. 119-128.

Scott, D.F., "Evidence on the importance of financial structure," *Financial Management*, 1, Summer 1972, pp. 45-50.

Scott, D.F. and J.D. Martin, "Industry influence on financial structure," *Financial Management*, 4, Spring 1975, pp. 67-73.

Senbet, L.W. and R. A. Taggart, Jr., "Capital structure equilibrium under market imperfections and incompleteness," *The Journal of Finance*, March 1984, pp. 93-103.

Williams, J., "Perquisites, risk, and capital structure," *Journal of Finance*, March 1987, pp. 29-48.

CAPITAL BUDGETING AND ASYMMETRIC INFORMATION

P. V. Viswanath

ABSTRACT

In a world of asymmetric information, the market's valuation of firm value may differ from the true value. A manager issuing risky securities in such a situation will not receive the proper price for these securities and would therefore not want to use a strict cost-of-capital rule. Myers and Majluf (1984) derived modified NPV rules for projects financed by new equity issues when asymmetric information invalidates the usual decision rule. In this paper, we extend their analysis in several ways. First, we show that, in some circumstances, even when a true cost-of-capital rule cannot be applied, an approximate market-value-based cost of capital may be used. Second, we devise a simpler version of the Myers-Majluf NPV rule that can be used for decentralized project selection. Third, we extend the analysis to projects financed by security issues other than equity. Fourth, we cast the modified NPV rule in an IRR framework.

Advances in Financial Planning and Forecasting,
Volume 5, pages 319-333.
Copyright © 1994 by JAI Press Inc.
All rights of reproduction in any form reserved.
ISBN:1-55938-421-2

INTRODUCTION

An important problem in capital budgeting is the determination of the cost of capital (COC) for a new project. If we assume that the risk of the new project is the same as that of the existing firm,[1] the manager should use the cost of capital[2] of the whole firm as a hurdle rate. However, recent research in finance has pointed out that investment decisions cannot always be evaluated in a vacuum. In particular, interactions between the investment and financing decisions have to be taken into account (Myers & Majluf, 1984; Ravid 1985).

An important source of these interactions is asymmetric information. Given the manager's access to the day-to-day workings of the firm, he often has information that is not available to the capital markets. Consequently, the market's valuation sometimes differs from the correct value of the firm. A manager issuing risky securities in such a situation will not receive the proper price for these securities. If this is the only way he can finance a new project,[3] he would not want to always stick to a true cost of capital rule.

Myers and Majluf (1984) derived modified NPV rules for projects financed by new equity issues when asymmetric information invalidates the usual decision rule. However, as in Myers' pecking order hypothesis, one would expect firms to issue less risky securities such as debt if there is asymmetric information. Furthermore, in their formulation of the decision rule, it is not possible to separate the evaluation of the project's cash flows and the adjustment for the asymmetric information.[4] Finally, since most firms use the IRR framework it would be desirable to specify the decision rule in that framework as well. In this paper, we extend their analysis in several ways. First, we show that, in some circumstances, even when a true cost-of-capital rule cannot be applied, a market-based cost of capital may be used. Second, we devise a simpler version of the Myers-Majluf net-present-value (NPV) rule that can be used for decentralized project selection. Third, we extend the analysis to projects financed by security issues other than equity. Fourth, we cast the modified NPV rule into an internal rate of return (IRR) framework.

CAPITAL BUDGETING WITH
ASYMMETRIC INFORMATION

It is not unreasonable to assume that, in general, the manager of the firm has superior information about the existing assets of the firm (assets in place) and/or the new project. There is a large literature that looks at various means by which the manager can credibly signal his superior information to the market. For example, Ross (1977) suggests that the debt-equity ratio might be such a signal. John and Williams (1985) look at dividends as a signaling mechanism. These papers derive conditions under which signaling equilibria will exist.

However, in spite of all these ways that the manager can signal his information, it is likely that some information asymmetry will still persist. Furthermore, as a practical matter, it is unlikely that the manager can signal on a continuous basis to keep the degree of asymmetric information low. In fact, the phenomenon of strong market reactions to the information content of financial decisions (such as stock price drops when equity is issued[5]) suggests that there is usually quite a bit of information asymmetry between managers and the market. In this paper, we will assume that there is some residual asymmetry of information between the manager and the market regarding the new project and/or the assets in place. Given this asymmetry, we wish to investigate the extent to which the usual capital budgeting rules need to be modified to evaluate new projects. Since the problem is created in the first place by the divergence of market values from true values, it may be conjectured that the substitution of market values for true values may produce the right decision, after all.[6] We consider this question first.

When Is a Market-Based Project Selection Rule Correct?

We first define the market-based project selection rule as follows:

> Accept the project if the market value of the project's cash flows is greater than the investment required.

Assuming that the capital markets are efficient, the market value is the present value of the market's estimate of the project's cash flows discounted at the cost of capital deemed appropriate by the market. When does this rule provide the correct decision? Obviously, if there is no information asymmetry at all, it will be correct. However, it could give the right answer even if the firm's assets in place are undervalued,[7] provided, however, that there is no information asymmetry regarding the new project. The additional condition required is that it be possible to finance the project separately. Under these conditions, the project would be accepted if the NPV is positive using the discount rate that is appropriate to the agreed-upon risk of the project itself. The information asymmetry is irrelevant in this case and the true value of the NPV will be equal to the market estimate. Hence, whenever the manager can obtain separate financing for the project, perhaps by spinning it off as a separate entity, and there is no information asymmetry regarding it,[8] the market-based capital budgeting rule would work properly.

Spinning off the project, however, may not always be possible. For example, the cost of issuing separate securities for each project may be too great, if there are fixed costs or if there are economies of scale in administering the securities. Furthermore, if the new project is closely tied up with the firm, high monitoring costs may have to be incurred to ensure that the manager keeps the cash flows from the project separate. In such cases, the project must be financed with funds raised from an issue of securities using the entire firm as a base. In such a case, a market-based rule would not necessarily be in the current shareholders' interests. This is because, since the existing firm is undervalued, the existing shareholders will have to give away too much of the firm to acquire the financing for the new project.[9] As long as the new securities bear any of the risk of the firm, the existing stockholders will share at least some of this unrecognized firm value with the new security holders without being paid for it.

This can be illustrated with an example. Suppose the true worth of the existing firm is $100, but the market values it at $80. Now, the firm has the opportunity to invest $15 in a new project that has an NPV of $5. The present value of the project is, therefore, $20. Let us assume that there is no information asymmetry regarding the new project. If the existing firm has 100 shares, how many new shares will it have to issue to raise the required investment of $15? Since the market value of the new firm (i.e., including the project) will be $100 (=$80 + $20), the new investors will demand a 15% share in the new firm, in exchange for putting up 15% of its market value. This means that 17.65 new shares will have to be issued. However, the true value of the new firm will be $120 (=$100 + $20). Hence, the 17.65 shares that have been issued are really worth 15% of $120 or $18. This means that the NPV that accrues to the existing shareholders is only $2 (=$20—$18). In this case, the new project is still worthwhile. However, if the initial investment required had been $85 with the NPV still being $5, the new investors would have demanded a 50% share of the new firm (market value of new firm =$80 + $90). Hence the 100 new shares the firm would have to issue would have had a true value of $95 (true value of new firm =$100 + $90), which means that there is a net decrease in the value of the existing shareholder equity, of $51! Under these circumstances the new project should not be adopted, although it has an NPV > 0, and would have passed muster under the usual capital budgeting rules. In this case, it is clear that using market values instead of true values makes no difference, since there is no divergence between true and market values for the new project; the NPV > 0 project would still be rejected.

In the following subsection, we first present appropriate NPV rules for project selection when the new project cannot be spun off, and then the corresponding IRR versions. We will show that there are other cases, where even though a strict market-value-based rule will not work, modified versions based partly on market values will lead to the right decision. The following section provides numerical illustrations of the quasi-market valuation rule and the last section gives conclusions.

Quasi-Market Project Selection Rules

We consider two different cases: case I, where the degree of asymmetry of information is the same for the new project as for the existing firm, and case II, where there is no asymmetry of information regarding the new project. We will show that a quasi-market NPV rule can be used in case I. In case II, the quasi-market NPV rule is not absolutely correct; however, the error caused by this quasi-market NPV rule may often be ignored.

First, we make two assumptions to make our problem manageable.

Assumption 1:   (a) None of the existing security holders of the firm other than the equity holders derive any benefit from the new project. (b) There is no wealth transfer from other existing security holders to the equity holders as a result of the new project.

Assumption 2:   No more projects will be available before the current asymmetry of information is resolved.

Assumption 1 serves to isolate the current problem of project selection under asymmetric information from moral hazard problems relating to previous issues. This implies both that equity holders write contracts to ensure that none of the benefit from a new project goes to the existing security holders and that the security holders ensure that the contracts are written to preclude any unforeseen wealth transfer from them to equity holders. Assumption 2 allows us to focus on the trade-off between the current dilution and the NPV of the current project.[10]

Define the following notation:

E — true value of the existing equity,

E^m — market value of the preexisting equity just after the securities are issued,

I — amount of new financing required,

P — true value of the new project,

P^m — market value of the new project.

Now, suppose equity is issued to finance the new project. Then, the rule derived by Myers and Majluf is to invest if condition (1) is satisfied:

$$\left(1 - \frac{I}{E^m + P^m} \right) (E + P) > E \tag{1}$$

The fraction $1 - I/(E^m+P^m)$ in this condition is the proportion of the equity of the new firm retained by the old equity holders.[11] Condition (1) can be rewritten as

$$P - I (E - E^m + P - P^m) / (E^m + P^m) > I) \tag{1$'$}$$

The interpretation of (1$'$) is that the new equity holders capture $I/(E^m+P^m)$ proportion of the difference between the true value and the market value of the existing equity and of the new project. Alternatively, it says that if the NPV, after taking dilution effects into account, is greater than zero, then the project should be accepted.

Rule (1$'$) is not, however, completely satisfactory, because it is precisely in cases of asymmetric information that we would expect a pecking order of financing to apply. In such cases, we would expect the firm to use retained earnings or riskless debt to finance new projects. This would allow the equity holders of the firm to accept all positive NPV projects, since they do not have to worry about dilution. If retained earnings are not available and it is not possible to issue riskless debt, then the firm will do the next best thing; it will issue secured debt or some other similar security that would minimize the dilution. Many factors have been discussed in the literature as relevant to the financing decision: tax factors, asset characteristics, bankruptcy costs, the stage of the business cycle, and finally asymmetric information. The manager weighs all these factors and decides on the appropriate security to issue to finance the current project. What concerns us here is that the manager is quite likely to use some security other than equity. Hence, we need to extend the project selection rule in (1´) to security issues other than equity.

Define a security to be α-sensitive if the sensitivity of the value of the security to an unexpected and exogenous change in the value of equity is α.[12] Equity itself, by definition, would have a sensitivity of unity; risky debt would have a sensitivity between 0 and 1 and riskless debt (e.g., debt guaranteed by the government) would have a sensitivity of zero. If the market for new issues is competitive, then the true value of the newly issued securities will be I, in the absence of any asymmetric information and independent of the value of equity. If there is asymmetric information (i.e., $E+P{\neq}E^m+P^m$) and equity is issued, then we have seen that the true value of the new equity holders is equal to I times a dilution factor of $1+(E-E^m+P-P^m)/E^m+P^m)$. Consequently the true value of a-sensitive securities in the presence of asymmetric information will be equal to I multiplied by a dilution factor, $1+\alpha(E-E^m+P-P^m)/E^m+P^m)$.[13]

Given assumption 2, we do not need to worry about future implications of the present decision. Hence, a natural extension of rule (1´) when an α-sensitive security is issued to finance the new project is to invest if

$$P - \alpha I\,(E - E^m + P - P^m)\,/\,(E^m + P^m) > I \tag{2}$$

This can be rewritten as:

$$P\left[\frac{E^m + P^m}{(1-\alpha)\,(E^m + P^m) + \alpha\,(E+P)}\right] > I \tag{2´}$$

We now discuss two extreme cases, one where the project has the same information asymmetry as the equity and one where the project has no information asymmetry.

Case I: Information Asymmetry for Equity and New Project Equal

Suppose the new project essentially involved an expansion of the existing firm. In such a case, all the characteristics of the existing firm would apply to the new project, including the degree of information asymmetry. This implies the relationship $P^m=P(E^m/E)$. Substituting in (2´), the modified rule is to invest if

$$P^* - P\left[\frac{E^m}{(1-\alpha)\,E^m + \alpha E}\right] > I \qquad (3)$$

We can think of P^* as a quasi-market valuation of the project. If the new security were equity, then $\alpha=1$ and we have $P^*=P(E^m/E)=P^m$, and we get our market-based rule. For $\alpha \neq 1$, the manager adjusts the true value of the project by the factor $E^m/[\alpha E+(1-\alpha)E^m]$. Alternatively, we could write condition (3) as

$$P > I^* - \frac{(1-\alpha)\,E^m + \alpha E}{E^m} \qquad (3´)$$

This allows us to use a standardized rule for all projects, since the NPV of the project is evaluated the same as without asymmetric information and the modified cutoff is the same for all projects.

Case II: No Information Asymmetry for New Project

An argument can be made that asymmetric information is generated when the manager actually operates the project (once it has been accepted) and gets to know the detailed requirements and contributions of the project. Furthermore, when financing is sought for a new project, the firm may have to provide documented information regarding the project to potential investors, either through the prospectus, if it is a public issue of securities, or directly to private lenders. Hence, although there may be an asymmetry of information regarding the existing assets in place, this may not hold for the new project. We therefore assume in this section that the project has no information asymmetry at all.[14] In this case, an application of (2´) requires that we invest in the new project if

$$P\left[\frac{E^m + P}{(1-\alpha)\,(E^m + P) + \alpha\,(E + P)}\right] > I$$

This can be rewritten as

$$P\left[\frac{E^m}{(1-\alpha)\,E^m + \alpha E} + \frac{(P-I)}{(1-\alpha)\,E^m + \alpha E}\right] > I \qquad (4)$$

If the NPV of the project, *P-I,* is not too large as a percentage of the value of the equity, we can ignore the second term on the left-hand side. We then have the familiar condition of Equation (3), $P^* > I$. In other words, we use the same rule as in case I. Once again, we could also use rule (3 ´) if we prefer a standardized rule.

The error introduced by using rule (3) is given by the second term on the left-hand side of (4), and can be estimated given the NPV of the project. We see that the error decreases in size the smaller the NPV of the project relative to the value of the existing firm. In the limit, if the NPV of the project is zero, then using rule (3) produces the correct decision.[15] In the next section, we will present numerical illustrations of this error.

We have not explicitly considered the effect of taxes on our decision rules. However, the introduction of taxes does not necessarily invalidate our rules. Obviously, if a Miller-type (1977) equilibrium applies,[16] where taxes have no impact on the capital structure of the firm, we do not have to modify our rules at all. If a Miller-type equilibrium does not apply, these rules can still be used if the adjusted-present-value method is employed——the tax effects will then be simply added to P^* before comparison with *I.*

In this section, we extended the Myers-Majluf project selection rule for equity issues to the case of other securities. We showed that we could reach the correct decision by using a quasi-market valuation of the project and applying the usual criterion of positive NPV. In the special case where the information asymmetry for the new project is the same as for the firm, and equity is issued, the correct method is in fact to use a market valuation rule. In addition, we formulated the rules in such a way as to be useful in a decentralized project selection situation. In the next section, we cast these project selection rules in terms of the IRR.

An IRR Formulation

Here we will assume that the conditions in case I apply, that is, that the information asymmetry for the existing firm and the new project are equal.[17] Under these conditions, rule (3) adjusts the NPV rule for the effects of asymmetric information. However, many managers may prefer to use a hurdle rate decision rule in addition to, or instead of, the NPV rule. Many surveys show that financial managers use the IRR or the accounting rate of return (ARR) to a large extent.[18] Hence, it is important to reformulate the modified NPV rule as a hurdle rate rule. We will first derive an IRR rule for infinite-lived projects and then provide a correction for finite-lived projects. We assume, for convenience, that the degree of information asymmetry for the project is the same as that for the assets in place.

Infinite-Lived Projects

Assume that the cash flows of the firm are perpetual. Denote the market's evaluation of the firm's cash flows in year 1 by C^m and that of the manager by C. Let the true growth rate in cash flows for the firm be g and the market's evaluation of the growth rate of the firm be g^m. The manager's evaluation of the required rate of return on the firm is r, while the market-determined cost of capital is given by COC. Then $E = C/(r-g)$ and $E^m = C^m/(COC-g^m)$. If C^p denotes the true first-period cash flows on the project, and g^p is the true growth rate of the cash flows for the project,[19] we can use the relations $P = C^p/(r-g^p)$ and $I = C^p/(IRR-g^p)$ to substitute in Equation (3) and find that the optimal rule reduces to the rule that the manager should invest if:

$$\text{IRR} > \text{COC*} = \frac{(r-g^p)}{(r-g)}\left[(1-\alpha)(r-g) + \alpha\frac{C}{C^m}(\text{COC}-g^m)\right] + g^p \qquad (5)$$

where COC* can be thought of as a quasi-market cost of capital. Again, we retain the standardization property, since right-hand side provides the common cutoff for all projects.

In practice, C^m could be measured by analysts' forecast of the firm's earnings for the next year, while C would be the manager's estimate. If the growth rates are zero, then the quasi-market COC is just a weighted average of (1) the true required rate of return and (2) the market-based COC, multiplied by the factor C/C^m. Furthermore, if the disagreement between the market and the manager is solely with reference to the riskiness of the firm (i.e., the appropriate discount rate) so that $C=C^m$, and all growth rates are the same, then the adjusted COC is simply a weighted average of the true required rate of return and the market-based COC.

Finite-Lived Projects

However, the above formula only applies to infinite-lived projects. We would like to know how the finiteness of project life affects our investment rule. We continue to assume, however, that the firm is infinite-lived and assume that cash flows are constant. In this case, the formula can be easily shown to be

$$\text{IRR} > \frac{(r-g^p)}{(r-g)}\left[(1-\alpha)(r-g) + \alpha\frac{C}{C^m}(\text{COC}-g^m)\right]k + g^p \qquad (5')$$

where

$$k = \frac{1-[(1+g^p)/(1+\text{IRR})]^N}{1-[(1+g^p)/(1+r)]^N}$$

The term k is less than 1 if $r >$ IRR and is greater than 1 if $r <$ IRR and can be easily computed. Of course, as N becomes large, k gets close to unity and can be dropped altogether, and we revert to rule (5).

ESTIMATES OF THE NPV CORRECTION FACTOR

It is difficult to say how large a degree of market mispricing may exist for the firm's securities. Some idea may be obtained by looking at the revaluation of a firm's stock upon announcement of new equity issues. It has been suggested (Myers & Majluf, 1984) that the issue of new equity signals negative information about the value of a firm. Under this hypothesis, the drop in the price of the firm's stock around the announcement date will measure the degree of overpricing. Masulis and Korwar (1986), in a study of 338 seasoned equity offerings by industrial firms, document an average negative abnormal return on days 0 and -1 relative to the equity issue announcement of 3.25 percent. Twenty percent of the firms in their sample had a price drop of over 6.5 percent and 10 percent had a price drop of more than 8.5 percent. Since the firms in this sample were fairly large, with an average value of \$949 million for total assets, it is likely that this figure represents a lower estimate on the degree of mispricing that exists in the market due to information asymmetry.

In Panel A of Tables 1 and 2, we provide some idea of the effect that such mispricing could have on project valuation when the degree of information asymmetry is the same for both the existing firm and the new project. In this case, condition (3) tells us if it is optimal to accept the new project. The factor $E^m/[(1-\alpha)E^m+\alpha E]$ in condition (3) is a correction factor that must be applied to the computed NPV (based on market-required rates of return). We compute values for the NPV correction factor for three different assumptions regarding the extent of the firm's over and undervaluation: 5 percent, 10 percent, and 25 percent. For $\alpha=1$, the correction factor is exactly equal to the degree of over- or undervaluation as we saw in the previous section. In this special case, using market quantities in the capital budgeting rule provides just the right amount of correction, as we also saw in the previous section. For values of $\alpha \neq 1$, the correction factor is less than the degree of over- or undervaluation.

Panel B of Tables 1 and 2 computes values for the correction factor when there is no information asymmetry at all for the new project. In this case, we use condition (4). The value of the correction factor is higher here than the corresponding value in Panel A if the true NPV of the project (P-I) is positive and less than the corresponding value in Panel A otherwise. If the true NPV of the project is positive, the formula inclines us more toward accepting it, than if it were negative or zero.[20] Hence the correction factor goes up, both for under-and overvaluation cases. A similar statement could be made for the negative-NPV cases.

Table 1. NPV Factors for Use in Conjunction with the Capital Budgeting Rule: Accept if P^x (NPV Factor) >I; Undervaluation Case

A: Same information asymmetry for existing firm and new project

α \ E^m/E:	0.95	0.90	0.75
0.10	0.9948	0.9890	0.9677
0.20	0.9896	0.9783	0.9375
0.30	0.9845	0.9677	0.9091
0.40	0.9794	0.9574	0.8824
0.50	0.9744	0.9474	0.8571
0.60	0.9694	0.9375	0.8333
0.70	0.9645	0.9278	0.8108
0.80	0.9596	0.9184	0.7895
0.90	0.9548	0.9091	0.7692
1.00	0.9500	0.9000	0.7500

B: Positive NPV projects   No information asymmetry for new project

	E^m/E					
	0.95		0.90		0.75	
α \ $(P-I)E^m$:	0.01	0.05	0.01	0.05	0.01	0.05
0.10	1.0047	1.0445	0.9989	1.0385	0.9774	1.0161
0.20	0.9995	1.0391	0.9880	1.0272	0.9469	0.9844
0.30	0.9943	1.0337	0.9774	1.0161	0.9182	0.9545
0.40	0.9892	1.0284	0.9670	1.0053	0.8912	0.9265
0.50	0.9841	1.0231	0.9568	0.9947	0.8657	0.9000
0.60	0.9791	1.0179	0.9469	0.9844	0.8417	0.8750
0.70	0.9741	1.0127	0.9371	0.9742	0.8189	0.8514
0.80	0.9692	1.0076	0.9276	0.9643	0.7974	0.8289
0.90	0.9643	1.0025	0.9182	0.9545	0.7769	0.8077
1.00	0.9595	0.9975	0.9090	0.9450	0.7575	0.7875

Negative NPV projects

	E^m/E					
	0.95		0.90		0.75	
α \ $(P-I)E^m$:	−0.01	−0.05	−0.01	−0.05	−0.01	−0.05
0.10	0.9848	0.9450	0.9791	0.9396	0.9581	0.9194
0.20	0.9797	0.9401	0.9685	0.9293	0.9281	0.8906
0.30	0.9746	0.9352	0.9581	0.9194	0.9000	0.8636
0.40	0.9696	0.9304	0.9479	0.9096	0.8735	0.8382
0.50	0.9646	0.9256	0.9379	0.9000	0.8486	0.8143
0.60	0.9597	0.9209	0.9281	0.8906	0.8250	0.7917
0.70	0.9548	0.9162	0.9186	0.8814	0.8027	0.7703
0.80	0.9500	0.9116	0.9092	0.8724	0.7816	0.7500
0.90	0.9452	0.9070	0.9000	0.8636	0.7615	0.7308
1.00	0.9405	0.9025	0.8910	0.8550	0.7425	0.7125

Table 2.   NPV Factors for Use in Conjunction with the Capital Budgeting
Rule: Accept if P^x (NPV Factor) $>I$; Overvaluation Case

A: Same information asymmetry for existing firm and new project

α \\ E^m/E:	1.05	1.10	1.25
0.10	1.0048	1.0092	1.0204
0.20	1.0096	1.0185	1.0417
0.30	1.0145	1.0280	1.0638
0.40	1.0194	1.0377	1.0870
0.50	1.0244	1.0476	1.1111
0.60	1.0294	1.0577	1.1364
0.70	1.0345	1.0680	1.1628
0.80	1.0396	1.0784	1.1905
0.90	1.0448	1.0891	1.2195
1.00	1.0500	1.1000	1.2500

B: Positive NPV projects   No information asymmetry for new project

	E^m/E					
E^m/E	1.05		1.10		1.25	
α \\ $(P-I)E^m$:	0.01	0.05	0.01	0.05	0.01	0.05
0.10	1.0148	1.0550	1.0193	1.0596	1.0306	1.0714
0.20	1.0197	1.0601	1.0287	1.0694	1.0521	1.0938
0.30	1.0246	1.0652	1.0383	1.0794	1.0745	1.1170
0.40	1.0296	1.0704	1.0481	1.0896	1.0978	1.1413
0.50	1.0346	1.0756	1.0581	1.1000	1.1222	1.1667
0.60	1.0397	1.0809	1.0683	1.1106	1.1477	1.1932
0.70	1.0448	1.0862	1.0786	1.1214	1.1744	1.2209
0.80	1.0500	1.0916	1.0892	1.1324	1.2024	1.2500
0.90	1.0552	1.0970	1.1000	1.1436	1.2317	1.2805
1.00	1.0605	1.1025	1.1110	1.1550	1.2625	1.3125

Negative NPV projects

	E^m/E					
	1.05		1.10		1.25	
α \\ $(P-I)E^m$:	−0.01	−0.05	−0.01	−0.05	−0.01	−0.05
0.10	0.9947	0.9545	0.9991	0.9587	1.0102	0.9694
0.20	0.9995	0.9591	1.0083	0.9676	1.0313	0.9896
0.30	1.0043	0.9638	1.0178	0.9766	1.0532	1.0106
0.40	1.0092	0.9684	1.0274	0.9858	1.0761	1.0326
0.50	1.0141	0.9732	1.0371	0.9952	1.1000	1.0556
0.60	1.0191	0.9779	1.0471	1.0048	1.1250	1.0795
0.70	1.0241	0.9828	1.0573	1.0146	1.1512	1.1047
0.80	1.0292	0.9876	1.0676	1.0245	1.1786	1.1310
0.90	1.0343	0.9925	1.0782	1.0347	1.2073	1.1585
1.00	1.0395	0.9975	1.0890	1.0450	1.2375	1.1875

The tables allow us to evaluate projects in two kinds of situations. In the first kind of situation, the true NPV of the project may be zero or negative; nevertheless, if the existing firm is currently overvalued by the market, it may be worthwhile to accept the investment (assuming that there is no other way to capitalize on the market overvaluation). Alternatively, the true NPV of the project may be positive; nevertheless, if the existing firm is undervalued, the project may have to be rejected because of the need to sell undervalued securities. The formulas derived in this paper allow the firm to evaluate this trade-off in a systematic fashion.

Assuming that a bond issue would have a much lower α than an equity issue, we see from Panel B of the tables that a positive-NPV project is more likely to be accepted if it can be financed by a bond issue even if the market tends to undervalue the firm's securities. On the other hand, even if the firm's securities are overvalued, a negative NPV project has a greater chance of being accepted only if it can be financed by equity or equity-like securities.

CONCLUSION

The use of COC rules for project selection generally depends on the assumption that there are no interactions between project selection and financing. It has been shown that when there is asymmetric information between the manager of a firm and the market, this assumption is not always valid. It is, therefore, important to reevaluate the cost of capital under these circumstances.

In this paper, we have formulated a modified quasi-market-value-based capital budgeting rule that can be used under asymmetric information. The market-value-based rule is a special case of this more general rule. In two situations, this quasi-market-value-based rule degenerates to the market-value-based rule itself: (1) if the project can be financed independently of the firm, and (2) if the project is equity financed and the asymmetry of information affects the existing firm and the new project in the same way. We have also reformulated the quasi-market-value-based rule for use in decentralized project selection situations. Finally, we derive an IRR formulation of this rule.

ACKNOWLEDGMENTS

I thank Ivan Brick and Michael Frierman for helpful comments. Support from the New Jersey Center for Research in Financial Services at the Graduate School of Management, Rutgers University, is gratefully acknowledged.

NOTES

1. In what follows, we maintain the assumption of similarity of risk between the new project and the existing firm. However, this is only for convenience. If both market and manager use the same model of risky asset valuation, then this assumption is not required.

2.   If the firm only has debt and equity, then the COC is a weighted average of the costs of equity and debt financing, with the true values of debt and equity used to determine the weights. It is straightforward to determine the formula if there are other securities also.

3.   If he can use retained earnings, this problem may not occur. See Myers and Majluf (1984) and their discussion of passive versus active investors.

4.   Such a separation may be desirable for decentralized decision-making, where the person with the most information about the new project (the division manager) may not be the same as the person with the information regarding market underpricing or overpricing (head office).

5.   See Asquith and Mullins (1986), Masulis and Korwar (1986), Mikkelson and Partch (1986), and Schipper and Smith (1986).

6.   For example, we may use market estimates of cash flows or risk, instead of the true values known by the manager.

7.   The analysis would proceed similarly in the case of overvaluation. The case of undervaluation is treated here for concreteness.

8.   Nanda (1991) suggests that such situations provide a raison d´être for spin-offs.

9.   If the firm is overvalued and the manager follows a market-based capital budgeting rule, the shareholders incur an opportunity cost, in that the manager would reject some projects that would add to shareholder wealth through the sale of overvalued securities.

10.   If there were other decision points before the asymmetry were resolved, it would be necessary to solve a dynamic intertemporal problem, which would give us the optimal investment-financing path over time. For example, if we expect to have a shortage of cash flows in the future, we may prefer to retain current earnings in order to avoid rejecting worthwhile projects in the future, even if this exposes us to some dilution at present. While consideration of such eventualities could change our current decision, solving such a problem would, on the one hand, be tremendously difficult. On the other hand, it might be argued that if the expected cash flow in future periods is not lumpy, it may be reasonable to treat the problem in a myopic manner.

11.   If $E^m = E$ and $P^m = P$, then the investment rule boils down to the familiar: Invest if $P^m = P > I$.

12.   The measurement of the α-sensitivity of different securities can be undertaken by a combination of conceptual and empirical methods. Theoretically, the α-sensitivity can be measured using an option-pricing framework. It is known (Black and Scholes, 1973) that contingent claims on the firm can be modeled as options on the value of the firm V. The α-sensitivity of a security B is just the ratio of $\partial B/\partial V$ to $\partial E/\partial V$, where the Black-Scholes option pricing model can be used to obtain these partial derivatives. Alternatively, α could be measured as the ratio of the beta of the security to the beta of the equity. In addition, the manager might be able to estimate the α-sensitivity from previous experience.

13.   This can be shown somewhat more formally as follows. Let MV(s) denote the market value of any security s and MV(e) denote the market value of equity. Then the change in market value of security s, caused by an exogenous change of ΔV, can be written as

$$
\begin{aligned}
\Delta\, d\mathrm{MV}(s) \quad &= \quad [d\mathrm{MV}(s)/dV]\ \mathrm{cap}\ dV \\
&= \quad [d\mathrm{MV}(s)/d\mathrm{MV}(e)]\ [d\mathrm{MV}(e)/dV]{*}\mathrm{cap}\ dV \\
&= \quad a{*}\mathrm{cap}\ d\mathrm{MV}(e)
\end{aligned}
$$

Now, we can think of the true value of a security as being equal to what the market value would be if the inside information of the manager could credibly be made known immediately to the market. Hence the above relationship also applies when we substitute for $\Delta\, d\mathrm{MV}(\cdot)$, the difference between the true and market values of each security.

14.   It is possible to allow for arbitrary differences in information asymmetry between the new project and the existing firm. This has not been done here in order to preserve simplicity. Also, these extreme cases probably approximate reality to a great extent.

15.   Later, we will present some estimates of the effect of a nonzero NPV on the capital budgeting decision.

16.   The phrase *Miller-type equilibrium* is used to allow for nontax reasons for an optimal capital structure.

17.   Or if case II applies, that the conditions for ignoring the second term on the left-hand side in rule (4) hold.

18.   In a sample studied by Schall, Sundem, and Geijsbeek (1978), fully 90 out of 101 financial managers used either the IRR or ARR method. Ross (1986) studied capital budgeting practices in 12 large manufacturing concerns. In 10 out of the 12, the IRR method was used. None used NPV, although it was calculated.

19.   Since we are assuming that $P^m/P=E^m/E$, we do not make a separate assumption regarding the market's evaluation of the growth rate for the project's cash flows.

20.   The question may be raised as to why this NPV factor does not appear in the case where the information asymmetry is the same for the existing firm and the new project. The answer is that it does so implicitly. The fact that the correction factor in (4) is higher for positive-NPV projects than the correction factor in (3) actually turns out to be irrelevant; the reason is that the absolute value of P^*-I is not relevant, only its sign is. A careful examination of formulas (3) and (4) will reveal, furthermore, that we will never accept a project using (4) unless we also accept it using (3).

REFERENCES

Asquith, P. & Mullins, D.W., (1986). Equity issues and stock price dilution. *Journal of Financial Economics, 15,* 61-89.

Black, F. & Scholes, M. (1973). The pricing of options and corporate liabilities. *Journal of Political Economy, 81,*(May-June), 637-659.

John, K. & Williams, J. (1985). Dividends, dilution and taxes: A signaling equilibrium. *Journal of Finance, 40,*(September), 1053-1070.

Masulis, R.W. & Korwar, A. (1986). Seasoned equity offerings: An empirical investigation. *Journal of Financial Economics, 15,* 91-118.

Mikkelson, W. & Partch, M. (1986). Valuation effects of secondary offerings and the issuance process. *Journal of Financial Economics, 15,* 31-60.

Miller, M. (1977). Debt and taxes. *Journal of Finance, 32,* 261-275.

Myers, S. (1984). The capital structure puzzle. *Journal of Finance, 39*(July), 575-592.

Myers, S.C. & Majluf, N.J. (1984). Corporate financing and investment decisions when firms have information that investors do not have. *Journal of Financial Economics, 13,(June),* 187-221.

Nanda, V. (1991). On the good news in equity carve-outs. *Journal of Finance.* (December), 1717-1737.

Ravid, S.A. (1985). Interactions between investment and financing decisions. *Financial Management.*

Ross, M. (1986). Capital budgeting practices of twelve large manufacturers. *Financial Management* (Winter), 15-22.

Ross, S.A. (1977). The determination o f financial structure: The incentive signaling approach. *Bell Journal of Economics* (Spring), 23-40.

Schall, L.D., Sundem, G. L. & Geijsbeek, W.R. (1978). Survey and analysis of capital budgeting methods. *Journal of Finance* (March), 281-287.

Schipper, K. & Smith A. (1986). A comparison of equity carve-outs and equity offerings: Share price effects and corporate restructuring. *Journal of Financial Economics, 15, 153-186.*

VALIDATION AND UNIFICATION OF MERGER THEORIES:
A CANONICAL CORRELATION APPROACH

Robert K. Su

ABSTRACT

This study uses canonical correlation analysis to validate and unify 5 merger theories. Empirically, it investigates the pattern of structural fit in terms of 10 financial ratios between 752 pairs of acquirees and acquirers of 1980 to 1990. A control sample of nonmerger firms was matched with the merger sample by the event year, size, and industry. The relationships between the merger groups and between the nonmerger groups were analyzed univariately as well as multivariately. The results indicate that profitable, cash-rich, but internal-opportunity-lacking firms took over efficient, low-leverage, high-liquidity, and well-valued targets in the recent merger wave. The findings support the resources redeployment theory most, management efficiency theory next, and financial synergy theory partially, but reject the economic disturbance theory and undervaluation theory.

Advances in Financial Planning and Forecasting,
Volume 5, pages 335-345.

INTRODUCTION

A new merger wave of an unprecedented size and intensity has just swept the United States. Hundreds of billions of dollars changed hands each year in the 1980s and the excess returns of mergers for target shareholders are consistently significant (Weston, Ching & Hoag, 1990]. However, no complete model exists to explain why companies merge.

Various theories have been proposed to determine merger motives (for instance, Peel, 1990; Krinsky, Rotenberg, & Thornton, 1988). But, they are not unified and often conflict. The lack of a unified merger theory is mainly because prior studies only examined the merger motives of either the acquiring company or the acquired company alone, but not both at the same time. The fact is that it takes two companies to make a merger deal. The interrelationship of the two companies involved in a merger should determine whether a good fit between them exists for them to merge. Further, the pattern of fit should explain why these two companies choose to merge while others do not. Without a simultaneous and thorough evaluation of the structural characteristics of both merger companies as compared to those of nonmerger companies in a controlled setting, no complete theory of merger could be meaningfully established.

To fill this theoretical gap, the present study uses canonical correlation analysis to investigate the structural relationship between acquirees and acquirers as well as between nonacquirees and nonacquirers. The two relationships are contrasted to explore the pattern of fit, if any, between merger firms so as to validate and unify merger theories.

Canonical correlation analysis is suitable for the purpose of this study because we are interested in analyzing the structural relationship between two groups. Stevens (1986, p. 373) described the method as "means of breaking down the association between two sets of variables, and is appropriate if the wish is to parsimoniously describe the number and nature of mutually independent relationship existing between the two sets." This method produces pairs of canonical variates and their canonical correlations to represent the overall structural association of two sets of variables. In addition, the method computes the correlation of individual variables with canonical variates to show the relative significance of the former in explaining the latter. In this study, we are interested in the overall correlation between the financial ratios of one group (say, acquirees) and those of another group (say, acquirers) as well as the correlation of individual ratios of the former with the entire set of ratios of the latter and vice versa.

The remainder of the paper is organized as follows. The next section discusses the methodology regarding the merger theories and variables under investigation, sampling process, data sources, and analytical techniques. The following reports the results of the univariate and multivariate analyses. The final section summarizes the major findings.

Table 1: Merger Variables, Attributes, and Theories

No. Variables	Attributes	Theories
1. Income/total assets	Profitability	Management efficiency
2. Quick assets/current liabilities	Liquidity	Financial synergy
3. Cash flows from operations/total assets	Cash flows	Resources redeployment
4. Total liabilities/owners' equity	Leverage	Financial synergy
5. Sales/total assets	Turnover	Management efficiency
6. Income/number of employees ($000)	Productivity	Management efficiency
7. Capital expenditure/sales	Expansion	Resources redeployment
8. Growth in sales	Growth	Management efficiency
9. P/E disturbance	Market valuation	Economic disturbance
10. Q ratio	Market valuation	Undervaluation

METHODOLOGY

Merger Theories and Variables

Although more than 10 merger theories have been proposed, not every of them is empirically testable due to data limitation.[1] For this reason, the present study considers only 5 merger theories: management efficiency (Manne, 1965), financial synergy (Ansoff, 1965), resources redeployment (Palepu, 1986), economic disturbance (Gort, 1969), and undervaluation (Tobin, 1969). The 5 merger theories and their operational variables are listed in Table 1.

The management efficiency theory predicts that acquirers are managed in a better way than acquirees. This study measures management efficiency by 4 variables for the various aspects of management: profitability in terms of return on assets, asset turnover, employee productivity in terms of profit per employee, and annual sales growth. As such, we would expect that acquirers have a higher return on assets, turn assets over more frequently, have a greater profit per employee, and have a higher sales growth than acquirees. We also expect that nonacquirees are better than acquirees in these aspects and that acquirers are better than nonacquirees in the same aspects.

The financial synergy theory suggests that the postmerger debt capacity of the combined firm can be greater than the sum of two firms' capacities before merger. The theory finds support from Rathinasamy et al. (1991), who reported that postmerger debt ratios were higher than the theoretical ratio. Given the need for a greater debt capacity, we would expect that, before merger, acquirers are more leveraged than nonacquirers, while acquirees are less leveraged than nonacquirees. Further, as liquidity is normally written into debt covenants as a restriction, we also view liquidity as a related financial synergy consideration. In terms of quick ratio, we therefore expect that acquirers are less liquid than nonacquirers, while acquirees are more liquid than nonacquirees.

The resources redeployment theory states that firms realign themselves with the changing environment through merger activities. When firms lack internal expansion opportunities, they likely would redeploy their resources, if abundant, on external mergers. We operationalize this theory by two variables: cash flows from operations and internal capital expenditure. Under the redeployment theory, we expect that acquirers have more cash flows than nonacquirers but spend less in internal expansions than nonacquirers. Also, we expect that acquirees have more cash flows and capital expenditure than nonacquirees such that the former are attractive to acquirers for the redeployment purpose.

The economic disturbance hypothesis of Gort (1969) implies that opportunities to gain from takeovers are greater when stock valuations of targets fluctuate more in a given period due to a temporary economic disequilibrium. We measure the economic disturbance by the maximal change in the P/E ratio within a year. Hence, we expect that acquirees have a greater annual disturbance in the P/E ratio than nonacquirees.

Finally, the undervaluation theory (Tobin, 1969) states that undervalued companies are attractive merger targets because it is cheaper to acquire them than to create the same firm from scratch. Using market value to book value as a proxy for the q ratio, we expect that acquirees have a lower q than nonacquirees.

Sample and Data

Four groups of sample firms are needed for the study: acquirees, acquirers, nonacquirees, and nonacquirers. The sample selection process started with a search for acquirees of 1980 to 1990. Near 3000 acquirees were located from the 1990 version of COMPUSTAT research annual file. Their acquirers were identified from the merger index of *Mergers and Acquisitions*. To qualify as a sample pair, both the acquiree and its acquirer must have data on the COMPUSTAT tapes for up to 2 years before merger. This requirement reduced the sample to 752 pairs of identifiable acquirers and acquirees. Further, a control sample of nonmerger firms was selected. To prevent confounding due to year, size, or industry difference, a nonmerger firm (nonacquiree or nonacquirer) was matched with the merger firm (acquiree or acquirer, respectively) by the event year, size in terms of total assets, and industry in terms of the 4-digit SIC code. On this basis, 752 pairs of nonacquirers and nonacquirees with the available 2-year COMPUSTAT data were selected. The final sample therefore consists of 752 pairs of firms that were involved in a merger in the 1980-1990 period and 752 pairs of matched nonmerger firms.

Annual data of the sample companies for 2 years prior to merger were extracted from the COMPUSTAT research and/or industrial annual files. The merger variables were calculated as defined in Table 1 to provide a general profile to measure the various merger-related characteristics of each sample group of firms.

Analytical Techniques

Finally, the merger profiles of the four groups in two pairs were analyzed univariately and multivariately. The univariate part includes a comparison of the profile of acquirees (nonacquirees) with that of acquirers (nonacquirers) to determine their relationship. The difference between each two groups was *t*-tested. As the four groups make 6 combinations, 6 two-tailed *t*-tests were conducted for each variable each year. The two relationships (i.e., acquirees/acquirers and nonacquirees/nonacquirers) were then contrasted to explore possible patterns of fit as well as to validate the merger theories on a univariate basis.

Since our ultimate goal is to unify the various merger theories, we therefore conducted canonical correlation analysis to determine the overall structural fit between acquirees and acquirers as well as which variables associate one group with the other. The same procedure was applied to the control sample of non-merger groups. First, we evaluated the canonical variates and their relative canon-ical correlations for the merger sample as compared with the nonmerger sample. Further, we assessed the correlation of individual variables with the canonical variates to determine the relative importance of the individual variables and the merger theory represented. As such, these analyses allowed exploration of the motives to acquire or to be acquired as well as the relative importance of the motives so as to validate and unify the merger theories under investigation.

FINDINGS

Univariate Analysis

Table 2 reports the means of merger variables and size for acquirees, acquirers, nonacquirees, and nonacquirers for 1 and 2 years before the merger in 1980-1990. The table also presents the *t*-test results for between-group differences.

Among the four groups, acquirers consistently were the most profitable (vari-able 1) and aquirees were more profitable than nonacquirees. This finding sup-ports the management efficiency theory of merger, which predicts that acquirers would be more profitable than their targets. Yet, the theory cannot explain why the most profitable firms (i.e., acquirers) did not take over the less profitable firms (i.e., nonacquirees) that were size and industry matched with the true target. Obvi-ously, profitability is not the only merger decision factor. A similar conclusion can be drawn based on employee productivity in terms of profit per employee (vari-able 6).

In terms of quick ratio (variable 2), acquirers and nonacquirers were less liquid than acquirees and nonacquirees, respectively. Acquirers' liquidity level improved before merger, while acquirees' dropped but remained the highest among the 4 groups. It is logical that acquirers preferred to take over more liquid

Table 2.   Mean of Variables

	(A) Acquirees	(B) Acquirers	(C) Nonacquirees	(D) Nonacquirers
Panel A: One year before merger				
1. Profitability	0.046(BC)	0.062(ACD)	0.037(ABD)	0.049(BC)
2. Liquidity	1.414(BD)	1.206(AC)	1.347(BD)	1.163(AC)
3. Cash flows	0.097(BC)	0.111(ACD)	0.087(ABD)	0.095(BC)
4. Leverage	1.321(BD)	1.468(AC)	1.338(BD)	1.535(AC)
5. Turnover	1.355(BD)	1.216(AC)	1.335(B)	1.259)A)
6. Productivity	3.477(BD)	6.239(AC)	3.125(BD)	5.147(AC)
7. Expansion	0.079(D)	0.079(D)	0.079( )	0.089(AB)
8. Growth	0.120(B)	0.159(AD)	0.127( )	0.117(B)
9. P/E disturbance	6.937(B)	6.126(AC)	7.475(BD)	6.485(C)
10. q ratio	1.633(D)	1.672(CD)	1.541(B)	1.521(AB)
Assets ($000,000)	319	3,239	250	1,723
No. of firms	580	580	614	614
Panel B: Two years before merger				
1 Profitability	0.054(B)	0.064(ACD)	0.054(B)	0.055(B)
2. Liquidity	1.423(BD)	1.176(AC)	1.350(BD)	1.145(AC)
3. Cash flows	0.100(B)	0.113(ACD)	0.099(B)	0.100(B)
4. Leverage	1.317(BD)	1.498(AC)	1.372(BD)	1.518(AC)
5. Turnover	1.381(BD)	1.286(AC)	1.364(B)	1.322(A)
6. Productivity	3.641(BD)	5.736(AC)	4.110(BD)	4.991(AC)
7. Expansion	0.081( )	0.082( )	0.078( )	0.085( )
8. Growth	0.136(B)	0.167(AD)	0.149( )	0.131(B)
9. P/E disturbance	7.460(BD)	6.209(AC)	8.027(BD)	6.428(AC)
10. q ratio	1.540( )	1.597(D)	1.576(D)	1.490(BC)
Assets ($000,000)	284	2,714	220	1,621
No. of firms	700	700	566	566

Notes: A letter in parentheses indicates that the mean of the group is significantly different at .05, based on a two-tailed *t*-test, from that of another group designated by the letter.

targets. Yet, no decisive conclusion can be drawn to support financial synergy theory based on the acquirers' motive to merge for liquidity improvement, because their liquidity level improved before merger and the least liquid firms (i.e., nonacquirers) did not come out to engage in merger activities.

Acquirers were consistently the richest in terms of cash flows from operations (variable 3) among the four groups. Since they possessed favorable cash flows but spent significantly less than nonacquirers in capital expenditure (variable 7) for internal expansions, it is likely that acquirers had excess cash but could not invest internally in a profitable way. On the other side, acquirees also had more cash flows from operations but were able to expand internally a little more than nonacquirees. These results together imply two things. First, acquirers were not able to expand internally and therefore sought external expansion opportunities. Logically, they chose to acquires cash-rich targets with expandable operations. Second, the small cash flows of nonacquirees did not make nonacquirees attractive takeover targets; meanwhile, nonacquirers' cash flows were not large enough to allow takeover of acquirees but were still sufficient for internal expansions. This analysis renders support for the resources redeployment theory of merger.

Acquirers were more leveraged (variable 4) than acquirees but less leveraged than nonacquirers, while acquirees were the least leveraged group. This finding supports the financial synergy theory of merger, which predicts that more-leveraged firms would merge less-leveraged ones. However, the support is partial because the most leveraged group (i.e., nonaquirers) did not engage in takeover. It is likely that nonacquirers' heavy debt load plus low cash flows precluded them from financial synergy opportunities from merger.

In terms of assets turnover (variable 5), acquirers were the least efficient among the four groups while acquirees were the most efficient. The finding that the least efficient firms (i.e., acquirers) acquired the most efficient ones (i.e., acquirees) goes against the management efficient theory. A logical explanation is that mergers in the recent merger wave were geared toward efficiency improvement.

Acquirers were growing faster in sales (variable 8) than any other group but acquirees grew less than nonacquirees. This finding well supports the management efficiency theory of merger if growth is viewed as an aspect of management efficiency. This result, taken together with the above analysis regarding cash flows (variable 3) and capital expenditure (variable 7) of the 4 groups, also points to the resources redeployment theory of merger. Acquirers managed their sales growth well, had rich cash flows, but hesitated to invest internally due to possibly limited internal investment opportunities. As a result, they redeployed resources on external expansion through mergers.

The last two variables involve stock market valuation of firms. The P/E disturbance relates to how consistently a firm is valued on the stock market. As Table 2 shows, nonacquirees consistently had a much higher level of annual P/E disturbance than acquirees but remained unacquired. Therefore, the hypothesis that firms with a high level of economic disturbance within a period would make attractive merger targets receives no support at all. In fact, nonacquirees had the highest level of P/E disturbance among the 4 groups. By contrast, acquirers consistently experienced less P/E disturbance than nonacquirers, suggesting a stable valuation of acquirers' stock.

Finally, the q ratio depicts the market valuation of firms as a surrogate for replacement cost to book value. The undervaluation theory of merger predicts that undervalued firms are favored merger targets. Like the economic disturbance hypothesis, this theory is not supported by the empirical results. In the year before merger, acquirees were valued more favorably by the stock market than nonaquirees. On the other hand, acquirers (nonacquirers) were consistently valued most (least) favorably by the market. Contrary to the theory, high-q-ratio firms

Table 3.   Canonical Correlation Analysis Results for the Year before Merger

	Acquirees vs. acquirers	*Nonacquirees vs. nonacquirers*
Panel A:	*Correlation (%) between the Pair of Canonical Variates*	
First	96.42	95.89
Second	50.66	45.54

Panel B: *Standardized Variance (%) Explained by the Canonical Variate of the Opposite Group*

First	48.34	60.42	45.27	52.37
Second	1.34	1.07	1.01	1.10

Panel C: *Variables and Their Squared Correlation
with the First Canonical Variate of the Opposite Group*

Variable	*Correlation*	*Variable*	*Correlation*	*Variable*	*Correlation*	*Variable*	*Correlation*
#10	(.7734)	#10	(.7839)	#10	(.7652)	#10	(.7679)
#5	(.7393)	#3	(.7565)	#5	(.7002)	#2	(.7579)
#2	(.7046)	#5	(.7531)	#2	(.6957)	#5	(.7090)
#4	(.6190)	#2	(.7325)	#4	(.5958)	#3	(.6781)
#3	(.5349)	#4	(.7087)			#4	(.6128)
		#7	(.5699)				
		#1	(.5464)				
		#9	(.5359)				

merged between themselves and low-q-ratio firms made no moves at all. Th
favorably and stably valued shares of acquirers, coupled with their rich cas.
flows, might have facilitated the mergers.

Canonical Correlation Analysis

Canonical correlation analysis was conducted to analyze the structural relationship between merger groups (acquirees and acquirers as a pair) and between nonmerger groups (nonacquirees and nonacquirers as another pair). Table 3 reports
the major findings of this multivariate analysis for the year before merger. The
results for the prior year are similar and therefore are not reported.

Panel A shows the correlation for the first two pairs of canonical variates for
both merger and nonmerger groups. The correlation between the first pair of
canonical variates is 96.42 and 95.89 percent for merger and nonmerger groups
with an F-value of 23.22 and 21.78, respectively. Both correlations are significant
at the .0001 level.

Clearly, acquirees are highly associated with acquirers and the same is true for
nonmerger firms, but the two canonical correlation coefficients differ only
slightly. This result is not surprising because merger and nonmerger firms were

year, size, and industry matched. The second pair of canonical variates has dramatically lower correlations: 50.66 and 45.54 percent.

Panel B reports the percentage of standardized variance of a merger (nonmerger) group explained by the first two canonical variates of the other merger (nonmerger) group. As the figures show, the first canonical variate of acquirees (acquirers) explains 60.42 (48.34) percent of the variance of acquirers (acquirees). The corresponding figures for the nonmerger groups are 52.37 and 45.27 percent.

It appears that merger groups can better explain each other's variance than nonmerger groups. The greater percentage of variance explained, as well as the greater canonical correlation reported in Panel A, between acquirees and acquirers than between nonacquirees and nonacquirers suggests a better fit between the merger groups than between the nonmerger groups. The second pair of canonical variates has little power to explain the association between either paired groups (less than 1.35 percent) and deserves no further attention.

Panel C reports the variables of a merger (nonmerger) group that has a more than 50 percent squared correlation with the first canonical variate of the other merger (nonmerger) group. The squared correlation of a variable represents the association of the variable of a group with the overall structure of the opposite group. A close examination of the squared correlations and variables reported in this panel reveals a pattern of fit between acquirees and acquirers and the relative importance of variables as merger decision factors.

Four findings are noteworthy. First, q ratio (variable 10), assets turnover (variable 5), quick ratio (variable 2), and leverage (variable 4) in descending order of squared correlation for each group except nonacquirers consistently correlated highly with the overall structural of its opposite group. This result suggests that market valuation, efficiency, liquidity, and leverage are the major considerations in merger decisions. Not surprisingly, q ratio has the highest squared correlation for both merger and nonmerger groups. As discussed earlier in the univariate analysis subsection, both acquirees and acquirers (nonacquirees and nonacquirers) were more (less) favorably valued by the market. Efficiency in terms of assets turnover is also an important merger motive, as acquirers were the least efficient but took over the most efficient firms. In addition, the high correlation for quick ratio and leverage suggests that financial synergy generally is another major merger decision factor.

Second, these four ratios of acquirees were respectively more associated with acquirers' overall structure than those of nonacquirees with nonacquirers' structure. The same is true for acquirers except for liquidity (variable 2, 73.25 vs. 75.79 percent). These findings point out a better fit in general between acquires and acquirers based on the four variables than between nonacquirees and nonacquirers such that a merger took place between the former pair rather than between the latter pair. The lower association of acquirers' liquidity with acquirees' structure further confirms the less importance placed by acquirers on financial synergy as a major motive of merger.

Third, acquirees' cash flows position (variable 3) was prominently associated with acquirers' structure (53.49 percent) but that of nonacquirees was much less associated with nonacquirers' structure (44.38 percent, a 9.11 percent difference). This results indicates that targets' cash flows was weighted seriously by buyers. Moreover, acquirers' cash flow (variable 3) level was the second most explanatory variable of acquirees' structure, while that of nonacquirers ranked fourth (75.65 vs. 67.81 percent). This difference suggests that the rich cash flows of acquirers played a major role in their decision to acquire the target.

Finally, three additional variables of acquirers were also prominently associated with acquirees' structure but it is not true for nonacquirers. This finding suggests that internal expansion (variable 7), profitability (variable 1), and stock price stability (variable 9) also played a role in merger decisions of acquirers, after consideration is given to the major merger variables. The significance of cash flows and internal expansion on the acquirers' part further supports the resources redeployment theory.

Overall Analysis

To sum, the above univariate and multivariate results reveal that a better fit existed between acquirees and acquirers than between nonacquirees and nonacquirers and nonacquirers. The difference in fit is subtle but discernible. Factors such as market valuation, assets turnover, liquidity, leverage, profitability, and internal expansion all played a role in the recent merger wave. The overall merger picture in 1980-1990 is that profitable, cash-rich, but internal-opportunity-lacking firms took over efficient, low-leverage, high-liquidity, and well-valued targets. The major motives of mergers were redeployment of resources and management efficiency. The financial synergy theory received partial support, while economic disturbance theory and undervaluation theory found no evidence at all.

CONCLUSIONS

This study investigates the pattern of fit between acquirees and acquirers of the recent merger wave to validate and unify 5 merger theories. A control sample of nonmerger groups was matched with the merger sample by the event year, size, and industry. The relationships between the merger groups and between the nonmerger groups were contrasted first univariately and next multivariately through canonical correlation analysis. The results indicate that in the recent merger wave, profitable, cash-rich, but internal-opportunity-lacking firms took over efficient, low-leverage, high-liquidity, and well-valued targets. The findings support the resources redeployment theory most, management efficiency theory next, and financial synergy theory partially, but reject the economic disturbance theory and undervaluation theory.

NOTE

1. See Weston, Chung, and Hoag (1990) for a review of merger theories (pp. 190-217) and related empirical evidence (pp. 249-275).

REFERENCES

Ansoff, K.I. (1965). *Corporate strategy: An analytical approach to business policy for growth and expansion.* New York: Penguin.

Gort, M. (1969). An economic disturbance theory of mergers. *Quarterly Journal of Economics, 83,* 624-642.

Krinsky, I., Rotenberg, W.D. & Thornton, D.B. (1988). Takeovers—A synthesis. *Journal of Accounting Literature,* 243-279

Manne, H.G. (1965). Mergers and the market for corporate control. *Journal of Political Economy, 73,* 110-119.

Palepu, K.G. (1986). Predicting merger targets. *Journal of Accounting and Economics, 8,* 3-55.

Peel, M. (1990). *Liquidation and merger alternatives.* Ashgate UK: Avebury Pub.

Rathinasamy, R.S. (1991). Mergers, debt capacity, and stockholder-bondholder wealth transfer. *Journal of Applied Business Research, 7,* (3), 92-103.

Stevens, J. (1986). *Applied multivariate statistics for the social sciences.* Hillside, NJ: Lawrence Erlbaum.

Tobin, J. (1969). A general equilibrium approach to monetary theory. *Journal of Money, Credit, and Banking* (February), 15-29.

Weston J.F., Chung, K.S., and Hoag, S.E.(1990). *Mergers, restructuring, and corporate control.* Englewood Cliffs, NJ: Prentice-Hall.

MERGERS CAN REDUCE
SYSTEMATIC RISK

Cheng-few Lee and K. Thomas Liaw

ABSTRACT

The motivations for mergers and acquisitions include synergy, undervalued assets, tax considerations, inefficient management, market power, debt capacity, agency problems, reduction in employment risk, and control. Diversification for shareholders has been regarded as a dubious reason for mergers. This is not necessarily correct. It is shown in the paper that, under some conditions, mergers lead to a lower systematic risk, which is beneficial to investors but cannot be achieved on their own homemade portfolios. The systematic risk will be reduced if the market is imperfectly competitive in the case of horizontal mergers. The same benefit can be obtained if there are economies of scope in the case of a conglomerate merger.

Advances in Financial Planning and Forecasting,
Volume 5, pages 347-353.
Copyright © 1994 by JAI Press Inc.
All rights of reproduction in any form reserved.
ISBN:1-55938-421-2

INTRODUCTION

Reasons proposed to explain merger activities include synergy, market power, debt capacity, tax considerations, inefficient management, undervalued assets, agency problems, and control (Silberston, 1972; Sullivan, 1977; Kim, McConnell, and Greenwood, 1977; Brealey and Myers, 1988; Martin, Cox, and MacMinn, 1988). Also, there has been much research in the area of mergers and acquisitions focusing on who benefits from the takeover activities. Jensen and Ruback (1983) summarize the literature and indicate that shareholders of the acquiring firm do not benefit, whereas shareholders of the target firm earn abnormal returns of 20-30 percent for successful attempts. Asquith, Bruner, and Mullins (1983), Dennis and McConnell (1986), and Jarrell and Poulsen (1989) demonstrate the existence of positive gains to the acquiring firms that prior studies had not observed. Martin, Cox, and MacMinn (1988) provide detailed documentation of the literature on the returns and takeover activities.

The risk aspect has not been fully examined. However, the literature seems to suggest that mergers can reduce employment risk for managers of the acquiring firm (Amihud & Lev, 1981) but are not beneficial for shareholders (e.g., Brealey & Myers, 1988). The basic argument is that the combination of two less-than-perfectly-correlated income streams will reduce the variability of these streams and hence reduce the employment risk for the managers of the acquiring firm. However, a merger does not provide diversification opportunities beyond what was available to shareholders before the merger.

This paper employs the capital asset pricing model (CAPM) to show that it is possible, under some conditions, for mergers to reduce systematic risk for stockholders and that this risk reduction is not obtainable by their homemade portfolios. The rest of this paper is organized as follows. The next section investigates risk and horizontal mergers and demonstrates that the outcome depends on the product market structure. The risk facing the shareholders remain the same if the product market is perfectly competitive. On the other hand, the reduction in risk is possible provided that the product market is imperfectly competitive after the merger. The subsequent section derives the relationship between a conglomerate merger and the systematic risk. Risk reduction through mergers is obtained if economies of scope exist. The last section concludes the paper.

HORIZONTAL MERGERS

The main issue studied in this paper is whether mergers can affect the systematic risk that investors take. We begin the examination with horizontal mergers, the combination of firms producing the same products. Suppose that there are N firms, producing a homogeneous product, in this market. The mark price of the product is p_i, the quantity produced by firm i is q_i, the unit variable cost for firm i

is vc_i, and the fixed costs incurred by firm i are F_i. Let R_i denote the return for firm i, Then

$$R_i = [\,(p_i - vc_i)\,q_i] - F_i\,]/V_i$$

where

V_i = expected value of the firm which is

$$\{\,[p_i - vc_i)\,(q_i^e - F_i)\,] - \lambda\ \text{Cov}\,[\,(p_i - vc_i)\,q_i, R_m\,]\,\}\,/\,(1 + r)\,,$$

q_i^e = expected output for firm i,

R_m = return on market portfolio,

Cov = covariance oprator,

λ = market price of risk,

r = risk-free rate.

From the CAPM, the systematic risk of firm i can be expressed as (Narayanaswamy, 1988)

$$\beta_i = \frac{\text{Cov}\,(R_i, R_m)}{\text{Var}\,(R_m)} = \frac{\text{Cov}\,\{\,[\,(p_i - vc_i)\,]\,q_i - F_i\,]\,/\,(V_i, R_m)\,\}}{\text{Var}\,(R_m)}$$

$$= \frac{\text{Cov}\,[\,(p_i - vc_i)\,q_i, R_m\,]}{\text{Var}\,(R_m)\,V_i} \tag{1}$$

where Var is the variance operators.

In expression (1), $(p_i\text{-}vc_i)\,q_i$ is the variable profits for firm i. The covariance between the variable profits and the return on market portfolio affects the beta coefficient. Also, the systematic risk is dependent on the expected value of the firm. The formation of expression (1) is the foundation of the following analysis.

Suppose that there are $n(<N)$ firms in the industry merge. The systematic risk before merger for these n firms is defined as the value-weighted average of their beta coefficients:

$$\beta_n = \frac{\displaystyle\sum_i^n \text{Cov}\,[\,(p_i - vc_i)\,q_i, R_m\,]}{\displaystyle\sum_i V_i\ \text{Var}\,(R_m)} \tag{2}$$

where ΣV_i is the total expected value of these n firms before merger. The systematic risk for the (postmerger) n-merged firm is

$$\beta_{\text{merge}} = \frac{\text{Cov} \left[(p - \text{vc}) \, q, \, R_{\text{m}} \right]}{(V_{\text{merge}}) \, \text{Var} \, (R_{\text{m}})} \tag{3}$$

where p is the postmerger product price, vc is the unit variable cost, and q is the amount of output produced by the merged firm. If the market is perfectly competitive and the merger does not change the market structure, then we obtain

$$\sum_{i=1}^{n} (pq_i - \text{vc}_i q_i) = pq - (\text{vc}) \, q, \quad \sum_{i=1}^{n} V_i = V_{\text{merge}}$$

The variable profits remain the same after the horizontal merger, and the combined value for these n independent firms is the same as that of the merged firm. Therefore, $\beta_n = \beta_{\text{merge}}$, that is, the merger is not beneficial for risk reduction.

Now suppose that the product market is imperfectly competitive after merger, regardless of the premerger market structure. The merger will enhance the market power of the merged firm. As a result, the variable profit will increase. The concept can be demonstrated by comparing the variable profits for a monopolist and for a perfectly competitive firm. A monopolist faces a relatively more inelastic demand curve than a perfectly competitive firm. Hence the monopolist's variable profit is greater than that of a perfectly competitive firm. We could conclude that a firm with a higher market power is accompanied by a higher variable profit, other things being equal. An increase in the variable profits (p–vc) will lower the systematic risk.[1] This can be obtained by differentiating the beta coefficient with respect to the variable profits. The negative relationship between the beta coefficient and market power has also been shown by Chen, Cheng, and Hite (1986) and Subrahmanyam and Thomadakis (1980) using different approaches.

In summary, gains in product market power via mergers will reduce the systematic risk of the firm. The next section will analyze the case of conglomerate mergers.

CONGLOMERATE MERGERS

The risk associated with manager's income is often closely related to the firm's performance. Such risk, the risk of losing job or professional reputation, cannot be effectively diversified in his/her personal portfolios. Conglomerate mergers can be used to stabilize the firm's income stream and hence reduce manager's employment risk (Amihud & Lev, 1981). Is it possible for a conglomerate merger to reduce risk for the shareholders? This is the issue to be examined in this section.

Consider the case when h firms from h different industries merge (conglomerate merger), with one firm from each industry. It is assumed that each firm produces only one product before the merger. After the merger, the merged company is a multiproduct firm. The premerger systematic risk is

$$\beta_h = \frac{\sum\limits_{i}^{h} \text{Cov}\,[\,(p_i - vc_i)\,q_i, R_m]}{\sum\limits_{i} V_i \ \text{Var}\,(R_m)} \tag{4}$$

where β_h is the value-weighted average of firm's beta coefficients and Vi is the expected value of firm beta coefficients and V_i is the expected value of firm i. The systematic risk after merger is

$$\beta_{\text{merge}} = \frac{\sum\limits_{i}^{h} \text{Cov}\,[\,(p_i - vc_i)\,q_i, R_m]}{V_{\text{merge}} \ \text{Var}\,(R_m)} \tag{5}$$

where β_{merge} and V_{merge} are the systematic risk and the value of the merged firm, respectively. Expressions (4) and (5) differ in the denominators only. This is because conglomerate merger does not affect the market structure in each product market. The market conditions and hence the product price in each market remain unchanged. As a result, the total revenue will remain the same. On the cost side, some resources are complementary. For example, a golf equipment store could merge with a ski equipment store to make better use of store capacity and reduce costs. Therefore, a conglomerate merger could possibly affect the total fixed costs and hence the firm value if there exist economies of scope,[2] that is,

$$V_{\text{merge}} \begin{array}{c} > \\ = \\ < \end{array} \sum_{i=1}^{h} V_i, \quad \begin{array}{l} \text{if there are economies of scope} \\ \text{if there are no economies of scope} \\ \text{if there are diseconomies of scope} \end{array}$$

The value of the merged firm will be greater, less than, or equal to the combined value of these h independent firms if there exist economies of scope, diseconomies of scope, or no scope economies.

Comparison of expressions (4) and (5) suggests that the systematic risk is reduced if scope economies exist, since the numerators are the same and the denominator in (5) is greater than that in (4). In the absence of economies of scope or diseconomies of scope, the systematic risk of the merged firm is the same as the value-weighted average systematic risk before mergers, that is, there is no reduction in risk for shareholders.

The important implication is that conglomerate mergers will reduce the systematic risk if there are economies of scope. Therefore, diversification for shareholders is not necessarily a dubious reason for (conglomerate) mergers. Also, divestitures may be beneficial for risk reduction in the presence of diseconomies of scope.

CONCLUSION

Diversification for shareholders or reducing systematic risk has been regarded as a dubious reason for mergers. This is not necessarily correct, as shown in this paper. It is possible to reduce risk for shareholders through mergers. The benefit of risk reduction cannot be obtained by the shareholders via portfolio manipulation.

For horizontal mergers, the risk can be lowered if the market is imperfectly competitive. In the case of conglomerate mergers, the risk will be reduced if economies of scope exist. A conglomerate merger is not beneficial for risk reduction in the presence of diseconomies of scope.

The analysis in the paper assumes that each firm produces only one product before the merger. The model can be extended to the multiproduct firm case before merge. The results then will be determined by the postmerger market power in each product market and the degree of scope economies in multiproduct production.

ACKNOWLEDGMENTS

We thank P. Worthington and M. Wong for valuable comments.

NOTES

1. Lev (1974) and Narayanswamy (1988) use the variable profit as a proxy for operating leverage.
2. See, for example, Panzar and Willig (1981) for the concept of scope economies, and Chang (1988) for the relation to the value of a firm in the context of CAPM.

REFERENCES

Amihud, Y. & Lev, B. (1981). Risk reduction as a managerial motive for conglomerate mergers. *Bell Journal of Economics, 12*, 605-617.

Asquith, P., Bruner, R.F., & Mullins, D.W. Jr. (1983). The gains to bidding firms from mergers. *Journal of Financial Economics,* 121-139.

Brealey, R.A. & Myers, S.C. (1988). *Principles of corporate finance, 3rd ed.* McGraw-Hill.

Chang, P. (1988). Economics of scope, synergy, and the CAPM. *Journal of Financial Research, 11*, 255-263.

Chen, K.C., Cheng, D., & Hite, G.L. (1988). Systemaic risk and market power: An application of Tobin's *q. Quarterly Review of Economics and Business, 26*, 58-72.

Dennis, D.K. & McConnell, J.J. (1986). Corporate mergers and security returns. *Journal of Financial Economics, 15*, 143-187.

Jarrell, G.A. & Poulsen, A.B. (1989). The returns to acquiring firms in tender offers: Evidence from three decades. *Financial Management, 18*, 12-19.

Jensen, M.C. & Ruback, R.S. (1983). The market for corporate control. *Journal of Financial Economics, 12*, 5-50.

Kim, E., McConnell, J., & Greenwood, M. (1977). Corporate mergers and the co-insurance of corporate debt. *Journal of Finance, 32*, 346-363.

Lev, B. (1974). On the association between leverage and risk. *Journal of Financial and Quantitative Analysis, 9*, 627-641.

Martin, J.D., Cox, S.H. and MacMinn, R.D. (1988). *The Theory of Finance*. Florida: Dryden Press.

Narayanaswamy, C.R. (1988). A mean-variance synthesis of corporate financial theory: A note *Journal of Finance, 43*, 529-530.

Panzar, J.C. & Willig, R.D. (1981). Economies of scope. *American Economic Review, 71, 268-272*.

Rubinstein, M.E. (1973). A mean-variance synthesis of corporate financial theory. *Journal of Finance, 28*, 167-182.

Silbertson, A. (1973). Economies of scale in theory and practice. *Economic Journal, 82*, 369-391.

Subrahmanyam, M. & Thomadakis, S. (1980). Systematic risk and the theory of the firm. *Quarterly Journal of Economics, 94*, 437-451.

Sullivan, T. (1977). A note on market power and returns to stockholders. *Review of Economics and Statistics, 59*, 108-113.

GOVERNMENT FINANCING POLICIES FOR SMALL- AND MEDIUM-SIZED BUSINESS IN TAIWAN:
A FURTHER ANALYSIS

Gili Yen and Eva C. Yen

ABSTRACT

In the present study, the authors update Yen's earlier empirical findings and reevaluate the effectiveness of government financing policies for small- and medium-sized businesses (SMBs) in Taiwan implemented over the period from 1972 to 1989. It was found that the past SMB-oriented government financing policies fell short of expectations in the first two subperiods (1972-1976, 1977-1981) and achieved a limited success in the more recent subperiod (1982-1989). Nonetheless, it should be pointed out that the share of banking credit extended to SMBs in the past two decades falls far behind the corresponding share of economic activity undertaken by the SMBs. Viewed from this perspective, much remains to be done.

Advances in Financial Planning and Forecasting,
Volume 5, pages 355-361.
Copyright © 1994 by JAI Press Inc.
All rights of reproduction in any form reserved.
ISBN:1-55938-421-2

RESEARCH BACKGROUND, OBJECTIVE, AND OUTLINE

In recognition of the prominent role played by small- and medium-sized business (hereafter SMB), Yen (1985) provided a chronological listing of government industrial policies implemented over the period 1970-1984 and found that the industrial policies directed toward SMBs were concentrated in the financial area. It was found that the banking system has indeed allotted an increasing share of its loanable funds to SMBs during the period under investigation. In this follow-up study, we make use of more recent data and allow for definitional changes in SMBs to reevaluate the effectiveness of SMB-promoting policies from the financial perspective.

Following this brief description of our research objective, the remaining portion of the paper is organized as follows, the first section delineates advantageous factors facilitating the growth of SMBs. The next section discusses disadvantageous factors limiting the growth of SMBs. Then, drawing on recent studies, we summarize in the latter part of this section the primary problems facing SMBs. The subsequent section reevaluates the overall effectiveness of past SMB-oriented financing policies. Concluding remarks are presented in the final section.

POSITIVE CHARACTERISTICS OF SMBs

Before we turn to the difficulties SMBs face, we must keep in mind that there are several positive characteristics that make them viable.[1] Otherwise, how could we possibly observe so many prosperous SMBs in Taiwan? Although no attempt is made here to exhaust all the possibilities, there are six salient factors worth mentioning:

1. SMBs are usually family-owned and family-operated. This means that decision planning, decision control, and the residual claims are concentrated in a limited number of key family members. Accordingly, agency costs are substantially reduced, if not completely eliminated.[2]
2. In some cases, materials and/or inputs are geographically dispersed. For such SMBs, it does not make economic sense to try to develop into big businesses if the transportation costs of moving materials or inputs exceed the amount of added value thereby created.
3. Similarly, when markets are primarily local or regional, SMBs rather than large businesses emerge.
4. Often the entire production process can be divided into several independent stages, resulting in cost savings. SMBs, under such circumstances, are better able to capture the benefits of specialization.

Table 1. Difficulties Encountered by SMBs[a]

Items Author	Financing	Marketing	Technological Improvement	Other Difficulties Mentioned	Industries Surveyed
Pan (1980)	1	2	3	Materials, business diagnostics, accounting system & financial management, quality control, managerial skills, others	Construction, textiles, transportation equipment, machinery equipment, electronics & electrical machinery, plastics, food, petrochemicals, metal products, others
Chang (1983)	2	1	3	Employee training	Watches and clocks, machine tools and parts, medical instruments and appliances, agricultural machinery and equipment, toys, parts and accessories for transportation equipment, chemical products for particular use, equipment for telecommunications and information systems, metal molds, musical instruments, precision instruments and equipment for measuring and controlling, parts and accessories for electronics, nonmetal furniture and ornaments, machinery for small industries, household electrical appliances
Sheen (1983)	4	—	2	Cutthroat competition (1), high selling expenses (3), management, materials, obsolete machinery, employer-employee relations, inadequate demand	Textiles, electronic products, footwear, machinery, furniture, hardware, plastics, automobile parts, athletic appliances, apparatus, parts, and accessories, toys, works of art & gifts, canned foods
Liu (1983)	2	2	2	Acquisition of information, accounting system, employee training	Cotton textiles, knitted garments, textile garments, wood furniture and ornaments, nonmetal furniture and ornaments, chemical products for particular use, metal molds, agricultural machinery, machinery for small- and medium-sized industries, machine tools, parts and accessories, equipment for telecommunications and information systems, household electrical appliances, electronic parts and accessories, accessory parts for transportation equipment, accuracy instruments for measuring, checking, and controlling

Notes: [a]Numbers in cells or parentheses indicate the order of priority.

Source: Yen (1985).

5. Relatively labor-intensive SMBs are unlikely to try to substitute capital for labor in the production process and so it does not make economic sense for them to try to develop into big businesses.

6. SMBs have a better chance of survival when economies of scale (scope) in production, financing, and marketing operations are nonexistent or unimportant.

These advantageous factors, all together, help explain why SMBs can manage to coexist with big enterprises in numerous industries in Taiwan.

NEGATIVE CHARACTERISTICS OF SMBs

Now, we look at the other side of the coin to see what the major obstacles are to the expansion of SMBs. Because of space limitations, we have summarized the main findings of recent studies concerning Taiwan's SMBs in Table 1. From Table 1, four primary problem areas stand out: (1) poor procurement of funds; (2) .ineffective marketing channels; (3) the slow pace of technical change; and (4) inefficient management. If we think carefully for a moment about these obstructions, we quickly realize that they are interrelated products of a common root: a shortage of funding. Deficiencies in working capital, inadequate resources to invest in research and development, and inefficiency in management can, to some extent, all be attributed to either capital shortage upon establishment or limited borrowing capability thereafter.

It is therefore come to us as no surprise that the government has focused its policies on the financial area. This is the very reason that the effectiveness of SMB-related financial policies was the primary concern in Yen (1985) and will be reevaluated in the present study.

REEVALUATING THE EFFECTIVENESS
OF SMB FINANCING POLICIES

By incorporating more recent data into Yen's original analysis, Table 2 summarizes the percentage of loanable funds of the whole banking system extended to SMBs over the period 1972-1989.

In Table 2, we observe that the banking system has been allotting an increasing share of its loanable funds to SMBs over time. Taken at face value, this finding seems to suggest that governmental policies have indeed helped SMBs obtain a larger portion of loanable funds, and are therefore successful. Before we jump to such a sanguine conclusion, we must examine the problem of defining the SMB. Otherwise, the rosy figures may reflect nothing but a definitional change. It can be legitimately argued that a larger portion of the banking credit is extended to SMBs

Table 2.   Loans of All Banks to SMBs in Taiwan (1972-1989)[a]

Year	Loans to SMBs (NT$Million)	Loans to SMBs as a Percentage of Total Loans (%)
1972	21,719	22.71
1973	34,125	23.11
1974	47,629	23.69
1975	60,797	21.64
1976	70,366	20.76
1977	85,029	23.86
1978	170,641	33.38
1979	191,829	33.01
1980	231,012	31.89
1981	261,701	32.60
1982	317,674	32.50
1983	399,709	34.76
1984	462,386	35.54
1985	506,913	36.00
1986	575,720	37.15
1987	739,421	40.19
1988	1,076,462	41.95
1989	1,346,629	40.74

Notes: [a]Figures for 1972-76 are end of June figures; the rest are year-end figures.

Source: *Financial Statistics*, Ministry of Treasury.

simply because they now include within their ranks a higher percentage of all business establishments.

The definition of SMB has been changed twice during our sample period: the first time in July 1976, when the maximum amount of capital used to define SMBs was raised from NT$10 to 20 million; and in July 1982, when the amount of capital was raised once again from NT$20 to 40 million. In view of these definitional changes, we decided to divide the sample period into three periods: 1972-1976, 1977-1981, and 1982-1989.

Since all numbers are end-of-June figures, data from the first subperiod correspond perfectly to SMBs under the same official definition. It can be seen that SMBs borrowed only 20.76 percent of total loanable funds at the end of June 1976, which is approximately 2 percent lower than the 22.71 percent figure for the end of June 1972. Therefore, SMB-oriented financing policies in this period can be characterized as a failure.

As we move on to the second stage, leaving out 1977 for the time being, we observe a similar pattern. Although the percentage of banking credits extended to SMBs has increased to a level slightly higher than 30 percent as a result of definitional change, on the annual basis we do not observe any significant increase in the period 1978-1981. Moreover, it should be pointed out the biggest jump took place some time around 1977, when the maximum amount of capital used to define SMBs was raised from NT$10 to 20 million. As a consequence, a larger number of SMBs was included. So, we suspect the favorable jump was caused primarily by the definitional change rather than government policies.

Over the period 1982-1989, we do observe a slow yet steady increase in the percentage of loanable funds extended to SMBs. Whether the trend will continue remains to be seen.

Based on the preceding analysis, it seems fair to say that the SMB-oriented financial policies implemented over the first period (1971-1976) and second period (1977-1981) fell short of expectations. In contrast, figures in the third period paint a more optimistic picture. However, it should be emphasized that SMBs in terms of the number of establishment have accounted for more than 90 percent of the Taiwanese economy. Although the figure becomes somewhat smaller when restated in terms of the value of exports, it remains as high as 70 percent. Accordingly, if the marginal efficiency of capital employed by SMBs is superior to or at least on par with that of their larger counterparts as shown in Shea et al. (1985), then it is doubtful that we can call the government policies in question a success.

CONCLUDING REMARKS

In view of the fact that past industrial policies were directed toward making access to financial institutions easier for SMBs, Yen (1985) attempted a preliminary evaluation. In this follow-up study, we reevaluate the effectiveness of SMB-oriented financing policies.

It was found in the present study that past government policies fell short of expectations in the first two periods (1972-1976, 1977-1981) and registered a better record in the more recent period (1982-1989). Nonetheless, it should be pointed out that the share of banking credit extended to SMBs in the past two decades falls far behind the corresponding share of economic activity undertaken by SMBs. Viewed from this perspective, much remains to be done.

NOTES

1. This section and the following section are based primarily on the excellent discussions of White (1982) and four major recent studies dealing with Taiwanese SMBs. For a detailed discussion, the interested readers should consult the cited paper or Yen (1985).

2. For definitions, see Jensen and Meckling (1976); for analysis, see Fama and Jensen (1983a, 1983b).

REFERENCES

Fama, E. F. & Jensen M.C. (1983a). Separation of ownership and control. *Journal of Law and Economics* (April), 301-326.

Fama, E. F. & Jensen M.C. (1983b). Agency problems and residual claims. *Journal of Law and Economics*. (April), 327-350.

Jensen, M., & Meckling, W. (1976). Theory of the firm: Managerial behavior, agency costs, and ownership structure. *Journal of Financial Economics* (October), 305-360.

Pratten, C. (1991). *The competitiveness of small firms*. Cambridge: Cambridge University Press.

Shea et al. (1985). On the financial system in Taiwan. *Economic Papers* No. 65, Chung-Hua Institution for Economic Research, Taipei, Taiwan, Republic of China.

White, L.J. (1982). The determinants of the relative importance of small business. *Review of Economics and Statistics*. (February), 42-49.

Yen, E. C. (1989). *How to promote small- and medium-sized businesses*. Research Report, Division of Small and Medium Business, Ministry of Economic Affairs, Taipei, Taiwan.

Yen, G. (1985). Industrial policies as they relate to SMBs in Taiwan: A financial perspective. *Asian Economic Review* (April and August), 63-83.

INTERNATIONALIZATION OF TAIWAN'S FINANCIAL MARKETS IN THE 1980s

Jia-Dong Shea and Gili Yen

ABSTRACT

This paper examines the internationalization of Taiwan's financial markets in the 1980s. In addition to a brief description of the newly established foreign currency call loan market, this paper considers in detail the accessibility to domestic markets by foreign banks, the establishment of an offshore banking center, and the setting up of foreign branches by domestic banks. The authors have found that, aside from attracting a larger number of foreign banks to establish branches in Taiwan, financial internationalization policies adopted by banking authorities in the 1980s in Taiwan have fallen short of expectations.

OBJECTIVE AND OUTLINE

The Asian Pacific economies are playing an increasingly important role in the changing world economy. It is therefore not surprising that both economists and

Advances in Financial Planning and Forecasting,
Volume 5, pages 363-375.
Copyright © 1994 by JAI Press Inc.
All rights of reproduction in any form reserved.
ISBN:1-55938-421-2

businessmen are paying close attention to the financial and capital markets in the region, including those of Taiwan.

The present study examines some recent developments in the financial markets of Taiwan. Repeatedly, officials and scholars in Taiwan have mentioned "institutionalization," "liberalization," and "internationalization" in their discussion of strategies for further economic development. Institutionalization is too intricate and elusive a concept to be exposed to a simple economic analysis, and will not be dealt with in this paper. Liberalization in the financial area, generally speaking, refers to opening up of the financial sector, the privatization of government-owned banks, elimination of restrictions on the free movement of capital, and loosening regulations on interest rates and/or exchange rates. Internationalization covers relaxation of foreign exchange control, easing of access to domestic financial markets by foreigners, establishment of offshore financing units, setting up of financial institutions abroad, and establishment of foreign currency call loan markets.

In broader terms, internationalization can then be viewed as a part of liberalization. In our opinion, internationalization deserves its own separate treatment for the following two reasons. First, several recent papers by local scholars have already addressed the general issues involved in liberalization of financial markets in the 1980s.[1] Second, and more importantly, internationalization is perhaps the most significant feature of the changing world economy. As Van Horne (1989) rightfully points out in comments about the world and Asian financial markets, "With the ever changing environment, several themes emerge which help us chart the waters ahead. ... The first theme to explore is globalization, a dominant one in many respects." For these reasons, the authors have decided to emphasize the international aspect of financial developments in Taiwan.[2]

This paper is organized as follows. The preceding introductory remarks give a brief description of the importance of financial internationalization and the focus of the present project. The next section reviews the factors that have forced the authorities to embark upon financial internationalization. The following section investigates the accessibility to domestic markets by foreigners. Then the discussion is directed toward the establishment of an offshore banking center in Taiwan. The subsequent section examines recent developments in setting up financial institutions abroad by domestic banks. The next section briefly introduces the Taipei foreign currency call loan market. The final section contains concluding remarks.

THE CAUSES OF FINANCIAL INTERNATIONALIZATION

Several domestic as well as foreign factors have pushed the authorities in Taiwan to move in the direction of financial internationalization.

Domestic Contributing Factors

The bad experience of past regulatory intervention and the changes in the domestic economic and political climates are two major driving forces for financial internationalization. The contributing factors arising from these two forces can be summarized as follows:

1. The private sector has accumulated a great amount of wealth through a high savings rate over the past 30-40 years. The excess of domestic savings over domestic investment in the 1980s, accompanied by huge trade surplus and a rapid expansion of the money supply, have created a serious problem of excess liquidity. A limited variety of domestic financial assets and investment channels can no longer satisfactorily accommodate the demands of asset holders. Their desire to invest in the international financial market has been intensified.
2. As a result of too much liquidity in the mid-1980s, the prices of stocks and of real estate skyrocketed, and the financial investment companies that took deposits illegally from the general public, paying monthly interest rates of 4-9 percent, expanded very quickly. These phenomena not only threatened financial stability, but also endangered social justice, caused deterioration of income and wealth distributions, and sparked speculation. To resolve these problems, providing more legal instruments and investment channels through both financial liberalization and internationalization has become a necessity.
3. In the last few years of his life in the mid-1980s, the late President Chiang Ching-Kuo relaxed social and political control in Taiwan to a great extent. This liberalization movement has spilled over from the political to the economic arena. The call for financial liberalization and internationalization has thus gained additional support.

Foreign Contributing Factors

In the 1970s and early 1980s, financial deregulation became increasingly fashionable in the international community. This trend certainly has boosted the morale of financial reformers and exerted pressure on the conservative decision-makers in Taiwan. More importantly, a huge trade surplus in the 1980s, of which surplus from trade with the United States constituted a major part, ushered in pressure from the outside world, especially from the United States to force Taiwan to open up its domestic financial markets, to have less governmental involvement in the determination of the exchange rate, and to relax foreign exchange controls. Without foreign pressure financial deregulation in Taiwan would undoubtedly have proceeded at a much slower pace.

ACCESSIBILITY TO DOMESTIC FINANCIAL MARKETS BY FOREIGNERS

When U.S. economic aid was about to end in 1965, government authorities began to allow foreign banks to establish branches in Taipei in order to encourage foreign investment. Although foreign banks hesitated to set up branches in Taiwan for both political and economic reasons, the number of local branches of foreign banks increased gradually from 1 in 1964 to 13 in 1979.

The termination of formal diplomatic relations with the United States in 1978 and the withdrawal from the IMF in 1980 spurred the authorities to allow foreign banks, especially European ones, easier access to domestic financial markets. One of the main purposes was to strengthen economic ties with the outside world; the other was to improve domestic banking operations through competition and technology transfer. With the easier access, 25 more local branches of foreign banks have been added since 1980, bringing the total number of such branches to 38 at the end of 1989. (See Table 1 for the number of local branches of foreign banks and geographical distribution of their mother companies.)

As indicated by Table 1, the number of foreign banks remains small in Taiwan, yet the number has been growing steadily and there were nearly three times as many branches in 1989 as in 1979.

In addition to the banking business, the insurance market and securities market have opened for foreigners. Every year since 1986, 2 life and 2 property insurance firms from the United States have been permitted entry into the Taiwan market. Under the 1988 Securities and Exchange Law, foreign nationals may participate

Table 1.   Local Branches of Foreign Banks (1978-89)

		Geographical Areas		
	Number of Branches	*North America*	*Europe*	*Southeast Asia and Others*
1978	13	9	0	4
1979	13	9	0	4
1980	21	12	5	4
1981	24	14	6	4
1982	25	15	6	4
1983	28	16	7	5
1984	31	16	9	6
1985	32	16	10	6
1986	33	16	10	7
1987	35	17	11	7
1988	35	16	12	7
1989	38	16	13	9

Source: Central Bank of China, R.O.C., *Financial Statistics Monthly,* various issues.

in the securities business through investment in and management of local securities firms. Moreover, there is no restriction on foreign investment in securities investment consulting companies. In June 1989, the Securities and Exchange Commission took further steps by accepting the applications of foreign securities firms to establish local branches in Taiwan.

Aside from policies meant to make entry easier for foreign financial institutions, the government authorities in Taiwan have also gradually relaxed restrictions regarding the operations of foreign banks. An alternative measure—and, in our judgment a more accurate measure of accessibility to domestic financial markets by foreigners—is the relative share of banking activities over time. Before we analyze business activities of local branches of foreign banks, however, some discussion on the imposition and relaxation of restrictions on banking operations is necessary.

To protect domestic banks and maintain financial stability, the authorities in Taiwan have put strict control on the operations of local branches of foreign banks. However, in company with the relaxation of entry barriers, some of the operational restrictions have been lifted in recent years. The major changes include the following:

1. According to the revised banking law in July 1989, foreign bank branches are permitted, upon approval by the Ministry of Finance, to set up savings and trust departments, through which they can accept passbook savings and time savings deposits, extend long-term loans, and apply for licenses as securities underwriters, brokers, and dealers.
2. If a foreign bank has been operating a branch for more than 5 years and the branch has not been punished for violating the relevant provisions of the banking law in the latest year, it may apply to establish an additional branch in another city (Taipei or Kaohsiung). This change was adopted in October 1989.
3. The restriction that foreign banks are not allowed to receive time deposits of over 6 months was abolished in October 1986.
4. Since April 1985 foreign banks have been permitted to extend their lending operations to cover individuals as well as enterprises.
5. To help foreign banks manage their reserve positions, the Central Bank of China has provided access to secured short-term accommodation facilities since March 1985, in addition to the unsecured short-term accommodation facilities already open to them.
6. Local branches of American banks were permitted in 1986 to participate in the Join Credit Information System of the Bankers' Association in Taipei, enabling them to issue credit cards.

Although several of the above deregulatory policies were adopted under pressure from foreign countries, they without doubt have contributed to the develop-

Table 2.   The Share of Local Branches of Foreign Banks
in Depository Financial Institutions[a] (in NT $ Million)

End of Year	Total Assets		Total Deposits		Loans and discounts	
	Amount	%	Amount	%	Amount	%
1980	94,436	6.08	3,618	0.36	85,584	8.40
1981	143,274	7.63	5,116	0.43	112,804	9.82
1982	173,491	7.34	7,662	0.51	104,419	7.76
1983	192,418	6.72	11,730	0.61	101,144	6.38
1984	216,624	6.43	18,410	0.79	104,285	5.83
1985	223,447	5.55	29,488	1.03	99,392	5.18
1986	218,387	4.45	26,822	0.77	117,473	5.57
1987	275,867	4.71	42,706	1.00	135,842	5.47
1988	236,583	3.53	53,646	1.04	150,780	4.46
1989	284,353	3.53	66,385	1.06	194,469	4.50

Notes: [a]Depository financial institutions include domestic banks, local branches of foreign banks, medium business banks, credit cooperative associations, and credit departments of farmers' and fishermen's associations.

Source: Central Bank of China, R.O.C., *Annual Report of the Operations of Financial Institutions, Taiwan District, R.O.C.*, various issues.

ment of the financial system in Taiwan by enhancing market competition and introducing financial know-how. More importantly, the opening up of domestic financial markets to foreign participants has also provided ammunition for local scholars and the general public to ask the authorities to open up the markets for local participants as well.

Table 2 summarizes the asset holdings and the activities of local branches of foreign banks for the most recent 10 years.

Contrary to what we found in Table 1 regarding the number of branches, we see in Table 2 that the share of net total assets of local branches of foreign banks has been steadily declining in the 1980s. This is a somewhat surprising development in the presence of the less strict regulatory environment for the branches. In our opinion, it is largely the result of the combined influence of worldwide sluggish business conditions, the continuing appreciation of the New Taiwan dollar, and bad business judgment due partly to ignorance of Taiwan's business climate and partly to misdemeanor, or fraud, by local borrowers. Despite the negative trend, the asset shares of foreign banks might yet increase if the government continues to deregulate foreign bank activities. Particularly important is whether the Ministry of Finance goes through with plans declared in July 1987 to permit foreign banks to receive savings deposits and engage in trust business.

ESTABLISHMENT OF AN
OFFSHORE BANKING CENTER

Given that foreign exchange control cannot be lifted completely in the near future, high-ranking government officials have viewed the establishment of an offshore banking center as a major step toward financial internationalization. The idea was initiated in 1982 with the primary purpose of raising funds from international financial markets and lending them to foreigners and nonresident domestic borrowers. It was hoped that through this endeavor Taiwan could emerge as a financial center in the Far East. Additional motivations for the project included (1) improving the managerial efficiency of domestic banks by greater exposure to the international financial market, and (2) providing training and education for the staffs of domestic banks to familiarize them with the operation of international financing.

According to Article 4 of the Regulatory Code of Offshore Banking, offshore banking can be operated through branches only and the scope of its operation is limited to the following:

1. Receiving foreign deposits from nonresident individuals, legal persons, or governmental agencies.
2. Receiving foreign deposits from financial institutions.
3. Borrowing funds from international financial markets.
4. Lending funds through international financial markets.
5. Buying or selling foreign currencies; acceptance is also allowed.
6. Extending loans to individuals, legal persons, governmental agencies, or financial institutions.
7. Managing debt and keeping books for loans lent in the form of foreign currencies.

Additionally, in handling foreign deposits, the receiving offshore branch is not allowed to receive foreign deposits in cash form or to pay withdrawn deposits in NT dollars (Article 7). Finally, to keep the existing foreign exchange management system intact, the offshore branches are not allowed to conduct money transaction or money exchange in cases where a conversion between foreign currencies and NT dollars is involved except with approval form the Central Bank of the Republic of China (Article 8).

After two years of preparation, the International Commercial Bank of China set up the first offshore banking unit in June 1984, followed by 4 other domestic commercial banks and 2 foreign banks later in the same year. At the end of December 1989, there were 23 offshore banking units established by 11 domestic banks and 12 foreign banks. As shown in Table 3, the total assets of offshore banking units increased from U.S.$ $4,262 million at the end of 1984 to U.S.$ $16,686 million at the end of 1989. Judging from the number of offshore banking units and total assets, the size of the offshore banking center in Taiwan is still relatively small.

Table 3. Structure of Assets and Liabilities of Offshore Banking Units   (Unit: %)

End of Month	No. of OBU	Total Assets= Total Liabilities (US$ million)	Loans to Non-financial Institutions (%) Residents	Loans to Non-financial Institutions (%) Nonresidents	Portfolio Investment (%)	Claims of Financial Institutions (%) Subtotal	Domestic Banks	Inter OBU	Foreign Financial Institutions	Other Assets (%)
December 1984	7	4,262	1.27	1.52	1.65	94.27	9.46	12.27	72.36	1.29
June 1985	8	5,262	1.40	1.17	1.49	94.44	6.15	3.43	84.87	1.50
December 1985	11	6,572	1.73	0.91	3.07	92.73	6.73	2.56	83.44	1.84
June 1986	13	5,905	1.57	11.79	9.78	75.08	11.85	0.79	62.44	1.77
December 1986	15	6,208	1.45	9.72	10.78	76.85	37.95	4.40	34.50	1.20
June 1987	15	7,636	1.06	7.47	9.11	81.10	60.16	2.47	18.48	1.26
December 1987	16	11,690	0.62	4.61	7.41	85.36	67.19	5.05	13.11	2.00
June 1988	20	11,335	0.61	4.33	6.56	86.77	58.21	1.63	26.93	1.73
December 1988	20	12,738	0.55	3.17	4.79	89.47	59.53	2.67	27.27	2.02
June 1989	20	12,852	0.50	2.82	4.26	90.47	63.43	4.43	22.40	1.95
December 1989	23	16,686	0.36	2.15	3.57	92.43	50.69	4.01	37.73	1.49

End of Month	Deposits of Non-Financial Institutions (%)	Due to Financial Institutions (%) Subtotal (%)	Domestic Banks	Inter-OBU	Foreign Financial Institutions	Securities Issued (%)	Other Liabilities (%)
December 1984	0.36	98.91	58.83	12.27	27.82	0	0.73
June 1985	0.45	98.42	71.03	3.43	23.98	0	1.13
December 1985	0.49	98.51	76.90	2.56	19.05	0	1.00
June 1986	0.60	97.69	62.67	0.79	34.24	0	1.70
December 1986	0.69	98.24	33.50	4.40	60.35	0	1.07
June 1987	0.58	98.13	23.25	2.47	72.42	0	1.29
December 1987	0.85	97.62	7.08	5.05	85.49	0	1.53
June 1988	0.97	97.71	13.96	1.63	82.12	0	1.32
December 1988	0.94	97.81	12.81	2.67	82.33	0	1.25
June 1989	1.71	96.72	8.51	4.33	83.88	0	1.57
December 1989	2.37	96.45	26.71	3.96	65.78	0	1.18

A closer examination of the structure of assets and liabilities in Table 3 reveals the following:

1. Interbank transactions constitute the lion's share of the financial activities of offshore banking units. More than 96 percent of the liabilities are due to financial institutions, and the share of claims on financial institutions on the assets side has been maintained at a level never less than 75 percent. On the other hand, the shares of deposits of nonresidents and loans to nonresidents are comparatively very low.

2. By definition, the offshore banking center is an outside-to-outside financial market, that is, the offshore banking units are supposed to use the money collected from abroad to finance the needs of the outside world. Before June 1986, however, the major function of the offshore banking units in Taiwan had been simply to rede posit the foreign exchange of domestic banks into foreign financial institutions. Since June 1986, the offshore banking units have reversed the trend, borrowing from foreign financial institutions to meet the demand of domestic banks. Note that since 1984 the financial institutions in Taiwan have been inundated with deposits due to the huge trade surplus. As a result the offshore banking units set up by domestic banks naturally became the channel to make use of the accumulated foreign exchange. However, when the Central Bank of China's intention of maintaining a slow, steady appreciation of the New Taiwan dollar relative to the U.S. dollar became clear, the domestic banks joined the speculators in borrowing heavily from abroad, again through their offshore banking units. The offshore banking units have in fact become a tool for foreign exchange speculation by the domestic banks.

From figures on either the assets of liabilities side, we see then that the primary business activities lie in interbank transactions, and that the original goal of obtaining funds and utilizing them outside the country's border has not been effectively achieved. Worse yet, in a time when exchange rates fluctuate over a wide range and are subject to intervention by the central bank, shrewd domestic bankers can obtain substantial capital gains at the expense of the central bank. When that happens, the offshore banking units come close to being just a bastion of speculation for domestic banks. Based on the observations above, it seems fair to say that although the policy of establishing offshore units was a right one, the results have been far from satisfactory.

SETTING UP FINANCIAL INSTITUTIONS ABROAD

Setting up financial institutions abroad is regarded as one of the most effective means of internationalizing the financial sector. Unfortunately, Taiwan's development in this respect is also unsatisfactory.

Following the structure of the previous two sections, let us discuss briefly the necessity and objectives of setting up financial institutions abroad before we move on to analyze the current state of affairs.

Generally speaking, commercial banks in the early stages of developing overseas can establish relationships with foreign banks to help conduct international operations. However, if business picks up and the market diversifies geographically, it can become economically attractive for commercial banks to launch their own overseas units. The establishment of such units can help achieve both long-term and short-term objectives.

Concerning the long-term objectives, the following three goals stand out: (1) To become a global bank and take part in global financial transactions, (2) to enlarge the service area and, by doing so, improve the quality of domestic service, obtain funds at more attractive terms, and achieve a better balance of foreign exchange holdings, (3) to accumulate and diversity assets. In view of Taiwan's huge foreign reserves, it is reasonable to expect commercial banks to be large net lenders through their foreign operations.[3]

As for short-term objectives, the following four are most often mentioned: (1) to cultivate staff expertise in the area of international financing, (2) to provide more attractive services to commerce and industry, (3) to enlarge the channels of obtaining funds abroad, (4) to tighten control of funds used in foreign countries so that the undesirable outcomes of either fund excesses or fund shortages can be better avoided.

At the end of 1989, only 5 banks had set up a total of 24 overseas financial institutions, including 15 branches, 6 representative offices and 3 subsidiaries abroad. The geographic distribution of these institutions was as follows: United States (8), Japan (2), Singapore (2), Panama (2), Australia (1), Canada (1), France (1), West Germany (2), United Kingdom (1), the Philippines (1), Saudi Arabia (1), Thailand (1) and Benin (1). Their major function has been providing trade-related financial services for trading firms, and most of their customers are overseas Chinese.

The following factors have hindered the establishment of financial institutions abroad:

1. Most of Taiwan's principal trading partners and the countries in which major international financial centers are located have broken formal diplomatic ties with the Republic of China. Therefore, domestic banks lack the official channels to negotiate with foreign authorities to set up branches.

2. The top authorities in Taiwan have long been very conservative in promoting the establishment of overseas financial institutions. Guidelines for screening and approving domestic banks' applications to establish overseas financial institutions have never been provided. The authorities have usually turned down applications with a "let's discuss it later," response without giving explanations. Moreover, the government has seldom

invoked the reciprocity principle to ensure that countries that have been allowed to set up branches or representative offices in the Republic of China accept our financial institutions.

3. Most of the important banks that are capable and in need of setting up overseas branches are government owned. The limitations facing the government-owned banks have handicapped domestic banks' ability to compete effectively with foreign banks in foreign countries. Moreover, some countries do not encourage the government banks from the Republic of China to set up branches in their territory for political reasons.

4. Until recently, direct investment abroad was not encouraged. As a result, there are only a few big companies from the Republic of China operating internationally and the demand for the services of overseas financial institutions is hence limited.

Recently, applications to set up more overseas financial institutions by the First Commercial Bank, Hua-nan Commercial Bank, Chang-hua Commercial Bank, and United World Chinese Commercial Bank have been approved in principle by the Ministry of Finance. More applications are expected to follow after the further relaxation of foreign exchange controls. However, if both the short-term and long-term goals of setting up financial institutions abroad are to be achieved, the hindering factors mentioned in this section need to be effectively conquered.

ESTABLISHMENT OF THE TAIPEI FOREIGN CURRENCY CALL LOAN MARKET

The Taipei foreign currency call loan market was set up on August 7, 1989, in order to better use the foreign exchange reserves held by the central bank, to improve the efficiency of the management of foreign exchange funds held by the authorized foreign exchange banks, as well as to promote Taipei as an international financial center. The central bank allocates part of its foreign exchange reserves to finance the authorized foreign exchange banks to conduct transactions through the call loan market. Many local branches of foreign banks are also transacting in the market.

The daily transaction volume has increased rapidly from U.S.$122 million on the first day to an average of U.S$729 million and U.S.$586 million, respectively, in February and March 1990. The outstanding balance of total borrowings in the market reached about U.S.$4.8 billion at the end of April 1990, and the maturities ranged widely from overnight to 6 months. It appears that the foreign currency call loan market still has ample room for expansion.

CONCLUDING REMARKS

In this paper, the recent developments of Taiwan's financial markets were investigated from an international perspective. Specifically, the accessibility to domestic markets by foreign banks, the establishment of an offshore banking center, and the setting up of foreign branches by domestic banks were examined in some detail.

It was found that, other than attracting a larger number of local branches of foreign banks, policy changes in the area of international financing have fallen short of expectations. Based on such findings, it seems safe to say that, unless drastic action is taken by authorities in Taiwan to improve the far from satisfactory state of the highly regulated and the predominantly government-owned banking system, the goal of internationalizing Taiwan's financial markets will remain beyond our reach.

Afterward

Since this paper was finished in July 1990, Taiwan's financial internationalization has continued rapidly. Domestic banks have been actively expanding into various world financial and trading centers, with a total of 26 branches, 14 representative offices, and 5 subsidiaries having been established overseas by 10 domestic banks as of March 1992. Meanwhile the number of OBUs has increased to 34 as of June 1992, with total assets amounting to approximately U.S.$25.2 billion. The scope of the Taipei foreign currency call loan market in terms of transaction volume, eligible participants, tradable currencies, and degree of integration with Singapore, Hong Kong, and Tokyo has also greatly expanded, and the authorities have made serious attempts to develop Taipei into a regional financial center in Asia. For these recent developments, the readers are referred to Samuel C. Shieh's speech, "Financial Liberalization and Internationalization: The Development of Taipei as a Regional Financial Center in Asia," delivered at a meeting sponsored by the Royal Institute of International Affairs, April 15, 1992, in London; and to Kuo-Shu Liang and Ching-ing Hou Liang, "Challenges in the 1990s for Banking and Financing Markets in Taiwan," *Journal of Asian Economics* (Fall 1991), pp. 399-413.

ACKNOWLEDGMENTS

The authors are indebted to J.T. Chen, M.T. Chen, R. Harbaugh, and especially C.F. Lee for their generous assistance in preparing this draft.

NOTES

1.   Among others, Lee and Peng (1985), Lee and Tsai (1988), Chang (1989), and Kuo (1989) are eminent examples.

2.   Since we are primarily concerned with the international financial interaction between Taiwan's financial markets and world financial markets, the relaxation of foreign exchange control, which is more closely related to aggregate output and the employment level, is not discussed in detail.

3. On top of these three goals, some government officials view establishing financial institutions abroad as an effective means of promoting de facto diplomatic recognition.

REFERENCES

Chang, Chi-Cheng. (1989). Financial liberalization in the Republic of China. Keynote speech, the Inaugural International Conference on Asian-Pacific Financial Markets, Taipei, Taiwan, Republic of China, March 13-15.

Kuo, Shirley (1989). Liberalization of the financial market in Taiwan in the 1980s. Keynote speech, the Inaugural International Conference on Asian-Pacific Financial Markets, Taipei, Taiwan, Republic of China, March 13-15.

Lee, Yung-San & Peng, Huai-nan. (1985). Financial liberalization in Taiwan, R.O.C. In *Proceedings of the Annual Conference on Industrial Policies of the Republic of Korea and the Republic of China*, Conference Series 86-01, Korea Development Institute, Seoul, Republic of Korea, November.

Lee, Yung-San & Tsai, Tzong-rong. (1988). Development of financial system and monetary policies in taiwan. In *Proceedings of Conference on Economic Development Experiences of Taiwan and Its New Role in an Emerging Asia-Pacific Area*, Institute of Economics, Academia Sinica, Taipei, Taiwan, Republic of China, June 8-10.

Shea, Jia-Dong. (1988). Internationalization of the financial sector in Taiwan, Republic of China. In *Proceedings of Annual Conference on Industrial Policies of the Republic of Korea and the Republic of China*, Seoul, Republic of Korea, February.

Van Horne, James (1989). Changing world and Asian financial markets. Keynote speech, the Inaugural International Conference on Asian-Pacific Financial Markets, Taipei, Taiwan, Republic of China, March 13-15.

THE INFORMATION CONTENT OF PRICE-BASED EARNINGS FORECASTS

Srinivasan Kannan and J. Kenton Zumwalt

ABSTRACT

Prior research provides evidence that stock prices change in anticipation of analysts' revisions of earnings forecasts. In addition, studies that have examined "the information contents of security prices" in the forecasting of corporate earnings conclude that stock price information produces better forecasts of earnings per share than models that use only historical EPS information. This study uses a stock-price-based methodology developed by Beaver, Lambert, and Morse to provide EPS forecasts that are compared with the EPS forecasts of financial analysts. The results support much of the earlier empirical work and indicate that although analysts' forecasts are not completely reflected in market prices, prices reflect most of the information contained in analysts' expectations.

INTRODUCTION

Research pertaining to the predictability of corporate earnings typically falls into one of two categories: an analysis or comparison of alternative statistical forecasting models, or a comparison of statistical forecasts with the forecasts of

Advances in Financial Planning and Forecasting,
Volume 5, pages 377-392.
Copyright © 1994 by JAI Press Inc.
All rights of reproduction in any form reserved.
ISBN:1-55938-421-2

financial analysts. Early statistical forecasting models generally use extrapolations of historical data of forecast earnings per share (EPS), while later studies utilize ARIMA time series models and quarterly earnings per share data in forecast analyses. These research efforts generally conclude that the earnings series can best be described as random-walk processes or random-walk-with-drift.[1]

More recently, the forecasts of both the simple extrapolation of historical data and the ARIMA models have been compared with the forecasts of financial analysts. These more current studies indicate that financial analysts outperform the extrapolative and/or time-series models.[2] Beaver, Lambert, and Morse (1980; hereafter BLM) examine "The Information Content of Security Prices" in the forecasting of corporate EPS. Their interest is in determining "whether analysts provide information via their forecasts which is not already reflected in security prices." The BLM study examines whether stock prices can be used with historical EPS data to improve EPS forecasting ability. They conclude that, indeed, security prices contain information use in predicting EPS.

In an update, Beaver, Lambert, and Ryan (1987) take "a second look" at the information content issue. Utilizing a more efficient method of data analysis, their empirical results support the earlier study: "[P]rice changes reflect information earlier than earnings do."

Both BLM "information content" studies compare the efficacy of a price-based earnings prediction model with earnings predictions based solely on past earnings. Since price movements reflect changes in market perceptions and financial analysts influence these perceptions with the publication of earnings forecasts, it remains to be seen if the price-based forecasts can outperform the forecasts of analysts. In fact, BLM suggest future research to examine whether financial analysts provide information not already found in security prices.

This study follows BLM's suggestion: First. the BLM model is used to develop EPS forecasts for companies in the electric utility industry. Then, these forecasts are compared with the forecasts of analysts as reported by the Institutional Brokers Estimate System (IBES) in order to determine whether security prices provide information not already reflected in IBES analysts' forecasts.

A BRIEF LITERATURE REVIEW

Givoly and Lakonishok (1984) observe that after stock recommendations, earnings forecasts are probably the second most important output of security analysts. They also note the results of an earlier study by Fried and Givoly (1982), which "suggests that analysts utilize a considerable amount of information which is independent of the time series and cross-sectional properties of the earnings series captured by the two naive model."

In a test of market reaction to forecast revisions, Givoly and Lakonishok report significant abnormal returns in the month preceding the revision, in the month of the revision, and in the two months following the revision. Their finding indicates that price changes may precede earnings forecast revisions.[3] They conclude that: (1) analysts' forecasts outperform mechanical prediction models that only utilize historical earnings; (2) investors use analysts' earnings forecasts to predict future returns; and (3) the forecasts are useful for formulating profitable investment strategies.

While studies prior to the Givoly and Lakonishok study have shown that analysts' forecasts outperform forecasting models that use only historical data, the results also suggest that stock prices may be useful in predicting subsequent earnings.

Brown, Foster, and Noreen (1985) observe, "An important but unresolved issue is the extent to which analysts use prior security returns as a basis for revising their earnings forecasts." They then provide evidence that stock price movements precede EPS forecast revisions by analysts.

Stickel (1990) and Abaranell (1991) provide evidence on the impact of the relationship between security price changes and analyst forecast revisions. Stickel reports that while the change in security prices is significantly related to subsequent forecast revisions, changes in the consensus forecasts and deviations of the individual analyst forecast from the consensus forecast account for most of the explanatory power. The three variables explain approximately 38% of the variation in individual analyst forecast revisions. Abarbanell observes that the sign and magnitude of analyst forecast revisions is positively associated with the sign and magnitude of prior security price changes. He reports that "the empirical evidence fails to support the hypothesis that analysts' forecasts fully incorporate prior price changes." The Stickel and Abarbanell studies provide evidence that, although prior price changes impact analyst forecast revisions, the revisions do not fully incorporate price change information.

The studies of Cragg and Malkeil (1968, 1982) and Malkiel and Cragg (1970) were among the first to investigate the relationship between analysts' predictions and stock prices. They reported that security analysts' expectations were "quickly and thoroughly impounded into the prices of securities."

In a similar vein, the impact of new information on stock prices was the focus of a study by Bjerring, Lakonishok, and Vermaelen (1983; BLV). BLV report that the recommendations produced by a major Canadian brokerage firm achieved positive abnormal returns during the period being considered. Unlike the results reported by Cragg and Malkiel, BLV report that "the information content of the recommendations is not 'immediately' reflected in market prices" and "market prices adjust to new information only if informed investors have enough clout to adjust the market price." Finally, BLV observe that "although the *data* may be publicly available, the *information* content is clearly not."

However, as pointed out by Brown, Richardson, and Schwager (1987), the *reason* for analysts' superiority is not well understood. The dimensionality of the information set used by financial analysts and the timing of the market's reaction to new information have been suggested as reasons for the predictive superiority of financial analysts. In a related study, Kross, Ro, and Schroeder (1990) provide insight on why analysts should outperform models based on only historical information. Specifically, they argue that analysts enjoy an information advantage when the earnings stream is highly variable.

A number of studies have examined whether forecasting accuracy can be improved by combining analysts' forecasts with forecasts from time-series models and/or information from security prices. Newbold, Zumwalt, and Kannan (1987) report that short-term earnings forecasts are improved by combining analysts' forecasts with those from a time-series model. However, Chatfield, Hein, and Moyer (1990) examine the electric utility industry and report that long-term earnings forecasts by analysts cannot be improved through a combined model.

Brown, Hagerman, Griffin, and Zmigewski (1987; BHGZ) use a regression procedure to examine measurement errors associated with a number of alternative proxies for forecasts of corporate earnings unexpected by the market at the time of the earnings announcement. They first examine the proxies individually and then combine the proxies. BHGZ report that *Value Line* analysts' earnings forecasts outperform forecasts generated by time-series models, that measurement error is reduced when forecasts are combined, and that when stock returns over a prior period are included in the model, measurement error is further reduced. Hence, combining analysts' forecasts and stock price information produces lower measurement errors.

O'Brien (1988) examines the timing of analysts' forecasts in order to determine if more current forecasts contain less forecast error than consensus forecasts. She reports that the more current the forecast, the more accurate it is, and that the most current forecast is more accurate than either the mean or median of the IBES forecasts. She also finds the forecasts of analysts to be more accurate than those of time-series models. O'Brien also observes that when the most out-of-date forecasts is eliminated, accuracy can be improved by aggregating forecasts.

Ou and Penman (1989) use 68 account variables and regression procedures to develop a measure to assess the probability of one-year-ahead earnings increase. They report that P/E ratios provide information about future earnings and that accounting statements provide similar earnings information. They suggest their empirical results show that accounting information filters out transitory earnings components. While "price changes reflect information about future earnings, they also reflect transitory elements of current earnings that are negatively correlated with future earnings changes." Butler and Lang (1991) present evidence that analysts' earnings forecasts are persistently optimistic or pessimistic relative to consensus forecasts. They conclude that the optimism or pessimism relative to consensus forecasts persists over time.

Ali, Klein, and Rosenfeld (1992; AKR) use market information in examining analysts' forecast errors. They report that the prior year's stock return is significantly positively related to forecast errors. This indicates past stock price information is not being used efficiently by the analysts. AKR also find that forecast errors exhibit significantly positive serial correlation. They also report the existence of bias, which indicates that the time-series properties of earnings are not properly recognized by analysts. AKR indicate analysts can partially differentiate between permanent and temporary components of reported earnings.

The studies mentioned above appear to have contradictory conclusions. The real difference is perhaps in the degree to which information is reflected in prices. BLM hypothesize that prices convey information about future earnings that is not conveyed by past earnings in their analysis. The methodology used by BLM is designed to "infer market participants' expectations regarding future earnings from observed changes in security prices." Most research prior to BLM had inferred a stochastic earnings-generated process from observing only past earnings. The BLM results indicate security prices contain information that is not contained in historical earning data.

In the follow-up study of Beaver, Lambert, and Ryan, a reverse regression procedure is used to increase the efficiency of the analyses. Their results support the earlier BLM study, which indicates prices can be used to develop better EPS forecasts than models that use only historical EPS.

In a related study, Pari, Carvell, and Sullivan (1989) report statistically significant relationships between firm P/E ratios and IBES forecasts of earnings growth. Their report lends support to BLM's notion that information about future earnings can be elicited from current stock prices.

As mentioned earlier, Abarbanell (1991) used *Value Line* EPS forecasts to examine the relationship between security price changes and subsequent analyst forecast revisions. Abarbanell concludes that "a positive association between price changes and subsequent earnings forecasts exist [*sic*] whether or not the price changes are combined with analyst private signals to formulate their forecasts." He observes that this is consistent with analysts forming forecast revisions without utilizing all price change information available.

Lys and Sohn (1990) utilize changes in analysts' earnings forecast with market return data to examine the information content of analyst forecast revisions. They observe that because of analyst-specific factors, a particular news event does not result in simultaneous earnings estimate revisions by all analysts. They conclude that, "individual analyst forecasts are informative [but] contain only roughly 66 percent of the information reflected by security prices."

DESIGN OF THE STUDY

The Beaver-Lambert-Morse Model

The model developed by BLM is designed to "infer a characterization of the stochastic process generating earnings, as *perceived by market participants*" (emphasis in original). BLM observe that the expected value of future earnings conditional on past earnings will not equal the expected value of future earnings conditional on past earnings *and* past prices if earnings are the result of a compound process involving more than one stochastic variable. Stated mathematically::

$$E\left(X_{t+k} \mid X_t, X_{t-1}, \ldots\right) \neq E\left(X_{t+k} \mid P_t, X_t, P_{t-1}, X_{t-1}, \ldots\right)$$

where E is the expectations operator, X refers to reported earnings per share, and P refers to price share.

BLM point out that actual earnings per share may be a compound process. In this case, X_t, the observed earnings, may be viewed as: $X_t = x_t + e_t$, where x_t is the earnings series, which also reflects price-affecting events, and e_t represents the impact on earnings of events or adjustments that have no impact on security prices. That is BLM divide reported earnings into the portion related to price and the portion unrelated to price.

Information regarding x that cannot be extracted from the X due to the compound process can now be obtained from P since the price conveys information about x. Stated differently, price P_t is directly impacted by changes in x_t, but not by changes in e_t.

Based on this reasoning, BLM developed the following forecasting model:

$$F\left(X_{t+1}\right) = F\left(g_{t+1} \mid P_t/X_t\right) X_t + X_t = \left[1 + F\left(g_{t+1} \mid P_t/X_t\right)\right] X_t$$

This formula shows that the forecast $F(X_{t+1})$ for observable earnings at period $t + 1$ is a function of the forecasted growth for the period given the P/E ratio at time t.

It should be noted that the BLM model uses observable earnings X instead of the more appropriate, but unobservable x. This creates an errors-in-variables problems that is minimized by using a grouping procedure in the empirical analysis.

BLM compared the forecasts generated by this model with those from a random-walk-with-drift model:

$$F(X^{t+1}) = X_t + d_t$$

where d_t is the security-specific drift term and is the average of earnings changes over prior years. They use the mean absolute error and the mean squared error to measure forecast accuracy and conclude that, indeed, the price-based model outperforms the model based solely on historical earnings information.

In contrast to the comparison of a price-based forecasting model with a random-walk-with-drift model, this study compares the forecasts of the BLM model with those of financial analysts.

The Data

Consensus EPS estimates for electric utilities from IBES are used as the analysts' forecasts. Price and earnings data from the Compustat tapes are used to develop a forecasting model similar to the one used by BLM. To obtain the BLM model, P/E ratios and earnings growth rates are calculated annually for all NYSE and AMEX firms with December fiscal year-end data available on the Compustat tapes from 1965 through 1987.

P/E Model Forecasts

Following the procedures used by BLM, all firms are ranked from high to low with respect to the P/E ratio and grouped into 10 portfolios. Each year the firms are reranked and portfolios are reformed.

The growth in EPS for each stock is calculated and the median growth rate for each portfolio of stocks is determined. This produces 10 earnings growth rates for each year—one growth rate for each portfolio. Historical EPS growth rates are used to develop the forecast for future earnings growth. For example, the median growth rate for the fourth portfolio for the 1966-1975 period is used as the growth rate expected in 1976 for those stocks that were assigned to Portfolio 4 at the end of December 1975. The forecasted earnings for 1976 are

$$EPS_{76} = EPS_{75}(1 + g_4)$$

where g_4 is the 10-year median growth rate for portfolio 4.

METHODS OF ANALYSIS

Two methods are used to evaluate the predictive effectiveness of the P/E-based forecasts and the forecasts of the IBES analysts. First, the mean absolute error (MABE), the mean squared error (MSE), and the MSE components are used to examine the forecasts errors. Second, a two-step regression procedure is used to determine if the forecasts of the P/E model contain information not found in the analysts' forecasts, and vice versa.

Measurement of Forecast Errors

As indicated above, both the MABE and MSE are utilized in the measurement of the forecast errors. In addition, following Mincer and Zarnowitz (1969), the MSE is divided into its components of bias, inefficiency, and random error in order to determine possible reasons for the forecast error. The MABE is calculated as

$$MABE = \frac{1}{n} \sum_{i=1}^{n} |P_i - A_i|$$

where P_i and A_i are the predicted and actual earnings for the ith firm and n is the number of firms.

The MSE is calculated as

$$\text{MSE} = \frac{1}{n} \sum_{i=1}^{n} (P_i - A_i)^2$$

and the MSE component is determined to be

$$\text{MSE} = (\bar{P} - \bar{A})^2 + (1 - b_1)^2 S_p^2 + (1 - R_{p,A}^2) S_A^2$$

where $\bar{P}$ and $\bar{A}$ are the means of the predicted and the actual earnings, respectively; b_1 is the slope coefficient of actual earnings A, regressed on predicted earnings P; S_p^2 and S_A^2 are the sample variances of the predicted and actual earnings, respectively, and $R_{p,A}^2$ is the coefficient of determination of the regression of actual on predicted earnings. The first component, $(\bar{P} - \bar{A})^2$, is the bias term and represents the portion of the MSE due to over- or underestimation of the mean. The second term, $(1 - b)^2 S_p^2$, is the inefficiency term and represents the portion of the coefficients from the expected value of 1.0 in the regression of actual earnings on predicted earnings. The random error component, $(1 - R_{p,A}^2) S_A^2$, is the final term.

The Two-Step Regression Procedure

In this procedure, the forecast of the P/E model is first regressed on the IBES forecast, and the residual term is determined:

$$\text{P/E (forecast)} = \alpha_0 + \alpha_1 \text{ IBES(forecast)} + \varepsilon$$

The residual term ε indicates the portion of the P/E forecast not explained by the IBES estimate. Next, the actual EPS for the year are regressed on the residual. This provides evidence as to whether the portion of the price-based forecast not explained by IBES is related to the subsequent actual EPS:

$$\text{actual EPS} = \beta_0 + \beta_1 \varepsilon + \mu$$

If the slope coefficient b1 is significant, then there is information contained in the P/E model forecast that is not contained in the IBES forecast.

The converse of this procedure is also employed. That is, the IBES earnings forecasts are regressed on the P/E model earnings are regressed on the residual to determine if there is information in the IBES forecasts that is not in the P/E model forecasts.

Table 1.   Magnitude of Forecast Errors

| | Percentage of Forecast Errors Less Than: | | | | | | |
| | 5% | | 10% | | 15% | | |
Year	P/E	IBES	P/E	IBES	P/E	IBES	N
1976	32.1	25.0	57.1	50.0	67.9	66.0	56
1977	22.0	24.0	44.0	52.0	60.0	62.0	50
1978	27.7	41.5	47.7	60.0	66.2	72.3	65
1979	33.3	33.3	54.6	60.6	62.1	68.2	66
1980	23.9	23.9	39.4	49.3	47.9	66.2	71
1981	21.8	28.2	46.2	56.4	64.1	73.1	78
1982	31.5	34.2	54.8	61.6	69.9	79.5	73
1983	20.3	40.5	55.4	56.8	75.7	78.4	74
1984	26.8	25.4	59.2	49.3	73.2	64.8	71
1985	15.7	31.4	31.4	64.3	50.0	78.6	70
1986	27.4	31.5	52.1	58.9	68.5	75.3	73
1987	16.7	34.5	36.9	53.6	57.1	65.5	84
Overall	24.7	31.4	48.0	56.2	63.5	71.1	831

EMPIRICAL RESULTS

Before examining the MABEs and MSEs, the magnitudes of the forecast errors are presented. Table 1 shows the percentage of firms with forecasts within 5, 10, and 15% of actual EPS. For example, in the 1987 data, 16.7% of the P/E-based forecasts are within 5% of subsequent actual EPS, while 34.5% of the IBES estimates are within 5% of actual EPS. Continuing across the row, 36.9% of the P/E model forecasts and 53.6% of the IBES forecasts are within 10% of actual year-end EPS. Finally, the P/E model produces estimates that indicate 57.1% of the estimates are within 15% of actual EPS, while 65.5% of the IBES forecasts are within 15% of actual earnings per share.

Overall, the IBES forecasts are better in 10 of the 12 years. Only in 1976 and 1984, does the P/E model outperform the IBES forecasts.

Summaries of the results involving the MABE and the MSE are presented in Table 2. The information is divided by the number of analysts following the particular companies. For example, the columns headed by "five or more" refer to the estimates for those companies followed by five or more analysts. The column labeled "all" refers to the entire dataset.

Several observations should be made concerning the MABEs and the MSEs. First, the means of the errors show that, on average, the IBES forecast error is less than the P/E model forecast error for all three groups for both error measures. In addition, the dispersion of the IBES errors (as measured by the standard deviation) is less than the dispersion for the P/E model. The mean absolute errors associated with the IBES estimates are lower than the errors associated with the P/E model in all years except 1984.

Table 2.   Mabe and MSE by Number of Analysts Estimates

	All Analysts		Three or More Analysts		Five or More Analysts	
Year	P/E	IBES	P/E	IBES	P/E	IBES
Panel A: MABE						
1976	0.258	0.247	0.242	0.236	0.275	0.252
1977	0.298	0.262	0.308	0.253	0.295	0.196
1978	0.272	0.241	0.260	0.246	0.270	0.258
1979	0.268	0.241	0.270	0.252	0.261	0.259
1980	0.341	0.269	0.334	0.279	0.328	0.275
1981	0.320	0.268	0.328	0.269	0.318	0.249
1982	0.306	0.286	0.309	0.269	0.321	0.277
1983	0.331	0.286	0.341	0.257	0.319	0.225
1984	0.366	0.401	0.361	0.409	0.380	0.388
1985	0.566	0.383	0.581	0.386	0.571	0.385
1986	0.586	0.432	0.601	0.435	0.617	0.443
1987	0.690	0.564	0.675	0.555	0.681	0.557
Mean	0.383	0.323	0.384	0.320	0.386	0.314
Std. dev.	0.139	0.096	0.141	0.097	0.142	0.102
Panel B: MSE						
1976	0.131	0.100	0.114	0.093	0.141	0.105
1977	0.146	0.107	0.157	0.106	0.145	0.065
1978	0.127	0.124	0.120	0.122	0.129	0.134
1979	0.130	0.109	0.133	0.118	0.122	0.127
1980	0.204	0.130	0.201	0.140	0.190	0.137
1981	0.180	0.131	0.189	0.138	0.172	0.119
1982	0.190	0.185	0.196	0.164	0.207	0.171
1983	0.212	0.183	0.224	0.139	0.178	0.102
1984	0.338	0.361	0.337	0.374	0.373	0.306
1985	0.895	0.717	0.952	0.757	0.978	0.799
1986	1.688	1.335	1.755	1.386	1.871	1.482
1987	1.364	1.170	1.304	1.149	1.349	1.189
Mean	0.467	0.388	0.473	0.390	0.488	0.395
Std. dev.	0.519	0.423	0.528	0.434	0.561	0.465

As seen from the MSEs, the IBES estimates exhibit less forecast error than the P/E model estimates except: in 1978, when the three-or-more and five-or-more estimates for IBES are greater than for the P/E model; in 1979, when the IBES estimates for five or more analysts exceed the error from P/E; and in 1984, when the IBES forecast errors are greater than the P/E errors for all analysts and for three or more analysts.

The results associated with the different number of analysts must be viewed with caution. There is no systematic relationship between the size of forecast errors and the number of analysts following the stock.

Table 3.   Results of the Two-Step Regression Procedure[a]

	IBES Model		P/E Model	
	Coefficient	*T-value*	*Coefficient*	*T-value*
1976	0.054	0.149	0.791	2.119
1977	−0.002	−0.006	0.845	2.1
1978	0.366	1.241	0.482	1.48
1979	0.21	0.6	0.699	1.947
1980	−0.081	−0.237	1.033	2.728
1981	0.217	0.789	0.814	2.476
1982	0.64	2.1	0.253	0.615
1983	0.346	1.276	0.611	1.888
1984	0.773	3.308	−0.025	−0.082
1985	−0.043	−0.074	1.364	1.906
1986	0.03	0.078	0.992	2.175
1987	0.5	4.4	0.247	1.067
Overall	0.426	6.185	0.469	5.128

Notes: [a]The results designated "IBES model" were obtained by first regressing the P/E model forecasts on the IBES analysts' forecasts and then regressing the actual EPS on the residuals of the first regression.
The results designated "P/E model" were obtained by first regressing the IBES analysts' forecasts on the P/E model forecasts and then regressing the actual EPS on the residuals of the first regression.

Finally, the magnitude of the forecast errors for both models increases dramatically over the time period. The MABE more than doubles, while the MSE increases by a factor of 10, with most of the increases occurring in 1985 and 1986.

Overall, the results indicate that IBES forecast errors are less than the errors associated with the P/E model. However, due to the magnitude of the standard deviations, the means of the MSEs and the MABEs are not statistically significantly different at traditional levels of significance.

Results of Two-Step Regression Procedure

As mentioned above, the MSE and MABE results suggest that the IBES estimates are superior to the estimates of the price-based model. Because a statistically significant difference cannot be observed, the regression procedure is used to examine the information content in the two forecasts.

Table 3 presents the results associated with the two-step regression procedure. The left section of the table shows the regression coefficient and the *t*-value for each year when the actual EPS are regressed on the residuals obtained by regressing the P/E forecasts on the IBES analysts' forecasts. As can be seen, the coefficient is significant in 1982, 1984, and 1987.

The right section of the table presents the results when the first-step equation is reversed. That is, the IBES forecasts are entered as the dependent variable and the P/E model forecasts are entered as the independent variable in the first step of the

Table 4.   Bias, Inefficiency, and random Error

Year	All Analysts		Three or More Analysts		Five or More Analysts	
	P/E	*IBES*	*P/E*	*IBES*	*P/E*	*IBES*
			Bias			
1976	0.0010	0.0122	0.0012	0.0098	0.0024	0.0142
1977	0.0034	0.0155	0.0025	0.0146	0.0012	0.0032
1978	0.0045	0.0195	0.0160	0.0293	0.0182	0.0318
1979	0.0200	0.0273	0.0261	0.0386	0.0263	0.0434
1980	0.0222	0.0167	0.0165	0.0156	0.0219	0.0178
1981	0.0034	0.0108	0.0028	0.0117	0.0011	0.0106
1982	0.0153	0.0003	0.0225	0.0000	0.0239	0.0002
1983	0.0058	0.0248	0.0078	0.0291	0.0034	0.0183
1984	0.0560	0.0070	0.0515	0.0061	0.0526	0.0068
1985	0.1603	0.0105	0.1702	0.0146	0.1511	0.0123
1986	0.2054	0.0414	0.2171	0.0517	0.2223	0.0503
1987	0.1572	0.1049	0.1375	0.0951	0.1362	0.1038
Mean	0.0545	0.0242	0.0560	0.0264	0.0551	0.0261
Std. dev.	0.0714	0.0264	0.0718	0.0250	0.0703	0.0277
			Inefficiency			
1976	0.0252	0.0082	0.0129	0.0021	0.0094	0.0005
1977	0.0323	0.0082	0.0366	0.0070	0.0330	0.0020
1978	0.0212	0.0065	0.0181	0.0078	0.0166	0.0080
1979	0.0120	0.0034	0.0242	0.0094	0.0161	0.0085
1980	0.0284	0.0011	0.0194	0.0009	0.0169	0.0013
1981	0.0200	0.0015	0.0226	0.0022	0.0174	0.0028
1982	0.0200	0.0000	0.0290	0.0007	0.0337	0.0017
1983	0.0297	0.0000	0.0304	0.0008	0.0336	0.0000
1984	0.0572	0.0251	0.0519	0.0310	0.0663	0.0271
1985	0.0004	0.0510	0.0006	0.0449	0.0000	0.0465
1986	0.0614	0.0005	0.0674	0.0003	0.0686	0.0006
1987	0.3975	0.0053	0.4077	0.0071	0.4491	0.0151
Mean	0.0588	0.0092	0.0601	0.0095	0.0634	0.0095
Std. dev.	0.1034	0.0142	0.1062	0.0134	0.1180	0.0135
			Random Error			
1976	0.1044	0.0793	0.0999	0.0806	0.1294	0.0906
1977	0.1104	0.0837	0.1180	0.0841	0.1109	0.0597
1978	0.1009	0.0977	0.0860	0.0851	0.0944	0.0942
1979	0.0982	0.0786	0.0825	0.0700	0.0799	0.0746
1980	0.1534	0.1121	0.1653	0.1240	0.1513	0.1179
1981	0.1564	0.1185	0.1634	0.1236	0.1534	0.1057
1982	0.1549	0.1849	0.1441	0.1629	0.1490	0.1690
1983	0.1763	0.1586	0.1860	0.1095	0.1409	0.0832
1984	0.2245	0.3289	0.2338	0.3369	0.2542	0.2722
1985	0.7346	0.6557	0.7809	0.6972	0.8268	0.7400
1986	1.4216	1.2933	1.4710	1.3335	1.5805	1.4312
1987	0.8096	1.0600	0.7585	1.0467	0.7633	1.0697
Mean	0.3538	0.3543	0.3575	0.3545	0.3695	0.3590
Std. dev.	0.3990	0.4024	0.4101	0.4143	0.4400	0.4430

regression. The actual EPS are then regressed on the residual term. The coefficient is statistically significant at the 5 percent level in 8 of the 12 years. Overall, the results indicate that, in general, there is more information contained in the IBES estimates than in the P/E model estimates.

Since the regression procedure indicates the IBES forecasts contain more information than the P/E model forecasts, but the MSE and MABE results show no statistically significant differences, the components of the MSE are examined to gain additional insight.

MSE Components: Bias

The top panel in Table 4 presents the bias component of the MSE. The average bias associated with the IBES estimate is slightly less than one-half of that for the P/E estimate. The size of the bias component is more pronounced for the P/E model in the years 1985-1987. The dispersion of the bias component, as measured by the standard deviation, is also lower for the IBES estimates.

MSE Components: Inefficiency

The middle panel shows that the inefficiency associated with the P/E model estimate is substantially greater than for the IBES estimate. The P/E model outperforms the IBES model in 1985, but exhibits substantially larger errors in 1987. Because of the large inefficiency component in 1987, the standard deviation of the estimates for the P/E model is much higher than for the IBES model.

MSE Components: Random Error

The bottom panel presents the random error component. The results indicate that, in general, the random errors associated with the P/E model and the IBES model are reasonably similar. The random error components are much greater than the bias and inefficiency components, and are of similar magnitude throughout the time period. As has been previously observed, the forecast error in 1985 increases substantially, and the increase is due primarily to the increase in the random error term.

As with the bias and inefficiency components, the number of analysts following a particular stock does not seem to be important in the size of the random error term. In some years, the random errors associated with five or more analysts are least, and in other years, the greatest.

SUMMARY AND IMPLICATIONS

Prior research indicated that stock prices contain information for forecasting EPS beyond the information contained in historical EPS. However, these studies had *not* compared the price-based forecasts with financial analysts' forecasts. The methodology involved comparing analysts' forecasts with forecasts generated from historical EPS patterns.

This study compares IBES EPS forecasts with the forecasts from a model based on the work of Beaver, Lambert, and Morse. A price-based model is developed and earnings are forecasted using the model. The forecasts are then compared with subsequently reported earnings per share. Mean absolute errors, mean squared errors, and a two-step regression procedure are used in the analyses of forecast errors. The results indicate that the IBES analysts' forecasts are marginally superior to forecasts based on prices, suggesting that most, but not all, of the information contained in the IBES estimates is reflected in the price-based estimates.

The results of the study support earlier works by Brown, Richardson, and Schwager, and Bjerring, Lakonishok, and Vermaelen. Even though the analysts' forecasts outperform the forecasts of the price-based model, the differences are marginal. Two conclusions can be drawn: (1) the closeness of the forecasts indicates that most of the information incorporated in one model is incorporated in the other; and (2) the market does not immediately reflect all new information, as suggested earlier by Givoly and Lakonishok. Further research into both the earnings-generating process and the impact of earnings information on stock prices is necessary in order to better understand valuation processes.

ACKNOWLEDGMENTS

The authors are indebted to IBES, Inc., for providing the data and to R.D. Johnson, C.F. Lee, and an anonymous referee for their helpful comments. Computational assistance by Sandeep Bhuwania is also appreciated.

NOTES

1. For a comprehensive summary of the early time-series studies see Bao, Lewis, Lin, and Mane-gold (1983).

2. For example, see Brown and Rozeff (1978, 1979), Collins and Hopwood (1980), Elton, Gruber, and Gultekin et al. (1984), Givoly and Lakonishok (1979), Moyer, Chatfield, and Kelley (1986), Rozeff (1983), and Guerard (1989).

3. The results also suggest that prices do not immediately incorporate all new information. More recently Dowen and Bauman (1991) report similar results contradicting the semistrong form of the efficient-market hypothesis.

REFERENCES

Abarbanell, J.S. (1991). Analysts' earnings forecasts. *Journal of Accounting and Economics, 14,* 147-165.

Ali, A., Klein, A., & Rosenfeld, J. (1992). Analysts' use of information about permanent and transitory earnings components in forecasting annual EPS. *Accounting Review, 67,* 183-198.

Bao, D.H., Lewis, M.T., Lin, W.T., and Manegold, (1983). Applications of time-series analysis in accounting: A review. *Journal of Forecasting, 2*, 405-423.

Beaver, W., Lambert, R., & Morse, D. (1980). The information content of security prices. *Journal of Accounting and Economics, 2*, 3-28.

Beaver, W.H., Lambert, R.A., & Ryan, S.G. The information content of security prices: A second look. *Journal of Accounting and Economics, 9*, 139-157.

Bernard, V.L. & Thomas J.K. (1990). Evidence that stock prices do not fully reflect the implications of current earnings for future earnings. *Journal of Accounting and Economics, 13*, 305-340.

Bjerring, J.H., Lakonishok, J., & Vermaelen, T. (1983). Stock prices and financial analysts' recommendations. *Journal of Finance, 38* (March), 187-204.

Brown, L.D., Hagerman, R.L., Griffin, P.A., & Zmijewski, M.E. (1987). An evaluation of alternative proxies for the markets assessment of unexpected earnings. *Journal of Accounting and Economics, 9*, 159-193.

Brown, L.D., Richardson, G.D., & Schwager, S.J. (1987). An information interpretation of financial analyst superiority in forecasting earnings. *Journal of Accounting Research, 25*, (Spring) 49-67.

Brown, L.D., & Rozeff, M. (1978). The superiority of analysts forecasts as measures of expectations: Evidence from earnings. *Journal of Finance, 33*, (March) 1-16.

Brown, L.D., & Rozeff M. (1979) Adaptive expectations, time-series models, and analysts forecast revision. *Journal of Accounting Research, 17*, 341-351.

Brown, P., Foster, G. & Noreen E. (1985). Security analyst multi-year earnings forecasts and the capital market. *Studies in Accounting Research, 21*.

Butler, K.C., & Lang, L.H.P. (1991). The forecast accuracy of individual analysts: Evidence of systematic optimism and pessimism. *Journal of Accounting Research, 29#1, (Spring) 150-156*.

Chatfield, R.E., Hein, S.E., & Moyer, R.C. (1990). Long term earnings forecasts in the electric utility industry: Accuracy and valuation implications. *Financial Review, 25#3, (August) 421-439*.

Collins, W.A., & Hopwood, W.S. (1980). A multivariate analysis of annual earnings forecasts generated from quarterly forecasts of financial analysts and univariate time-series models. *Journal of Accounting Research, 18*, 390-406.

Cragg, J.G., & Malkiel, B.G. (1968). The consensus and accuracy of some predictions of the growth of corporate earnings. *Journal of Finance, 23*, (March) 67-84.

Cragg, J.G., & Malkiel, B.G. (1982). *Expectations and the structure of share prices*. Chicago: University of Chicago Press.

Down, R.J. & Bauman, W.S. (1991). Revisions in corporate earnings forecasts and common stock returns. *Financial Analysts Journal* (March-April), 86-90.

Elton, E.J., Gruber, M.J., & Gultekin, M.N. (1984). Professional expectations: Accuracy and diagnosis of errors. *Journal of Financial and Quantitative Analysis, 19*, 351-363.

Fried, D., & Givoly, D. (1982). Financial analysts' forecasts of earnings: A better surrogate for market expectations. *Journal of Accounting and Economics*, (October) 85-107.

Givoly, D. & Lakonishok, J. (1979). The information content of financial analysts' forecasts of earnings: Some evidence of semi-strong inefficiency. *Journal of Accounting and Economics*, (Winter) 165-185.

Givoly, D. & Lakonishok, J. (1984). The Quality of analysts' forecasts of earnings. *Financial Analysts Journal*, (September/October 40-47.

Guerard, J.B. Jr. (1989). Combining time-series model forecasts and analysts' forecasts for superior forecasts of annual earnings. *Financial Analysts Journal*, (January-February) 69-70.

Kross, W., Ro, B. & Schroeder, D. (1990). Earnings expectations: The analysts' information advantage. *Accounting Review, 65,#(2, April), 461-476*.

Lys, T. & Sohn, S. The association between revisions of financial analysts' earnings forecast and security-price changes. *Journal of Accounting and Economics, 13*, 341-363. (1990).

Malkiel, B.G., & Cragg, J.G. (1970). Expectations and the structure of share prices. *American Economic Review, 60*, (September) 601-617.

Mincer, J., & Zarnowitz, V. (1969). The evaluation of economic forecasts. In *Economic Forecasts and Expectations* (J. Mincer, ed.). New York: National Bureau of Economic Research.

Moyer, R.C., Chatfield, R.E., & Kelley, G.D. (1986). "The accuracy of long-term earnings forecasts in the electric utility industry. *International Journal of Forecasting, 1*, 241-252.

Newbold, P., Zumwalt, J.K. & Kannan, S. (1987). Combining forecasts to improve earnings per share prediction: An examination of electric utilities. *International Journal of Forecasting, 3*, 229-238.

O'Brien, P.C. (1988). Analysts' forecasts as earning expectations. *Journal of Accounting and Economics, 10*, 53-83.

Ou, J.A. & Penman, S.H. (1989). Accounting measurement, price-earnings ratio, and the information content of security prices. *Journal of Accounting Research, 27*, 111-141.

Pari, R., Carvell, S. & Sullivan, T. (1989). Analyst forecasts and price/earnings ratios. *Financial Analysts Journal* (March-April), 60-62.

Rozeff, M.F., (1983). Predicting long-term earnings growth. *Journal of Forecasting, 2*,(October-December), 425-435.

Stickel, S.E., (1990). Predicting individual analyst earnings forecasts. *Journal of Accounting Research, 28*, 409-417.

Advances in Pacific Basin Business, Economics and Finance

Edited by **C. F. Lee**, *Department of Finance, Rutgers University*

Volume 1, In preparation, Winter 1994
ISBN 1-55938-737-8   Approx. $73.25

CONTENTS: PART A: MACROECONOMICS. Outlook for Japan-EC-United Staes Political-Economic Relations, *Richard J. Sweeney.* New Economic Policies for the U.S., *John Clark Francis.* Japan and the Threat of Laura Tyson, *Jeremiah J. Sullivan.* An Overview of Recent Economic Development in China, *Wuu-Long Lin and Thomas P. Chen.* Linkage Effects of Foreign Enterprises on Chinese Economy: Problems and Prospects in the 1990s, *Peter C. Y. Chow.* Linkage Effects of Foreign Enterprises in China: Problems and Prospects - Comment, *Chao-Nan Liu.* Financial System in China, *Frank C. Jen.* Trade Policy of Taiwan, *Rong-I Wu.* A Re-Evaluation of Taiwan Domestic Economic Policy: A Political-Economy Approach, *Pai-Hsien Pang and Shih-Ming Chen.* Chinas Foreign Exchange Rate Policy, *Jizu Wang.* Trade and Investment Across the Taiwan Straits: Maintaining Competitive Advantage, Pursuing Complementarity, *Koong-lian Kao.* Privatization and Productivity Growth in China: 1979-1990, *Chi-Chu Chou.* Japans ODA and its Role in Chinas Economic Reform, *David C. Cheng.* A Comparative Study of Economic Development: The Case of Shanghai, *Hong Kong and Taiwan, Chang-Hsien Chang, Chen and Zhang, and Peter Koveos.* Economic Relationships between Taiwan and CHina, *M. Jan Dutta.* Globalization of the Taiwanese Economy and U.S. - Taiwan Trade Relations, *Frank S. T. Hsiao.* The Pattern of U.S. - Asian Pacific Rim Trade, 1965-1987, *Ira N. Gang, Catherine Y. Co.* PART B: BUSINESS, FINANCE AND ACCOUNTING. An International Comparison of the Accuracy of Analysts Forecasts of Earnings, *Jang Youn Cho and Andrew Pitcher.* Earnings Forecasting in Efficient Japanese Portfolios, *John B. Guerard Jr., Suzuki Makoto and Unmesh Bhide.* A Comparative Study of the Weekend Effects in the United States, British and the Pacific Rim Stock Markets: An Application of the ARCH Model, *,Bwo-Nung Huang, Yu-Jane Liu and Chin W. Yang.* Corporate Ownership Structure and Corporate Governance Mechanism: With Experience of Korean Firms, *Ungki Lim.* On the Pricing of the Deposit Insurance Liabilities of the CDIC of Taiwan, *Jin-Chuan Duan, Mao-Wei Hung and Thomas Liaw.* The US, Japan and the Emerging Stock Markets of the Pacific Basin: A Test of Regional and Intertemporal Stability, *Richard Ajayi, Jongmoo Jay Choi and Seyed M. Mehdian.* Excess Returns of Unseasoned New Issues in taiwan: An Institutional Perspective, *Gili Yen, E.C. Yen and S. Chen.* An Analysis of Mergers Between Mutual Banks and Credit Cooperatives in Japan, *Yasuo Hoshino.*